GREAT CANADIAN LIVES

Great Canadian Lives

A Cultural History of Modern Canada Through the Art of the Obit

Sandra Martin

Foreword by William Thorsell

ANANSI

Hardcover edition first published in 2012 by House of Anansi Press Inc. with the title *Working the Dead Beat: 50 Lives That Changed Canada*.

This edition published in 2014 by
House of Anansi Press Inc.
110 Spadina Avenue, Suite 801
Toronto, ON, M5V 2K4
Tel. 416-363-4343
Fax 416-363-1017
www.houseofanansi.com

Distributed in Canada by
HarperCollins Canada Ltd.
1995 Markham Road
Scarborough, ON, M1B 5M8
Toll free tel. 1-800-387-011

House of Anansi Press is committed to protecting our natural environment. As part of our efforts, the interior of this book is printed on paper that contains 100% post-consumer recycled fibres, is acid-free, and is processed chlorine-free.

18 17 16 15 14   1 2 3 4 5

Library and Archives Canada Cataloguing in Publication

Martin, Sandra, 1947–, author
Great Canadian Lives: A Cultural History of Modern Canada Through the Art of the Obit / Sandra Martin ; foreword by William Thorsell.

Includes bibliographical references.
Issued in print and electronic formats.
ISBN 978-0-88784-246-7 (bound).—ISBN 978-1-77089-448-8 (pbk.).
—ISBN 978-1-77089-906-3 (html)

1. Canada—Biography. 2. Canada—History—20th century—Biography.
I. Title.

FC541.A1M37 2012   971.06092'2   C2012-902958-0
                          C2012-902959-9

Cover design: Alysia Shewchuk
Text design and typesetting: Alysia Shewchuk

Cover images (clockwise from top left): Great Northern Railway's Chinese track gang (1909)/Vancouver Public Library; [P.E. Trudeau at the] Liberal [Leadership] Convention, [Ottawa, Ont.](6 Apr., 1968) © Library and Archives Canada/Duncan Cameron/Duncan Cameron fonds/PA-111213; Oscar Peterson plays piano (1977)/Hans Bernhard/Wikimedia Commons; Portrait of Celia Franca in an evening gown (ca. 1943-1948)/Library and Archives Canada/Celia Franca fonds/e008300164; A line of soldiers from Newfoundland (March 1945) © Hulton-Deutsch Collection/CORBIS; Kananginak Pootoogook, president of the West Baffin Co-operative, Cape Dorset, Nunavut (1960) © Library and Archives Canada/ Rosemary Gilliat Eaton/Rosemary Gilliat Eaton fonds/ e010975349; Maurice Richard (November 1970) © Government of Canada/Library and Archives Canada/ National Film Board of Canada fonds/e003525241; Mrs. Jane Jacobs, chairman of the Comm. to save the West Village holds up documentary evidence at press conference at Lions Head Restaurant at Hudson & Charles Sts (5 December 1961)/World Telegram & Sun photo by Phil Stanziola/Wikimedia Commons

Canada Council Conseil des Arts
for the Arts   du Canada

ONTARIO ARTS COUNCIL
CONSEIL DES ARTS DE L'ONTARIO

We acknowledge for their financial support of our publishing program the Canada Council for the Arts, the Ontario Arts Council, and the Government of Canada through the Canada Book Fund.

Printed and bound in Canada

MIX
Paper from
responsible sources
FSC
www.fsc.org   FSC® C004071

ANCIENT FOREST ™
FRIENDLY

For Hazel and Elle
From a time before you were born

CONTENTS

FOREWORD

S ANDRA MARTIN OBSERVES that "context is everything" in writing obituaries, defending the role of the journalist as disinterested observer in
parsing a dead person's nature and deeds. In this volume of fifty lives spent
and done, Sandra Martin provides context about the obituary form itself,
which makes her telling of tales all the more pungent. She demonstrates
through these often gripping portraits that rumours of the obituary's death in
the digital age have been grossly exaggerated. The gauzy eulogy is ultimately
no competition for journalism's obituary, whose purpose is "to bring the subject alive for readers — warts and all."

"As skinny as a preying mantis, tottering on platform shoes, sucking on a
cigarette, her hair a cumulus of auburn curls..." — that could only be Jackie
Burroughs to anyone who has been around Canadian theatre in the past fifty
years. Great obituary writers must be mordant observers of fragile creatures,
without becoming morbid or indulging in the easy game of post-mortem ridicule barely disguising envy. They must combine the sometimes cruel objec-
tivism of journalism with appreciation of the human condition, and perhaps
even a dollop of that dangerous potion known as empathy. And all this with a
sense of humour, black to ribald, wry to dry, never gratuitous.

Obituaries serve various purposes. The core is social history, one individual at a time, using the vector of one person's life to illuminate the situation of
many. In this light, even eulogies, generally the nature of the *Globe and Mail*'s

"Lives Lived" column written by friends and family of "ordinary people," fill in the blanks of the daily news, present and past. But there is also fascination in individuals alone: "In my view, there is no such thing as an uninteresting life, but there are badly researched and written accounts. The difference between humdrum and compelling rests in documenting weaknesses, celebrating strengths, and placing the people's lives in context of what else was happening here and abroad," says Martin. She demonstrates that well in this volume, including individuals of meager fame but telling detail.

The devil may be in the wings for some of Martin's subjects, but the devil is in the details when it comes to the facts of dead people's lives. Her career in daily journalism gives Sandra Martin a properly obsessive concern for accuracy and "the whole truth" — meaning contextual information that illuminates motivation and constraints. She has gone beyond the *Globe and Mail*'s published obituaries in these portraits, adding considerable information based on additional sources (and adding several individuals to boot). In effect, her newspaper obituaries served as the first draft of these biographies, tight to be sure, but rounded and deepened beyond the constraints wrought by deadlines and short notice. "Noteworthy people always die late in the afternoon," she writes with an eye to the first edition, contributing to the "immediacy and finality" of the job, which she describes as "terrifying." If so, her terror bans complacency, and finality turns out to be an illusion. She has returned to these stories even more convincingly with the assistance of time.

Obituary writers perform acts of resurrection in the immediate context of internment. That is why the craft can be so delicate and dangerous, speaking truth to grief, exposing intimacies at the precise moment when intimacies can be most wounding. This is where both tact and courage come into play, abetted by allusion sometimes, but sometimes unavoidably not. "I am writing for the readers, not the family." Thus of Scott Symons, Martin reports with literary punch: "His life was his art. Alas it was not a masterpiece." Her compilation of the facts supports such conclusions in all too many lives.

Sandra Martin brings a deeply observant and informed mind to her subjects, rooted in years of experience as a journalist, author, and citizen. Her references draw on her own memory of life in Canada over the past half-century or so, enriching the insights she brings to each story. If you knew these people, you will utter sounds of recognition in reading the accounts of their individuality and times. And you will appreciate Sandra Martin's elegant and surgical use of the language in restoring life to the dead in the garment of literature.

William Thorsell
Toronto, Ontario
June 2012

INTRODUCTION

Five Myths about the Dead Beat

S OME OF YOU may think that writing obituaries is an odd — perhaps even
whacky — occupation for an able-bodied journalist. After all, I could be
chasing fires, sniffing out political sleaze, or even waxing editorial about the
state of the nation. I used to feel that way too, I confess, until I changed sides
from writing about the living to documenting the dead.

I've grown accustomed to the arched eyebrow, the flash of revulsion, the
involuntary step backwards, and the exclamation "But that's so morbid"
when I tell people what I do for a living. I ignore cracks about the "Siberia of
journalism," pointed queries about who's "on your slab today," and the oh-so-
clever jokes: *How's life on the dead beat? What's happening in God's anteroom?*
As for the real killer — metaphorically speaking — "Why would you want to
write about dead people? They're finished," I smile mordantly and murmur,
"I'll keep that in mind if I write your obituary."

Most journalists have a beat — crime, fashion, arts, health, business, politics. Obituaries encompass all those areas and more, because everybody,
from scientists to visual artists, comes under my scrutiny eventually. My
tenure as the *Globe and Mail*'s chief obituary writer has taught me that writing obituaries is the most interesting and often the most terrifying job on
any newspaper.

Aside from learning something new every day, which is the spur driving
most journalists to get out of bed in the morning, the dead beat has another

decided advantage: You never repeat yourself. Literally. That is one of the aspects that appealed to me about obituaries after several years in the arts section writing about books and authors.

On the obituaries desk there is no next year, no next book, no next achievement, no new angle. An obituary is the final word on a subject's life — until a posthumous biography appears several years down the road. Getting it right, therefore, is daunting, given the urgency of the 24/7 news cycle.

That's one of the reasons why I have written this book. I wanted to produce a second draft of the lives of fifty Canadians who died in the first decade of this century. Some of them I wrote amid a blur of phone calls and Internet searches; some I didn't write about at all because they died when I was away or on other assignments. I'm calling these biographical portraits "lives" because they don't adhere to the rigid deadline and format constraints of the traditional newspaper obituary. They are a bit more expansive, a bit more personal, and a bit more reflective.

ALTHOUGH MY SUBJECTS all died between 2000 and 2010, their lives span the twentieth century, beginning with head-tax survivor Ralph Lung Kee Lee. Born in 1900, he sailed to Canada when he was twelve with two younger cousins, all of them wearing identifying tags around their necks. Mabel Grosvenor, who was born five years later, was the granddaughter of Alexander Graham Bell. As a small child she watched the earliest attempts at manned flight in this country, at Bell's estate in Baddeck, Nova Scotia.

Many of my subjects are famous, others are known only to a coterie of admirers and family members, but each has done something to shape this country in big ways or small. They include politician Pierre Trudeau, hockey legend Maurice "The Rocket" Richard, writer Mordecai Richler, social activist June Callwood, Native rights advocate Donald Marshall, architect Arthur Erickson, economist John Kenneth Galbraith, and Celia Franca, founder of the National Ballet of Canada. I have included rogues as well as champions. Both exist in life, and so too they reside between the covers of a book that uses obituaries to comment on Canadian society. Taken together, they contribute to a composite picture of Canadian politics and society in the twentieth century, from before the First World War to the Internet age.

You will note that men outnumber women. That was still the reality in the late twentieth century, not in numbers but in opportunities for women. One of my subjects, Bertha Wilson, was the first woman appointed to the Supreme Court of Canada. As I write, in April 2012, four of the nine judges on the Supreme Court, including Chief Justice Beverley McLachlin, are women. That change has been a long time coming. We need more women in public life, more female politicians and corporate leaders, if the gender balance is to be redressed in a future anthology of Canadian obituaries.

It isn't just the country that has changed over the lifetimes of the fifty Canadians I have chronicled in this book. Obituary writing itself has also been transformed. Once the preserve of the rich, the noble, and the worthy, obituaries now encompass scoundrels as well as saints, eccentrics as well as celebrities. The style has changed as much as the subjects. There is a new frankness, an unwillingness to camouflage warts under layers of unctuous hyperbole and — thanks to technology — fresh, innovative ways to augment obituaries with photographs, interviews, and even videos.

Technology is a tool, but, for all the advantages of downloads and social networking opportunities, there are also ethical dangers lurking in cyberspace. Even while embracing technological wizardry we must safeguard the journalistic principles that gave authority to print obituaries. Balancing speed versus credibility and objectivity versus melodrama are huge considerations if we are to keep the best of print in new narrative modes geared to a younger and more expansive audience.

WHEN I STARTED on the dead beat, editors wanted the definitive obituary in the next morning's paper even if the gap between my subject's last breath and the deadline to send the page to the printers was ludicrously short. Too bad if a worthy Canadian had the bad luck to die late in the day, or at the same moment when a world leader succumbed to a heart attack or a rock star injected a fatal overdose. A few lines below the fold, cobbled together from a wire service, was probably the best the poor departed's family could expect to read through their tears at breakfast the next morning. Whatever could be scrabbled together became the final word.

Consequently, the whiff of death catapulted reporters into default mode. They would hit the phones, gathering quotes like black bunting from anybody and everybody willing to comment. Often these reaction pieces told you a lot about friends and family members but offered little concrete or coherent information about the subject.

Now it is more likely that a news story announcing the death of a signifi-cant person will break on the Web and the obituary will follow at a pace that sometimes seems too leisurely, even to me. *They are still dead* is the crude but accurate rationalization for scheduling major obituaries as the "big read" for Saturday, because weekend circulation figures generally dwarf the number of weekday subscribers.

Having more time to research and think about a life — although the more important the person, the faster inevitably the turnaround — is a windfall of "the Web is for news, the paper is for analysis" syndrome. The combination of the newsflash on the Web with the promise of "full obituary to follow" in the paper allows for more thoughtful and accurate obituaries, the kind that peo-ple want to clip and preserve for second and even third readings. That is one of the continuing pleasures of printed obituaries.

At the beginning of this chapter I said that I had the most interesting job in the newsroom. There is another reason my job is so compelling. I am writ-ing obituaries at a pivotal moment in a long and venerable tradition — the transition from print to digital. Long gone are the days when newspapers published several editions a day to break news and update stories. Many local dailies, especially in the United States, have merged or shut down.

Even now at a robust news organization such as the *Globe and Mail*, news flashes occur on the Web and are often digitally updated, as quickly as you can hit the Refresh button. Analysis, background features, and wide-ranging commentary — some of it curated from other news agencies or websites — have replaced breaking news as the mainstay of the morning newspaper.

The immediacy and the voracious appetite of the 24/7 news cycle, along with the informality and the way gossip dressed up as news goes viral around the globe on social media, has affected everything about the way I do my job. That's why a key component of this book is the history and craft of writing obituaries, from the printing press to the Internet age. I don't think there is another area of journalism that has undergone such a dramatic change in style and form. Those changes are largely unheralded, so I would like to lift the shroud and discuss the problems and pleasures, the pressures and rewards of writing obituaries.

Let me begin by dispelling five myths about the dead beat.

Myth Number One: The Dead Beat Is a Dead End

AFTER I WAS appointed to the *Globe*'s obituary beat, a colleague several years my senior approached me with a wistful look and confided that he had thought seriously about applying for the job.

"Why didn't you?" I asked.

"I thought I still had a few good stories in me before I was put on the shelf," he replied with the kind of candour that probably explains his long list of former wives and girlfriends.

That's the way it used to be on the dead beat: obituaries were the domain of junior reporters and old-timers waiting for their pensions or a buyout. Author Tom Rachman describes an over-the-hill obituary writer in his novel *The Imperfectionists*: "It has been nine days since his last obit, and he hopes to extend the streak. His overarching goal at the paper is indolence, to publish as infrequently as possible and to sneak away when no one is looking."

Obituary writing has changed. "The last decade of the twentieth century and the early years of the twenty-first will be looked on as a golden age for newspaper obituaries," according to James Fergusson, the inaugural obituaries editor of the *Guardian*. "The rules have all changed: once an obscure genre, obituaries are now a necessary weapon in any serious paper's armoury," he argues in "Last Words," an essay in the *London Library Magazine*. Why? The answer is simple: the Internet encouraged the formation of obituary websites and discussion groups in which readers and writers could read, comment on obituaries, and connect with each other around the world.

Unlike British newspapers, there really wasn't an obituary beat or even a dedicated obituary editor at most North American newspapers before the 1960s. News editors would look around the newsroom and assign obituaries to whomever was available. Seasoned reporters were reluctant to take them on because anonymity ruled, as it still does in most quality papers in the U.K. No matter how sparkling your prose, how diligent your research, how incisive your commentary, there was no byline to give you credit for a job well done. As John L. Hess noted in a 1985 *Grand Street* article, "On the Death Watch at the *Times*," writing obituaries was a mug's game, for "editors would no more identify [the reporter] than they would the embalmer."

The situation was even worse when it came to writing advances — the obituaries that news organizations like to have prewritten in case a famous person dies suddenly. Reporters, accustomed to seeing their efforts immortalized in print within hours or minutes, could update an obituary three or four times, retire, or even die themselves before the subject of an advance obituary finally breathed his or her last breath.

Reluctance to research and write a story that might not appear for years, and even then wouldn't add to a reporter's pool of credited stories, gave obituaries a bad rap. Consequently, editors began handing out these assignments to junior reporters as a training ground in writing fast human-interest stories about local worthies, expecting a minimum of research and a few hasty phone calls to friends and next of kin.

That was the management theory, but writing obituaries unleashed the hidden writer in many a novice journalist, including the celebrated long-form writer Gay Talese, acclaimed author of several books, one of the founders of "new journalism," and a Pulitzer Prize–winning writer whose numerous profiles—including such classics as "Frank Sinatra Has a Cold" and "[Muhammad] Ali in Havana"—are routinely taught in magazine and journalism classes. Back in the mid-1950s he worked for the *New York Times* as a junior political reporter, covering the state legislature in Albany, New York. He floundered so badly that his editors "punished" him by reassigning him to write obituaries. "I was never happier," he wrote in "When I Was Twenty-Five," a memoir essay. "Obituary writing was in the realm of personal history, biography, a summation of an individual's worth and consequence, and anyone who commanded an obituary in the *Times* was doubtless an individual of distinction and singular achievement—which was considerably more than I had seen during my brief career."

After a decade as an investigative reporter, Jim Nicholson reluctantly took on the dead beat, becoming the first obituary writer at the *Philadelphia Daily News* in 1982. More than twenty-five years later he could still remember how the "faces of my long time colleagues betrayed expressions people can't hide when looking at a terminal patient with that 'there but for the grace of God go I' look in their eyes."

Nicholson carved out his own niche according to a formula worked out with Tom Livingston, the paper's managing editor. "The newsroom handles the big guys, Nicholson writes about the nobodies," Nicholson recalled in "The Making of an Obituary Writer—and a Man," an article for the fall 2006 edition of *Nieman Reports*. "I started writing obits like they were personal columns, with a lot of subjective slants on philosophy, religion, cabbages, and kings, all meant to enhance the life, times, and character of the deceased." By the time Nicholson retired in 2001, he considered obits not only "the best job" he had ever had in journalism but also one that had vanquished his journalistic cynicism and made him believe that "most men and women are good; most when given a chance will do right; most will show honor."

I'm not sure I'm ready to go that far, but here's one thing I do know: writing obituaries teaches you that there is no such thing as an uninteresting or insignificant life. Far from a dead end, it is an invitation to expand your horizons and your empathy. One of the ways that I have stretched mine has been finding new ways to tell the story of a life. You can't recycle an obituary by topping it with a new lede (journalists' term for the article's opening paragraph) as you can with a developing news story, but you can repackage your research to produce different treatments in other parts of the paper and on the Web.

Space on the Web is infinite, so you can write at length and add timelines and list film and book titles in sidebars — context and details that are usually trimmed to make an obituary fit the increasingly truncated space of the shrinking newspaper page. For example, late in 2008 I wrote an advance obituary of Jean Pelletier, former mayor of Quebec City and chief of staff to Prime Minister Jean Chrétien. I did a massive amount of research on the sponsorship scandal, the 1995 Quebec referendum, and other aspects of Pelletier's life and career, as well as several audio interviews that included a conversation with former prime minister Chrétien. I couldn't possibly cram all that material into the finite space of an obituary page, so when Pelletier died on January 10, 2009, I let the obituary run long, complete with sidebars, on the Web. Then an enterprising *Globe* videographer and I put together a web package using slides, audio from my interviews, music, and a voice-over that I wrote and recorded to tie it all together as an enhancement of the printed obituary. In the process I used material that otherwise would have hit the floor, learned other skills, and got an additional and different byline.

Sometimes a life is too complicated for a single page; sometimes words alone can't suffice. I was on holiday when jazz pianist Oscar Peterson died two days before Christmas in 2007, so I wasn't involved in writing his obituary (that's one of the reasons I am glad to include him in this book). Instead I read about Peterson growing up in the Depression in Montreal, his determination to play music, and the tributes attesting to his musical genius, just like any other newspaper subscriber. How much better it would be, I thought at the time, along with the biography and the accolades, to provide a video link to give readers a chance to hear and see him performing. On radio and television I saw and heard lots of clips of Peterson playing the piano, but those media skimped on the biographical details that imbued his life and his music with colour and resonance. The authority of print plus the vibrancy of the Web can create a synergy that produces an obituary that lives far beyond the typical news cycle.

Myth Number Two: Obituaries Are Depressing

Obituaries are about life, not death. In the same way that a birthday or an anniversary provides the opportunity to reflect on a milestone, death is the occasion for setting an entire life in context. The sad and even tragic fact of somebody's death is a news flash; the laments of mourners are reaction pieces; public utterances at funerals for the deceased are eulogies. But the obituary is something else. It is an account of a life in all its complexity — the light as well as the shadow, the achievements as well as the failings — set within the context of the times in which the person lived.

That makes an obituary a combination of biography, history, analysis, and reportage. I rarely write about accident or murder victims or young soldiers killed in war zones — people whose lives were snuffed out by bad luck or tragic circumstance before they had a chance to realize their potential. Usually my subjects are people who were once famous, at least in this country, until the klieg lights of public attention dimmed. Their names are familiar to older readers but unknown to a younger generation. The goal is to chronicle their successes along with the controversies that dogged them and the challenges they overcame. What I have learned is that every life is fascinating in its own way, if only I can dig deep enough into the past and learn the personal and public details of my subject's life and career — usually in time for the next day's paper.

Research makes the difference between capturing a life in all its complexity and slipshod accounts. When people ask me for advice about how to write obituaries, I always say, "Before you pick up the phone, go to the library." Sometimes, research puts paid to an intriguing story, but so be it.

Legendary sportswriter Trent Frayne was revered in newsrooms across the country for his stylish writing, incisive commentary, and generosity to cub reporters, but he was also a serious drinker. He was arrested for driving under the influence in October 1964. According to newspaper accounts, a provincial police officer was forced to drive onto the median of Highway 401 near Milton to avoid a head-on crash with a motorist going west in the east-bound lanes. The police officer was only shaken up but another motorist was rear-ended. Frayne pleaded guilty, was fined $400, and had his licence suspended for two years. That humiliation changed his behaviour. He gave up the sauce and never relapsed, not even when his youngest child, twenty-year-old Casey, was killed by a drunk driver on Highway 401 in 1982.

I'd found that information on microfiche in the *Globe* library when I was researching his wife June Callwood's life before she died in 2007, and filed it away. When Frayne died at the age of ninety-three, on February 11, 2012, I included his drunk-driving arrest and subsequent sobriety in his obituary. Then I heard a tale allegedly told by Callwood, who had been married to Frayne for more than sixty years. Apparently Frayne, who had worked for at least three newspapers in Toronto during his long sportswriting career, had dipped into the clipping files at each of those news outlets and surreptitiously removed the story about his arrest. Lots of people go to extraordinary lengths to obscure embarrassing details about their past, so it was possible, though it didn't gibe with what I knew about Frayne as an ethical reporter. Still, journalists are notoriously lousy interviews — cagey, controlling, even sullen when asked questions about their own lives — because they know what can happen after the tape recorder is turned off and the typing starts. The story was a good one and I wanted to use it, but first I needed to check it out. I retrieved the yellowed envelope bearing Frayne's name and rifled through the clippings in the *Globe* library. And there it was — the account of his arrest. Who knows if I would have found it at the *Toronto Star* or *Maclean's*, but it was definitely in the *Globe* files. To tell the truth, I was glad to find the clipping, even though it ruined a juicy anecdote, because it spoke to the man I thought Frayne was — honourable even about his own failings.

Sometimes the research changes your own life. After I wrote anthropologist Bruce Trigger's obituary, I wanted to stand on a street corner like a contemporary ancient mariner stopping passersby to draw their attention to the significance of our loss. Trigger, who died at sixty-nine of pancreatic cancer on December 1, 2006, had a wide-ranging intellectual curiosity that roamed across civilizations, from ancient Egyptians in Africa to the Huron Confederacy in eastern Canada. Yet few people know his name. Of his two dozen books, three are considered masterpieces: *The Children of Aataentsic: A History of the Huron People to 1660*; *A History of Archaeological Thought*;

and *Understanding Early Civilizations: A Comparative Study.* As long ago as 1986, the journalist Boyce Richardson called *Aataentsic* "a work of such historical imagination and literary quality that Trigger deserves to rank with Harold Innis, Northrop Frye, and Marshall McLuhan — Canadian academics known abroad for their critical imaginations and honoured at home for their contributions to Canadian self-knowledge."

What made Trigger different from almost anyone else as a teacher, a scholar, and a human being was the thoroughness and integrity of his work. "He let the evidence speak, he didn't rearrange history to fit his theory," said Ursula Franklin, professor emeritus at the University of Toronto, in an interview. And in contrast to many archaeologists, he had an expansive attitude to diverse sources — science, folklore, oral history — but subjected them to rigorous scrutiny.

But he wasn't just an academic. He was a patriot who believed in building an intellectual life here. After university he went on scholarship to do a PhD in anthropology at Yale; at the time there "was no alternative to going abroad to study," as he wrote later in a biographical essay for *The Archaeology of Bruce Trigger: Theoretical Empiricism.* He joined the Pennsylvania-Yale expedition to Egypt that was rescuing artifacts before the area was flooded for the Aswan Dam project, which led to his dissertation, "History and Settlement in Lower Nubia." Despite warnings from his American colleagues that Canada was an academic backwater, he accepted an appointment at McGill University in 1964 and remained there for the next four decades. Although he continued to receive prestigious offers from abroad, he preferred to build a department and a discipline at home rather than chase international scholarly accolades.

I rarely write about people I know personally. I'd heard of Trigger but I'd never met him or studied his work. Writing his obituary gave me an insight into his research and his life. I talked to students he inspired and to his family, who spoke of the man behind the scholarship, the father who loved to chat expansively at the dinner table and who was so dear that his younger daughter hastily organized her wedding hoping it could take place in his hospital room before he died. Alas, the nuptuals had to take place without the father of the bride. I still haven't met any of Trigger's family, but he made such an impact on me that, after death, he was transformed from a stranger into a friend. Learning about his achievements and humanity enhanced my own life.

MYTH NUMBER THREE: OBITUARIES ARE PREWRITTEN AND LEFT TO MOULDER IN A DRAWER

NOBODY CAN PREDICT who will be the next to die; there is no launch complete with press kits, media tours, or scheduled interviews to help you cover a subject's life with authority and dispatch, the way it is with elections, literary prizes, and film premieres. The immediacy and the finality of writing obituaries make my job terrifying. That's why many obituary writers have nightmares about car crashes and heart attacks carrying off people on their "to-do" list.

As practitioners we know far too well that the well-stocked "morgue" of meticulously researched, luminously written, and conscientiously updated obituaries ready to roll as soon as the death knell tolls is the biggest myth in the business. "Some newspapers, I'm told, have hundreds of obituaries ready," Ann Wroe, obituaries editor of the *Economist*, wrote in 2008. "There are ten obituaries in [our morgue] as I write, and I have never yet been able to pluck one out and use it." In my own experience, having a prewritten obituary on file is the best guarantee of immortality, because nobody in the morgue ever seems to die. They live on, if only to haunt you for having had the effrontery to anticipate their deaths. As Ann Wroe says, they "achieve a kind of eternal life, getting wirier and stronger by the day."

When I started writing obituaries for the *Globe and Mail*, I quickly discovered that the advances we did have were woefully inadequate. The previous obituary writer had died several years earlier and had not been replaced during one of those periodic downswings in the newspaper business. So nobody had been updating, revising, and writing new obituaries for ages. There were people in the advance queue — a much more delicate term than *morgue* — whose accomplishments had faded into obscurity, and others who had gone through career moves or political campaigns that had resulted in dynamic lifestyle changes since the advances had been filed.

Delving into our morgue was akin to winning an election and then being shown the empty coffers in the national treasury. But that shock was nothing compared to being knocked sideways by the tsunami of relief emanating from all the other reporters in the newsroom when they realized they were no longer on the hook for the advance obituaries they had postponed writing. As the official obituary writer, I had absolved them of that nerve-wracking burden.

One of my colleagues in the arts section, for example, had been working on an obit of the significant and prolific poet Irving Layton for a decade. He continued to say that he was just writing up his notes for me until the day Layton died in 2006, at age ninety-three, after suffering from dementia for nearly a decade. That was a scramble, I can tell you. Layton, who had won a Governor General's Literary Award in 1959 for his breakthrough collection, *A Red Carpet for the Sun,* had both a huge oeuvre and a Byzantine personal life that involved myriad wives, partners, feuds, and offspring.

One of the best examples of writing obituaries under pressure comes from a profile of Alden Whitman, a legendary obituary writer and editor for the *New York Times.* As an editor, Whitman had broken the byline embargo and transformed the obituary from a news story into a biographical and literary essay, hence establishing standards he himself was forced to meet as a writer. The *Times* had an astounding two thousand obits in its morgue (today that figure is more like 1,300) but there wasn't a word on Adlai Stevenson, the U.S. ambassador to the United Nations, when he died suddenly in 1965 while on a trip to England. A huge obituary was required because Stevenson, a former governor of Illinois, had twice run for president against Dwight D. Eisenhower, had been John Kennedy's ambassador to the United Nations during the Cuban Missile Crisis, and was still in that office under Lyndon Johnson when he succumbed to a heart attack at age sixty-five. My chest tightens just thinking about it.

Whitman heard the sorry news from his wife, who also worked at the *Times.* That is so often how I hear about a death too — not from my wife, of course, but from a friend or family member. *Is it true?* That is always my first reaction before my heart starts thudding and I scroll through my electronic Rolodex for somebody who can confirm or deny the news.

Instead of hitting the phones, Whitman, according to journalist Gay Talese's account in *Esquire* magazine, "broke into a cool sweat, slipped out of the City Room," and went to lunch upstairs in the NYT cafeteria. "But soon he felt a soft rap on his shoulder. It was one of the metropolitan editor's assistants asking: Will you be down soon, Alden?"

Rather like being told that the time has come for your execution. The chilly equivalent of that tap has happened to me dozens of times. I'm sure I can't prove this scientifically, but I'm convinced that noteworthy people always die late in the afternoon — or at least that's when I hear about their demise.

Certainly that's what happened when documentary filmmaker Allan King died of a malignant brain tumour on June 15, 2009. I had seen several of his films, including *Warrendale, A Married Couple,* and *Dying at Grace,* but I knew little about his life. The more I found out while researching and writing simultaneously to create a full-page obituary in a couple of hours, the more I realized that King's early life had been bleaker than a Victorian melodrama. What fascinated me was the way he had channelled the deprivations of his childhood into a fascination with other people's lives — not to ridicule or exploit his subjects, but to empathize with the frailties of the human condition.

King was born Allan Winton in Vancouver on February 6, 1930, the elder child of an alcoholic father. His parents separated when he was six; his mother became destitute and had to put her children into foster care. She was allowed to visit them only once a month, until she found a job that paid well enough for her to reclaim them. As a teenager he discovered film: watching it, programming it at the Vancouver Film Society, and eventually making his own gritty documentaries in the early days of CBC Television in Vancouver. The films always coincided, however subtly, with the emotional traumas of his own life, from his first documentary, *Skid Row* (about alcoholics like his own father who lived in flophouses on Vancouver's Eastside), to *A Married Couple* (about the disintegration of a marriage) to one of his last and most poignant films, *Dying at Grace* (portraits of people in palliative care at a Salvation Army hospital in Toronto). I suppose I could have rebelled and said: "Call the film critics; they know his work better than I do." But then I wouldn't have learned the outlines of the life of a cinéma-vérité pioneer who influenced a generation of filmmakers and whose work was heralded by, among others, Jean Renoir.

Knowing the pressure of writing an obituary on deadline, I can empathize with Whitman's sweat and urge to flee before facing the inevitable. What I don't share is the "occupational astigmatism," as Talese put it, that caused Whitman to cross people off his list so definitively once the advance was filed. Having written their lives, he began thinking of his subjects in the past tense — literally. Because they were deceased on paper, they were dead in reality, at least as far as he was concerned.

I've never had such overweening pride of authorship that I have wished my subject would drop dead, and soon, so that I could see my masterpiece in print. On the contrary, my subjects become like relatives — the close kind. I know them so well by the time I have written about them that I hope they will live forever. I take comfort from seeing them resting quietly in my advance queue, knowing that at least the groundwork is there. No matter when they die, I invariably rewrite and revise until an editor gives me the electronic equivalent of the tap on the shoulder that interrupted Whitman's lunch.

Myth Number Four: The Dying Don't Want to Talk about Their Lives

WHEN I WAS offered the job as obituary writer, I was asked if I would be willing to interview politicians and other significant Canadians before writing advance obituaries. I can remember agreeing and then asking what the typical approach was in requesting an interview with, say, Brian Mulroney. "Oh, you just say you're preparing an interview for the files," was the reply.

So that is what I did the first time I wrote an advance. I phoned Hamilton Southam, a prominent but aged cultural figure. He agreed to see me, we settled into his den, and we had an absorbing discussion about his life as a journalist, veteran, diplomat, founder of the National Arts Centre in Ottawa, and key figure in establishing the Canadian War Museum, among many other cultural initiatives. I became more and more uneasy as the interview continued, realizing that I was there under ambiguous circumstances.

Finally we said our goodbyes and he turned to me and asked the perfectly obvious question: "When will the piece appear?"

"Not sure," I mumbled. "I'll be in touch."

And a good thing too, as Southam lived for three more years. Within that time I added another civic accomplishment and a romantic wrinkle to his story. But it didn't end there. Southam died in 2008 on Canada Day, a national celebration that he had pioneered back in the late 1970s. As a death date it was pleasingly symbolic for a ninety-one-year-old man who had devoted his life to Canadian life and culture. Alas, the holiday meant that there were few people on the news desk; consequently, Southam's demise slipped under the radar and, even though I had a long obit waiting in the morgue, we were a day late in reporting his death.

That conversation with Southam was the first and last time I relied on the "piece for the files" ruse to get an interview. The deception still makes me cringe. From then on I resolved to tell the truth, however difficult. Novelist Tom Rachman has a variation on that scenario in his chapter about obituary writer Arthur Gopal in *The Imperfectionists*. Sent to interview Gerda Erzberger, a terminally ill Austrian intellectual who has been championed and then dumped by feminist activists, he arrives, notebook and tape recorder in hand, to interview her for a "profile" for the paper, although the only newsworthy thing about her is her approaching demise. She has no time for subterfuge and pinions him with a direct question: "'So can I assume,' she asks, half turned toward the kitchen, 'that you're writing my obituary?'"

As Rachman's character learns, people who are elderly or ill know full well that their lives are coming to an end. They are thinking about their impending deaths and interested in reflecting on their lives. Sometimes they have things they want to say, especially if they trust you to keep their confidences until after they are dead.

In my experience, it is the people around the dying—the dear friends, close colleagues, and devoted family members—who are squeamish, not the person who is actually dying. Still, there is nothing worse than going on a fishing expedition for biographical facts with somebody who is ill. I research the life to figure out the themes and the questions that I want to ask, then I make the phone call. I introduce myself and say that I would like an interview to talk about their significant contribution to Canadian life, explaining that while I hope the obituary may not be needed any time soon, I want to do the best job possible by preparing in advance.

I let this sink in and then I make sure I promise that nothing said to me will be printed before "such time as it may be necessary." (So far nobody has confessed to stealing the Crown Jewels or to other misdemeanours that would put my vow of confidentiality into conflict with the laws of the land or the news imperatives of my employers, but I am cognizant of the ethical dilemmas such a disclosure would present.) Another long pause, and then I explain that in my experience the only people who die are the ones I haven't written about. Besides, I conclude, I update every five years. When I made that pretty speech several years ago to politician Flora MacDonald, who was then in her late seventies, she retorted: "You'll have to do that, because my mother lived well past a hundred."

By chance, in 2005 I was in the audience for one of William Hutt's farewell performances at the Stratford Festival. He was Prospero in *The Tempest*, a role he had first played on that stage more than forty years earlier. Looking like a haggard bloodhound after a fruitless hunt for a rabbit, he delivered his final lines: "As you from crimes would pardon'd be / Let your indulgence set me free." I was haunted by the poignancy with which he stood alone on the stage, garbed in a white bedsheet of a robe and holding a bouquet of red roses, while the waves of applause and love lapped over him. When I heard nearly two years later that Hutt was suffering from leukemia, I phoned and asked him for an interview for an eventual obituary.

"I will be happy to talk with you, but my days are short," he said, in a voice that was commanding yet courtly. "I am looking on my demise as a project, and I am the project manager." He had already chosen a cemetery plot and decided on his epitaph: "Soldier and Actor."

Ten days later I rang his Stratford doorbell. Wearing a loose brown patterned shirt over casual trousers and with terribly swollen ankles showing above a pair of moccasins, Hutt sat in a wing chair beside a window. He was attached to a portable oxygen tank and did not rise to greet me — an indication from an unfailingly courteous man that his strength was failing. His face had a waxy pallor and, having smoked for sixty years before he finally butted out, he was often racked with coughing spells. But his conversation was thoughtful and engaging.

For ninety minutes we had a frank and wide-ranging conversation about his disaffection with his parents, the war and his introduction to death before he had had a chance to know much about life, his bisexuality, and how he had found a home on stage at the Stratford Festival. Although completely lucid, he seemed to have transcended the quotidian world and was in a contemplative space I felt privileged to share.

Unlike so many young men who charge onto the battlefield deluded by visions of glory, Hutt was a pacifist. He had "no intention of shooting anybody" but he wanted to serve his country in the Second World War, so he enlisted in an ambulance unit as a corporal, thereby probably seeing more trauma and gore than the most gung-ho combatants. Just north of Monte Cassino, Italy, he volunteered to traverse a heavily mined and booby-trapped field, under constant mortar fire, to attend to wounded soldiers and to find a suitable site for a first-aid post. For his gallantry and initiative he was awarded the Military Medal in the field.

Hutt had no false modesty about his capacity as an actor. "I will leave the word 'great' to history," he said that afternoon, "but I do know that in some kind of way, my career as an actor has paralleled the growth of theatre in this country." He said he had always been very practical as an actor, and that his decision to stay home rather than to chase fame in London and New York came from an "arrogant pride" in Canada. "I had no intention of leaving this country until I was invited. I wasn't going to beg." And by doing so, he showed that it was possible to have both a stellar career here and attractive offers to work elsewhere.

Growing philosophical, he said there are three major stages in life: The first is adolescence, when things happen to your body and your mind. The second stage is when you are in your twenties and your parents become your friends rather than authority figures (the war had interrupted that process for him and left him divided from his parents). The third stage, the one he was entering, is death and wondering what that will be like. He wanted to go on living, but he wasn't afraid of death.

Sensing his fatigue, I turned off my tape recorder, put away my notebook, and walked across the room to shake his hand and make my goodbyes. "How are you going to use this?" he asked, locking my eyes with his and holding on to my outstretched hand. "By the time I write your obituary, in ten years' time," I said with what I hoped was a disarming smile, "this moment we have shared will have evaporated." He nodded, and then, after struggling to get up, he pulled my face down and kissed me on both cheeks, a farewell that only later I realized was permanent. Fewer than five days afterwards he died, to the shock of friends, colleagues, and this obituary writer.

How I wish now that I'd had a video camera in my journalist's toolkit that afternoon, so that the final interview with Canada's most majestic actor could have been captured for posterity. Would the magic connection that I felt with William Hutt that hot afternoon have been destroyed by cameras and technicians? I can't say for certain, but I don't think so. He was an actor, after all, and it is my experience that people forget about the tape recorder and the camera if the conversation is engaging.

Nothing is completely dispassionate in this world, but the process in which I, the journalist, interview and write an obituary of a significant Canadian figure comes closer to the ideal of objectivity than eulogies and tributes from family and friends that appear in print and on the Web.

Myth Number Five: Obituaries Don't Tell the Real Truth

Somebody asked me while I was in the final stages of writing this book if I had thought about including Clifford Olson, the murderer who abducted, tortured, and killed eleven children in British Columbia in a heinous nine-month rampage in the early 1980s. Yes, I replied, but I couldn't because he died in September 2011, which was outside my time frame of the first decade of this century.

There was nothing good to say about Olson the habitual criminal, his revolting "cash for bodies" deal with authorities so families could recover the remains of their murdered children, or his prison-cell antics to negotiate a new trial, parole, and other concessions. But his diabolical behaviour both in and outside prison changed the justice system in Canada. Measures that we take for granted nowadays, such as victim impact statements at sentencing and parole board hearings, were nonexistent back then. Amber Alerts, the National Missing Children's Registry, and amendments to strengthen the Criminal Code with respect to sexual assault, child abduction, and sexual abuse have also become standard. Many of those changes came about because the families of Olson's victims, outraged and traumatized by the treatment they endured during his prosecution and incessant jailhouse appeals, petitioned and lobbied the justice system on behalf of their murdered children. That's why Olson's worth writing about.

"Never speak ill of the dead" is an aphorism attributed to Chilon of Sparta, a sixth-century BCE Greek sage and civic leader who is said to have encouraged the rise of militarism in Sparta. Essentially he was saying that the dead can no longer harm the living or defend themselves against criticism, so it is better to ignore their faults and remember their virtues. That is a fine sentiment, especially as proclaimed by a politician eager to ensure his own legacy, but it doesn't apply to obituary writers. We stand apart from the family and friends of the deceased because we are journalists, not eulogists.

In my view there is no such thing as an uninteresting life, but there are plenty of badly researched and written accounts. The difference between humdrum and compelling rests in documenting weaknesses, celebrating strengths, and placing people's lives in the context of what else was happening here and abroad. ("Did they serve in the Second World War?" is a question I always ask when I look at the resumés of people born in the early decades of the twentieth century. If yes, where? If not, why? I'm not interested in ridiculing decisions made long ago but rather in seeking an understanding of how a pivotal event of the past century affected my subject.) My goal is to make my subjects breathe one more time on the page, and that means a portrait that includes shadow as well as light, or "warts and all," as

Oliver Cromwell allegedly said to court painter Sir Peter Lely back in the seventeenth century.

Nevertheless, writing about the dead means observing and sometimes even sharing the grief of those they have left to mourn, as the euphemism has it. "Dead people can't sue" may be a legal truism in most jurisdictions, but that doesn't mean the departed and their survivors don't deserve respect. An obituary writer often dwells in the slippery territory between the blunt truth and the subtle reference. Nothing is omitted, but unflattering traits aren't shouted out in neon headlines either.

Denounce the practice as burying the lede, if you will, but I think delivering the facts in a tactful way is important at a distressing and sad time. Besides, canny readers delight in deciphering the code and learning that somebody described as "restlessly romantic" was probably a chronic philanderer, or a person "who enjoyed a drink or three before dinner" was a borderline alcoholic.

There is a delicate balance between telling the truth and respecting the grief of family and friends. How much life is too much information in an obituary? That is the eternal question. I have evolved a working rule: if the information can be documented and it had a fundamental impact on my subject's life, I include it, however unseemly.

The family of entertainer Jack Duffy pleaded with me to expunge his alcoholism from my proposed obituary. I refused because it was true and had been widely reported, and he himself had spoken publicly about the binge drinking that threatened to ruin his career and end his life. A ringer for Frank Sinatra, Duffy was a skinny, sad-faced crooner who toured with Tommy Dorsey's band in the late 1940s, singing lead vocals and doing sardonic imitations of his look-a-like heartthrob. His career spanned nearly sixty years of Canadian and American radio, television, and film, including a long stint on *Party Game*, a TV variety showed based on the old parlour game charades.

While touring with the revue *Spring Thaw* in the mid-1960s, Duffy met a petite red-haired actress named Marylyn Stuart. They became a couple both professionally and romantically. By the time they were performing at Expo 67 in Montreal, Duffy was such a serious alcoholic that a doctor gave him a death sentence and told him not to marry Stuart if he truly loved her, because otherwise he would merely be saddling her with his problems. The message penetrated, and that summer, when everybody else was celebrating Canada's centennial, Duffy was drying out.

He put the cap on the bottle and kept it there until he died at age eighty-one on May 19, 2008. Duffy's sobriety was an accomplishment that said something about him as a person, and so it needed to be included in his obituary. What his family feared was a headline that blared "Former Drunk Also Sang and Acted." In the end they were happy about the frankness of the obituary because the tough parts were presented in the context of a redeemed life.

Not everybody is as reasonable as the Duffy family. I have suffered the wrath of family and friends who feel they have the right to dictate the terms and conditions of what I write. I have learned that the most innocuous detail — at least to me — can be a trigger unleashing pent-up grief camouflaged as rage. The anger is misplaced, for I am only the messenger. It is far easier for the grief-stricken to get mad at me for allegedly speaking ill of the dead than it is for them to blame a loved one for leaving them alone and bereft.

Obituary writers constantly walk a tightrope between assessing a life and respecting the feelings of the bereaved. This is most poignant when it comes to people who "die suddenly," as the family death notices say, from no apparent cause — the traditional euphemism for suicide. When I read those words, I always check the person's age and scan the list of charities for clues as to what really happened. I haven't written about too many suicides, but one I will always remember is the death of poet Richard Outram.

Outram had both a tragic and a transcendent life. Born in Oshawa, Ontario, on April 9, 1930, he studied at the University of Toronto under philosopher Emil Fackenheim and literary critic Northrop Frye, two illustrious scholars who greatly influenced the way Outram saw the world. After earning an honours degree in English and philosophy in 1953, he went to England, where he found work as a stagehand at the BBC. It was in London that he began writing poetry and where he met the Canadian artist Barbara Howard, the woman who would share his life and his artistic vocation.

They returned to Canada, married, and had a baby daughter, Sarah, who died a day after her birth, a grief that Outram expressed in several poems. He kept his day job as a stagehand until he turned sixty, consciously spending his days at physical labour and his evenings exercising his imagination and his literary sensibilities. Although Outram never achieved glory or celebrity as a poet, he had a coterie of devoted readers who admired his acute sense of the natural world, his rhyming, and the metaphysical coherence of his work. The typographical designer Allan Fleming (who created the CN and Ontario

Hydro logos, among many other projects) designed and published Outram's first chapbook, *Eight Poems*.

After Howard died unexpectedly in 2002 during a routine operation, Outram was devastated. For nearly three years Outram staggered on alone. Then, on a bitterly cold winter night in January 2005, after consuming a quantity of pills and drink, he settled down on the side porch of his house in Port Hope, Ontario, and in a grand Blakean gesture allowed himself to die alone under the night sky. "The two of them fed each other beautifully and with enormous intensity. They were the closing of the couplet," writer Barry Callaghan observed. "So, what are you going to do with a one-line couplet? He really was his work and his love for her." Outram's suicide was a gentle but determined act of wilful hypothermia, a death that in the telling said much more about Outram as a romantic and a poet than the weasel expression "died suddenly" could possibly convey.

Suicide has always been with us, but as the population ages a new way of dying — doctor-assisted suicide or hastened death — is going to become a much more pressing issue, not only for society but for those who write about people who end their lives when and how they choose, should the state allow them to do so.

It is not only the way we die, but how we deal with death that is changing. Uploads on social networking and video-sharing websites, streaming coverage of funerals for the ordinary person as well as for public figures, provide an emotional platform for friends, families, and even strangers to deliver heartfelt (and sometimes mawkish) messages about the departed. These sites, which can turn ordinary people into celebrities, aren't restricted to mourners. Recently I received an e-mail request from the sales manager of an entrepreneurial legacy website. He wanted me to write a story about his company, which offers people the opportunity to record virtual final messages so they can be delivered in the future to family and friends, turning the expression "voice from beyond the grave" into a dubious reality. Ghoulishness aside — and some of these sites offer maudlin deathbed scenes worthy of the fictional tales of Charles Dickens — they pose a challenge to traditional media outlets.

The Internet is the greatest boon and the trickiest pitfall for the contemporary obituary writer. It offers you anything and everything, everywhere and all the time. There are few filters unless you are searching a legitimate journalistic or scholarly site. The urge to be first with the news encourages journalists to relax standards and accept Twitter feeds as gospel without double-sourcing to ensure that the news of a celebrity's death is fact and not rumour. "Is it accurate?" is the question you have to keep asking as you wade through a swamp of information. Being first is useless if you are wrong.

If we journalists are to maintain our lead in preparing dispassionate, authoritative obituaries of recently departed notables — and by that I mean biographical essays that set a life in context, pay tribute to achievements, and account for failures and faults — then we too must embrace the new technology. But there's a huge caveat: we can't abandon traditional journalistic standards in a rush to compete with streaming funerals, mydeathspace.com, or *The Blog of Death*.

In writing about the fifty people I have selected for this book, I have tried to cover a range of occupations, achievements, locations, and aspirations. Most of all I wanted to write about individuals whose stories moved me and whose lives said something larger about the country and our collective history. The past is a different country, but if we don't know its geography we can't map our way into the future. In recounting the achievements and the vulnerabilities of my fifty subjects, I hope I have conveyed an abiding sense of their humanity.

ICONS

"This Is Bigger Than Bush"

I T WAS JUST before six p.m. on November 30, 2004. I had written an obituary of Phyllis Mailing, a mezzo-soprano and avant-garde musician. A former wife of composer R. Murray Schafer, she premiered many significant musical pieces, inspired several composers, and for decades taught aspiring vocalists at Simon Fraser University. I had filed my piece, the page had been edited, and I was thinking of slipping out of the newsroom and heading home.

My phone rang. I debated letting it go to voice mail, but something compelled me to pick up the receiver. The female voice on the other end was hoarse. "Sandra," was all she said.

Immediately I knew two things: the voice belonged to Elsa Franklin, the long-standing producer, confidante, and publicist for Pierre Berton, and that she was calling with bad news.

"He's died, hasn't he," I said.

"Yes," she replied.

I was sad for her, for his family, for all of us, but what I also felt was the shock of knowing my day was only beginning, even though I had already done a full and productive shift. Fortunately I had been working on Berton's obituary and it was more or less finished — not to my satisfaction, of course, but it had a beginning and a middle and now I could write its inevitable end. But it was way past deadline and my piece on Berton was too long to fit on the obituary page.

I sent an electronic note to my section editor. He responded the way editors always do. He decided that maybe it was time to read my piece. He pulled it up on his screen and then he informed his superiors that Berton was dead.

Here is what happens when somebody significant dies: You no longer own the file. Everybody wants a piece of it because journalists are like baying hounds that have caught a whiff of fox. That's another reason to prepare in advance. Invariably you will end up jockeying for position in what amounts to an editorial scrum, but you have the advantage of reworking and updating an existing piece rather than staring frantically into a blank screen seeking inspiration.

Of course, the 24/7 news cycle of the Internet has made all of these machinations even more frenzied. Journalist Christopher Hitchens was only the latest in a long list of celebrities who fell into that category when he died of cancer of the esophagus on December 15, 2011. Prince Philip fought off the Grim Reaper late in that same month, but I can tell you that I mentally reviewed his file while I stirred the gravy for my family's Christmas turkey.

Nobody in this mortal coil can accurately predict who will be the next to die, although there are several Internet sites that do their best to shine klieg lights on ailing celebrities. Mostly I find the notion of death watches offensive, especially when they involve sound trucks and camera crews camped outside a hospital like a Greek chorus waiting for its cue to move onto centre stage.

Still, I have to do my job. So I often wish close family or friends would give me a warning when somebody is nearing the end, on the understanding that I will quietly prepare the obituary for when it is "needed," as the euphemism has it. Otherwise, the tension ramps up and I worry even when I am on vacation — especially when I am on vacation — that one of my subjects will die before I have finished researching and writing his or her life. A couple of years ago I drove across the country with my husband; every morning I was a wreck until I had scoured the local newspaper or browsed the Web to check on the health of Nelson Mandela, one of the people on my to-do list. He's still with us.

It's easy enough to man the phone lines and collect quotes about the enormity of the loss, but that, as I've said before, makes for a reaction piece, not an obituary. I want to capture the life of my subjects, and that involves finding out where they went to school, their mother's maiden name, and who and why they married. It requires hours, even days, of research and writing.

Sometimes the timing is eerily close between drafting an obituary and a subject's death, almost as though he or she were patiently waiting for me to finish typing. For example, the call announcing the death of Beland Honderich, former publisher of the *Toronto Star*, came in one hour after I had saved and closed his file on my computer. More often, though, people die unexpectedly, or when you have set aside a half-written obituary of a living subject to work on somebody who is actually dead.

The other inevitability about death is that editors — the still mostly men who decide what goes on the front page — are only interested in the top six paragraphs of your story. The rest, or what is often called the "turn," is left to copy editors. But the senior editors want their paws on the lede and the "nut," the summary paragraph that gives readers the gist of your story in a nutshell. They were happy enough with my Berton lede, but there was a complication. You can't turn from the front page to another section of the paper, so either Berton had to reside in a secondary part of the paper or two pages of national and foreign news had to be dumped to accommodate the passing of Mr. Canada.

His death wasn't the only front-page contender that day. U.S. president George W. Bush was arriving from Washington for his first state visit to Canada, a visit that was scheduled to last only until the next day. Space on the front page had been reserved for the Ottawa bureau to file late accounts of Bush's dinner with Prime Minister Stephen Harper.

(Of course, whatever I might have been planning to do that evening was also shelved. My friends have become used to a frenzied call or email from me cancelling lunch or dinner or the movies with the terse message "Somebody's died. I can't make it." In the early days of my tenure on the dead beat, people often responded to this message with condolences on my loss, assuming I was in deep mourning over a sudden death in my own family.)

Warily I went to the news desk to see what nightmare awaited me and my long but incomplete obituary. As I approached, I saw seven or eight men standing in a circle in earnest conversation, weighing the merits of George W. Bush versus Pierre Berton and the next day's front page. Elsa Franklin may have called me first, but I wasn't the only one on her media list. We had an advantage, but not a big one. Suddenly the front-page editor looked up and exclaimed: "This is bigger than Bush." There was a moment's silence as everybody looked at him. Then slowly, beginning with the editor-in-chief, several heads nodded sagely.

"Yes, it is," I said to myself, resisting the impulse to thrust my fist into the air in triumph. "A genuine Canadian champion has died, and thank God these hard-news guys have the sense to realize that cultural history is as significant as daily politics."

And then the work began. The obituary page was called back and poor Phyllis Mailing, the avant-garde mezzo-soprano, had to give way to the greatest popularizer of our country's history. I wrote a news piece for the front section after calling a list of people for reaction to Berton's death, and then I polished and revised my obituary while the obituary page editor designed a stand-alone two-page spread on the expanded obituary pages. By nine p.m. the copy had been ripped from my hands, final revisions made, and the Send button pushed.

THE WORD *ICON* is not hyperbolic for the ten lives, including Berton's, in this section. They have all made an outsize impact on Canadian life and culture, from Arthur Erickson's monumental designs for buildings that rise out of the landscape to Oscar Peterson's virtuosity as a jazz musician to Pierre Trudeau's political leadership in preserving national unity and transforming Canada into a modern multicultural society. They begin with the economist John Kenneth Galbraith and end with the writer Mordecai Richler. Their lives encompass the emotional depth of Maureen Forrester's singular contralto, the urban activism of Jane Jacobs, and the searing power of hockey legend Maurice "The Rocket" Richard.

The public grief for Pierre Trudeau or Rocket Richard, who both died in 2000, (or for NDP leader Jack Layton, who died of cancer in August 2011, only three months after achieving Official Opposition status for his party in Parliament) was overwhelming, but these men, heroes to so many, each had a ceremonial lying-in-state followed by a public funeral. People could express themselves by lining up to pay tribute, signing a condolence book, and sharing the experience collectively with other mourners. The same release occurred when Oscar Peterson's music was played on radio and television and celebrated in a free public memorial concert.

The memorials for other icons in this chapter, including Berton, Mordecai Richler, and June Callwood, were private affairs, so mourners took to print and broadcast venues to remember them and to express their grief. The reaction to Berton's death from readers was staggering. You have no idea how

many people wrote in with reminiscences about Mr. Canada, including variations on his famous recipe for roasting a turkey—by basting the bird with soy
sauce, of all things. People felt Berton's loss keenly for the simple reason that
he had taught us to revere the past the way the Group of Seven had shown us,
with their broad, impressionistic strokes, how to appreciate the rugged,
untamed landscape of the Canadian Shield.

Over his lifetime, Berton's heroic narrative style gave way to a different
kind of storytelling—one that is regional, multicultural, and diverse—which
I think was another reason to mark his passing. With his death we were also
saying goodbye to an era of cultural nationalism and a monolithic narrative
about our country. The past is no longer tidy. It is now a territory claimed by
women, aboriginals, immigrants from Africa, Asia, Eastern Europe, and
other places around the world. Instead of a lone voice telling a heroic story
about the past, we have a social and ethnic chorus that embraces both scholars and informed enthusiasts.

If the voices have changed, so have the stories. The writers who emerged
after Berton's generation—the ones such as Margaret Atwood who came of
age in the 1950s and 1960s, or Michael Ondaatje, who arrived in the great
waves of non-European immigration in the 1960s and 1970s—tended, if they
wrote about the past, to do it in fiction and poetry. Partly that was because
literary writing is not constrained by national borders and markets: the imagination does not speak to a local audience.

Print has long since been eclipsed as the primary storytelling conduit
from writer to audience. Network television has demanded an increased role,
with dedicated programming, such as the History Channel, and institutional
boosters, such as the Historica-Dominion Institute and the National History
Society, collecting and championing storytelling circles, groups, and vehicles.
The Internet, with Wikipedia and specialty websites, homes in on all manner
of arcane subjects and events.

Even as more people are telling their personal and collective stories, the
tools that are available for researching the past have improved enormously.
Researchers still dig their way through boxes of letters in public archives, but
they are just as likely to be searching for online references in Wikipedia, the
Dictionary of Canadian Biography, or *The Canadian Encyclopedia* (pioneered
by another lone voice, Mel Hurtig of Edmonton, and now part of the Historica-
Dominion Institute). None of these tools was readily available when Berton
began writing popular history half a century ago.

THE ICONS IN this chapter stretch in time from the first decade of the previous century through the first decade of this one — a hundred years in which bloody wars were fought; men landed on the moon; and women won the vote, acquired the means to control their fertility, and found leadership roles outside the home. Their power to change minds and attitudes has had an enormous impact and has made us think about the contribution each made to our collective society. Their legacies endure.

John Kenneth Galbraith

Economist

October 15, 1908 – April 29, 2006

T HE MOST POPULAR American economist of the past century was actually a Canadian.

John Kenneth Galbraith, the lanky six-foot, eight-inch Keynesian pundit and advisor to Democratic presidents — from Roosevelt through Clinton — was born on a farm in southwestern Ontario when Laurier was prime minister and Canada was still part of the British Empire.

In the academic discipline known as the dismal science, Galbraith was in the troika of our most internationally celebrated practitioners. The other two are economic historian Harold Innis (whose work, and whose influence on other academics such as Marshall McLuhan, is still internationally revered) and political economist Stephen Leacock, who is remembered today chiefly as a writer and humorist. Galbraith, as political scientist Stephen Clarkson once quipped, was "Canada's greatest contribution to civilizing American capitalism."

He learned his populist politics on his father's farm before the First World War and discovered his inherent writing skills at the Ontario College of Agriculture during the Depression. As for his mordant wit, charisma, and social cachet, they seemed to come naturally. An economic and political confidant of President John F. Kennedy, he contributed the pivotal sentence "Let us never negotiate out of fear, but let us never fear to negotiate" to Kennedy's inauguration speech.

He never won the Nobel Prize, nor did he spawn any schools of economic thought — as did his arch-rival, Milton Friedman. Still, Galbraith wrote more than forty books, many of them bestsellers; coined the expressions *conventional wisdom*, *affluent society*, and *countervailing powers*; and was said to have been the only economist invited to Truman Capote's Black and White Ball in New York in 1966.

He was awarded the Order of Canada, nearly fifty honorary degrees, and the Presidential Medal of Freedom twice — by Harry S. Truman in 1948 and Bill Clinton in 2000. His books include *American Capitalism: The Concept of Countervailing Power* (1952), *The Affluent Society* (1958), *The New Industrial State* (1967), *The Age of Uncertainty* (1977), and three satirical novels.

Galbraith taught at Harvard for more than thirty years, but he wasn't a typical academic. He used his wit and his flair for the well-honed phrase to write for a popular market rather than a scholarly one, rarely presenting his ideas in peer-reviewed scholarly papers where they could be vetted by the profession. Many economists resented him for hanging out in presidential enclaves and op-ed pages instead of sticking to the seminar rooms and the lecture halls, but Galbraith, who was never criticized for being excessively modest, was unchastened.

He had learned early on — working in the Office of Price Administration for the Roosevelt administration during the Second World War — that nobody paid any attention to dense academic arguments, so he deliberately wrote for the general public about economic issues, gambling that when an idea caught on with the masses, the profession would pay attention too. And that's exactly what happened As his friend the economist Paul Samuelson observed to Galbraith's biographer Richard Parker, he "will be remembered, and read when most of us Nobel Laureates will be buried in footnotes down in dusty library stacks."

Galbraith was so popular with the public and so prominently connected with government leaders that the profession couldn't disregard him: they elected him president of the American Economic Association in 1972. True to his Canadian roots, he insisted that the association's annual meeting be held in Toronto, the first time it had ever met outside the United States.

As a populist, he contended that economics had failed as a field of study by pretending to be something it wasn't — a hard science. As for economists, they had lost touch with the way economies actually operate in relation to political, social, and environmental factors by adhering like barnacles to mathematical modelling. "In making economics a non-political subject," Galbraith once wrote, "neoclassical theory destroys the relation of economics to the real world...it manipulates levers to which no machinery is attached."

Economist Richard Parker described the Galbraithian method, in *John Kenneth Galbraith: His Life, His Politics, His Economics*, as dealing with issues as they emerge. "You don't proceed from an abstract, atemporal, ageographical model, but from what you see around you and what you can feel around you," Parker explained in a public lecture.

Today Galbraith's reputation rests on his talents as a writer of masterful prose, his historical influence as a presidential advisor, and his work as a pragmatic liberal economist who believed in government intervention as a countervailing economic force to unbridled capitalism. "I'm for a socially pain-free, decently egalitarian society," he told the *Globe and Mail* in 2005, when he was ninety-six, still writing books and still in demand as a pundit.

JOHN KENNETH (KEN) Galbraith was born on October 15, 1908, in the back bedroom of a two-storey farmhouse in Iona Station, a hamlet on the railway line connecting Detroit and Buffalo. He was the third of five children (although one sister had died of whooping cough before he was born) of schoolteacher and farmer William Archibald (Archie) Galbraith and his wife, Sarah Catherine (Kate) Galbraith (née Kendall).

His parents weren't rich but they weren't poor either, owning two farms that together amounted to 150 acres. Although the Galbraiths were staunchly Liberal in their politics, Archie Galbraith was sufficiently disgruntled to become active in the United Farmers of Ontario, a protest movement that gained enough political momentum to win the provincial election of 1919.

Many years later, Galbraith sardonically memorialized his family, which had emigrated from Scotland in 1819, in *The Scotch*, one of his most popular books. He recalled attending a political rally with his father in the middle of the First World War, when he was about eight. Needing a podium, the senior Galbraith mounted a large pile of manure and addressed the crowd. "He apologized with ill-concealed sincerity for speaking from the Tory platform," Galbraith wrote. "The effect on this agrarian audience was electric. Afterward I congratulated him on the brilliance of the sally. He said, 'It was good but it didn't change any votes.'"

His mother died after a short illness when he was fifteen, a tragedy that he mentioned briefly in his memoirs, *A Life in Our Times*, when he wrote: "My mother, a beautiful, affectionate and decidedly firm woman, died when her children — my brother, my two sisters, and I — were not yet all in their teens." The family was devastated.

Her husband, Archie, remote in his grief, never remarried and became even more active in community affairs. As for Ken, an avid reader, he found solace in books, taking advantage of the local library's decision to change its lending policy from two books every two weeks to unlimited borrowing. Even so, he let his assigned schoolwork slump. He travelled the six miles to school in a horse and buggy with his siblings but was frequently late for class. Gangly, awkward at sports, and humiliated by his clumsiness in the compulsory cadet corps, he had to repeat his senior year of high school.

After he finally graduated in 1926, he went to the Ontario Agricultural College (now the University of Guelph), about eighty miles northeast of home, because his father decided he should. Years later, Galbraith referred to the oac in an interview in *Time* magazine as "not only the cheapest but probably the worst college in the English-speaking world."

He spent five years at the oac partly because of his inadequate high school education and partly because he was diagnosed with "an incipient tuberculosis." What made the difference for this decidedly indifferent student was the academic requirement that all students had to write weekly compositions. And this is where the physically inept but bright Galbraith came into his own.

Buoyed by his newly discovered aptitude for the written word, he helped to found a college newspaper, the *oacis*, which gave him a touch of campus celebrity and the nickname Spike, which he much preferred to his high school moniker, Soupy. He began freelancing and produced a few pieces on agricultural issues for local papers, the *St. Thomas Times-Journal* and the *Stratford Beacon Herald*. His earnings — five dollars per column — enabled him to go to the 1930 International Livestock Exhibition in Chicago, a trip he said later was "the greatest triumph of my college days."

The Depression was eradicating farmers' hard-won prosperity. That economic reality, which Galbraith and his family were experiencing on a visceral level, led him to conclude that "something was terribly wrong with the way agricultural markets worked," according to biographer Richard Parker. That problem, an opportunity to do something about it, and a potential direction for his own future coalesced when Galbraith spotted a poster advertising graduate fellowships in agricultural economics at the University of California. He applied and was accepted. Late in July 1931, his father drove him to Port Stanley, where he boarded the Lake Erie steamer for its daily run to Cleveland and met up with the nephew of a family acquaintance. The two young men drove across the country in a gas-guzzling 1926 Oakland sedan to Berkeley, an academic institution that made more intellectual demands and offered greater opportunities than anything he had encountered at home.

When he was asked by the *Globe and Mail* why he stayed in the United States, rather than returning to Canada after graduating from Berkeley with his doctorate in agricultural economics in 1934, he replied: "I had a choice between Washington and Ottawa, and my hesitation was non-existent. I was personally invited by William Lyon Mackenzie King and the alternative was the Roosevelt administration and the New Deal. And I have no recollection of a problematical or passionate struggle over the choice."

As a new graduate, he had a five-year teaching contract at Harvard University in Boston and summer jobs working for Roosevelt's Agricultural Adjustment Administration. In 1937 he married Catherine (Kitty) Atwater, a Radcliffe student and linguist, and became an American citizen — the U.S. didn't allow dual citizenship back then. The Galbraiths went to Europe on their honeymoon, where he hoped to meet with his hero John Maynard Keynes. That ambition was thwarted because Keynes, who would die a decade later, had suffered a heart attack.

When Galbraith's contract at Harvard expired, he taught at Princeton and then moved to Chicago to work in the U.S. Farm Bureau. Early in 1941, he became deputy administrator of the Office of Price Administration, responsible for setting U.S. prices to prevent wartime inflation and to encourage the production of military supplies. John S. Gambs, one of his early biographers, described Galbraith as "virtually the economic czar of the United States" he ran afoul of Republican congressman Everett Dirksen from Illinois. Accused of having "communistic tendencies," Galbraith was fired in 1943.

With a wife and two small boys to support — the Galbraiths would eventually have four sons — he actively solicited an editorial position with *Fortune* magazine, having rejected job offers there three times in the past. Publisher Henry Luce, the genius who had invented *Time, Life, Fortune,* and *Sports Illustrated,* didn't share Galbraith's liberal economic and political views, but he recognized the value of having them expounded in his pages. Years later, Luce wrote to President John F. Kennedy, "I taught Kenneth Galbraith to write. And I can tell you I've certainly regretted it ever since."

Galbraith worked at *Fortune* for five years, elucidating the tenets of Keynesian economics to American business leaders. He took a leave at the end of the Second World War, when he was seconded as one of several directors of the U.S. Strategic Bombing Survey, to study the effectiveness of the Allied bombing of strategic and civilian German targets. He concluded that the carpet bombing of German cities had not hastened the end of the war, although the final reports of the survey were not as strongly worded as he would have liked.

With Eleanor Roosevelt, widow of the recent U.S. president, and Hubert Humphrey, he co-founded the liberal interest group Americans for Democratic Action in 1947. The following year he left *Fortune* and went back to teaching at Harvard, occupying the Paul M. Warburg Chair in Economics, a position he held until his retirement in 1975. His colleagues, perhaps with some envy, called him "the most famous professor at Harvard."

By 1950 Galbraith had tenure and had signed a publishing contract for what would become his breakthrough book, *American Capitalism*. Success often beckons tragedy to test the mettle of a supposedly lucky individual, and so it was with Galbraith. That March his second son, six-year-old Douglas, was diagnosed with leukemia. For Kitty Galbraith, the horror of watching her son die was compounded by her mother's coincidental diagnosis with a brain tumour, tearing her from one bedside in Boston to another in New York City. Days after she returned from her mother's funeral, Dougie, as he was called, died, shortly after his seventh birthday. Biographer Parker writes that the child's grieving parents had given him the bicycle he had wanted for his birthday, all the while knowing he would never ride it.

American Capitalism, which Galbraith dedicated to his dead son, was a bestseller in 1952 and is still in print more than half a century later. "Like a slingshot, *American Capitalism* propelled him beyond the gravitational pull of university life and professional economics," according to Parker. *Business Week* was more explicit: "A brilliant and provocative book, witty, irreverent, and utterly merciless."

That bestseller was only the beginning. In 1954 he published *The Great Crash*, a book detailing the excesses and follies that had precipitated the Depression and which, Galbraith suggested, could make another crash inevitable. Two years later, on a visit to poverty-riddled India, Galbraith realized that a society begins to produce "unnecessary" goods as it becomes wealthier, with corporations creating artificial demand for their products through advertising. That insight led to *The Affluent Society* in 1958, a bestseller that made Galbraith's name internationally. He portrayed a society in which consumer culture had run amok, social services were being neglected, and the private sector was being indulged at the cost of the public one — all of which increased the likelihood of both inflation and recession.

Meanwhile he was also working as a speechwriter for Adlai Stevenson's failed 1952 and 1956 presidential campaigns, later admitting he had erred in tailoring Stevenson's message too much to the "intellectual elite." That didn't stop him from serving as an economic advisor to John F. Kennedy's 1960 presidential campaign and working the floor at the Democratic convention. He also became a speechwriter and advisor to the young president.

He was Kennedy's ambassador to India from 1961 to 1963, persuaded First Lady Jacqueline Kennedy to undertake diplomatic journeys to the subcontinent, and was an early critic of the disastrous Vietnam War. While his observations and insights were circulated at the highest levels of the Kennedy administration, they were often dismissed by other economists and, in the case of the Vietnam War, by Kennedy's military advisors, including the then hawk Robert S. McNamara.

After Kennedy was assassinated, Galbraith worked as an advisor and speechwriter for Lyndon Johnson, drafting speeches for the "Great Society" legislation aimed at eradicating poverty and racism. After splitting with Johnson over the Vietnam War, he campaigned for Eugene McCarthy in 1968 and then worked for Democratic presidential candidates George McGovern in 1972 and Morris Udall in 1976. He supported Senator Edward Kennedy's failed effort to run against Jimmy Carter in 1980.

Following his retirement from Harvard, Galbraith remained in Cambridge, Massachusetts, and spent his summers at an "unfarmed farm" in Newfane, Vermont. He continued to criticize prevailing economic thought, attacking control of U.S. politics by the wealthy in *The Culture of Contentment* (1992). In *The Good Society* (1996) he set forth his vision of a just, equitable society politically organized to help the poor. In 2004, when he was ninety-five, he wrote *The Economics of Innocent Fraud: Truth for Our Time*, an essay arguing that corporate managers manipulate consumers and the government.

Although Galbraith essentially said goodbye to his native country in 1925, he often reflected on his early days on the farm and the hard physical labour they entailed. His vision was clearly not clouded by nostalgia. "My mind on many matters still runs back to those early Ontario years," he allowed the year before he died of complications of pneumonia in Cambridge, on April 29, 2006, at age ninety-seven, "particularly to the farm and particularly to the hard work on the farm. I consider one of the fortunate parts of my life escape from the routines of early agriculture." His willingness to move on never stopped us from claiming him as one of our favourite sons.

JANE JACOBS

Writer, Urban Thinker, Social Activist

MAY 14, 1916 – APRIL 25, 2006

TWO UNRELATED ACTS of civil disobedience disrupted Toronto mayor William Dennison's annual levee on January 1, 1970. A girl of thirteen tried to shake hands with His Worship at the men-only event, and the Provocative Street Players, an offshoot of the Stop Spadina movement, arrived with a twenty-foot-long sign denouncing a proposed expressway through the downtown core. Security guards escorted the provocateurs outside the building, where they gave full voice to their musical lament "The Bad Trip." The times were changing in Toronto the Good.

The lead vocalist was the nineteen-year-old son of writer, activist, and urban theorist Jane Jacobs, the acclaimed author of *The Death and Life of Great American Cities.* She and her husband, architect Robert (Bob) Jacobs, had arrived in Toronto in June 1968, seeking a refuge for their draft-age sons from the voracious demands of fighting the American war in Vietnam.

Almost immediately, the citizen-activist, who had brought a crosstown expressway to a screeching halt in New York City, was embroiled in a fight in her new country against the "single greatest menace" to the "most hopeful and healthy city in North America." Before she was through, the expressway that would have cut a vicious swath through downtown neighbourhoods had been abandoned, and many of the local citizenry had been emboldened to have faith in their inherent good sense and ability to think for themselves.

As a public speaker Jacobs was feisty, as a writer she was provocative, as a thinker she was original. Curiosity and common sense are the drivers coursing through her eight books, from her classic *The Death and Life of Great American Cities* (1961) through her final clarion, *Dark Days Ahead* (2004). Largely self-educated, she was an acute observer and an intellectual scavenger, storing facts and incidents in her prodigious brain for later analysis. From the small and the concrete — the street under her feet — she worked upwards and outwards, drawing a complex web of activity connecting neighbourhoods, cities, economies, and human behaviour to explain why some systems worked and others failed.

The ideas that fascinated her have a common theme: local control, biodiversity, and how an organic harmony can reside in what, at first glance, seems chaotic. Nothing exists in isolation; the principles that underlie the workings of the natural world apply equally well to the economic one. A pragmatist rather than an ideologue, she didn't tell readers what to think; she inspired them to look around with fresh insight and to have the confidence to act upon their own conclusions.

"I studied city planning, and when I read her book [*Death and Life*] all of my city planning was turned upside down because she looked at it from a different angle — from the angle of the human being," architect Eberhard Zeidler said after Jacobs died on April 25, 2006. "It changed my architecture because I started to think of architecture — no matter if you design a hospital or a factory or a house — not as a thing you do, but as a thing you do for people."

Her theory that cities are ecosystems that can be smothered by rigid, authoritarian planning; that busy, lively sidewalks help cities thrive as safe, healthy places; and that good urban design mixes work, housing, and recreation are now taken as gospel, but they were heretical when *Death and Life* was first published. It is often linked to other epochal works that were written in the early 1960s, books such as *Growing Up Absurd* by Paul Goodman (1960), *Silent Spring* by Rachel Carson (1962), *The Feminine Mystique* by Betty Friedan (1963), *Understanding Media* by Marshall McLuhan (1964), and *Unsafe at Any Speed* by Ralph Nader (1965).

She was "completely original," according to her editor, Jason Epstein. In his view, her later works, such as *The Economy of Cities* (1969) and *Cities and the Wealth of Nations* (1984), were just as important as *Death and Life* and will eventually become part of mainstream thinking and reading. Describing Jacobs as a "genius of common sense" with a "20/20 vision for reality," he said she "saw something academic economists hadn't seen because they get so caught up in other people's abstractions that they can't see what is really happening."

But because she was an original, people had trouble categorizing her. She was called everything from a self-styled economist to an urbanologist. Because she helped defeat the Spadina Expressway, she was branded a left-wing activist; because she believed competition is essential for communities to thrive and that subsidies are counterproductive, she was sometimes stamped a right-wing conservative; because she advocated in her most controversial book, *The Question of Separatism: Quebec and the Struggle over Sovereignty* (1980, 2011), that Quebeckers should decide for themselves if they wanted to remain in Canada, she was denounced as a separatist.

Jacobs reviewed the history of Quebec from the British victory on the Plains of Abraham in 1759 through the Quiet Revolution in the 1960s; looked at the separation of Norway from Sweden in 1905, among other examples; described how cities influence the development of nation-states; and concluded that Quebec sovereignty would be a good thing. Otherwise, Montreal might eventually become a mere regional centre in the Toronto hinterland and Québécois culture and language be overwhelmed. "In sum," she wrote, "Montreal cannot afford to behave like other Canadian regional cities without doing great damage to the economic well-being of the Québécois. It must instead become a creative economic centre in its own right... Yet there is probably no chance of this happening if Quebec remains a province."

The label that irked her most was *amateur* — gifted, but an amateur nonetheless — because she had dared to write about planning in *Death and Life* without professional credentials. "I am a professional writer, I'm not an amateur writer," she insisted in an interview with the *Globe and Mail* in 2000, pointing out that when she wrote about planning, she was making a living as a professional critic at *Architectural Forum*.

In reality, Jacobs was two personalities: the ferocious intellect who talked about issues and a gentle-natured woman interested in the lives of complete strangers. A friendly figure, she wandered the streets of her midtown Toronto neighbourhood, her magpie eyes peering out from behind the owlish glasses that rested on her apple cheeks. She shopped in local stores and appeared at citizen-organized meetings to present cogent opinions that countered bureaucratic bombast and wrong-headed platitudes. Her attire was casual rather than stylish. She usually wore sneakers and a denim jumper over a white long-sleeved turtleneck. Over the years her straight hair, cut in a chin-length bob with bangs, mutated from brunette to pewter to chalk.

Many thought her intimidating — and she was when confronting cant and artifice — but mostly she was unassuming and idiosyncratic. After Christmas, instead of discarding her tree, she would hang it from a hook in the ceiling of her porch, letting it dangle about an inch off the floor, where it danced and swayed like an evergreen dervish until summer finally had its way and turned it brown. Like everything else about Jacobs, it was transformed from commonplace to unique.

JANE BUTZNER WAS born in Scranton, Pennsylvania, on May 14, 1916, the year before the Americans entered the First World War. She was one of four children of John Decker Butzner, a doctor, and Bess Mary Butzner (née Robison), a teacher and nurse. An independent, curious child and an avid reader, she took great advantage of the riches to be found in the local reference library, museum of natural history, and zoo. By the time she had completed high school, she was "thoroughly sick of attending school and eager to get a job."

She worked as a reporter for the *Scranton Tribune* before moving to New York to live with her older sister in the early 1930s. Jobs were scarce during the Depression, and she scrambled to find short-term secretarial work. Between assignments she wrote four articles about working districts of the city that she sold to *Vogue* — her first real literary sale.

Her parents wanted her to go to university, so she went to the School of General Studies at Columbia; however, she was bored by the courses required for completing a degree. "I went for a couple of years to university because I wanted to learn, not because I wanted to sit in custodial care or wanted credentials," she said later about her decision to quit university to embark on her own curriculum of reading, observing, wondering, thinking, and trying to assemble her thoughts into a coherent piece of writing.

To support herself, she worked in magazines and as a feature writer for the Office of War Information. She met her husband, Robert Hyde Jacobs (who was working at the same defence plant as her sister), when her sister invited him to a party in the apartment the two young women shared. "I walked in the door," Bob Jacobs said later, "and there she was, in a beautiful, green woollen evening dress, and I fell in love. It took me a little longer to convince her." Four months after they met in March 1944, they were married.

After peace came, she found a job at *Architectural Forum*, a journal that she read frequently because her husband was a subscriber. It never occurred to her to stay home and be a full-time wife and mother after her children, James Kedzie (April 1948), Edward (Ned) Drecker (June 1952), and Mary (Burgin) Hyde (January 1955), were born. Her female forebears had always worked in their communities, so "I grew up with the idea I could do anything," she said later.

At the magazine she was assigned stories on urban life and structures and was stunned to discover that "city planning had nothing to do with how cities worked successfully in real life." One of her readers was William H. Whyte, editor of *Fortune* magazine and author of *The Organization Man,* who hired her to write an article on cities. She concluded in her essay that "Designing a dream city is easy. Rebuilding a living one takes imagination."

The *Fortune* article caught the attention of the Rockefeller Foundation, which asked her if she had any other ideas about cities. She did, envisaging "writing a series of articles, which might be a book, of about ten chapters, mostly about city streets, and that it would take me a year." The foundation offered her a grant in 1958 and she set to work on the manual Remington typewriter that she used for the rest of her life.

It took more than two more years and as many grants to complete *The Death and Life of Great American Cities*, a book that has never been out of print since it was first published in 1961. She was challenging not simply the mistakes she saw around her but the very idea that an urban utopia could be designed. Her argument was that cities begin at the pavement level and grow organically in a self-organizing mix of commerce and domesticity. Zoning by function — a prime example being the razing of neighbourhoods to build isolated public housing projects — deprived whole areas of the interactive human oxygen they needed to survive as dynamic entities.

Many urban planners and architectural writers were aghast, but the book found a receptive audience. Partly it was the writing, which was clear, concise, and jargon-free; partly it was the argument, which moved from the concrete — a city sidewalk — to the abstract; partly it was the fact that her book connected with a generation of young adults who were trying to make sense of the postwar world.

She was barely back at work from her book leave when the City of New York decided to appropriate her own neighbourhood for urban renewal — a case study of the "intellectual idiocies and ignorance of city workings that I had been writing about." She protested along with her neighbours and was made chairman of the Committee to Save the West Village. The journalist and critic had been transformed into an activist.

About this time, opposition to the Vietnam War was coming to a boil on many American campuses. Jacobs joined a protest march on the Pentagon in 1967 and found herself smack up against a row of soldiers in gas masks. "They looked like some big horrible insect, the whole bunch of them together, not human beings at all. And I was also not only appalled at how they looked, but I was outraged that they should be marching on me, an American," she said in an interview with the *Boston Globe*, explaining her decision to move to Toronto with her family in 1968.

Her husband, a hospital architect, found work with architect Eb Zeidler, a friend and colleague. The Jacobs family moved into a flat on Spadina Avenue — in the path of the proposed expressway — and then into a house on Albany Avenue, in the nearby Annex area. She was still unpacking when she found new foes to combat with the radical activism she had learned on the streets of New York City: developers who wanted to tear down historic properties to erect high-rises, and politicians who wanted to build expressways to bring cars from the suburbs into the downtown core.

She made a profound impression on reformist city politicians such as Mayor David Crombie and alderman John Sewell, who were opposed to the expressway. They had known her reputation as an activist and her writing before they met her in the flesh. In addition to giving them a living, breathing, pragmatic model of an ethical thinker, she gave them and other activists who cared about the city in which they lived the confidence that their ideas mattered and that it was essential to act upon them.

She was not above civil disobedience. Besides her Spadina antics — lobbying, writing, marching — she helped save a historic inner-city neighbourhood. In 1973, developers had erected hoardings around a row of Victorian houses at the corner of Sherbourne and Dundas Streets and were about to demolish them. During a protest, Jacobs told Alderman Sewell to rip down the hoardings, because she knew that it was against the law to demolish a building unless there was a hoarding surrounding it. He said, "I can't." She said, "You must." And it was done. That act of vandalism led to the city's first non-profit housing project.

After Bob Jacobs died of lung cancer in 1996 — in a hospital he had helped design — she remained in their Annex house, continuing to write books and to respond to calls to engage in neighbourhood and city protests, including an unsuccessful struggle against the amalgamation of the City of Toronto with its outlying boroughs in 1998.

Her adopted city of Toronto honoured her in 1997 by sponsoring a conference titled "Jane Jacobs: Ideas That Matter," bringing together a wide range of diverse thinkers who shared a proclivity for thinking outside the box. The conference spawned a book by the same name and the Jane Jacobs Prize, which offers a $5,000 annual stipend for three years to an "unsung hero" engaged in "activities that contribute to the city's vitality."

No matter how frail Jacobs became — she had a hip replacement in 2000 — many people thought of her as indestructible and remembered that her mother had lived past a hundred. But her mother had never smoked, a habit that Jacobs had enjoyed with furious intensity for decades before she finally butted out her cigarettes. Smoking she could give up; working was something else. Even in her late eighties she was under contract to write a short history of the human race and an anthology of her thoughts about economics.

Inevitably old age caught up with her and "her body wore out," according to her son Ned Jacobs. In announcing her death at Toronto General Hospital on April 25, 2006, at age eighty-nine, her family said in a statement: "What's important is not that she died but that she lived, and that her life's work has greatly influenced the way we think. Please remember her by reading her books and implementing her ideas." And if you don't, her son warned, "there's a *Dark Age Ahead*."

PIERRE TRUDEAU

Statesman

OCTOBER 18, 1919 – SEPTEMBER 28, 2000

AS ENIGMATIC AS he was complex, as combative as he was charismatic, Pierre Trudeau was the fifteenth prime minister of Canada. He championed bilingualism, multiculturalism, and national unity; he patriated our constitution and gave us the Charter of Rights and Freedoms, which has defined modern Canada and become a model for the world.

Trudeau arrived in the House of Commons in 1965, as the junior member of the federalist trio led by Jean Marchand and Gérard Pelletier, whom Prime Minister Lester Pearson had recruited to bolster the Quebec wing of his caucus. A law professor and a neophyte politician who had worked briefly in the Privy Council Office more than a dozen years earlier, he was an intellectual who had studied at Harvard, the London School of Economics, and L'institut d'études politiques in Paris and then travelled the world, juxtaposing theory with the rough realities of life on the road. An athlete and an outdoorsman, he was given to testing himself on rugged canoe trips, punishing treks, and daredevil ski runs. A shy and introspective bachelor who lived with his widowed mother well into his forties, Trudeau was also a renowned ladies' man who cut a mean figure on the dance floor. Abidingly Catholic, independently wealthy, a graduate of the elite Jesuit-run Collège Jean-de-Brébeuf, he had flirted with militant ultra-nationalism as a student at the Université de Montréal, protested against conscription in the Second World War, and failed to enlist in the armed forces. Yet he grew out of his insular pro-nationalist phase, emerging as a civil and human rights activist who defied repressive Quebec premier Maurice Duplessis in *Cité libre*, the political magazine he co-founded in 1950.

In their book *Trudeau Transformed*, Max and Monique Nemni argue that they could have written several biographies of Trudeau, concentrating on him as an athlete, a scholar, an adventurer, a heretic, a believer, or a ladies' man. None of these would have worked, they contend, because they would provide only slices of the man. His strength and his appeal came from the powerful and often odd contrasts among the myriad components of his character and upbringing. His many private sides and personal angles — above all his belief in individual liberty, social justice, and federalism — combined in unusual and unexpected ways to make him the most memorable Canadian politician of the twentieth century.

JOSEPH PHILIPPE PIERRE Yves Elliott Trudeau was born in Montreal on October 18, 1919, the middle child of Grace Elliot, an anglophone of Scottish descent, and Charles-Émile Trudeau, a rural Québécois lawyer-turned-entrepreneur. Growing up, Pierre moved from one language to another like a paddle slicing through the still waters of a northern lake (what other francophone politician of his day had the linguistic ammunition to sneer, "Zap, you're frozen," at a stunned Robert Stanfield to deride the Opposition leader's campaign pledge to freeze wages and prices to combat stagflation in 1974?).

His father grew rich after selling his string of automobile service stations to Imperial Oil during the Depression for the then-staggering sum of more than a million dollars, but the family always lived modestly, even after they moved to Outremont, an affluent section of Montreal. "My father taught me order and discipline," Trudeau once said, "and my mother taught me freedom and fantasy."

After his father died suddenly of a heart attack in the spring of 1935, when Trudeau was fifteen, he grew even closer to his mother. He also grew more introspective and took up karate and boxing, developing the pugilistic skills and the stance of the solitary warrior that he would later use to his rhetorical advantage in debates and on the campaign trail. A team player he was not.

When he accepted Pearson's invitation to run in the safe Liberal riding of Mount Royal in the 1965 federal election, Trudeau was forty-seven, a law professor at the Université de Montréal — the theory of the law had always appealed more to him than its practice — a critic of Pearson's decision to allow American nuclear-armed Bomarc missiles to be deployed in Canada, and politically aligned with the social democratic aspirations of the New Democratic Party. Far too much of a pragmatist to settle for moral rather than electoral power, Trudeau decided that if he was going to enter politics, he wanted to run for the Liberals, a party with a likelihood of governing the country. After winning his seat, he served as parliamentary secretary to the prime minister and was appointed minister of justice a little more than a year later.

He excelled in the role. Late in December 1967, at the end of an exuberant, self-confident centennial year, he introduced two pivotal pieces of legislation to bring the antiquated divorce laws and the stringent Criminal Code in line with the behaviours and attitudes of a younger generation of Canadians, even if the changes contravened religious codes and mores. The omnibus amendments to the Criminal Code, which proposed legalizing contraception and decriminalizing homosexual acts between consenting adults, provided Trudeau with one of his most celebrated quotes — albeit lifted from an editorial in the *Globe and Mail* — that "the State has no place in the bedrooms of the nation."

Enshrining individual rights and personal freedom was one of his core beliefs and would become a hallmark of his political career and his legacy. He showcased another political and philosophical tenet — a strong federal government surmounting its constituent provinces and territories — at a televised federal-provincial conference on constitutional affairs in Ottawa in February 1968. Union Nationale leader Daniel Johnson had been elected premier of Quebec in 1966 after a campaign of "*égalité ou indépendance*," and he brought that mandate and the idea of a new kind of federalism — based on the notion of two equal nations: Quebec and the rest of Canada — to the conference.

Trudeau eviscerated the argument coolly but with merciless logic, and humiliated the man on national television. "His tone ever more biting, his voice metallic, Trudeau responded to Johnson's reference to him as the 'député de Mont-Royal' by describing the premier as the 'député de Bagot'" (his provincial riding in the Eastern Townships of Quebec), as John English relates in *Just Watch Me: The Life of Pierre Elliott Trudeau*. At a coffee break hastily called by Pearson to allow the tension to dissipate, Trudeau "curtly nodded at Johnson and muttered that the premier was seeking to destroy the federal government. Johnson sneered that Trudeau was acting like a candidate, not a federal minister." Here was an early example of the lone combatant in action, yet another side of the dashing, eloquent bachelor who sported a rose in his lapel, wore a leather coat, and drove a silver Mercedes 300SL convertible.

A little more than a week later, Trudeau announced that he would be entering the leadership race to succeed Pearson as party leader and prime minister at the Liberal convention in April 1968. He had agonized over the decision to run and he didn't win the contest easily — it took four ballots. But in the wider world, the one reached by television, he was already generating emotional crushes normally reserved for rock stars.

From the beginning he envisaged a goal far beyond the mundane pragmatism of party politics. "By building a truly just society," he promised dubious Liberals, "this beautiful, rich and energetic country of ours can become a model in which every citizen will enjoy his fundamental rights, in which two great linguistic communities and people of many cultures will live in harmony and in which each individual will find fulfillment." He was sworn in as prime minister on April 20. Three days later he asked the governor general to dissolve Parliament and call an election for June 25, 1968.

The swarming that had begun even before the leadership convention became known as Trudeaumania. Partly it was timing. Trudeau emerged on the federal political scene just as the swaggering postwar baby-boom generation, the first to be reared on television, got the vote. Trudeau's taut, sculpted face with his glittering eyes and implacable stare was ideal for television. As media guru Marshall McLuhan, a friend, pointed out, he had "the perfect mask — a charismatic mask...the face of a North American Indian."

His appearance, his mannerisms, his eligibility, his ambiguities, and his dangerous flair lured boomers like moths to his charismatic flame. Communications theorist Don Tapscott suggested in an interview that baby boomers, who had grown up with television, looked to the box to find leaders they could follow. By that reasoning, Trudeau — "the command and control, top down, great visionary" — was the quintessential man of his time. "We were passive recipients in a one-way, one size fits all, one-to-many medium, where the messages could be architected and controlled," said Tapscott, identifying himself as a boomer. "It was about the powerful central authority pushing something out to passive recipients. Trudeau, with his gunslinger mode, was a great master of that."

At times, especially in the middle of his long political career, Trudeau's connection with Canadians attenuated into Trudeauphobia as his economic policies failed to ameliorate the recession driven by the OPEC oil embargo in the mid-1970s, or when the West bristled about the forced sharing of gushing oil revenues under the National Energy Program in the early 1980s. By the mid-1980s, with the first sovereignty referendum defeated, the constitution patriated, and the Charter of Rights and Freedoms enshrined, he seemed to lose interest in Canadians and politics, and they with him, as the deficit soared close to $40 billion and interest rates spiralled. As economist Sylvia Ostry told *Maclean's* after Trudeau's death, "He was highly intelligent and intellectual: he read all of his briefing documents, including the footnotes. He just wasn't interested in economics. He listened to everything and understood it. But in the end, he had one priority: national unity."

He wanted an international platform for his final crusade: a world without nuclear arms. He was nominated for the Nobel Peace Prize but the momentum fizzled, largely because of the opposition of those dogged Cold Warriors Margaret Thatcher of Britain and Ronald Reagan of the United States. But the link with Canadians was never severed, even after he left office on June 30, 1984, moved back to Montreal with his three sons, and joined the law firm Heenan Blaikie.

Most of us who lived through those years, and even those who were too young to be startled by a Canadian prime minister pirouetting saucily behind the Queen's back at a Buckingham Palace reception, impressed by his dignity in dealing with his flamboyantly rebellious wife, or shocked by reports of him giving the finger to protesters at a B.C. whistle stop in what came to be called the "Salmon Arm salute," carry contrary images of Trudeau in our heads. Here are five evocative moments from his life.

THE DEFIANT PRIME MINISTER

THE 1960S WERE tumultuous times, no more so than in 1968. In France, students were marching through the streets of Paris; in the United States the Vietnam War was tearing the country apart, especially after the military launched the Tet Offensive in January and civil rights leader Martin Luther King was murdered in April and Senator Robert Kennedy in June. Canadians watching TV reports of rioting and looting south of the border knew they weren't immune. Quebec separatists had been blowing up mailboxes and delivering package bombs for years in their terrorist campaign to secede from the rest of Canada, a movement that would gain political strength and credibility in 1968 with the formation of the Parti Québécois.

Trudeau confronted the fear of politically motivated violence when he insisted on appearing at the annual Saint-Jean-Baptiste Day parade on the eve of the federal election he had called for June 25, 1968. Trudeaumania had swept much of the country, but in Quebec he was hated by many for his pro-federalist stand, a situation he had inflamed with his belligerent and uncompromising remarks. Montreal mayor Jean Drapeau advised him to stay away from the parade and so did others, but he refused. Trudeau, along with other dignitaries, including Mayor Drapeau and the archbishop of Montreal, Paul Grégoire, sat on a reviewing stand on Sherbrooke Street across from Lafontaine Park. A group of hardcore separatists led by Pierre Bourgault of the Rassemblement pour l'indépendance nationale (RIN) started heaving bottles and shouting, "*Trudeau au poteau*" (Trudeau to the stake). More than forty police and eighty civilians were injured and nearly three hundred rioters arrested.

Several dignitaries fled and two RCMP officers threw their coats over Trudeau and tried to force him to the floor of the reviewing stand. He shook them off and sat upright, staring defiantly at the protesters, his eyes flashing as he sent an unmistakeably tough message to voters across the country watching the late-night news. Here was a politician willing to stand up to the separatists. By the time the ballots were counted the next evening, he and the Liberals had won a majority government, the first since Louis St. Laurent's victory in 1953 and John Diefenbaker's landslide triumph for the Progressive Conservatives in 1958.

If Trudeau's performance on the reviewing stand made a difference in the outcome, his message was heard loudest in Quebec (56 seats), Ontario (63 seats), and, surprisingly, in British Columbia (16 seats). It was the first of five federal elections that Trudeau fought in his nearly two decades in public office. He won four of them.

THE BELLICOSE PRIME MINISTER

EVEN BEFORE TRUDEAU went to Ottawa, small and disparate incendiary groups, inspired by revolutionary movements in Algeria, Cuba, and other despotic states, had been terrorizing the citizenry under the guise of freedom fighting. Their specialties were Molotov cocktails, bomb blasts in mailboxes, vandalism to monuments of Anglo heroes, and infiltration into labour disputes in foreign-owned factories. In the spring of 1963, a war veteran on the eve of his pension was killed and an explosives expert maimed as he tried to defuse a bomb in a Westmount mailbox. Early in 1969, bombs ripped through the Montreal Stock Exchange, injuring close to thirty people.

Then, on October 5, 1970, a Front de libération du Québec cell kidnapped British trade commissioner James Cross at his Redpath Crescent mansion on the southern slopes of Mount Royal, issued a manifesto urging the people of Quebec to rise up against their oppressors, and demanded concessions for Cross's release, including freedom for twenty-three "political prisoners," $500,000 in gold, and broadcast and publication of the FLQ manifesto.

Trudeau refused to negotiate, although the manifesto was read in French and English on radio and television. Police raids on suspected troublemakers began on the morning of October 7. Two days later, on Saturday afternoon of the Thanksgiving weekend, another FLQ cell abducted Quebec labour minister, Pierre Laporte, while he was playing touch football in a field across from his home in Saint-Lambert, Quebec. The following day, under coercion from his kidnappers, Laporte sent a *"Mon cher Robert"* letter to Premier Bourassa, begging for his life. At Quebec's request, Trudeau sent in the army to patrol the streets in the search for Cross and Laporte, transforming Montreal from the hippest city in Canada into a film set for a war movie. He also ordered the military to patrol significant sites in Ottawa.

Then, as Trudeau was bounding up the steps on the way to his office in the Parliament Buildings on the morning of October 13, he encountered a covey of journalists with microphones, tape recorders, and television cameras. One of them, CBC reporter Tim Ralfe, scrummed him about the trade-off between armed security forces in the streets and the potential risk that prominent people might be kidnapped. The debate went back and forth with Trudeau the civil libertarian — but also the prime minister charged with maintaining "peace, order, and good government" — arguing that it was "more important to get rid of those who are committing violence against the total society and those who are trying to run the government through a parallel power by establishing their authority by kidnapping and blackmail."

Ralfe refused to concede his larger philosophical point about what risks are reasonable in order to live in a democratic society. That's when Trudeau lost his patience. Hands on hips, his nostrils flaring, he shifted into attack mode and snarled, "There are a lot of bleeding hearts around who just don't like to see people with helmets and guns. All I can say is, go on and bleed, but it is more important to keep law and order in the society than to be worried about weak-kneed people who don't like the looks of a soldier's helmet."

Other leaders might have walked away from the cameras. Trudeau, ever competitive, continued to joust verbally with the reporter. Ralfe, no doubt sensing the terrific sound bite he had for the evening news, pushed for more: "At any cost? How far would you go with that? How far would you extend that?" To which Trudeau snapped his famous riposte, "Well, just watch me."

In fact, we couldn't watch him, because the decision about what to do next was taken behind closed doors. Cabinet documents and books released by researchers who have had access to Trudeau's papers all indicate that the decision to impose the War Measures Act, last invoked after Canada declared war on Germany in September 1939, was not a unilateral move by the prime minister but the result of ongoing discussions and consultations, over most of a week, with his own Cabinet, the government of Quebec, and the municipality of Montreal.

Early in the morning of October 16, after formal requests from Quebec and Montreal, the federal government imposed the War Measures Act, giving the state extraordinary and draconian authority to suspend civil liberties and arrest and hold people without charge and without access to legal counsel. Within forty-eight hours the police had reportedly carried out more than 1,500 raids. More than 250 people were arrested, including the singer Pauline Julien, the poet Gérald Godin, and the journalist Nick Auf der Maur. By the end of the year, the total arrested had risen to 468, of whom 408 were released without charges being laid.

Later that same morning, Trudeau announced in the House of Commons that the government had imposed the War Measures Act; he made a televised address that evening to the nation — one of the few times when he read from a script. The following night, Laporte's body was found at Saint-Hubert Airport in the trunk of a car belonging to Paul Rose, one of the kidnappers.

He had been strangled with the gold chain carrying a small crucifix that he wore around his neck.

Many believed he had been murdered in retaliation for the War Measures Act. Margaret Sinclair, who was secretly dating Trudeau, wrote later in her tell-all memoir *Beyond Reason* that she had been in bed with him at Harrington Lake when the phone rang at one a.m. with the news that Laporte's body had been found. She heard him crying after he put the phone down. "I watched him grow old before my eyes. It was as if Laporte's death lay on his shoulders alone: he was the one who wouldn't negotiate, and he was the man who would now have to take responsibility for the murder of an innocent man."

At the time there was widespread approval of the government's action. As an indication of the prevailing mood, reporter Tim Ralfe was formally and publicly reprimanded for his aggressive questioning of the prime minister, and a letter was placed in his file by CBC executive news producer Peter Trueman — actions the broadcast executive later regretted.

The bill passed 190 to 16 in the House of Commons, with the only concerted opposition coming from Tommy Douglas and most of his NDP caucus. When Douglas suggested that the prime minister was using a sledgehammer to smash a peanut, Trudeau replied that "peanuts don't make bombs, don't take hostages, and don't assassinate prisoners. And as for the sledgehammer, it was the only tool at our disposal."

Whatever people said later — and many did renounce the War Measures Act, including some of those sitting around the Cabinet table — polls taken at the time showed overwhelming support for the actions taken by the federal government. Indeed, both Douglas and René Lévesque, who had also opposed the War Measures Act, were pilloried, and Lévesque, who had founded the Parti Québécois two years earlier, failed to win a seat in the 1973 provincial election.

As for Trudeau, he never changed his mind about negotiating with terrorists and never conceded that there was a link between the "six kids trying to make a revolution," as James Cross labelled his kidnappers, and Trudeau himself as a vocal revolutionary in the 1940s. Of course, Trudeau never acted out his ultra-nationalist agenda and never resorted to violence like the FLQ cell members who murdered Laporte. There can be no doubt, however, that Trudeau destroyed violence as a tactic for sovereignty. After the October Crisis, the struggle for independence was fought with words and arguments, not bombs and abductions.

The Prime Minister Takes a Wife

"Trudeau Marries Vancouver Girl, 22" blared the headline in large type on the front page of the *Globe and Mail* on March 5, 1971. Below it was a photograph of the prime minister boogying with Margaret Sinclair, one of the five daughters of Lester Pearson's former fisheries minister, James Sinclair. The headline, along with the picture, which had been taken during their first public date in 1969, at the National Arts Centre in Ottawa, conveyed the bewildered tone of editorialists and readers. What will he do next? was the rhetorical question. The best reaction came from former Prime Minister John Diefenbaker, when he suggested that Trudeau had had two choices: marry Sinclair or adopt her.

Pictures of the wedding, which had taken place the evening before, followed, with the dark-haired bride wearing a hooded caftan that she had made herself during a course put on by the Singer sewing machine company. The pair had met in Tahiti the Christmas of 1967, when she was nineteen and he was deciding whether to run for the leadership of the Liberal Party. Before they married, she converted to Roman Catholicism. She bore him two sons, Justin and Alexandre (Sacha), on Christmas Day two years apart, in 1971 and 1973, which somehow made the union both more improbable and yet somehow preordained by a higher order. Michel completed the trio with his birth on October 2, 1975.

Isolated and alienated in Ottawa, where she had few friends, trapped by the protocols and security regulations attendant on the wife of the prime minister, exhausted by the demands of three small children, Margaret Trudeau was bored, lonely, and feeling ignored by a husband who was away all day and worked long into the night on what she later called those "damned brown boxes." In one of their fights she ripped out the hand-stitched letters in *La raison avant la passion*, the prized French version of artist Joyce Wieland's famous quilt, which he had bought and hung on a wall at 24 Sussex.

The public was curious about this flower child with the hedonistic past, and Trudeau and his advisors found a way to slake its thirst: showcasing his young wife on the campaign trail in the 1974 election. "In 1972, my campaign never really got off the ground," he told reporters, "but this year, I've found the secret. I have a train, and I have Margaret." She travelled with him and introduced him to huge crowds, once going so far as to say at a rally in

Vancouver: "He's a beautiful guy. He taught me a lot about loving." Afterwards, she said she had felt "used."

In following his heart, Trudeau had married a naive and narcissistic — she would later be diagnosed as bipolar — young woman less than half his age. For a time it seemed that the dashing (and ageing) bachelor had found a way to harness the beauty and energy of the baby-boom generation, but marriage wasn't an affair, it was a lifelong commitment. She was certainly not ready for that, and he wasn't willing to give up his day job.

After humiliating him with obscene outbursts at diplomatic functions, hanging out with the Rolling Stones in Toronto, dancing lewdly and drunk-enly at Studio 54 and other New York discos, and having affairs with, among others, Senator Ted Kennedy, Margaret Trudeau finally fled. The couple sepa-rated in 1977 and divorced in 1984. He never complained publicly about his rebellious wife, expressing compassion for her in interviews, but he drove a hard bargain: he got sole custody of their three sons and she got little if any alimony. "I'll win in the end," she told him, "because I'm going to live longer. When the boys are grown up, I'll still be around." Little did she realize that she would ultimately need them to keep her life in order and that his legacy would grow with time.

He never remarried, although in May 1991, when he was in his early seven-ties, he had a daughter, Sarah, by lawyer Deborah Coyne, a constitutional advisor to then Newfoundland premier Clyde Wells.

THE PRIME MINISTER AS ARCHITECT OF MODERN CANADA

IN 1973, TRUDEAU said on the CTV program W5 that he had entered politics for two reasons: "to make sure that Quebec wouldn't leave Canada through separatism" and "to make sure that Canada wouldn't shove Quebec out through narrow-mindedness." In a way he tried to remake Canada in his own image — bilingual, rational, and confident of its rights and responsibilities — and he succeeded perhaps better than he could have imagined. Those goals underlie official bilingualism, the push to promote francophones in the civil service, the Charter, his vision of a strong federalism, and his obsession with patriating the Constitution, which more than a century after Confederation remained an act of the British Parliament that could be amended only by sending a request to Westminster.

Several prime ministers before Trudeau had tried to wrest the British North America Act from Britain but had always failed to come up with an amending formula that all ten provinces and the federal government could accept. He first tried to make constitutional change at the federal-provincial conference in Victoria in 1971, with a proposal to patriate the constitution with an amending formula, entrench French and English as official languages, and codify rights such as freedom of expression and religion.

All the provinces agreed, and then Robert Bourassa got chilblains after he returned home and was pilloried by politicial allies and opponents for giving away too much. He called Trudeau, reneged on the verbal agreement, and so the proposal foundered. Trudeau blamed the electoral victory of the Parti Québécois five years later and Brian Mulroney's Meech Lake Accord in the late 1980s on Bourassa, because the Quebec premier had denied his province an opportunity to sign on to a constitutional accord when he had the chance. "Much of Bourassa's subsequent career," Trudeau wrote in his *Memoirs*, "has been spent trying to regain what he was once so unwise as to refuse."

After the Liberals were defeated by Joe Clark's Progressive Conservatives in the May 1979 election, Trudeau announced that he was retiring from politics. Quebec premier René Lévesque, leader of the separatist Parti Québécois, who had campaigned on offering Quebeckers a referendum on separation, thought he would have an easier time winning it with Trudeau out of power and sped up his agenda.

Fate intervened. The minority Clark government was defeated on a budget amendment in December 1979, only seven months after taking office, and Trudeau came roaring out of retirement — a convention had not yet been held to choose his successor — to lead the Liberals into the subsequent election. "Welcome to the 1980s," Trudeau quipped on election night, February 18, 1980, having trounced Clark's Progressive Conservatives 147 seats to 103, although his majority mandate was lopsided, with no seats west of Manitoba, in contrast with the distribution in the 1968 election.

An emboldened Trudeau, knowing this mandate would probably be his last, focused on the issues that mattered most to him and that in the end guaranteed his legacy. First among them was the referendum, and that led to ferocious public confrontations between Trudeau and Lévesque over the future of the country.

At a massive rally in the Paul Sauvé Arena in east-end Montreal — the same venue where the Parti Québécois had celebrated its election victory in

1976 — Trudeau, in full gunslinger mode, delivered a devastating speech, only six days before the referendum vote scheduled for May 20, 1980. He promised to reform the Canadian constitution if the *Non* side won. He was deliberately vague about the terms, allowing many Québécois to assume that he was planning to accede to their aspirations — a conclusion he said later was not "logical," based on his persistent stand against "special status." The secessionists were defeated 59.56 percent to 40.44 percent, a decisive 20 percent margin. "À *la prochaine fois*," a dispirited Lévesque said to his distraught supporters, from the stage of the very same arena where Trudeau had held his *Non* rally.

After the defeat of the referendum, Trudeau moved quickly to restart the constitutional talks by meeting with the premiers in Ottawa and giving them a twelve-point agenda. The eleven governments negotiated all summer and assembled at a First Ministers' Conference in Ottawa in September. Nobody could agree on a deal. Ever the samurai, Trudeau determined to go it alone. In October he unveiled what came to be called the "People's Package." After approval by the House and the Senate, the patriation proposal would be sent directly to Westminster. It proposed a modified version of the amending formula that had been accepted in Victoria 1971 and a Charter of Rights and Freedoms.

Much had changed on the political landscape in the ensuing decade, however, including the election of a separatist premier of Quebec. Ontario and New Brunswick accepted the resolution, Saskatchewan and Nova Scotia reserved judgement, and the remaining six provinces — an unlikely combination that included Alberta and Quebec — resolved to fight it in the courts, in their legislatures, and in London.

By April 1981, Saskatchewan and Nova Scotia, the two provinces that had stayed on the sidelines, had aligned themselves with their disaffected counterparts to form a "Gang of Eight" in opposition to the prime minister. Then, in September, the Supreme Court of Canada ruled that Ottawa's proposal, while legal, was unconstitutional because it violated traditional conventions. That forced Trudeau back to the negotiating table one more time, setting the scene for a *High Noon* confrontation with his old foe Lévesque and the Gang of Eight.

The weary combatants met in Ottawa early in November. After two days of wrangling, a frustrated Trudeau offered to take the amending formula and the Charter in a referendum to the people. Lévesque broke from the Gang of Eight to accept the referendum, a compromise that he later realized was a tactical error. Later that same evening of Wednesday November 5, some provincial premiers and their bureaucrats got together to hammer out a compromise, in which they offered to accept Trudeau's Charter with the inclusion of a notwithstanding clause in exchange for Ottawa accepting their amending formula. They presented this proposal to all the first ministers the following morning. With some modifications, Trudeau agreed, but Lévesque accused his fellow gang members of betrayal and stomped out. (This quickly gave rise to the myth of "The Night of the Long Knives," which in turn prompted Brian Mulroney's subsequent attempts to get Quebec's signature through the Meech Lake and Charlottetown Accords.)

Over the next weeks, all but Quebec made modifications to the patriation package, which was then sent to Westminster, where it was duly approved by the British Parliament. Later Trudeau wrote in his *Memoirs*: "I always said it was thanks to three women that we were eventually able to reform our Constitution. The Queen, who was favourable, Margaret Thatcher, who undertook to do everything that our Parliament asked of her, and Jean Wadds [a former Progressive Conservative MP who had been appointed High Commissioner to the United Kingdom by the government of Joe Clark in 1979], who represented the interests of Canada so well in London."

The Queen and Prince Philip travelled to Canada to sign the act into law on April 17, 1982. Wearing a teal-blue coat and matching hat with a jaunty tassel, she sat outdoors at a small wooden table on Parliament Hill for all her subjects to observe her signing the final act that would symbolize the independence and maturity of Canada as a sovereign nation. Trudeau, bareheaded and wearing a morning suit, sat at the head of the low table, holding down the parchment in a sudden gust as his sovereign picked up the pen and signed her name.

"What we are celebrating today," he told the crowd, "is not so much the completion of our task but the renewal of our hope, not so much an ending but a fresh beginning." Of all the images of Trudeau the statesman, this is the one where he looks most carefree. There was no hint of a mocking pirouette, although he couldn't resist executing one at the airport after the Queen's plane rose into the sky for her return flight to London.

The Prime Minister in Retirement

After Trudeau stepped down as prime minister on June 30, 1984, he returned to Montreal, the law, and private life. He emerged twice as the solitary warrior stalking the battlefield of constitutional wars.

The first time, he sabotaged Prime Minister Brian Mulroney's attempt through the Meech Lake Accord — endorsed by ten provincial premiers on April 30, 1987 — to have Quebec belatedly sign on to the patriated constitution. The Accord offered Quebec status as a "distinct society" and a constitutional veto (a right also demanded by the other provinces), among other accommodations. Trudeau vociferously denounced the Accord in articles in the French and English press and in a lengthy interview with broadcaster Barbara Frum on CBC. Watching that interview now, with Frum at her persistent best, you have to admire (and wonder at) his steely logic, his confidence and ease with being the sole opponent to ten premiers; of course, he had been there before and won the day, albeit with some tough compromises, including the notwithstanding clause.

Later, Ontario premier Bob Rae likened Trudeau to Isaiah Berlin's concept of the hedgehog, an animal that knows one big thing. Political scientist Wayne Hunt, countered in "The Branding of Trudeau," that Trudeau was a hedgehog who used the tactics of a fox, a sly animal that knows many things, to achieve his big goal of national unity.

Trudeau's opposition to Meech was delivered with chilling logic: there could not be "two Canadas" in the same country. Later, before a special joint committee of the Senate and the House, he spoke tenaciously for more than three hours about the Canada he had reinvigorated as "a federation that was set to last a thousand years," until it fell "into the hands of a weakling [Mulroney]" who had "sold out" to the provinces. Trudeau's fervent opposition, combined with regime changes in several provincial governments and growing resentment against a "special deal" for Quebec, precipitated the failure of the Accord to be ratified by its three-year deadline in 1990.

Mulroney tried again with the Charlottetown Accord, which, unlike Meech, offered Canadians a referendum in order to express their opinions. Again Trudeau lashed on his battle gear, writing a denunciation in *Maclean's* and delivering an impassioned speech at an event in La Maison du Egg Roll restaurant in Montreal, arguing that the new accord would lead to the destruction of the federal government and the disintegration of Canada, and saying that the "big mess deserves a big 'no.'" And that's what it got, in simultaneous referenda in Quebec and the rest of the country on October 26, 1992. Charlottetown was defeated by a vote of 54.3 percent to 45.7 percent, a difference of 8.6 percent. The failure of Meech and Charlottetown boosted the pro-sovereignty forces in Quebec.

Trudeau bore a heavy cost for these constitutional victories. He was so demonized in Quebec, his native province, that he was asked to stay on the sidelines by the *Non* committee during the second Quebec sovereignty referendum, in 1995. That referendum, issued by Parti Québécois premier Jacques Parizeau, asked for support for sovereignty combined with a new economic and political partnership with the rest of Canada. Three days before the vote, the *Non* side organized a huge demonstration called the "unity rally" in the streets of Montreal with supporters hitchhiking, busing, and driving from across the country to profess their love of a united country. Nobody asked Trudeau to speak at the 100,000-strong gathering about Canadian unity, his "magnificent obsession," or even to "join the current leaders on stage," as John English reports in *Just Watch Me*. "Alone and rejected, the once fiery orator watched the massive rally in the square below his office window at Heenan Blaikie's office, perched high above Boulevard René Lévesque . . ." The vote, which occurred on October 30, 1995, was desperately close. The pro-sovereignty side was defeated by 50.58 percent to 49.42 percent, a shadowy margin of just over 1 percent. Afterward, a bitter Parizeau blamed the loss on "money and the ethnic vote."

The last time Trudeau emerged from private life was heartbreaking. He appeared as a desolate father mourning the death of his youngest son. Michel Trudeau, twenty-three, was killed in an avalanche while on a skiing expedition with friends in Kokanee Glacier Provincial Park, north of Nelson, B.C., on November 13, 1998. His body was never recovered.

There was nothing belligerent about the ashen-faced Trudeau at the memorial service on Friday, November 20, 1998, at Saint-Viateur Church in Outremont, where he himself had worshipped as a young man. During the Mass he read a passage from 1 Corinthians, chapter 15, about life everlasting. Afterwards, the surviving Trudeau family walked out of the church as a four-some, a staggering Margaret held up by her eldest son, Justin, on her left side and her middle son, Sacha, on her right. Trudeau, his face tear-streaked, his eyes bleak and unseeing, walked on the far side of Sacha, upright and solitary in his grief.

The "mask" McLuhan had described, and which had made Trudeau so telegenic thirty years earlier, was now frozen in place by Parkinson's disease. He looked forlorn, vulnerable, frail, and heartbreakingly human as he endured the unimaginable — the death of a child, especially one more than fifty years his junior. Even from a distance, Canadians embraced him as never before, as the wounded warrior.

For a time Trudeau lost his faith, as biographer John English reports in *Just Watch Me*, but finally he "believed once more, and ultimately took refuge once again in the consolation of this faith and its Church." Still, he seemed tired of living and refused treatment for the prostate cancer that was beginning its deadly and inexorable creep through his body.

A FINAL SURGE

THE FIRST OFFICIAL inkling that Trudeau was dying came in a statement from his two surviving sons on September 7, 2000, saying their father was "not well" and asking for privacy. Of course the opposite happened. Reporters and camera crews camped outside Maison Cormier, his art deco house on avenue des Pins in Montreal, and well-wishers left flowers and notes. He appeared to rally but then, having received a few old friends and the last sacrament, died surrounded by his sons and his former wife at his Montreal home on September 28, 2000. He was three weeks shy of his eighty-first birthday.

Watching broadcasts of the Summer Olympics from Sydney was forgotten as thousands, many of them carrying roses, waited for hours to pay their respects when his flag-draped coffin lay in state in the Hall of Honour in the Centre Block of Parliament in Ottawa. Equal numbers lined the tracks as a special train carried his body back home to Montreal, where several thousand more mourners gathered to sign the condolence book and pass by his coffin in City Hall before his state funeral at Notre-Dame Basilica on October 3, 2000.

At Sacha Trudeau's request, Jean Chrétien read the same Bible passage about life everlasting that Trudeau had read at his son Michel's funeral less than two years earlier. "My father had particular fondness for Saint Paul's letters and this forceful argument for faith and eternal life fit his own deep convictions," Sacha Trudeau explained in an email. His brother Justin's emotive eulogy, ending with tears and "*Je t'aime, Papa*," caused the mourners to burst into applause in the Basilica, indicating for the first of several times that his mother's blood coursed more freely in his veins than his father's.

The spontaneous, naive, expectant thronging of the late 1960s had a final swell of grief and mourning. These two primordial surrenders to emotion, thirty years apart, were attempts to holster and harness the elusive and contrary man we longed to possess, the man who had transformed our country, our concept of ourselves as Canadians, and our place in the world.

PIERRE BERTON

Mr. Canada

JULY 12, 1920 – NOVEMBER 30, 2004

For more than half a century, Pierre Berton dominated print and broadcast media in Canada as a popular historian, crusading journalist, scrappy columnist, television personality, and cultural ambassador. He told us our story before we knew we had one.

Many of his fifty books were forgettable, but the best ones — his histories of the North, the building of the transcontinental railway, the War of 1812 — earned him three Governor General's Awards, fourteen honorary degrees, and the gratitude of ordinary Canadians for making their past come alive.

He wrote history like a journalist: sniffing out good stories, checking his facts, digging up vivid anecdotes, and spinning his yarns into dramatic narratives that aroused a huge popular audience and often got up the noses of professional historians. Jack Granatstein, an early critic who grew into an admirer, admitted he had once chided Berton in print for "consciously" making things "*interesting.*" "Of course I do," retorted Berton in a lengthy letter deriding academic arrogance. "I sure as hell don't consciously make it dull."

Berton enticed us with his muscular prose into learning the stories of the men and women who had come here as immigrants, fought against invaders, and opened the West and the North. He belonged to the generation born after the First World War, who lived through the Depression, survived the Second

World War, and prospered in the buoyant postwar years of cultural nationalism. A colourful storyteller with a respect for the past and an urge to celebrate it, he excelled in an era when television was coming into its own and before the Internet, the *Dictionary of Canadian Biography*, and other tools — including *The Canadian Encyclopedia*, Google, and Wikipedia — made the past instantly accessible to readers wanting a sense of our heritage and our place in the world.

A Bunyanesque figure who sported a trademark bow tie and (for a while) a Ronald Colman moustache, Berton had an aggressive style and a piercing stare. He was a tough guy who never backed down from a fight — I once saw him punch an uninvited guest at a publishing party who had insulted his publisher Jack McClelland's executive assistant.

Underneath the bluster, he was kind. "Whenever there is a disaster, and we all have them, the Bertons are always the first ones on your doorstep," recalled the journalist June Callwood in 2004. He was also a generous and mostly anonymous benefactor to writers and artists in need. He was a founding member of the Writers' Trust and the Writers' Union; in 1989 he bought his childhood home in Dawson City and turned it into a haven for professional writers.

A birdwatcher and yet a lover of cats — one of last books was *Cats I Have Known and Loved* (2002) — Berton inspired and demonstrated loyalty, especially from women. His wife, Janet, was his first and best proofreader; Janice Tyrwhitt edited all his books, beginning with *Drifting Home* in 1973; Barbara Sears researched *Hollywood's Canada* for him in 1975, the beginning of a working relationship that lasted through nearly twenty books; and Janet Craig was his perennial copy editor. And at the centre of his working life was Elsa Franklin, his producer and agent, who worked with him on television shows and other projects for forty years.

A workaholic and a dynamo — he could type a column while the potatoes boiled for dinner — Berton made newspapers, magazines, books, radio, and television into customized vehicles for his shoot-from-the-hip opinions and his straight-ahead prose. Whether he courted controversy or it dogged him, Berton had opinions on everything from organized religion, teenage sex, abortion, capital punishment, and civil rights to the best way to roast a turkey. A Canadian, he once said, is somebody who knows how to make love in a canoe. He cheerfully admitted to arrogance, saying that it was time Canadians learned to be arrogant. "This statement was considered to be so remarkable,"

he wrote in *My Times*, his 1995 memoir, "it was picked up by Canadian Press...
An Arrogant Canadian! It was like discovering a new species of marmot."

PIERRE FRANCIS DE Marigny Berton, the only son of Francis Berton, a civil
engineer, and Laura Berton (née Thompson), a part-time reporter, was born
in Whitehorse, Yukon, on July 12, 1920. His father, a graduate of the University
of New Brunswick, had gone to the North seeking adventure; his mother was
the daughter of newsman and socialist T. Phillips Thompson. Berton probably inherited his fearlessness from his father and his crusading journalism
from his mother.

When he was less than a year old, his parents moved to Dawson City,
where their daughter, Lucy, was born in the fall of 1921. Like many Canadians,
the Bertons suffered during the Depression, surviving with frugality, home-
made clothing, and scanty provisions. The radio was their conduit to what
was happening in the world.

The Boy Scouts became a huge outlet when Berton was an adolescent,
inspiring a lifetime of loyalty. He said later that joining the Scouts was the
only thing that kept him from turning into a juvenile delinquent. After graduating from high school in 1937, he headed south to Victoria, B.C., for
university.

His first conscious move towards moulding himself into "Pierre Berton,
famous Canadian" was transferring from Victoria College, across the Strait of
Georgia, to the University of British Columbia in 1939 for his final two years.
"Quite clearly, although I didn't know it at the time, I was going into journalism. I switched my courses and did everything I had to do to get to UBC so
that I could get to the *Ubyssey*," he said in a 2001 interview. During the summers, he worked in Yukon gold mines.

He embraced the student newspaper and its swashbuckling tradition of
chasing stories and skirts and skipping class. He wanted to be editor, but was
considered "too loose a cannon" for the UBC administration to accept as overall editor, according to A. B. McKillop, author of *Pierre Berton: A Biography*.
Still, he had a strong influence, redesigning the layout, writing his own pieces,
and editing the Tuesday edition of the twice-weekly paper.

He also became a campus correspondent for the Vancouver *News-Herald*.
In 1940 he was taken on full-time for the summer and got a permanent job
there after he graduated from UBC in 1941. Editors were in short supply

because many younger journalists had enlisted to fight in the Second World War. So Berton, at age twenty-one, became the youngest city editor in Canada.

He was not on the job for long. The Canadian Army beckoned and Berton served, first as a private in the Canadian Information Corps. He rose through the ranks, ending up as a captain and an instructor at the Royal Military College in Kingston.

After the war he returned to Vancouver, where on March 22, 1946, he married Janet Walker, an aspiring journalist whom he had met at the *Ubyssey*. (She edited the Friday edition of the paper and was later promoted to news manager, according to McKillop.) He quickly found a job at the *Vancouver Sun*, where his front-page scoops and headline-making adventures — including a series on the Nahanni Valley, which, with typical hyperbole, he called Headless Valley — caught the eye of Arthur Irwin, editor of *Maclean's*, the best magazine in the country. Irwin sent journalist Scott Young from Toronto to offer Berton a job as an associate editor, giving him the authority to negotiate a starting salary between $4,000 and $4,500. "I'll take $4,500," retorted Berton, clinching the deal that moved him from the sidelines to the centre of the journalism industry in Canada.

"He was huge and shy and brash and we didn't know what to make of him," said June Callwood in a 2004 interview. Like her husband, Trent Frayne, Callwood was a "regular" freelancer for the monthly magazine. At a "casserole and bottle of rye" party, soon after Berton arrived in Toronto in 1947, he recited Robert Service's "The Shooting of Dan McGrew" like "a kid trying to make a good impression."

Performing the Service poem became one of Berton's party tricks. In September 2004, two months before he died, he rose from his wheelchair at a fundraising dinner in Toronto for the Berton House Writers' Retreat and recited the whole thing off the top of his head.

At *Maclean's*, Berton was a writing dynamo. He banged out stories on the Arctic, Canadians serving in Korea, discrimination against Japanese and Jewish Canadians in the 1940s, and the need to end capital punishment. Editor Ralph Allen "used to say that Pierre had ten ideas every day for articles and two of them were brilliant," according to Callwood.

At the time, Berton thought of Toronto as merely a way station to a larger career south of the border. "My idea was always to go to the States and work for *Life* magazine or the *Saturday Evening Post*," he said later. In the end he stayed here, and instead of becoming part of the brain drain he became, under the tutelage of Allen and journalist Bruce Hutchison, instrumental in fostering a home-grown cultural nationalism. He never regretted that decision. "I've done much better here than I would have done in the States. I became a big frog in a little puddle."

By the mid-1950s the Bertons had several offspring (eventually they would have eight children, two of them adopted and seven of them given first names starting with the letter *P*). After a tip from broadcaster Lister Sinclair, a friend since *Ubyssey* days, the Bertons bought three and a half hectares of land in Kleinburg, northwest of Toronto, and built a sprawling house for their expanding family. The pressure to provide for all those mouths soon saw Berton moonlighting on radio programs such as *Court of Opinion*, becoming a panellist on *Front Page Challenge* (from 1957 until the program finally went off the air in 1995), and pounding away at book manuscripts. He got up very early, typed until it was time to go to *Maclean's*, and hit his keys again at home in the evening, establishing a twelve-hour workday regimen that he followed for the rest of his life.

By 1958 he had written three books, two of which, *The Mysterious North* and *Klondike: The Last Great Gold Rush*, earned him Governor General's Awards. That was the year that Berton was lured away from *Maclean's* to become a daily columnist for the *Toronto Star*, his third significant career switch.

His output was staggering. He wrote 1,200 words a day, five days a week, and on the sixth day he ran a column of letters. The column, which was by turns investigative, crusading, ruminative, and domestic, combined the best aspects of the rabble-rousing local journalist and pushed the genre in new directions. His writing hummed with energy and enthusiasm and was as interactive with readers as it was possible to be in those pre-Internet days.

After four years at the *Star* (and two books based on his newspaper columns), he went back to *Maclean's* as a columnist, a gig that was short-lived because of a notorious column he wrote in 1963 under the heading "Let's Stop Hoaxing the Kids about Sex." The column was really about hypocrisy, and Berton soon learned a lesson on that very subject from his employers.

As the father of four daughters, he wrote, he hoped his girls would be sensible, but if they wanted to have sex he wished they would do it in a comfortable bed rather than the back seat of a car. The public was outraged and all hell broke loose. "Church groups were formed to attack *Maclean's*, to cancel subscriptions and to withdraw advertising, and I was fired," he said later. "I didn't quit, I was fired. They published the goddamn thing, and now they were pushing me out."

Leaving *Maclean's* gave him more time to concentrate on books and his burgeoning career in radio and television. Besides regular radio debates with his friend Charles Templeton and his *Front Page Challenge* gig, he hosted *The Pierre Berton Show* on CTV from 1962 until 1973. His panoply of controversial guests included prostitutes, dope addicts, professional divorce co-respondents, and once, a Playboy bunny. Helen Gurley Brown, author of *Sex and the Single Girl,* should have been on the list, but skittish executives killed the program.

Mainly, though, he wrote books. For the next three decades he produced a book every autumn as regularly as the leaves fell from the trees. *Klondike: The Last Great Gold Rush, 1896–1899* (1958), a heroic book about the common people who went north seeking their fortunes, remained his favourite. "It is a lively book, it says something about human nature and I put my heart into it," he explained in 2001. That fondness was shared by historian Ramsay Cook. "That is where he came from and where his mother taught him how to write," he said in a 2004 interview with the *Globe.* "It is a wonderful book on almost every level. You can dig around and find a lot of things he probably didn't pay attention to and he probably tells some stories that are a little larger than life, but still it is a book that anybody who is going to visit the Yukon would have to read."

In the mid-1950s, Berton hooked up with legendary publisher Jack McClelland because his publishing house, McClelland & Stewart, was the Canadian distributor for Alfred A. Knopf, for whom Berton had written his book on the royal family in 1954. It was only after *Klondike* that M&S became his originating publisher. The two men shared an appetite for drink and the company of women and were co-founders of a notorious luncheon society, coyly called the Sordsmen's Club, in the early 1960s. Only men could belong; wives were not invited — except as the guests of men other than their husbands. Nobody enquired too closely when dalliances took place and couples sought secluded rooms after several courses and many libations.

For a while, Berton added editor-in-chief of M&S to his many titles. McClelland wanted to start an illustrated books division and persuaded Berton to head it up by promising him it would take only one day a week. When this proved illusory, Berton told McClelland that either he could stay on as editor-in-chief of M&S or he could quit and write another book. That book turned out to be *The National Dream* (1970), the first volume of his history of the Canadian Pacific Railway, and a mega-hit for Berton and M&S.

He wrote the manuscript in three weeks, although he took a year to revise it. The second volume, *The Last Spike* (1971), took longer to draft — a month — and the same amount of time to polish. Historian Michael Bliss agreed to be the academic reader for the CPR books. "I came to that job with much skepticism, thinking he was probably a phony who relied on researchers, and then was quite surprised that the manuscripts were so good and that in conversation he clearly knew his material extremely well," Bliss said in a 2004 interview with the *Globe*. "He obviously had high intelligence, good writing skills, and a flair for story-telling, and what more does one want in a popular historian?"

The Last Spike won Berton his third Governor General's Award. Both books sold about 130,000 copies each. It led to another triumph when the CBC produced *The National Dream* in 1974, eight dramatized documentaries based on his bestselling books. The series, introduced by Berton, netted 3.6 million viewers, a mammoth audience in English Canada at the time.

Flamboyant, daring, and fiercely patriotic, McClelland was the perfect marketer for Berton's colourful narratives about the building of the railroad, the opening of the West, the Great Depression, the War of 1812, and the Dionne quintuplets. Together they rode the roller coaster of cultural nationalism, with Berton providing the content and McClelland supplying the razzmatazz.

The relationship with M&S continued through dozens of books and the sale of the financially beleaguered firm to real-estate developer Avie Bennett in 1985, and only ended a decade later, when Berton took his memoir *My Times* to rival publishers Doubleday in a dispute about money. Bennett, who had taken a hard look at the balance sheet for *Starting Out* (1987), the first volume of Berton's memoirs, was unwilling to offer the advance that Berton demanded.

The blockbuster sales for Mr. Canada were over. So, too, were the days for the kind of history that he had made his own. When his forty-seventh title, *Onward to War*, a history of Canada's dutiful response to declarations of war in South Africa, Europe, and Korea, was published in 2001, it was less well received than earlier titles. Reviewing the book in the *Globe*, historian Modris Eksteins asked: "If the world changed in the last century as dramatically as Berton insists, can — or should — history be written in much the same way Carlyle and Macaulay presented it over a century ago?"

Eksteins had a point. Berton will not be remembered for any great archival discoveries or new theories or interpretations. His skill was in creating a large popular following for his re-creation of the characters and events of the past.

In his last years, Berton suffered from congestive heart failure, diabetes, and a slew of other lifestyle ailments. Although he had slowed down, he continued to work — he wanted to go out writing. In the fall of 2004, aged eighty-four, he began a monthly column for the *Globe* and published his fiftieth book, *Prisoners of the North*, a quintet of profiles of Arctic adventurers that included Klondike Joe Boyle, Vilhjalmur Stefansson, and Robert Service.

He also continued to make radio and television appearances, demonstrating his technique for rolling a joint on *Rick Mercer's Monday Report* on CBC TV, using a copy of *The National Dream* as a flat surface. Some viewers were reminded of the time he almost severed a finger on *90 Minutes Live* back in 1978, demonstrating the workings of the then-revolutionary Cuisinart food processor while aghast host Peter Gzowski watched his guest's blood flow onto the studio floor. The *Monday Report* segment was Berton's last television appearance, and it was a classic: self-parodying, flamboyant, and a poke up the nose of the Canadian lawmakers who refused to legalize the smoking of recreational marijuana.

In the middle of October 2004, Janet Berton fell and broke her hip. As soon as she was admitted to York Central Hospital for what turned out to be a prolonged stay, Berton's own decline accelerated. By the end of the month both Bertons were in separate wings of the same hospital. He was transferred on November 29 to Sunnybrook Health Sciences Centre. There, with his wife Janet and his daughter Peggy Anne at his bedside, the man everybody called Pierre died the following afternoon of complications from heart disease and diabetes. He was eighty-four.

MAURICE "THE ROCKET" RICHARD

Hockey Player

AUGUST 4, 1921 – MAY 27, 2000

MAURICE "THE ROCKET" Richard always insisted that he was just a hockey player. No matter how heartfelt and accurate, those denials didn't stop fans, politicians, team owners, and opportunists from appropriating his name and power for their personal, political, philosophical, and commercial goals. Even after he died of abdominal cancer on May 27, 2000, his state funeral — extremely rare for an athlete — threatened to become hijacked by politics. Should the coffin be draped with the fleur-de-lys flag, symbolizing the nationalist aspirations of Quebec, as Premier Lucien Bouchard wanted? Or should it be covered with the maple leaf of Canada, as Prime Minister Jean Chrétien desired in that tempestuous era of national unity debates? Wisely, Richard's family chose the apolitical route that the hockey legend himself had always tried to skate: they ordered a blanket of yellow roses, insisting that the final public ceremony be about the man, not other people's expectations or ambitions.

His career statistics are still staggering: He was the first player to score fifty goals in a fifty-game season and to amass a career total of five hundred goals, achieving 544 markers in regular play and 82 in the playoffs in his eighteen years skating with the Canadiens. He helped win the Stanley Cup eight times for Montreal, was captain for four winning years in a row between 1957 and 1960, and played in every annual NHL All-Star game from 1947 to 1959. He was also the only hockey player to single-handedly spark a riot in the streets of Montreal, on March 17, 1955 — St. Patrick's Day — after league president Clarence Campbell suspended him for the rest of the season after a violent altercation with a linesman four days earlier in Boston.

Why was it that Richard became more than just a hockey player in the hearts and imaginations of Canadians? Sure, Howie Morenz was already a star before Richard laced up his skates for *les Canadiens* in 1942, but Morenz was an anglophone from Ontario. The Rocket was the first French-Canadian hockey legend. He emerged as a jet-propelled scoring ace in the 1940s and early 1950s, when radio controlled the airwaves. An entire generation of Québécois boys, including future teammates Jean Beliveau and Bernie "Boom Boom" Geoffrion, grew up listening to the play-by-play, visualizing the Rocket tearing up the ice (and any defencemen) in his zigzag path as he roared from the blue line, eyes blazing, to slap a puck into the opposing team's net.

One of those kids was Roch Carrier, the distinguished playwright and short-story writer (*La guerre, yes sir!* and *Floralie, où es-tu?* among other titles), arts administrator, and author of the classic children's book *The Hockey Sweater*. Born in May 1937, Carrier turned eight the year that Richard scored fifty goals in fifty games. In *The Hockey Sweater* he describes his adulation for Richard and his chagrin when his mother ordered him a new sweater from the Eaton's catalogue and the retailer sent a Toronto Maple Leafs sweater by mistake. "We all combed our hair like Maurice Richard... We laced our skates like Maurice Richard, we taped our sticks like Maurice Richard.... On the ice... we were ten players all wearing the uniform of the Montreal Canadiens... [and we] all wore the famous number 9 on our backs."

Although Richard is often forced into the heroic mould of a hero of the Quiet Revolution, he is a reluctant and imperfect fit. He did grow up in Quebec at a time when anglophone commercial and cultural dominance was pronounced and he played in an era when the ultra-nationalist Maurice Duplessis was premier of the province, but Richard was always his own man. Moreover, he retired from hockey a year after Duplessis died in September 1959, just as the not-so-Quiet Revolution was beginning.

Richard never made a political speech other than to complain, quite rightly, that in his day the owners treated the players, who drew in the fans and filled their coffers, more like serfs than heroes. But that was a common grievance throughout hockey and not limited to francophone players.

Introverted and shy, Richard remained apart — not aloof, but apart — from the camaraderie in the locker room and the kibitzing on the hockey award banquet circuit. Richard led by example, not words, as Canadiens goalie Jacques Plante observed decades after the legendary player had hung up his skates. "The Rocket was a very quiet man and on the road trips, he would watch us play cards and laugh at the jokes." More important, "He always took the blame himself for a loss, never faulting anyone else. If a player wasn't working hard enough or playing smart, one glare from the Rocket usually corrected the problem."

That silence, that distance, left plenty of space for sportswriters and pundits to speculate about the extraordinary surge of emotion this smouldering-eyed, taciturn lumberjack on skates could summon from the stoniest heart. There isn't a single answer, but the best explanation is probably that fans and foes alike recognized in Richard a simple man driven by love — for the game, his family, and his country — all of those basic values that need no fancy filigree to shine brighter than precious metals.

JOSEPH HENRI MAURICE Richard, the eldest of eight children of Onésime and Alice Richard (née Laramée), was born on August 4, 1921, in Montreal. His parents, who were both from the Gaspé region, had moved separately to the city, seeking work during the First World War. They met, courted, married, and found a small house to rent in the east end, near Lafontaine Park. By the time Maurice was four, his father, a woodworker for the Canadian Pacific Railway at their Angus Yards, had saved up enough money to build a small house in the Bordeaux district, near rue Jean-Talon in the northeast part of the city. That's where Maurice learned to play hockey on a backyard rink flooded by his father.

Organized hockey teams began when he entered the school system. He played peewee, bantam, and midget while a student at Saint-François-de-Laval elementary school. After Grade 9 he went to the Montreal Technical School and played for its team as well as the community one in his neighbourhood. As a teenager he added boxing and baseball to his sporting repertoire while continuing to play as many as two games of hockey during the week and four on weekends — adopting aliases such as "Maurice Rochon" so he could be on more than one roster.

He even met his future wife, Lucille, through hockey: she was the younger sister of Georges Norchet, his hockey coach at the Paquette Club, in the Parc Lafontaine Juvenile League. Norchet often invited team members back to his parents' house after games. Unlike his more outgoing teammates, Richard would stand quietly off to the side, sipping a soft drink, when the rugs were rolled back and the gramophone wound up. Lucille, then only thirteen, was a petite and pretty redhead with a ready smile and easy social skills. "I took it upon myself to teach Maurice to dance and to act as his fashion consultant too," she reminisced later. Much to her parents' shock, the couple became engaged when she was seventeen. By then Richard had quit school and was working with his father as a machinist as well as earning some money as a player for the Canadiens' senior farm team in the Quebec league.

They married on September 21, 1942. The Richards had reared seven children and had been married for more than half a century when Lucille died of cancer in July 1994. Richard was so devoted to his wife that he refused to leave her side to accept a symbolic appointment to the Privy Council. The Queen herself was to convey the honour at Rideau Hall on Canada Day, 1992, in commemoration of the 125th anniversary of Confederation. Adding the designation *L'honorable* to his name paled next to comforting his ailing wife. The PMO offered to send a nurse to the Richard home, but the Rocket declined. Finally, Richard agreed to accept the honour in a special ceremony organized in his hometown.

As a player, Richard was fast and relentless. He got his nickname "Rocket" in 1942 from another player. Left-winger Ray Getliffe was sitting on the bench in the Forum watching Elmer Lach feed "a lovely pass" to Richard. "I leaned over [to one of the other players] and said, 'Wow, Richard took off like a rocket.'" The comment was overheard by *Montreal Star* sports writer Dink Carroll, who immortalized it in print.

In his short biography *Maurice Richard*, Charles Foran describes Richard as having the upper body of a logger, complete with barrel chest, broad shoulders, tree-trunk arms, thick hands, and permanently swollen knuckles. "He does not skate over the ice so much as impose himself upon it with each pressuring stride. His strokes are economical rather than elegant, commanded by force more than grace," Foran writes, having watched Richard's solitary skate in a 1975 CBC documentary. "Shoulders square and elbows at 90 degrees, chin up and gaze ahead...he manoeuvres the puck side to side on the blade of his stick with the ease of someone stirring milk into coffee."

Even more often than documenting Richard's glide, journalists and opposing players invariably commented upon Richard's gaze, especially the ferocious stare in his "anthracite eyes" as he barrelled towards the opposing team's goal. Over the years several opposing players described the effect. "When he came flying toward you with the puck on his stick, his eyes were all lit up, flashing and gleaming like a pinball machine. It was terrifying," said Hall of Fame goalie Glenn Hall.

In his memoir, *Tales of an Athletic Supporter*, Trent Frayne described Richard as the "most spectacular goal scorer who ever played hockey." Nobody "electrified onlookers the way the Rocket did, dashing from the blue line in. And nobody I've seen since had his hypnotic flair, either. When he was battling for the puck near the net, driving for it with guys clutching at him, you could actually see a glitter in his coal-black eyes, the look wild horses get."

Roch Carrier used the same animal image. "He's half wild horse, half well-disciplined soldier...with a face as rough as a stone in a Gaspé field and the piercing eyes of someone who has the gift of seeing things invisible to others," he wrote in *Our Life with the Rocket: The Maurice Richard Story*.

Richard's eyes even became part of the homily delivered by the archbishop of Montreal, Cardinal Jean-Claude Turcotte, at Richard's funeral at Notre-Dame Basilica on May 31, 2000. "What a look! Such strength, such intensity in those eyes. Poets have said that the eyes are the mirror of the soul. All of Maurice was in his eyes. We will not forget that look," the cardinal promised. And so it has become.

But, for all his power and spell-casting, Richard was injury prone. Even before he showed up at training camp for the Canadiens in 1942, the year he married Lucille, he had suffered a broken ankle and a broken wrist. That season he fractured his leg in December, after only sixteen games. Canadiens general manager Tommy Gorman tried to trade him to the New York Rangers, but the American team scoffed at the deal.

Despite the conscription crisis at the outbreak of the Second World War and the nationalist Québécois opposition to fighting for the British Crown, Richard wanted to enlist in the army and go overseas to fight the Germans. He tried twice to join the combat forces, beginning in 1939, but was refused as unfit because X-rays showed his injuries hadn't healed properly. Finally, in 1944, he applied as a machinist but was rejected because he had neither a high school diploma nor a technical trade certificate, even though he had been working at the trade in a local factory since he was sixteen. Frustrated but determined, he enrolled at the Montreal Technical School, but by the time he had earned his certificate, the war was over.

Instead of serving the war effort overseas, he kept the home spirits stoked by playing hockey. After Richard's wife, Lucille, gave birth to their first child on October 23, 1943, he went to Canadiens coach Dick Irvin and asked if he could switch his number from fifteen to nine to commemorate the lusty birth weight of his daughter, Huguette. For Richard, the number became a talisman symbolizing his love for his baby and his wife and his need to express that emotion, not in words but on the ice, as he skated, stick-handled, and scored goals. Hockey, plus whatever jobs he could get in the off-season, combined later with endorsements and commercials for a variety of products — from hair dye to fishing tackle — were essential in supporting a wife and seven children. Despite his fame and his prowess, Richard never made more than $25,000 a season playing hockey.

In 1944 the Canadiens won the Stanley Cup, with Richard scoring thirty-two goals in the regular season and twelve in the playoffs, including all five goals in a 5–1 victory over the Toronto Maple Leafs in the semifinals, a stellar achievement that culminated in Richard's being awarded all three stars at the end of the game that night. The following season Irvin switched the left-handed Richard to right wing, alongside Elmer Lach and Toe Blake in what came to be called the "Punch Line." That was the year he put fifty goals in the net in as many games.

Richard rarely started a fight, but he didn't back away from one either, often using his training as a boxer to give back more than he got. He had a notoriously short fuse and, once ignited, his temper exploded like a fuel-injected missile. Heckled by rival players, victimized by referees, Richard was drafted into a symbolic martyrdom by a francophone minority who felt persecuted in their home province — the way they felt he was abused on the ice — by the mercantile and political masters of the rest of Canada.

One cultural commentator, Benoît Melançon, author of *The Rocket: A Cultural History of Maurice Richard*, has actually gone so far as to compare a colour photograph of Richard in the April 1955 issue of *Sport* magazine with a seventeenth-century painting of Saint Sebastian, the early Christian martyr, by the Baroque painter Luca Giordano: "both bodies stand out against a black background; where one has an arrow in his side, the other holds fast to his stick." But Melançon isn't content with visual similarities between the painting of the martyr and the photograph of the hockey player. He contends that the photograph, which was hanging in the Montreal Forum before the March 1955 riot, gave marauders "the image of the martyr Richard was to become that very evening," an overstretched juxtaposition that collapses under its own hyperbole.

In a much more restrained and powerful article in *Saturday Night* magazine in January 1955, novelist Hugh MacLennan wrote presciently about the "gentleness and ferocity" that co-existed in Richard and warned of the danger in provoking his rage: "Every great player must expect to be marked closely, but for ten years the Rocket has been systematically heckled by rival coaches who know intuitively that nobody can more easily be taken advantage of than a genius. Richard can stand any amount of roughness that comes naturally with the game, but after a night in which he has been cynically tripped, slashed, held, boarded, and verbally insulted by lesser men he is apt to go wild. His rage is curiously impersonal — an explosion against frustration itself."

Less than two months later Montreal itself exploded in what came to be known as the Richard Riot. Tensions had been percolating for years between Richard and the unilingual, authoritarian NHL president Clarence Campbell, a Rhodes Scholar, former NHL referee, and lieutenant colonel in the Canadian Army.

A year earlier, Richard, in a ghostwritten column in a Montreal weekly that he hadn't even read, had called Campbell a dictator for the way he had "over-penalized" his brother Henri and Boom Boom Geoffrion for vicious behaviour in fights they had not initiated. Campbell went ballistic, with the result that Canadiens general manager Frank Selke persuaded Richard to offer an abject apology and to post a thousand-dollar bond. Campbell publicly released the details, which infuriated the French media. They accused the NHL of muzzling their hero, who by then had agreed to stop allowing his name to appear as a byline on somebody else's prose.

An anglophone referee named McLean seemed to be blind when Richard was under attack and yet omniscient when the Rocket retaliated. Encountering the referee in a New York hotel lobby, Richard grabbed him and began swinging. That earned him a $500 fine from Campbell. Then, in a losing game against the Bruins in Boston on March 13, 1955, Richard got into an altercation with opposing defenceman Hal Laycoe. Sticks were raised, and Laycoe opened a gash in Richard's scalp. Trent Frayne, who was there, described Richard attacking the defenceman with his stick: "wielding it across Laycoe's shoulders and neck as though taking an axe to a tree." The benches emptied, and in the ensuing brawl Richard punched linesman Cliff Thompson, a retired defenceman for the Bruins, in the face — twice. Campbell ordered that

Richard, the Canadiens' leading scorer, be suspended for the rest of the season, including the playoffs.

The lengthy suspension outraged fans and killed Richard's hopes of winning his first league scoring title. Everybody had an opinion on Campbell's verdict, including Mayor Jean Drapeau, who publicly warned him to skip the Canadiens' next home game because even showing up would look like a "provocation." Campbell refused, which inflamed the already angry fans. When he arrived at a game against the Detroit Red Wings, who were tied for first place with the Canadiens, Campbell was pelted with tomatoes and other debris. A fan punched him in the face, another hurled a canister of tear gas. The game was abruptly forfeited to the Red Wings and attendees were ordered to leave the arena, swelling the militant crowds rampaging through the streets of downtown Montreal.

The rioters caused an estimated $100,000 in property damage, thirty-seven injuries, and a hundred arrests before the police exerted control. Even the Rocket himself was persuaded to speak on radio the next morning, in French and English, to calm the crowd. Richard's teammate Boom Boom Geoffrion won the scoring title that season and the Detroit Red Wings took the Stanley Cup. The following year Richard returned to the ice and led his team to the first of five successive Stanley Cup victories.

After that, his glory days on the ice were over. He showed up at training camp in the fall of 1960, but nothing seemed the same, and impulsively he decided to retire in September, a month after his thirty-ninth birthday. He had put on some pounds, his reflexes were slowing down, and he had suffered injuries, including a broken bone in one of his ankles and a severed Achilles tendon, which had kept him from playing the full season in his last three years. Management wanted him to go while the crowds still roared as he slapped the puck into the net — sooner rather than later — and offered him a three-year post-retirement job in public relations at his playing salary.

Years later Richard admitted that he had left the game too soon. He really didn't know what to do with himself off the ice. Several post-playing positions, including as inaugural coach of the Quebec Nordiques, fizzled. Unlike his teammate Toe Blake, who had a distinguished post-playing career as coach of the Canadiens, or Jean Beliveau, who moved into the executive ranks of the organization, Richard was really only at ease on the ice or at home with his family. Eventually he split with the Canadiens and started a number of business ventures, including owning a tavern, selling fishing tackle, and appearing in commercials endorsing hair products.

What brought him back into the fold and the public eye was the closing ceremonies for the venerable Forum on March 11, 1996. The game itself was not memorable. Instead of one of their traditional rivals — the Leafs, the Bruins, or the Red Wings — the Habs were up against the upstart Dallas Stars. After the final whistle sounded and the three stars had been named in a game in which the *bleu-blanc-rouge* defeated the Stars 4–1, a work crew unrolled four red carpets stretching in a huge square from the blue lines. As funeral music was played, surviving Hall of Fame players, wearing their team sweaters, walked on to the ice as the crowd roared. The last to appear was Richard. The building erupted in a standing ovation that lasted nearly eight minutes, despite the Rocket's attempts to quell the cascading waves of applause. It was as though the fans — many of whom were too young to have ever seen him play — recognized the depths of passion in the vulnerable, ageing figure with the taciturn demeanour. They bathed him in love and admiration as though he represented all of their grandfathers. By the time francophone announcer Richard Garneau intoned, "*Mesdames et messieurs, vous avez devant vous le coeur et l'âme du Forum*," the crowd was spent and Richard himself was weeping.

It was a living tribute, one that would be echoed four years later, when more than 100,000 fans lined up around the clock and around the block to pay their last respects as his coffin lay in state in the new Molson Centre on May 30, 2000. They then thronged the streets the following day to watch the funeral procession wend its way to Notre-Dame Basilica in Old Montreal. It was the end of an era — and the birth of Rocket Richard, nationalist hero.

June Callwood

Writer and Social Activist

June 2, 1924 – April 14, 2007

A FTER SHE WAS diagnosed with terminal cancer in 2003, June Callwood talked about gliding over Georgian Bay, contemplating all the pain she had experienced in her life and wondering whether there was "anything spiritual" that could help ease her misery. "And I thought, floating up there, 'This is what it's all about. It's kindness. Not top-down kindness, giving a toonie to a street person and treating them like a slot machine, but stopping and talking to them. If people can behave well to each other, that's all that there is,'" she told *Globe* journalist John Allemang. An atheist, she took that philosophy of kindness, which was as close as she could come to a religious belief, and sprinkled it liberally as she carried on her personal campaign against injustice, even as cancer rampaged through her body.

Known as a doer, a "secular saint," a fundraiser, a civic activist, a fierce campaigner for human rights, and a "general nuisance," she wrote thirty-odd books, more than a thousand magazine articles, close to five hundred newspaper columns, and hosted at least two television shows, *In Touch* and *National Treasures*. She helped establish fifty organizations — more than most people join in their lifetimes. The institutions range across the arts, human rights, civil liberties, and social welfare. In recompense, she was given nearly twenty honorary degrees, named a Companion of the Order of Canada, and had a street, a park, and Ontario's volunteerism award named in her honour.

Life itself inspired her activism. Her mother and father were inept as parents, so she learned early on "to take care of myself and live in my imagination, and as soon as I could find books, I was reading them." Words became magic for Callwood. She used them to persuade, denounce, and describe. They were the source of her livelihood, her prodigious influence in effecting social change, and her solace.

She also had two grandfathers "who were crazy about me," so she didn't mind her parents' lack of attention, because she was loved and praised. "I grew up thinking people take care of one another and you have to do that to be a good person; you have to be available to help others. And I also grew up fearless, so that helped."

Her self-confidence took perennial tumbles when it came to her vocation. "Fear of failure is huge with me in writing. I have never written something I thought was good enough," she said in an interview five months before she died on April 14, 2007. Of all the books she wrote, she never attempted a memoir. "I'm not very introspective," she explained. "I don't think there are a lot of complications about me." Besides, she was never sure she could write about her life without colouring her memories, and the reporter in her wouldn't allow that.

JUNE ROSE CALLWOOD was born in Chatham, Ontario, on June 2, 1924, the elder daughter of Harold ("Byng") and Gladys (née Lavoie) Callwood. Her mother's family had settled in Quebec City in 1650 and could claim some native blood; her father's ancestry was British. He was a plumber by trade and an entrepreneur by inclination. "My father was a rake who made life very hard for my mother. She eloped with him at sixteen to escape her convent school," she told her friend, writer Sylvia Fraser, in a 2005 *Toronto Life* profile.

She spent her first two years in the town of Tilbury, the home of her grandfather, Harold Callwood, a magistrate. When she was two, her family moved to Belle River, a village near Windsor where her other grandfather, bootlegger Bill Lavoie, had built himself a massive stone house from the proceeds of running liquor across the Detroit River during Prohibition. Her father established the Superior Tinning and Retinning Company and set about, with his wife's help, recycling rusty milk cans using a re-coating process he'd invented.

At six, June entered Belle River's Catholic school and was immediately accelerated into Grade 3. An avid reader, she consumed books in the local library, acquiring general knowledge "so I wouldn't feel so helpless." By the time she was ten and her sister, Jane, was eight, her parents' business had gone bust.

A bigger loss was in the offing. Her father skipped out on his family (and his financial liabilities) three years later and found work threshing wheat on prairie farms for a dollar a day. Callwood's mother took in sewing, but she and her daughters were usually only half a step ahead of the bailiff, and there was one three-day stretch when they ate raw potatoes dug out of somebody else's garden.

The war improved their situation. With many men overseas, her mother landed a job as a bank teller. Callwood attended Brantford Collegiate and gained friends and status as a cheerleader. Television producer Ross McLean was a classmate. He once described her as "a definite original," saying: "Her beauty and her openness caught our fancy, for sure, but so did her unconventional ways."

Athletically she was a freestyle, backstroke, and high-diving champion, but she was also honing her writing skills by working on the high school newspaper and entering (and winning) a short-story contest. A man named Judge Sweet gave her the prize and told her she should look him up if she ever needed a job — a circumstance that emerged sooner than either of them had anticipated. After her mother complained in the middle of a quarrel that she was tired of supporting her rebellious daughter, the furious teenager went to see Judge Sweet, who was on the board of directors of the *Brantford Expositor*. He gave her a letter of introduction to the publisher, who hired her as a proofreader at $7.50 a week.

In 1942 the *Toronto Star* offered her a job for $25 a week. "I was eighteen, but I looked about twelve, despite the high heels, and when the editors saw me, they had no respect for me," she said later. She was supposed to answer the mail and write captions, but her editor fired her after only two weeks for writing a smartass letter to a sergeant who had complained that she'd misidentified an army tank.

She then applied to be a Spitfire pilot but was rejected by the Royal Canadian Air Force Women's Division because they didn't train women to fly. She was outraged. The *Globe and Mail* gave her a trial assignment covering an Ontario Medical Association convention at the Royal York Hotel, but her nerves got the better of her. Don Carlson, a reporter for the *Toronto Star*, took pity on her and wrote her piece after filing his own. On the strength of that

OMA story, the *Globe* hired her as a general-assignment reporter. After that break from a male reporter, she could never endorse second-wave feminist rage at the oppressions of the patriarchal society.

She met Trent ("Bill") Gardiner Frayne at the *Globe*; he was a journalist whose photograph and writing she had admired since her days at the *Brantford Expositor*. They were married on May 13, 1944. Callwood, who was nineteen, wore a grey flannel suit and white hat. She didn't change her name because the *Globe* wanted to keep her on staff; two reporters named Frayne — one male, the other female — would look suspicious in an era when married women were expected to stay home.

Being married to Frayne meant "everything" to her. "My dad was a rascal, and I fell in love with [Frayne] because he was a rock. I wanted somebody I could be safe with, who I could count on and who wouldn't walk out in the middle of the night like my dad did, never be promiscuous, never lie — just an honourable man," she said in November 2006. "And he was handsome as hell," she added with a grin. The added bonus was his sense of humour. "He's hilarious. Dear with his children, and the freaky thing was that it never occurred to him that his wife shouldn't work. It never crossed his mind." She always referred to him as "my guy" and they called each other "Dreamy."

The question of working was rendered moot when Callwood became pregnant three months after the wedding. "I wanted babies, I always wanted to be a mother and I assumed I was going to be a marvellous mother." She quit work before her first child, Jill, was born on May 24, 1945. Motherhood, which Callwood embraced enthusiastically, also turned her into a freelance writer, as a home-based way of earning money.

She wrote her first magazine article (for *Liberty*, earning fifty dollars) about Violet Milstead, the instructor who was teaching her how to fly a single-engine Aeronca Super Chief. Callwood loved flying, but she gave it up after nearly snaring her plane in power lines. The prospect of being seriously hurt or killed was too alarming, given that she had one small child and was expecting another. Brant ("Barney") was born on May 31, 1948.

By comparison, writing was harmless. She produced her first piece for *Maclean's* magazine on the Leslie Bell Singers, an amateur women's choir, in June 1947. Four years later, Callwood and Frayne cobbled together the down payment for a modest two-storey clapboard house on a large, maple-shaded lot surrounded by farmland in Toronto's west end. By then they had a third child, Jesse (born May 15, 1951). Although the house was renovated and expanded over the years, it remained their home and workplace.

Callwood was a whirlwind of activity in the 1950s, writing regularly for *Maclean's* to produce stories that varied from a profile of swimmer Marilyn Bell to the newfangled birth control pill, the death of the Avro Arrow, and even the meaning of the universe. She also began collaborating with Dr. Marion Hilliard — her own doctor — by ghostwriting a monthly column in *Chatelaine* when Doris Anderson was editor of the magazine.

"She was gay," Callwood said, remembering how Hilliard wanted her to say in a column on lovemaking that "it doesn't matter whether you are the same sex or not," but "I was too scandalized to do it." In 1957 Doubleday published *A Woman Doctor Looks at Life and Love*, a book that Callwood ghosted, based on the long-running magazine column. It became a bestseller, was eventually translated into forty languages, and launched Callwood on a prolific career as a ghostwriter for such celebrities as Barbara Walters, Otto Preminger, and Bob White, the Canadian labour leader.

And then everything crashed around her. Just when her three children were in school and she had a steady freelance income, she was whacked by depression. She sought help from a therapist and then turned the experience into a book, *Love, Hate, Fear, Anger and the Other Lively Emotions*, which was published in 1964 under her own name. She and her husband also had the surprise joy of conceiving their youngest, unexpected child, Casey, who was born September 12, 1961, when Callwood was thirty-seven.

The 1960s saw the emergence of Callwood the social activist. Like so many other things in her life, it happened because of a connection with one of her children. Teenaged Barney was living in Yorkville, then a hippie section of Toronto. Every so often he would bring home a destitute friend. "I was so shocked because I had seen us get out of Depression and scarcity and people not having enough," she said, "and then, all of a sudden, I got hit with the kids from Yorkville, and they had bad teeth and many of them had grown up in foster homes and I thought, 'What the hell is going on?'"

Eventually she founded Digger House (named after a group that had tried to establish self-supporting communes in England in the 1600s), a shelter for homeless kids. She paid the first month's rent of $600, the equivalent of the fee for a magazine article. It was the first of several hostels she would help organize, always in response to a directly perceived need.

She also became a street protester, joining a demonstration against the Vietnam War in July 1968. When she tried to help another demonstrator, who was in police custody, she was herself arrested, hauled off to the Don Jail, and charged with obstructing the police. Pierre Berton testified at her trial. She was acquitted, but the experience had turned her into an activist, albeit one who was always dressed to the nines, complete with earrings, high-heeled shoes, and matching handbag.

Over the next two decades she helped found Nellie's (1973), a shelter for abused women, and Jessie's (1982), a home for teenagers and their babies. She also became deeply involved with the Canadian Civil Liberties Association, the Canadian Council of Christians and Jews, the Writers' Union, the Writers' Trust, and PEN Canada. Callwood brought her enthusiasm, energy, contacts, and persuasiveness to all of these activities. Sometimes, though, she became frustrated with the politically correct tenor of the times. A start-up manager par excellence, she was probably too impatient and energetic to be an effective maintenance manager involved in the running of an organization on a day-to-day basis.

When poet M. Nourbese Philip complained that a PEN congress had put too much emphasis on white writers, Ms. Callwood exploded with a crude expletive. "She was being obnoxious so I told her to fuck off," she recalled. Years later, a black female staff member complained at a Nellie's board meeting that the white staff members were racist; Callwood challenged her remark. Tempers flashed, and somebody called Callwood herself a racist. Shaken, she left the meeting and eventually the organization.

In the chaos, the provincial government contacted Callwood with a stern reminder that the Nellie's operating grant would be cancelled if the enclosed forms weren't filed immediately. "To my eternal credit, I decided I had to save Nellie's so I phoned them and said they had to come and pick up this paperwork, but there was a moment there . . ." she said, five months before she died, her eyes glittering. The attenuated silence called to mind a comment she had made in the *Globe* in 2004: "It took me years to stop being angry, and I'm not over being hurt yet."

Diagnosed with CUP (cancer, unknown primary) in September 2003, she had surgery but declined aggressive treatment. When journalist Sylvia Fraser asked Callwood, the author of *Twelve Weeks in Spring*—an inspirational memoir about the care circle she had formed for Margaret Frazer, a friend who was dying of cancer—whether she could foresee a time when she might like home palliative care, Callwood made a "rude" noise and said: "Would you want your friends feeding you and emptying your bedpan?"

By then Callwood had confronted the unthinkable: the death of one of her own children. Casey "was a dandy," she said in that 2006 interview, with a quiver in her voice. "I used to say to him, if anything happens to you, I will never get over it." And she didn't. In April 1982, Casey, twenty, was riding his motorcycle back to Queen's University in Kingston when he was killed by a drunk driver going the wrong way on Highway 401.

Out of Casey's death and the palliative care experience with Frazer came the idea for establishing a residential hospice for people dying of AIDS. Callwood donated half the royalties from *Twelve Weeks in Spring* to help found Casey House hospice in 1988. It offers free services to more than one hundred clients and runs a thirteen-bed residential program in downtown Toronto.

For her eightieth birthday, in 2004, her family gave her a mahogany-coloured Mazda Miata, the latest in a string of small convertibles that she drove with the top down, especially on annual sojourns to Florida. Although the cancer was spreading, she seemed serene as she approached her inevitable death. She felt no fear and she admitted to very few regrets. "I'm a very healthy woman except for a lot of cancer tumours. They aren't scaring me, although I wish I could breathe better because it is hard to go up stairs and I can't walk very far." She remained irredeemably cheerful, partly because every time she looked up her disease on the Internet, "I read my life expectancy and give myself a six-month extension."

In her inimitable style she tried to organize her own departure, sending typewritten notes to friends and acquaintances — tidying up her desk, as it were — and then, on March 7, 2007, wearing a white shawl over a black trouser suit, she made a final public appearance at the Writers' Trust annual awards ceremony to accept a lifetime contribution award. Knowing full well that death had already claimed the award's two previous recipients, Pierre Berton and Bernard Ostry, she accepted a standing ovation with only a tinge of irony. And then she got down to business.

Never one to let a moment escape that could be turned to the advantage of others, Callwood reminded her admirers in a short speech that "If you see an injustice being committed, you aren't an observer — you are a participant." That didn't mean you had to intervene, she explained, but you couldn't pretend that you weren't a part of what was happening in front of you. It was her ultimate chance to deliver her activist mantra and to sprinkle a little kindness on a well-intentioned audience. And then, breathing heavily because of cancer's inexorable devastation, she left the building, the devoted Frayne at her side.

Two weeks later she entered the palliative care unit of Princess Margaret Hospital, where she said farewell to friends and family, nibbled on chocolate, sipped ice water and the occasional sherry, and exuded a calm acceptance of the manner in which her life was ebbing—a model, as always, for those around her. She was ready, but her strong heart wasn't; it kept pumping until it finally stopped at four a.m. on the morning of April 14, 2007. She was eighty-two.

ARTHUR ERICKSON

Architect

JUNE 14, 1924 – MAY 20, 2009

ARTHUR ERICKSON GREW up in the wet, lush climate of British Columbia, a land of grey skies, blue-green forests, towering mountains, crashing waves, ancient totem poles, and Haida longhouses. The scenery was rampant, the landscape was monumental, and both evoked a reverence and a wary respect for rigorous weather, and a desire to build shelters in harmony with their geography. Unlike so many architects, he absorbed the lessons of his environment and imagined buildings ensconced in their settings.

Erickson's innovative body of work changed the face and the structure of architecture in a legion of buildings that included the landscape-hugging University of Lethbridge; Roy Thomson Hall in Toronto; the Canadian pavilion at Expo 70 in Osaka, Japan; the Canadian Embassy in Washington; the Museum of Glass in Tacoma, Washington; Napp Laboratories in Cambridge, England; the Kuwait Oil Sector Complex in Kuwait; and the Kunlun Apartment Hotel development in Beijing. But the largest and architecturally richest repository of Erickson's work is in his native province, beginning with the Filberg house in Comox and including Simon Fraser University in Burnaby, the Museum of Anthropology at UBC, and the Robson Square complex in downtown Vancouver.

Innately curious, openly gay, raised in a family that encouraged independent thinking, he also got outside his own environment by travelling the world at three pivotal points in his life. The army sent him to India and Malaya during the Second World War before he had decided on a career in architecture; he won a graduate travel grant in the early 1950s before he had sharpened his pencil and hung out his shingle as a practising professional; and he received another travel grant in the early 1960s about two years before he and Geoffrey Massey — to their surprise and most everybody else's — won the design competition for Simon Fraser University.

On those two later, self-directed odysseys through the history of architecture in Europe and the Far East, Erickson learned the boldness of ideas, how style is inseparable from climate and place, the significance of light and cadence, and the paramount importance of site. Those trips were as influential as any seminar or encounter with architectural titan Frank Lloyd Wright in forming Erickson's aesthetic. For him, as he wrote in *The Architecture of Arthur Erickson*, "the dialogue between building and setting" became the "essence."

The result was a modernist architecture that combined classical Eastern elements and First Nations influences in signature buildings made out of contemporary materials, especially glass, wood, and his beloved concrete. Many architects are technically accomplished and build from the inside out, according to the principle of form following function. Erickson was the opposite. A visionary, he created from the outside in, invariably reminding you of the natural world on the other side of the glass wall, in buildings that weren't always waterproof but rarely failed to inspire. Phyllis Lambert, founder of the Canadian Centre for Architecture, commented after Erickson's death in 2009: "He created architecture of the earth and out of the earth and he has done it with extraordinary humanity."

ARTHUR CHARLES ERICKSON was born in Vancouver on June 14, 1924, the elder son of Oscar Erickson and his wife, Myrtle (née Chatterton). His parents had met in Winnipeg and became engaged before his father went overseas with the 78th Winnipeg Grenadiers in the First World War. The relationship nearly died on the battlefield. A shell burst between Erickson's knees at Amiens and he was left for dead until a nurse recognized him and arranged for him to be taken to a field hospital. After surgeons amputated what remained of his legs, everybody — including the patient — thought the marriage was off. His fiancée disagreed. As she said later, "I'd rather marry a man with wooden legs than a wooden head."

In a series of interviews with Edith Iglauer for the *New Yorker* (which later became the basis for her book *Seven Stones*), Erickson remembered his father as a conservative both socially and politically, but a kind and humble man who behaved as though he didn't have a disability. His mother was gregarious, an innovative cook, an aficionado of Canadian art, and an expansive hostess who kept the house teeming with visitors.

Erickson began painting when he was about thirteen, using the bedroom walls as canvases for a rich jumble of plants, fish, and animals. At sixteen he won an honourable mention for two of his abstract pastels in a show at the Vancouver Art Gallery and attracted the attention of Group of Seven artist Lawren Harris, who became a family friend. Beset with career suggestions and torn between a fascination with biology and a creative passion for painting, Erickson asked Harris what path he should follow and received the curt but excellent advice "it's your life, not mine," and, therefore, "it is your decision." Forever after, when aspiring acolytes asked Erickson the same question, he repeated Harris's mantra.

Erickson entered an engineering program at the University of British Columbia in September 1942, nine months after the Japanese bombed Pearl Harbor. Like so many other young men, he joined the Canadian Officers' Training Corps. Within a year he had taken intensive instruction at a Japanese-language school and had received a commission in the Intelligence Corps of the army. He was stationed in India as a commando in a field broadcasting unit waiting for deployment behind enemy lines in Malaya — a precarious proposition — when Japan finally surrendered. He was demobilized with the rank of captain.

Back in Vancouver in 1946, he began studying economics, history, and Japanese with a view to a diplomatic career or perhaps anthropology or archaeology. Then, by chance, he saw colour photographs of Frank Lloyd Wright's Taliesin West in *Fortune* magazine. "If you can do as imaginative and creative a thing as that in architecture, I want to be an architect," he remembered thinking. As a Westerner, he was curious about the East, and although it was barely a month before the academic year began, he wired a slew of universities, including Harvard, MIT, and the University of Toronto. McGill was the only one that replied, so that is where he headed.

Four years later he graduated first in his class with an honours degree in architecture. "I didn't listen to my teachers much, but I had three people who influenced me — all keenly observant, original spirits," he told Iglauer. The first and the strongest was his unconventional mother, then Lawren Harris, and finally Gordon Webber, a design professor at McGill. "He was very vague, never explained anything clearly, which forced you to see for yourself. I don't think I would be as receptive to everything as I am had it not been for Gordon Webber."

Surprisingly, he didn't mention Frank Lloyd Wright. The summer before his final year at McGill, he went to visit Wright at Taliesin East, in Wisconsin, which he later described as "an absolutely beautiful blending of building and landscape." When Wright invited him to spend the year at Taliesin, he gladly accepted and raced back to Montreal to pack. But he changed his mind when he learned that he was likely to win the travelling scholarship awarded to McGill's top graduating student in architecture.

Why would he give up a chance to study with Frank Lloyd Wright in favour of travelling to as many architectural sites as the $1,500 stipend would allow? "He was turning out little toy soldiers and I wanted to find my own way," Erickson replied in an interview in 2008. Intuitively, he knew he had to escape Wright's shadow and see the world with his own eyes. He eked out his funds over three years before returning to Vancouver and the workaday world of Canadian architecture in the mid-1950s.

Several firms hired him and a couple fired him before he began teaching at UBC in 1957 and hooked up with Geoffrey Massey, the architect son of actor Raymond Massey. Together they designed houses for friends and did solo projects such as Erickson's Filberg house in Comox, on Vancouver Island. He quit teaching in 1963, the same year that he and Massey scored their huge architectural coup to design Simon Fraser University in nearby Burnaby. Having ignored most of the competition specifics, they attended the award announcement only out of curiosity about the winning design and were stunned to hear their names announced.

The Erickson-Massey proposal combined visions of the Acropolis in Athens with the clusters of terraced houses clinging to the hillsides of Italy. It emphasized the horizontal rather than the vertical, as though the mountain itself was part of the design, and knitted the "learning elements" of the university together rather than separating them into isolated units or colleges, as in the Oxbridge tradition. Construction began in 1964 and the almost "instant university" opened eighteen months later, on September 9, 1965.

The success of Simon Fraser meant the duo was in demand for innovative, statement-making buildings, including the University of Lethbridge. As with

SFU, the Lethbridge design linked the disparate studying and living parts of the university. As always, the site influenced the design. Instead of perching atop a mountain, the University of Lethbridge is nestled into the tawny ravines of the headlands of the Oldman River Valley. The roofline remains a constant flat plane, barely rising above the horizon, while the building plunges into the crevices created by the barren, undulating landscape.

After the Erickson-Massey partnership dissolved, Erickson formed his own practice in 1972 and embarked on even bigger projects, such as the breathtaking post-and-beam construction of the Museum of Anthropology at UBC and the massive concrete headquarters of forestry giant MacMillan Bloedel in downtown Vancouver. The strong horizontals evoke Haida long-houses built out of mammoth cedar logs and planks.

The Robson Square redevelopment was a series of structures, built out of concrete, glass, and wood, that turned the twentieth-century skyscraper on its side and opened normally sequestered law courts to the gaze of the public. Nicholas Olsberg, author of *Arthur Erickson: Critical Works*, says that with this building Erickson "re-introduced a spiritual dimension to architecture."

Like his friend and intellectual soulmate Pierre Elliott Trudeau, Erickson was an iconoclast who railed against authority and regimentation. As prime minister, Trudeau overrode his own bureaucrats in the early 1980s and personally appointed Erickson to design the Canadian Embassy in Washington, D.C., on a prime site between the Capitol and the White House.

Confronted with a lengthy list of neoclassical design requirements to make the building conform to existing structures, Erickson sent up the process in his cheeky creation of *de rigueur* columns supporting a "Rotunda of the Provinces" at the southeast corner of the embassy. The twelve columns — one for each province and territory — are made from aluminum, so they are too lightweight to support anything. Instead of making visitors walk through the columns to enter the embassy, he created a tiny entrance off to the side, all to poke a little fun and to create a disparity between the appearance and the reality of the building. He even toyed with the idea of installing an empty chair in the rotunda facing the Capitol, as an ironic reference to the Lincoln Memorial, but thought better of the notion.

The more famous Erickson became, the more projects he took on. Eventually he opened offices in several locations around the world — at one point he was operating five concurrently — stretching his financial reach far beyond the management abilities of a single architect, especially one who was

more interested in design than administration. Thinking, creating, and envisaging were his strengths; the humdrum business of budgets and accounts
receivable he left to others. As he said to Iglauer in 1981, with what in retrospect seems like astonishing insouciance, "I don't want to go to meetings...I
hardly know who works for me. It is a great disadvantage to a client, I suppose, that I'm not running the office... [but] I'm involved in *all* the design.
That's what I enjoy... That's why I'm hired."

Not surprisingly, the firm became lumbered with debt in the recession of
the late 1980s. After closing his Toronto and Los Angeles offices, he formed a
new company, Arthur Erickson Architectural Corporation, in 1991, the year
before he declared personal bankruptcy, listing more than $10.5 million in
liabilities. The only asset he reported was his six-hundred-square-foot home
and garden in the Point Grey district of Vancouver.

Supporters formed a group called the Arthur Erickson House and Garden
Foundation, which became the registered owner of his house, allowing
Erickson to continue to live there at a modest rent. Sometime later he began
sharing offices and working with architect Nick Milkovich, a former student
and long-time colleague. The two men collaborated on a number of projects,
including the Portland Hotel, a public housing project in Vancouver's
Downtown Eastside; the Museum of Glass in Tacoma, Washington; and the
Waterfall Building in Vancouver.

As he approached his eighties, Erickson's health began to fail as he struggled with the combined effects of Parkinson's and Alzheimer's. At the same
time, some of his dearest friends and romantic partners were dying of HIV/
AIDS and related diseases. Particularly hard was the suicide in April 2000 of
his former lover and long-time collaborator, the interior designer Francisco
Kripacz, whom he had known since the 1960s.

At an interview early in 2008, in the offices he shared with Milkovich,
Erickson was exquisitely groomed as always. Wearing a finely tailored blue
suit, a matching striped shirt, and patterned blue tie, he looked almost dainty
because of his medium height and slender build. He was magnetic and
charming, but it quickly became apparent that his short-term memory was
wobbly. He could talk in detail about dinner-table conversations with his
parents when he was growing up in Vancouver, but larger queries about his
career left him straining to remember. It was as though he understood the
questions, and knew where he intended to go in answering them, but lost his
way en route.

On some points, though, he was very clear, such as why he chose concrete early on as a building material. "It was cheap and so it was very competitive in the market. And I think I just loved it because of its relationship to stone and to quarries."

When asked about the Graham house in Vancouver, which had been demolished, and Roy Thomson Hall in Toronto, which was modified to improve the acoustics, he grew philosophical about how he coped with the demands of clients and the way they might later use and abuse his vision. "You have to walk away," he said, "but you never leave it entirely. It is like mud being thrown in your face and you just have to put up with it."

The effort of being interviewed must have been exhausting for him, but he was so patient with himself and my questions that I was humbled by his grace, even as I was touched by his fragility. Once so opinionated and confident as a world traveller, teacher, and visionary architect, he now seemed as fragile as a wilting flower.

Although he loved living in his home and garden in Point Grey, he had reached the point where he needed more care and eventually moved into a nursing home. He died in Vancouver of complications from dementia on May 20, 2009, at age eighty-four.

Oscar Peterson

Jazz Pianist and Composer

August 15, 1925 – December 23, 2007

A GIANT OF a man stretching to more than six feet in height and weighing in excess of two hundred pounds, Oscar Peterson could caress the keys with gentleness, make them swing with abandon, and boogie as though tomorrow were an abstract concept. His large hands gave him a reach that allowed him to roam across the keyboard like a hereditary ruler inspecting his domain. Duke Ellington called him the maharajah of the keyboard; Count Basie said he "plays the best ivory box I've ever heard."

Art Tatum was Peterson's idol, but most jazz fans think Peterson was right up there with the legendary player. He was blessed with perfect pitch, but it was his determination, his obsessive practising, recording, and touring, and his infectious delight in playing that made him a star. He grew up in a lower-middle-class family in the Little Burgundy neighbourhood of Montreal, the same area where former governor general Michaëlle Jean and her family would settle after their arrival from Haiti in 1968. Prejudice was ubiquitous and opportunities were scarce and low-level, but Peterson, the son of an immigrant railway porter, was raised in a stable home where discipline was rampant and mastering a musical instrument was as rigorously enforced as church attendance.

Racism in Canada during Peterson's youth and early adulthood was not legalized or institutionalized, but it did exist as a nasty, unofficial blight directed sporadically at all those seen as alien to a primarily white-skinned

Anglo-Saxon Canada; reviled groups included not just blacks but also Asians and First Nations. Skin colour wasn't the only trigger for prejudice — anti-Semitism was rife, francophones were derided as priest-ridden rubes, and immigrants in general were suspect. The law might rule that all were equal, but custom dictated otherwise.

Peterson's soaring talent enabled him to surmount racial barriers that were more flexible in Canada than in countries with entrenched slave cultures such as the United States. As a teenager he played in the all-white Johnny Holmes Orchestra, the best swing band in Montreal, and he landed a solo radio show. In a career lasting more than sixty years, Peterson made jazz swing on both sides of the border, developed a musical community based in Canada that stretched around the world, and broke down racial barriers long before there was a Charter of Rights and Freedoms. He released more than two hundred recordings, won eight Grammy Awards, played thousands of live concerts, and composed pieces for piano, trio, quartet, and big band.

He even sang, in a voice that echoed the light baritone of Nat King Cole, who first became a big name in the late 1930s as the piano-playing leader of a jazz trio. After Peterson recorded an album of vocals in the mid-1950s in which he accompanied himself on the piano, Cole, who by then was a celebrated singer, jokingly said: "I'll make a deal with you, Oscar. You don't sing and I won't play the piano." And that's what happened, until Cole died in 1965 and Peterson released *With Respect to Nat*, a dozen tunes that Peterson sang in tribute to his mentor and friend.

Among Peterson's notable recordings are *The Complete Young Oscar Peterson*; *Swinging Brass with the Oscar Peterson Trio*; *The Oscar Peterson Trio at the Stratford Shakespearean Festival*; *The Way I Really Play*; *Exclusively for My Friends*; *Oscar Peterson: London House Sessions*; and *Oscar Peterson: The Trio*. His best-known compositions are "Hymn to Freedom," inspired by the civil rights movement in the United States in the 1960s, which appears on his album *Night Train*, a bestselling record from its release in 1962, and *Canadiana Suite*, a tribute to this country and to the memory of his father's work on the railway in the way it moves thematically across the country from east to west.

The intricacy and speed with which Peterson could stroke the keys was so daunting that some critics complained he was too much about technique and too little about interpretation. Peterson himself supplied the best rejoinder: "Technique is something you use to make your ideas listenable," he said to jazz writer Len Lyons. "You learn to play the instrument so you have a musical vocabulary, and you practise to get your technique to the point you need to express yourself, depending on how heavy your ideas are."

His signature style, which incorporated swing and bop, was set early on, which prompted conclusions that he wasn't innovative. True perhaps in the traditional sense of developing a new style of music, but Peterson's genius lay in another area: he set the standard for the modern jazz combo. He excelled at playing with others, as a sensitive accompanist to singers such as Ella Fitzgerald and trumpeter Roy Eldridge, in duos with pianist Count Basie and guitarist Joe Pass, and especially in the trios he formed with bassist Ray Brown, guitarist Herb Ellis, and, after Ellis joined Alcoholics Anonymous and gave up touring, drummer Ed Thigpen.

Instead of merely following Peterson's lead, all the musicians, Peterson included, played with, and off, each other. As Peterson himself once explained, "You have to listen to find how a tune expands or contracts, and each performance has its own pulsation. And a performance needs dynamics, where a tune grows or falls away. You can't perform a tune on one level."

Pianist Herbie Hancock, a jazz star from a younger generation, said in a tribute to Peterson that he "redefined swing for modern jazz pianists for the latter half of the twentieth century" and "mastered the balance between technique, hard blues grooving and tenderness." An even younger jazz pianist, Canadian Diana Krall, said he was her inspiration as a high school student.

Diligent and professional, Peterson didn't emote on stage or sate his angst with drink, drugs, or eccentricity when he was out of the spotlight. His celebrity was not of the headline-blaring kind, although he was honoured with many awards, including the Order of Canada and several honorary degrees, and had parks, schools, and streets named for him. But there was a toll from such a long career and the relentless touring and recording. He had three failed marriages before marrying his fourth wife, Kelly Green, by whom he had his seventh child, Céline.

He never retired and he never gave up; perhaps he continued to hear his father's demanding voice for the entirety of his life. A year after suffering a stroke in 1993 that paralyzed much of his left side, he was back performing before live audiences, causing his friend, politician and amateur pianist Bob Rae to declare: "a one-handed Oscar was better than just about anyone with two hands."

OSCAR EMMANUEL PETERSON was born in the Saint-Henri district of Montreal on August 15, 1925, the fourth of five children of Daniel Peterson, a Caribbean immigrant sailor. His father, who had always wanted to play the piano, bought himself a collapsible organ and a series of books on theory and practice, and he took them aboard in his luggage. He taught himself to play keyboard during his long voyages as a bosun's mate, and his son inherited that determination and work ethic. Oscar's mother, Kathleen Peterson (née John), who was also from the West Indies, was a domestic from a well-educated family.

After their marriage, Daniel Peterson worked as a sleeping-car porter for the Canadian Pacific Railway. Culturally ambitious, he loved to read poetry and the classics aloud, taught his children to read and write long before they went to school, and insisted that his wife and all of his offspring learn to play a musical instrument. He set his children lessons and exercises and expected the older ones to tutor the younger ones while he was away on his transcontinental stints. On his return he would listen to them play, and if they didn't perform flawlessly he punished them harshly, often beating them with a belt.

By the time he was five, Oscar was learning both the trumpet and the piano. Two years later he contracted tuberculosis and, according to the treatment of the day, was confined to bed at the Montreal Children's Hospital. He was "cured" thirteen months later. His father, worried that his lung capacity had been compromised, made him give up the trumpet and concentrate on the piano, like his older brothers, Fred and Chuck, and his sister, Daisy.

Oscar told biographer Gene Lees in *Oscar Peterson: The Will to Swing* that Fred was the best pianist in the family. Fred died of tuberculosis when he was fifteen, leaving his nine-year-old brother without a role model. Oscar's father may have been the family taskmaster, but his older sister, Daisy, was the natural teacher. Her tutelage and her brother's natural ability combined to impress pianist Lou Hooper, who'd played jazz in Harlem in the 1920s. He took on the eleven-year-old as a private student in 1936.

When Hooper joined the armed forces after the outbreak of the Second World War, Daisy found her brother another teacher, the Hungarian emigré Paul de Marky, a pianist and composer who had studied in Budapest with István Thomán, a pupil of Franz Liszt. "I taught him technique, speedy fingers, because that's what you need in modern jazz," de Marky told Lees in a 1982 interview. "I gave Oscar Chopin studies. And then mostly, as I found that he was so good at melodic ballad style, I gave him the idea of big chords, like Debussy has them."

For his part, Oscar told Lees that de Marky instilled "musical and artistic" confidence. "It's one thing to know you can play, to know you can skate up and down the rink, but as to how well you look doing it, how much finesse you have, how much confidence, how much interest you can create in your audience, I guess that all has to do with it. He made me believe that I did have something to offer the music world."

Through Hooper and de Marky, young Peterson's fingers were linked to the virtuosity of twentieth-century American jazz and nineteenth-century European expressionism. But there was another influence, from a pianist closer in age to Peterson, a virtuoso who made Peterson question his own talent and ability. The player was Art Tatum, a nearly blind, largely self-taught musician about fifteen years older than Peterson. Influenced by Fats Waller, he could play extremely fast and was a virtuoso of stride — the technique whereby the pianist plays chords with the left hand and the melody with the right. Fats Waller is alleged to have walked away from the piano bench when Tatum strolled into the club where Waller was playing, saying, "I only play the piano, but tonight God is in the house."

Daniel Peterson brought home a recording of Tatum playing "Tiger Rag" and played it for his son because he thought the boy was becoming too enamoured of his own prowess. Oscar was so overwhelmed that "I gave up the piano for two solid months; and I had crying fits at night," he later told his friend the pianist and conductor André Previn.

For the rest of his life Peterson described himself as an "Art Tatum-ite," saying, "he was and is my musical God, and I feel honoured to remain one of his humbly devoted disciples." Strangely, both his idol Tatum and his father, Daniel Peterson, died within a week of each other in 1956. A devastated Peterson said later that he had "lost two of the best friends I ever had."

Once he regained his confidence, Peterson was obsessive about practising and playing boogie-woogie on the school piano during recess and lunch breaks. Along with trumpeter Maynard Ferguson he played in a band called the Montreal High School Victory Serenaders. His sister, Daisy, pushed him into auditioning for a national amateur contest sponsored by the Canadian Broadcasting Corporation. He won the semifinals and the grand prize of $250 in a competition in Toronto, using the money to buy himself a piano. The contest led to a gig on *Fifteen Minutes' Piano Rambling*, a weekly radio show on

Montreal station CKAC, as well as other spots that included *The Happy Gang* on CBC. He was such a musical success that he dropped out of high school at seventeen to play full-time, a decision his father reluctantly accepted with the proviso that Peterson become not just another piano player but the best. And that is what he set out to do.

He played with the Johnny Holmes Orchestra from 1942 through 1947 as the "Brown Bomber of Boogie-Woogie," a reference that likened his two-handed playing to boxer Joe Louis's knockout punching style. Until joining Johnny Holmes, Peterson had played as a solo performer, free to suit only himself in style and repertoire; now he had to learn to play in concert with the rest of the orchestra, a discipline that helped him as a ballad player.

He was the only black member of the orchestra, which exposed him to blatant racism when they played at the Ritz-Carlton Hotel in Montreal and at resorts in the Laurentian Mountains north of Montreal. He mostly withstood the prejudice with dignity, but every so often his rage would surface and he would lash out physically at the injustice of being called a nigger or denied what other, lighter-skinned folks took as their due.

By his early twenties, Peterson had already made several recordings for RCA Victor and was leading a trio at the Alberta Lounge in Montreal, sessions that radio station CJAD broadcasted live to its listeners for fifteen minutes on Wednesday nights. That's how Norman Granz discovered Peterson — at least, according to a story that the American jazz impresario, concert promoter, and record producer loved to tell.

In the late 1940s, at the end of a visit to Montreal, Granz was in a cab heading to the airport when he chanced to hear a jazz trio with an electrifying pianist on the car radio. He asked the cabbie for the name of the station so he could find out the title of the disc. That's not a recording, the cab driver explained; that's live from the Alberta Lounge. Forget the airport, Granz ordered, take me there. That impromptu decision led Granz to become Peterson's manager, signing the young pianist to his Verve label.

The tale is a tall one, according to biographer Lees, who speculates that Granz was in Montreal specifically to catch Peterson's trio at the Alberta lounge. Peterson was known to several of Granz's other recording artists, and the Lounge, located around the corner from Windsor Station, was a popular destination for train-riding jazz lovers from both sides of the border, including Ella Fitzgerald, Dizzy Gillespie, Benny Goodman, and Coleman Hawkins. Whether the story is true hardly matters. It is a good yarn, Peterson and Granz stood by it, and the meeting was propitious for both men and for jazz.

Granz persuaded Peterson to expand beyond bop and embrace boogie-woogie and to appear as a "surprise" guest at one of his "Jazz at the Philharmonic" concerts at Carnegie Hall in New York City in September 1949. Peterson couldn't get a work visa to play professionally, so Granz planted him in a seat among the audience, pretended to spot his protegé, and invited him onstage to play as a favour to the crowd. Peterson played "Fine and Dandy" and "Tenderly," among other pieces. The crowd went wild, giving him his first big break in the U.S. market less than a month after his twenty-fourth birthday. Reporter Mike Levin wrote in *DownBeat* that Peterson had "stopped" the concert "dead cold in its tracks" with "a flashy right hand, a load of bop," and a good "sense of harmonic development" and had "scared some of the local modern minions by playing bop ideas in his *left* hand, which is distinctly not the common practice." That performance was immortalized on *Jazz at the Philharmonic.*

Early the following year, Peterson won the *DownBeat* readers' poll for the first of numerous times. Granz was Peterson's manager for most of Peterson's career, in a relationship that was as inspirational as it was rewarding. Granz, whose heritage was Jewish and Ukrainian, knew about prejudice and wasn't prepared to tolerate racism, especially when it affected his passion, which was jazz. He took freewheeling jam sessions out of after-hours clubs and put them on tour and into concert halls all over the U.S., refusing to accept bookings in segregated halls.

Granz's "Jazz at the Philharmonic" (JATP) tours and recordings of live concerts eventually travelled to Canada, Europe, and Japan. He made stars of many of his players, none more so than Peterson, finding them audiences far beyond their jazz base. He owned several record labels over the years: Clef, Norgran, Verve, and Pablo. As Peterson's manager, mentor, and friend, Granz was the one who suggested he should form his first major trio, with Ray Brown and Herb Ellis.

Peterson's career was soaring, but the incessant touring and performing played havoc with his home life. He had married Lillie Fraser, the daughter of a Montreal-based railway porter, in September 1944, when he was barely nineteen. The marriage couldn't survive the loneliness they both endured: she in a small apartment coping with five small children, he on the road for weeks at a time. He moved his family to Toronto in 1958 and tried to stay put by founding the Advanced School of Contemporary Music. He liked teaching, but touring and performing live were his adrenalin. Both the marriage and the school gave way to his international playing and recording schedule. In later years he was a mentor in the jazz program at York University and was chancellor of the university from 1991 to 1994.

Peterson played at the top of his form until his late sixties, but then ill-health began to catch up with him. He'd had arthritis in his hands since childhood, but it became more pronounced in his seventies. His expanding girth — his weight crept up to 280 pounds — affected his mobility so much that the journey from backstage to the piano often became painful to observe. He had hip-replacement surgery in the early 1980s.

Peterson was playing at the Blue Note in New York in May 1993 when he felt a strange sensation in his left side and realized his left hand wasn't responding to the music. He had suffered a stroke, which severely weakened his left side and robbed him of his two-fisted technique. At first he was depressed, but he was determined to overcome his disability. Within two years he was performing and recording "Side by Side" with violinist Itzhak Perlman and touring again, although at a much less frantic pace.

In 2003 he recorded A Night in Vienna with Niels-Henning Pedersen, Ulf Wakenius, and Martin Drew. He continued to tour, with rests between concerts to restore his strength. Among his accompanists were Wakenius on guitar, David Young on bass, and Alvin Queen on drums. There was a celebration with about two hundred friends for his eightieth birthday in 2005. Diana Krall sang "Happy Birthday" and performed a vocal version of his song "When Summer Comes," with lyrics written by her husband, Elvis Costello. That same year Canada Post issued a stamp in his honour, the first time a living person other than royalty had been commemorated in that way.

By 2007 kidney disease forced him to cancel a performance at the Toronto Jazz Festival and an appearance at a Carnegie Hall all-star concert in his honour. A little more than two weeks after he died of kidney failure — at home in Mississauga, Ontario, on December 23, 2007 — musical greats including Herbie Hancock, Nancy Wilson, and Quincy Jones assembled in a memorial concert at Roy Thomson Hall in Toronto. More than 2,500 people attended the free concert, many of them having lined up for hours to pay tribute to Canada's foremost jazz musician.

Maureen Forrester

Contralto

July 25, 1930 – June 16, 2010

Nobody will ever know where Maureen Forrester's voice came from, what combination of genetics and serendipity produced the marvellous velvet sound that will live on as long as recordings and digital archives last. What's important is what Forrester did with her gift, working as a clerk to pay for singing lessons, training with the best coaches she could find, travelling the world to perform—at her peak, she gave 120 concerts a year. No matter how crowded the auditorium, she poured the immensity of her emotions into her music, as though she was singing directly into the ear of each member of the audience.

A contralto who made Mahler her own, she "had a singular beauty of sound, intensity of musical focus and a haunting darkness of feeling," according to conductor Sir Andrew Davis. "She could fill the softest pianissimo with an eerie carrying power" and she "could weave a spell better than anyone," he told the *Globe and Mail* after her death in 2010.

Forrester, who dropped out of school at thirteen, could quickly master the most difficult music and sing fluently in several languages an expansive and versatile repertoire that included everything from lieder to oratorios to opera to torch ballads. She even belted out "When Irish Eyes Are Smiling" at Prime Minister Brian Mulroney's "shamrock summit" with U.S. president Ronald Reagan in Quebec City in 1985.

A buxom, flamboyant woman with a magnetic presence on or off the stage, Forrester looked like a Valkyrie but performed like a professional. She was the opposite of a haughty and imperious prima donna. She appeared under the baton of international maestros that included Bruno Walter, Eugene Ormandy, Leonard Bernstein, Andrew Davis, Mario Bernardi, and Seiji Ozawa and sang with nearly every major orchestra in the West and the East, in the northern and southern hemispheres, and on both sides of the Iron Curtain.

Primarily known for her mastery of German lieder and her interpretation of Mahler, Forrester was also a celebrated opera singer, although roles for contraltos invariably take second place to soprano parts. She made her Canadian debut as Orpheus in *Orpheus and Eurydice* at the O'Keefe Centre in Toronto in 1962. Other significant roles were Cornelia in *Julius Caesar* for the New York Opera in 1966, Erda in *Das Rheingold* at the Metropolitan Opera in 1975, and the Countess in *The Queen of Spades* at La Scala in 1990. She embraced the role of the witch in Norman Campbell's CBC production of *Hansel and Gretel* (a role she reprised at the Guelph Spring Festival in 1979) with such gusto that friends of her children regularly asked her if she could fly around the living room on her broom.

Internationally recognized and honoured at home with a succession of prizes and awards, including Companion of the Order of Canada, she always gave back, promoting the works of Canadian composers such as Harry Somers, R. Murray Schafer, Murray Adaskin, and Alexander Brott. When she was at the peak of her international acclaim, she served an arduous five-year term as chair of the Canada Council for the Arts from 1983 to 1988, putting her name and her energy on the line to boost the careers of other artists, to protect the arm's-length principle from government interference and lobbying hard for more public money and support for the arts. She also served as chancellor of Wilfrid Laurier University from 1986 to 1990, as well as donating time, money, and effort to myriad artistic causes.

No singer was too insignificant for her to encourage and coach; no audience was too small or too remotely located to command her presence. In 1994, when she had been a galactic star for nearly three decades, she accepted an invitation to sing in an operetta in Chicoutimi, Quebec. "They think, 'She'll never come,'" she said at the time. "But of course I'll come. These crowds are wonderful. They wait all year for you."

As frank about her facelifts as she was about her affairs, she jokingly bemoaned that she was invariably cast in the roles of "mothers, maids, witches, bitches, mediums, nuns, aunts and pants" but rarely as the bride. A lifetime of frenetic busyness, as she juggled home and career, became endemic for a woman who was intelligent but not an intellectual, who could focus intensely to learn a new piece of music but wasn't really interested in reading for pleasure or stimulation.

There was more to her frantic schedule than a love of audience and applause. She never forgot her church choir roots, remaining grateful for the opportunities she had been given as a teenager to sing in chapels and halls. Besides all that, she was the financial support for a brood of six children. In her prime she could command towering fees, but the expenses for her gowns, accompanists, travel, and housekeepers were huge. She had to keep working.

Although she loved luxury — her former husband, violinist Eugene Kash, once said she "lived on the gross and never considered the net" — she also relished scrubbing her own kitchen floor. For Canadians she was that rarest of creatures in the 1970s and '80s — a working mother with an international career who insisted on making her home in Canada.

MAUREEN KATHERINE STEWART Forrester was born on Fabre Street in the impoverished east end of Montreal on July 25, 1930, the youngest of four children of Thomas Forrester, a Glasgow-born cabinetmaker, and his wife, Marion Forrester (née Arnold), an aspiring singer from Belfast. Times were tough for the Scottish-Irish immigrant family in the wake of the stock market crash, and they didn't get better through the long, lean years of the Depression.

Forrester went to William Dawson Elementary School. By the age of eleven she was working after school and on weekends selling cigarettes and ice cream cones in a corner store on Laurier Street, earning enough to indulge in lipstick and twin sweater sets and to try smoking, a habit she never acquired because she couldn't inhale.

School bored her and she craved financial independence, so she quit at thirteen and got the first of a succession of clerical jobs, handing over her weekly paycheque to her parents, who gave her back a small amount as an allowance. Her life might have trundled along happily and anonymously enough had her older brother Arnold not intervened. Back from fighting overseas in the Second World War, he heard her singing as she went about her household chores and noticed that her voice had changed from soprano to alto. He suggested she take singing lessons from a woman named Sally Martin, and he offered to pay for them. Years later, after Forrester had begun paying for the lessons herself, she learned the real reason for her brother's patronage: he was keen to meet one of Martin's other students.

She began earning a little money singing in church choirs and found a new teacher in Frank Rowe, who improved her breathing technique and diction. Soon she began getting paid engagements on CBC radio and other places and entering competitions. At eighteen, while working as a secretary and switchboard operator at Bell Telephone, she realized she might make a career as a singer, a path she pursued with gusto and determination.

Eventually she found her way to voice teacher Bernard Diamant, a Dutch baritone who had fled Europe after the war. As she related in her 1986 memoir, *Out of Character* (with Marci McDonald), he listened to her sing and pronounced: "You certainly have a gift from God. That's a very big voice. But I must tell you something, my dear. You don't know how to sing." His first remedy was to order Forrester to quit her bread-and-butter freelance gigs and to stop singing entirely for at least six months. Her mother was horrified by the loss of income, but Forrester realized that Diamant was "building the inner core of my voice, expanding the range up and down." Finally Daimant let her sing and asked his accomplished musician friend John Newmark to work as her accompanist.

A German Jew from Bremen, Newmark had fled to England just before the war. Detained there as an enemy alien, he had been shipped to an internment camp outside Lennoxville, Quebec. Hitler's Nazis had destroyed Newmark's chances of a solo career; instead he provided Forrester and several others with the backing, support, and confidence of his superb training and musicianship. As an accompanist he provided "an integral part of each song, without being guilty of either too much or too little," as *Globe* critic John Kraglund said in a 1960 review.

Although they didn't like each other at first, Newmark and Forrester overcame their separate hostilities and developed a close friendship and an enduring partnership, touring the country and the world for many years. With Newmark accompanying her, Forrester made her recital debut in 1953 at the Montreal YWCA. Thomas Archer, music critic for the *Montreal Gazette*, wrote: "Few if any contraltos on this continent could challenge her." He became the first to compare her voice favourably to the great English contralto Kathleen Ferrier.

That recital, at age twenty-three, marked the true beginning of Forrester's career. It led directly to an invitation to make her concert debut, singing the small but significant alto part in Beethoven's Ninth Symphony with the Montreal Symphony Orchestra under the ageing and ailing but still magnificent Otto Klemperer in December 1953. She also won a touring contract to sing forty-five concerts at schools in northern Ontario and Quebec with Jeunesses Musicales du Canada. She made $25 per concert and learned essential techniques — how to pace a concert, hold the attention of the audience, modify the program according to what succeeded and what failed — and acquired discipline and endurance from performing day after day in small towns.

Forrester's next boost came from J. W. McConnell, the founder and publisher of the *Montreal Star*, who became her secret patron and benefactor (even paying her father's funeral expenses) so that she could have the time and the resources to continue studying voice. In her memoir, Forrester estimates that McConnell gave her at least $25,000 over the next several years — a sizable sum in the 1950s. "The big breaks came to me on their own," she wrote, "but they would have taken five years longer without J. W."

After touring extensively throughout Canada and Europe with Jeunesses Musicales, she made her New York City debut at the Town Hall on November 12, 1956, with McConnell supplying the $1,800 rental for the auditorium. She sang some Schubert, some Britten, and some Wagner and earned rave reviews, including a headline in the *New York Times*: "Canadian Contralto Displays Superb Voice." Critic Edward Downes praised the "generous compass and volume" of her voice and described her range as moving "from a darkly resonant chest register to a brilliantly focused top with a middle register that she makes velvet soft or reedy according to her expressive intent."

By then Bruno Walter, the German-born conductor and protegé of Gustav Mahler, had invited Forrester to sing for him. He coached her for a recording of Mahler's Symphony No. 2 ("Resurrection"), helping her develop her signature interpretation and technique. She also recorded Mahler's "Das Lied von der Erde" with Walter and sang at his farewell performances as a conductor with the New York Philharmonic in 1957.

While her career was on a trajectory into the stratosphere, her romantic life was on an operatic roller coaster. The cause was violinist and conductor Eugene Kash. They had met at a concert she gave on a Sunday afternoon in a high school gym in Ottawa in 1953. He was eighteen years her senior and "not the marrying kind," as he frequently reminded her. Besides, his mother would never approve of her son marrying a Gentile.

He had no such qualms about an affair. When Forrester became pregnant, Kash tried to persuade her to have an abortion. Failing that, he wanted her to put the child up for adoption. Instead Forrester secretly kept the baby, named Paula, in Germany while keeping up a rigorous European concert schedule — she sang a concert five days after the birth — and did her best to raise the little girl on her own. She again became pregnant by Kash in 1956 — these were the days before reliable birth control was readily available — and this time she did have an abortion.

Kash finally married her in London, England, on July 20, 1957, after the death of his mother and when the daughter he barely knew was two years old. Having finally given in, Kash became a devoted papa to their increasing brood; he later described himself as "one of the original stay-at-home dads." Forrester had five children in nine years and, by her own admission, would have had six if she hadn't fallen down the stairs and suffered a miscarriage.

Beginning in 1961, Forrester and Kash began appearing together at the annual Casals Festival in Puerto Rico, a commitment they kept up for nearly fifteen years. They moved their family to Pennsylvania while they both taught at the Philadelphia Academy of Music, among other assignments, from 1967 through 1971. After their return to Canada, Forrester taught voice students at the University of Toronto and gave master classes at the University of Alberta and in many other locations when she was visiting as a performer. Mainly though, husband and children stayed in Toronto while Forrester travelled the world, giving concerts in countries as varied as Australia, China, and the former Soviet Union.

The Kashes separated in the mid-1970s, when she left him after developing a *grande passion* for a married man. That affair ended badly three years later, when her lover dumped Forrester (and his wife) for a younger and richer woman. Forrester was devastated and for one of the few times in her life gave in to her emotions off the stage, lying on a chaise in her garden and weeping for three days while her children watched frantically, thinking she had been diagnosed with a terminal illness. "I felt like a bloody fool," she wrote in her memoir, for breaking up her marriage with Eugene — a "good and scrupulously honest" man who "truly loved" her — in favour of a "deceitful character." Nevertheless, she and Kash remained close until he died in 2004 at the age of ninety-one.

Forrester could probably have had a long and satisfying late career singing character parts as a mezzo-soprano, but her voice and her energy deteriorated under the twin demons of alcoholism and dementia, beginning in the mid-1990s. She could still perform, as her residual memory surfaced when she heard the opening bars and saw the faces in the audience, but getting her onto the stage became increasingly difficult. In one of her final public appearances — to receive the inaugural Creative Artist Award in 2000 — she spoke a few words and sang a simple children's song a cappella. It was the last time that Wayne Gooding, editor of *Opera Canada*, heard her perform live. Describing the scene as "poignant" and "moving," he said her unmistakable voice "had faded, but the artistry, stagecraft and drive to express herself in song were as strong as ever."

By then Forrester had been through several residential addiction programs such as the Betty Ford Clinic in Rancho Mirage, California, and the Homewood Health Centre in Guelph, and had been living in the subsidized Performing Arts Lodge in Toronto for almost a decade. Even the benevolent supervision of family, friends, and social workers couldn't keep her from wandering. To ensure her safety, her family finally admitted her to a nursing home in the east end of Toronto in the summer of 2001.

The years of living glamorously and donating generously to others had swallowed her earnings. And so she spent her last years befuddled, immaculately coiffed, unfailingly polite, and seemingly happy in an assisted-living facility, subsidized by the taxpayers she had served so well, her family, and the proceeds from selling her papers to Wilfrid Laurier, the university of which she had once been chancellor. She died on June 16, 2010, six weeks before her eightieth birthday.

MORDECAI RICHLER

Writer

JANUARY 27, 1931 – JULY 3, 2001

C ANADA HAS A few literary geniuses — Alice Munro and Michael
Ondaatje come to mind — but writers who are also public intellectuals,
whose opinions are sought on the tragedies and follies of the day, are rare.
Margaret Atwood's pronouncements do guarantee headlines, but nobody
could amuse, arouse, and antagonize like Mordecai Richler. He offended
everybody: Jews, cultural nationalists, and sovereignists — not to mention his
family of origin — for his unrelenting and hilarious pricking of pretensions
and hypocrisies and his refusal to cater to special pleading, whatever the
cause or the aspiration.

Richler was driven not by rudeness but by an unbending moral code. He
hated special pleading, double standards, and prejudice, and nobody was
exempt from his merciless arbitration. As early as 1960 he wrote an article in
Maclean's magazine complaining, from the perspective of a Jew returning to
Canada from abroad, that the community, which had come to this country
fleeing persecution, had forgotten its traditional respect for "the ethical, the
spiritual, and the intellectual" and had grown "flabby, money driven, and
prejudiced." Sure, there was anti-Semitism in Canada and yes, the murder of
six million Jews in the Holocaust was unforgiveable, but that didn't give Jews
the right to ignore the sufferings of others. Seeing his homeland with fresh
eyes, Richler charged that "Jews were not, as I had hoped, against discrimination. They were opposed to discrimination against Jews."

111

His argument was that Jews, of all people, should be the first to protest on behalf of other maligned minorities. He took a similar tack thirty years later in an article in the *New Yorker* in September 1991, when he ridiculed the passage of Bill 101, the Quebec law that forced stores and restaurants such as Eaton's and Ben's to modify their names and their commercial signs to make them sound and look more francophone. (A revised and extended version appeared as the book *Oh Canada! Oh Quebec! Requiem for a Divided Country* the following year.) His point was that francophones shouldn't pass arbitrary laws that restricted the rights of anglophones in pursuit of their own nationalist goals.

In setting the context for the prohibition of commercial signs in English, Richler outlined a tradition of anti-Semitism in Quebec, specifically targeting the Roman Catholic Church in the teachings and writings of Abbé Groulx and the editorial policy of *Le Devoir*, taking his examples mainly from the 1930s. To equate the current cultural and national aspirations of the Québécois with historical prejudice against other minorities was an outrage to many commentators, but to do so in an American magazine was an even bigger affront. It was all grist for Richler's journalistic mill, and newspapers such as the *Gazette* and magazines like *Saturday Night* were delighted to give him a podium, knowing that their readers would relish watching the master jouster taking on all contenders in a verbal brawl.

The best contemporary comparison to the bruising effects of Richler's scathing commentary was the late Christopher Hitchens, a writer who shared Richler's talent for punditry but who was a polemicist rather than a satirist. Besides, he lacked Richler's fictional imagination. That's what sets Richler apart. From 1951, when he fled claustrophobic Canada for Paris, following the typewriter spools of Ernest Hemingway, Morley Callaghan, and Mavis Gallant, until he died from complications of kidney cancer in a Montreal hospital on July 3, 2001, Richler was the ultimate freelance writer. He never had another job. A writer was all he was, but his prowess was extraordinary and he stretched the parameters of the form to include every mode except poetry.

Although he often scrabbled to pay his rent in cold and rat-infested garrets in the early days and to finance an increasingly affluent international lifestyle in his middle age, he invariably smoked, drank, and caroused with other expatriates in London, Paris, and Spain and with his cronies in Montreal and Toronto. But no matter how late or indulgent the evening, he always got up early the next morning to pound away at the keys of his manual typewriter, writing fiction, journalism, essays, screenplays, and children's books, maintaining the workaholic habits of a lifetime that had taught him his craft, made his name, and supported his family.

There were a few Mordecai Richlers, and not all of them appeared in public. The rude and sullen writer-in-residence and talk-show guest camouflaged his shyness and his fear of being observed and categorized. For someone whose own eye was so omniscient and whose writing depended on observed life, he hated being under the klieg lights of a television studio, in a classroom, or at a podium. He was a lousy interview, enduring questions with the baleful stare of a recalcitrant bull wearily pawing the ground to get up the steam to defend his turf.

Behind that bristly mask was the playful, loyal friend, the passionate husband, and the devoted father. Posthumous stories abound about his loyalty and generosity to pals in need or in poor health; while he was alive he insisted that his fax pranks and his good deeds remain under wraps, so it was his loutishness that generated notoriety — yet another public camouflage.

There was no way to hide his passion for his elegant wife, Florence, a connection that made other couples envy the way they looked at each other across the room at cocktail parties and restaurant tables. Kind, generous, devoted, but with a core of steel swathed in a velvet charm, she was his first and most trusted editor and the mother of his children (five altogether, although only four were his biological offspring). As much as Florence was the inverse of his own narcissistic and demanding mother, Richler turned himself into a paterfamilias who was doting, encouraging, and loving, the opposite of the father he had ridiculed in his second novel, *Son of a Smaller Hero*, in 1955. That's not to suggest that he changed diapers or made meals, of course.

Everything he read, wrote, and experienced fed into his fiction, the ten novels that included his early literary success *The Apprenticeship of Duddy Kravitz*, his mature works *St. Urbain's Horseman* and *Solomon Gursky Was Here*, and his ultimate achievement, *Barney's Version*. "To be a Jew and a Canadian is to emerge from the ghetto twice," he wrote in *Hunting Tigers under Glass*, a 1968 collection of essays. Some critics have charged that Richler endlessly repeated himself — "I love his book; I buy it every time he writes it" was a frequent taunt. Writing a negative review of *Joshua Then and Now* in the *New York Times Book Review* in 1980, the novelist and editor George Stade wrote: "It's as if a rich and unusual body of fictional material had become a kind of prison for a writer who is condemned to repeat himself ever more vehemently and inflexibly."

We are all trapped in the prism of our formative circumstances. Richler couldn't escape being born a Jew in the east end of Montreal on the eve of the Depression. He was too young to fight the Fascists in the Spanish Civil War or the Nazis in the Second World War, too old to grow a beard and march in the Vietnam War protests of the 1960s, join the counterculture, or fight against the Arabs in the Six-Day War. As Richler writes in *St. Urbain's Horseman*, "Always the wrong age. Ever observers, never participants. The whirlwind elsewhere."

Instead of repeating himself endlessly, what Richler has done is chart the emotional and psychological progress of a Jew (not unlike himself) who is making a tortured and stumbling odyssey through life, all the while trying to harmonize his embittered psyche with his vacillating environment. He once said that he wanted to "write one novel that will last, something that will make me remembered after death." Surely that is *Barney's Version*, the novel in which he imagines Barney Panofsky sliding into the fogginess of Alzheimer's while dictating his memoirs. The journalism, however lasting as a portrait of the foibles, vagaries, and nightmares of the second half of the twentieth century, was research, a way to make a living, and a means of keeping his name out there in the marketplace.

He won his share of literary prizes, including two Governor General's Awards, two Commonwealth Prizes, and a Giller Prize. As well, there have been four biographies since Richler's death, including Charles Foran's definitive and multiple-award-winning *Mordecai: The Life & Times*. The ultimate accolade, though, is that his books have outlasted him and continue to attract eager readers.

MORDECAI RICHLER WAS born on St. Urbain Street in the Jewish ghetto of Montreal on January 27, 1931, the younger son of Moses and Leah (née Rosenberg) Richler. His parents' arranged marriage was supremely dysfunctional. His mother, the daughter of an Orthodox rabbi, was socially ambitious; his father, the uncouth yet gentle son of a scrap dealer, was ruined by the Depression. The family often had to change lodgings in the middle of the night, hauling away their paltry possessions a step ahead of the bailiff.

The Richlers separated when Mordecai was thirteen and his older brother, Avrum, was a first-year student at Queen's University in Kingston. That left Mordecai estranged from his father, with whom he had quarrelled violently, and living with his mother and her lodger, a German Jew named Julius Frankel, who doubled as her lover. One morning, the prepubescent boy found his mother hiding under the covers in the lodger's back bedroom, and on other occasions he had to feign sleep while the lovers had noisy sex in the adjacent bed in the room he shared with his mother. Offensive behaviour by any account, but to a moralistic boy with an unforgiving nature it was a deep affront, one that later fuelled the devastating and hilarious fictional portrait of the licentious mother who performs a striptease at her son's bar mitzvah in *Joshua Then and Now*, among other caricatures. His mother attempted a rebuttal in her memoir *The Errand Runner: Reflections of a Rabbi's Daughter*, but she lacked her son's lacerating wit and coruscating talent.

As an adolescent, Richler was regularly outraging his relatives with his unruly and unorthodox behaviour — smoking in the street, skipping Hebrew school, claiming to be an atheist. An indifferent student at Baron Byng High School, he didn't have the marks to get into McGill University, let alone the tougher requirements to surmount the unofficial entrance hurdles for Jews. Instead he attended Sir George Williams (now Concordia) University but dropped out after a couple of years, cashed in an insurance policy, and headed to Paris to find his way as a writer.

He returned to Montreal in 1953 with a draft of *The Acrobats*, working at nights at CBC Radio International while he rewrote his novel. André Deutsch published it the following year in London — a coup for a twenty-two-year-old writer. Later he dismissed the novel as derivative and refused to have it republished during his lifetime, but it gave him an important entree to an innovative publisher and outstanding editor, Diana Athill.

By then Richler was romantically involved with Montrealer Catherine (Cathy) Boudreau, a divorcée a decade older than he, and a Gentile. His parents were horrified. Their reaction to their son's choice of bride was not ameliorated by his virulent depiction of his childhood in his second novel, *Son of a Smaller Hero*, in 1955. Richler claimed the novel is not autobiographical, bluntly stating in an author's note that readers looking for "real people" were "on the wrong track" and had misunderstood "my whole purpose." But, as biographer Charles Foran points out in *Mordecai*, "The novel wasn't looking to critique his family and Jewish Montreal; it was calling them out to a brawl, an Apostate taking on Everybody." The novel received good reviews in distant London, where the setting was considered exotic and the angry narrative voice deemed intense and refreshingly candid. Montrealers were generally aghast. The *Star* reviewer called it a "distasteful story" about a "blindly self-ish" young man of "limited intelligence" who "succeeds in reducing all those around him to rubble," according to Foran.

More turmoil was looming on both the creative and emotional horizons. His marriage was doomed because the principals were a turbid mix and also because Richler had fallen in love with a beautiful married woman, the model, actress, and script reader Florence Mann, an obsession that had begun with a chance meeting with mutual friends on the eve of his own wedding late in August 1954. Mann's marriage, troubled by her husband Stanley's womanizing, limped along, although she and Richler verbally acknowledged their mutual attraction when they met at a huge march in Trafalgar Square protesting the British intervention in Suez in early November 1956. She was seven months pregnant.

Bizarrely, but surely a reflection of the intermeshed nature of the expatriate community, when Daniel Mann was born just before Christmas that year, his father, Stanley Mann, suggested to Florence that their mutual friend Richler should be godfather. What's more, Richler agreed.

The following year, in September 1957, Richler, who had been paying the rent by writing scripts for film and television, published his third novel, *A Choice of Enemies*. In a thinly veiled portrait of the political machinations of the expatriate crowd in London, Richler borrowed characteristics and dialogue liberally from his friends, including the screenwriter Ted Allan, who had fought the fascists in Spain with the Mackenzie-Papineau Battalion and co-written a biography of Norman Bethune.

Having thoroughly slagged his family and his friends, Richler seemed to have detoxified himself. Cleansed of the particulars of his own disaffections, he began writing from absorbed rather than merely observed experience, and he had found his ideal partner and editor. By the time Daniel was eighteen months old, the Manns and the Richlers had split after a sojourn together at a rented house in Roquebrune on the Riviera. As Reinhold Kramer writes in *Mordecai Richler: Leaving St. Urbain*, "In the beginning of June 1958, there were two couples — the Richlers and the Manns. By July, there was one — Richler and Florence."

Richler's new novel, *The Apprenticeship of Duddy Kravitz*, propelled by the adventures of a gloriously irreverent, shamelessly opportunistic, and brash Jewish kid on the make from the Montreal ghetto, was gobbled up by critics and readers. Besides the memorable Duddy, a Sammy Glick character who is striving *for* something — ownership of a hidden lake in the Laurentians on which he dreams of building a grotesque holiday village — rather than merely rejecting everything he knows, there were a number of blackly comic set pieces, such as Duddy's scheme to produce films of bar mitzvahs directed by an auteur (and alcoholic) British director. Having lightened up, and with the benefit of Florence's discerning editorial eye, Richler was having fun with his material, and so too did readers.

Duddy made Richler's name at a time when his life was solidifying as well. Writing for the movies was padding his pocketbook and stoking his inventory of satirical subjects, and his unhappy marriage to Cathy Boudreau was finished and he and Florence were lovers, although discreet ones because of the arcane divorce laws and their custody worries about Daniel. All went well and the couple married on July 27, 1960, in Montreal, two days before their son Noah was born.

Can-cult and the film industry supplied the focus for Richler's next two satirical novels. *The Incomparable Atuk* (1963) parodied the boosterism of cultural nationalism and our neophyte star system that made broadcasters such as Nathan Cohen and Pierre Berton "world famous all over Canada," as a character boasts. *Cocksure* (1968) lampooned both the power structure within the film industry and the craziness involved in adapting novels for the screen. The movie business also supplied an occupation for Jake Hersh in *St. Urbain's Horseman*, Richler's bestselling and Governor General's Award–winning novel about the Montreal ghetto, its entangling alliances, and his own preoccupations as a Jew, a Canadian, and a man born out of sync with the huge battles occurring elsewhere. The novel was also shortlisted for the Booker Prize but lost out to one of V. S. Naipaul's lesser books, *In a Free State*.

The gap between books was growing larger, but so too were the ambitions of the novels, the size of his family, and the number of other projects, including journalism, essays, and film. As well as wanting him to adapt other people's books for the screen, producers and directors were clamouring to make films of his novels, especially *Duddy* and *Horseman*. After almost twenty years in England he had moved back to Montreal — although not to the ghetto — with his wife and five children in the early 1970s because he recognized that the city and the country supplied the writerly pulse that quickened his prose and whetted his imagination.

He had more books in him: the delicious children's story *Jacob Two-Two Meets the Hooded Fang*, the introspective *Joshua Then and Now*, and the innovative *Solomon Gursky Was Here*, a postmodern invocation of what it means to be a Canadian, as well as an excoriation of the Bronfmans, a family he had always despised because to him they seemed to care only about mammon. Years earlier, Saidye Bronfman (wife of Samuel, the patriarch of the distillery family) had said to him, at the premiere of *The Apprenticeship of Duddy Kravitz*, "Well, you've come a long way for a St. Urbain Street boy." Never one to sidestep a slight, Richler retorted, "Well, you've come a long way for a bootlegger's wife." *Solomon Gursky* was also short-listed for the Booker but lost to A. S. Byatt's *Possession* in the 1990 contest.

Above all, there was *Barney's Version*. The novel completes Richler's quasi-autobiographical odyssey of the Jew's progress through life, sharpens and refines his favourite satirical targets, and allows Barney to breathe with emotional depth even as he is wandering onto the foggy shoals of Alzheimer's. More than anything, it is a love song to Florence. The novel won his pal Jack Rabinovitch's glitzy Giller Prize, chosen by a jury that included his Parisian friend Mavis Gallant. Unlike many novelists whose creative energy seems spent in mid-career, Richler got better as he aged, like cognac.

Richler had proved you can go home again. He was more celebrated than reviled, except in Quebec, where he divided his time between a two-storey house on Lake Memphremagog in the Eastern Townships and a Montreal apartment — although he and Florence escaped the blustery winters for a flat in London. Most important, he wasn't ignored. Sought after as a contributor to magazines and newspapers on both sides of the Atlantic and on either side of the undefended border, he was that rarest of creatures — a prosperous Canadian writer. And if he was a celebrity at home he was an icon in Italy, where *Barney's Version* was such a spectacular success that it sparked a regular newspaper column in *Il Foglio* called "Andrea's Version" and a slang expression, "Barneyano," for a man who was politically incorrect and unapologetically so.

Life was good, especially with the arrival of grandchildren and the stirrings of an eleventh novel in the gnarled reaches of his imagination. Sedentary decades of smoking, drinking, and sitting in front of a typewriter every day for several hours exacted a price, however. His health was failing. He had survived surgery for kidney cancer in 1998, but in early May 2001 he was informed that a small-cell carcinoma in his lungs had metastasized to his abdomen and chest. The prognosis was one to three years. That proved optimistic. Richler died in hospital in Montreal after a series of hemorrhages on July 3, 2001. He was seventy.

A month before, he had handwritten an addendum to his will giving Florence power of attorney in medical matters and asking that he be buried in Mount Royal Cemetery, provided that an adjoining plot was reserved for his wife "so that eventually we may lie beside each other in death, as we did so happily in life." That final testament to his love for Florence was found after his death, as Foran writes in *Mordecai*. She had a double tombstone erected with their first names, his dates, and her incomplete ones. Then, in a public affirmation of their enduring love, she added Richler's poignant comment about lying together in death. Across from the stone she placed a bench for visitors to sit and planted a mulberry tree, an affecting reference to Ovid's tale of Pyramus and Thisbe and the lovers' union after death.

BUILDERS

Obituaries Are the Biographical Building Blocks of a Country's History

T HE TEN PEOPLE in this chapter combine daring, vision, dedication, and plain hard work. They lived in many parts of the country, from the Arctic to the Maritimes to northern British Columbia. A few of them were immigrants, two were First Nations — an Inuit and a Nisga'a — one could trace his ancestry to the United Empire Loyalists, while another had an impoverished childhood and died the richest man in the country. What appealed to me were their achievements: Bertha Wilson, the first woman to sit on the Supreme Court of Canada; Frank Calder, the First Nations chief who helped to persuade Pierre Trudeau to change his mind on aboriginal rights; Ken Thomson, the newspaper scion who could have coasted on the gushing profits from his father's investment in North Sea oil and instead built a global communications empire and shared his art collection with the rest of us; Celia Franca, the ballerina who built our premier dance company and trained the dancers who keep it strong; Louis Robichaud, the Acadian premier who hauled New Brunswick into the modern world and made it the first bilingual province in the country; Kananginak Pootoogook, the Inuit artist who helped his people make the transition from nomadic life on the land to self-sufficiency in built communities.

Their stories form a collective narrative that speaks to how this country matured as a nation. That is the power of obituaries. As a literary convention, they go back long before Canada existed as a nation. Sadly, we don't have a strong or lengthy tradition of writing or collecting obituaries or of using them as a resource in writing cultural history. Our record, with the exception of the monolithic *Dictionary of Canadian Biography*, is rudimentary at best.

Elsewhere, obituaries have spawned grand historical, social, and literary materials. You can trace the form as far back as the ancient Egyptians, who used hieroglyphics to record the lives of the pharaohs and the wealthy elites on tablets and sarcophagi and later on papyrus. Homer's account of the great warrior Achilles in *The Iliad* — his heroics, his rage, his vulnerability — was spoken, not read, but otherwise his epic poem has all the components of a modern obituary.

In the Middle Ages, religious scribes painstakingly created illuminated manuscripts detailing the lives of saints and martyrs. Over time the practice morphed from the spiritual to the secular and became more and more individualized. However, it wasn't until after the invention of the printing press by Johannes Gutenberg in 1440 that writings about notable lives could reach a non-scholarly audience. By the seventeenth century, printing and production methods and general literacy had all improved sufficiently to enable the dissemination of pamphlets and "relations," which were the precursors of newspapers. The first newspaper obituary, documenting the life and death of Captain Andrew Shilling, appeared in 1622 in a British journal called *The True Relation of Our Weekly News*, according to Australian journalist-turned-academic Nigel Starck.

Reportage on Shilling's death was tucked into an account of a sea battle between the rival fleets of the East India Company and Portugal, but the commentary was very similar to a modern obituary, according to Professor Starck in his book *Life after Death: The Art of the Obituary*, because "it offered some description of Shilling's life along with an attempt, albeit brief, of posthumous character assessment." The unnamed obituarist offers "a richer dossier on a life lived than does the simple chronicling of a death died," wrote Starck. There's even a Canadian note in that the Arctic explorer William Baffin, after whom Baffin Bay and Baffin Island are named, knew Shilling and sailed with him on the ship *London* to Surat for the British East India Company from 1617 to 1619.

Along with newspapers, books of biographical sketches were being published and consumed by a bourgeois audience interested in learning about the exploits of the celebrated and notorious characters of their times, especially with the return to court life, the reopening of theatres, and the end of overt

Puritanism in 1660. That's when Charles II was crowned, thus bringing back the monarchy after the bitterly divisive Civil War, the beheading of his father, Charles I, in 1649, and the demise of Oliver Cromwell and his republican Commonwealth.

Reports called "The Life and Death" began appearing in two English weekly newspapers, the *Intelligencer* and the *Newes*, in the 1660s. "The subjects were exclusively royalty, nobility, those in high office or those with distinguished roles in the armed forces," according to Elizabeth Barry, an associate professor in the department of English literature at the University of Warwick in England. "The obituaries were also, in the Restoration context, Royalist in outlook, the papers rewarding loyalty and service to the monarchy as part of the propaganda machine of the restored Crown," she writes in "From Epitaph to Obituary: Death and Celebrity in Eighteenth-Century British Culture."

Thomas Fuller, a clergyman who was made chaplain to Charles II, compiled *A History of the Worthies of England*, which was published in 1662, a year after his own death. Aboout the same time a researcher and compiler named John Aubrey (1626–97) began collecting materials for biographical sketches that even today are held up as exemplars of the obituarist's craft, especially in England.

Aubrey, an only child, was born into a prosperous gentry family in Wiltshire during the reign of Charles I. The English Civil War interrupted his studies at Trinity College, Cambridge, and although he pursued the law for a while at the Middle Temple in London, he never acquired a profession. Instead he collected books, explored, and wrote about the megalithic remains at Avebury, and, on his father's death in 1652, in the early years of Cromwell's Protectorate, inherited large estates and complex debts. In the 1650s he began to write *Lives of Scientists* and later embarked on a two-volume survey of his native Wiltshire.

In 1663, three years after Charles II's ascendancy, Aubrey became a member of the Royal Society. But by 1670 he had lost all his property and spent the rest of his life living on the generosity of others. He loved gossip and conviviality and collecting information about his vast circle, which included scientists, politicians, writers, aristocrats, and more common folk in trade, manufacturing, and service. As a charming guest at country estates and London houses, he jotted down his memories from the night before while his hosts were still sleeping and he himself was battling a hangover. Fascinated by people's thoughts, attitudes, and eccentricities, as well as their conversation, he brought a psychological curiosity to his scribblings, and as time went on he added notations about where his subjects were buried and what had happened to their books and pictures.

Two centuries after Aubrey's death, the Reverend Andrew Clark produced a transcript of his manuscripts (which had been deposited in the Bodleian Library in Oxford) with excisions to spare late Victorian sensibilities. It was published in 1898 and has been reissued at regular intervals ever since. In the late 1960s the British playwright Patrick Garland, who likened Aubrey to the diarist Samuel Pepys as a great chronicler of his age, wrote a one-man show based on *Brief Lives*. The actor Roy Dotrice gave 1,800 performances of *Brief Lives* over the next forty years, including one attended in the mid-1980s, as we shall see in Rogues, Romantics, and Rascals, by Hugh Massingberd when he was about to become obituaries editor of the *Daily Telegraph* in London.

Meanwhile, the nascent newspaper obituary continued to develop and to reflect the values and obsessions of the society that consumed it. As the middle class burgeoned, society became less secular. Improved printing and distribution methods encouraged the proliferation of newspapers and journals. The obituary evolved into a document recording a much wider range of worthies, determined by who they were, what they had accomplished — for good or ill — and how they had died (the more prolonged and gruesome, the better). Rather than simply extolling the virtues of the nobility or following an overt political agenda, these new publications aimed at a readership that embraced both the gentleman and his tailor and brought them together in the same, increasingly urban cultural arena.

"Celebrity — short-lived fame — became a feature of British society, and the untimely or dramatic death began to create as well as test...this new kind of fame," argues Barry in "From Epitaph to Obituary." She believes the obituary played a key role in this process and represented an important mechanism for introducing modern notions of fame and celebrity into British society. As the general population became more literate and newspapers more robust and prolific, obituaries developed a definitive purpose: to showcase exemplary lives, to record society's progress and achievements, and to chronicle the art of dying nobly, bravely, and stoically — traits that still appear in family-written death notices today.

The short-lived *Post-Angel* (1701–02), edited by John Dunton, produced graphic accounts of the pious deaths of the noble and religious, as well as the dastardly lives and evil ends of criminals and rogues as exhortations about the wages of sin. Even though it lasted only two years, the *Post-Angel* is a rich repository of extraordinary attempts to link behaviour in the temporal world with reward or damnation in the eternal one. Queen Mary, wife of William of Orange, apparently declared in her final breaths, "I believe I shall now soon die, and I thank God, I have from my youth learn'd a true Doctrine, that Repentance is not to be put off to a Death-bed." Not so the Scottish pirate Captain William Kidd. His botched execution, as recounted by the ordinary — the guard who accompanied him on his final journey to the scaffold in London on May 23, 1701 — is a vivid example: "But here I must take notice of a Remarkable (and I hope most Lucky) Accident which then did happen, which was this, That the Rope with which Capt. Kidd was ty'd, broke, and so falling to the Ground, he was taken up alive; and by this means had Opportunity to consider more of that Eternity he was launching into."

Whether Kidd considered himself lucky and actually took advantage of his bungled execution to make peace with the Almighty is not known. Certainly the ordinary felt assured that Kidd had had a change of heart, and it is from his perspective that the end of the tale is told: "This he said as he was on the top of the ladder, (the Scaffold being now broken down) and my self half way on it, as close to him as I could; who having again, for the last time, pray'd with him, left him, with a greater satisfaction than I had before, that he was Penitent." However Kidd left this world, his corpse was encased in chains and left to dangle over the Thames as a warning to other would-be pirates of the harsh justice that awaited them.

"It took the appearance of the more neutral *Daily Journal* in the 1720s," according to Barry, "for the obituary to gain a place in the print culture of the day entirely in its own right, as an authoritative account of the biography and death of significant persons" and not solely as a personal vehicle for the attitudes of its proprietor. By the time the *Gentleman's Magazine* appeared in 1731, moral commentary and political propaganda had been replaced by a much more democratic and bourgeois preoccupation with the middle classes and their activities, both social and vocational. Founded in London by Edward Cave, the *Gentleman's Magazine* gave Samuel Johnson his first paying gig as a writer. Barry and other scholars suggest that it created celebrities in its pages, similar to the way multimedia do today.

In 1780 a named obituary column was introduced into the magazine, in which the dead were recognized for the way they had died and for their prowess on the playing field, on the stage, and at the gaming tables, as well as achievements in more ordinary occupations. A Mr. Foster Powell was lauded for walking great distances very quickly; John Broughton was congratulated on his boxing skills, which would "ever be recorded in the annals of that science"; Isaac Tarrat was remembered for impersonating a doctor and telling fortunes in a "fur cap, a large white beard, and a worsted damask night gown"; and John Underwood was written up because of the way he pre-organized his own funeral: "No bell was tolled, no one invited but the six gentlemen, and no relation followed his corpse; the coffin was painted green."

An actress gone bad was irresistible to a magazine aimed at an audience with the leisure and the wherewithal to be fascinated by celebrity. In the unsigned obituary for Mrs. Baddeley, the author concentrated on her personal life, suggesting both financial and romantic misadventures by alluding to "private motives" that forced her to quit London for an engagement in Dublin, and which precipitated "the miseries into which she plunged by obeying the dictates of impetuous passions." The writer concludes by lamenting that her "fair form, her abilities, and her flatterers, have not been able to prevent her from falling into the distresses inseparable from misconduct and want of economy." Change the language and the time, and the piece could be about Anna Nicole Smith or even Diana, Princess of Wales.

The *Gentleman's Magazine* was not the only outlet for obituaries. Blackwood's *Edinburgh Magazine* published a long account in 1819 of the European life and death of John Sackeouse, an "Esquimaux" who had been born in Greenland in 1797 and been converted to Christianity, probably by Danish missionaries. The account, written by Captain Basil Hall, described Sackeouse as about five feet, eight inches tall, broad-chested, and with a very wide face and a great quantity of coarse black hair.

"The expression of his countenance, however, was remarkably pleasing and good-humoured, and not in the least degree savage." Sackeouse was considered modest, pious, fond of children, and eager to take instruction in religion, drawing, reading, and writing, although he proved a mediocre student in the latter. To modern eyes there is a condescending tone to sentences like this one: "He never expressed any of that idiotic surprise which savages sometimes evince, on seeing anything very different from what they have been accustomed to," but overall the writer seems genuinely fond of the deceased, especially in his deathbed description, which owes much to Christian redemption and belief in the afterlife. "His dying moments were soothed by the anxious attendance of his friends...but he said it was of no use, for his sister had appeared to him and called to him to come away. It must not be supposed, however, that this arose from superstition, or was anything more than the effect of the fever...for he was unaffectedly pious under...and...held in his hand an Icelandic catechism [published in Copenhagen in 1777] till his strength and sight failed him, when the book dropped from his grasp, and he shortly afterwards expired."

Perhaps the best-remembered obituary from this era, and one of the few that stand apart for its literary value, is philosopher and journalist William Hazlitt's essay "Death of John Cavanagh," published in the *Examiner* on February 9, 1819. Indeed, Hazlitt was himself so fond of the obituary that he reprinted it in his essay "The Indian Jugglers" in *Table Talk* in 1828. John Cavanagh was an athlete who was especially skilled at a form of handball called fives, a sport that Hazlitt himself loved playing. "When a person dies who does any one thing better than any one else in the world, which so many others are trying to do well, it leaves a gap in society," Hazlitt wrote effusively. "It is not likely that any one will see the game of fives played in its perfection for many years to come — for Cavanagh is dead and has not left his peer behind him. It may be said that there are things of more importance than striking a ball against a wall; there are things, indeed, which make more noise and do as little good, such as making war and peace, making speeches and answering them, making verses and blotting them, making money and throwing it away. But the game of fives is what no one despises who has ever played at it. It is the finest exercise for the body, and the best relaxation for the mind."

Although very pretty as a piece of writing, Hazlitt's essay is not much use as an obituary. We learn very little about the deceased — not even his birth or death dates. Instead Hazlitt tells us that Cavanagh, a devout Irish Catholic who never ate meat on Friday, had "a clear, open countenance" and was a "young fellow of sense, humour, and courage" who had suffered a "burst blood vessel" two or three years earlier but was "fast recovering" when "he was suddenly carried off." That's it. No details about his family, his schooling, his livelihood. Instead Hazlitt has used the occasion of Cavanagh's death "on a Friday" to demonstrate his own poetic prowess and to score a few cheap literary points: "His blows were not undecided and ineffectual — lumbering like Mr. Wordsworth's epic poetry, nor wavering like Mr. Coleridge's lyric prose, nor short of the mark like Mr. Brougham's speeches, nor wide of it like

Mr. Canning's wit, nor foul like the *Quarterly*, not *let* balls like the *Edinburgh Review*. Cobbett and Junius together would have made a Cavanagh."

By championing Cavanagh's athletic skills over the poetics of Wordsworth and Coleridge, Hazlitt is clearly snubbing his former literary heroes, their achievements, and their fame. But his hyperbolic text also has another purpose: to create a lasting legacy for the temporal achievements of an athlete — especially important in the days before sporting matches could be recorded on film — when "the noisy shout of the ring happily stood him instead of the unheard voice of posterity." Hazlitt is trying to cheat death by using his skills as a wordsmith to render Cavanagh immortal. And he has succeeded, even though the essay is read today not as a tribute to Cavanagh but as an example of Hazlitt's own talents as an essayist.

This kind of literary exercise — in which the writing outweighs the significance of the subject — is not restricted to the nineteenth century. The *Economist* devoted a page in August 2009 to the death of a legendary trout named Benson. The fish, which reached an epic size of sixty-four pounds, two ounces (twenty-nine kilograms), was compared to Marilyn Monroe and Raquel Welch and described by the unnamed obituarist as "lither than either as she cruised through the water-weed, a lazy twist of gold" with lips that "were full, sultry or sulking" and an "unblinking expression." Hyperbole could not be tamed in the obituary, which finally ended with a description of Benson, having died probably of overeating, lying "like Wisdom drawn up from the deep: as golden, and as quiet." Frankly, I have always had a personal rule: no animals, although I might have made an exception for Northern Dancer.

As social historians have amply demonstrated, the texture of lives and the context of the times are the glue connecting the legal, military, political, artistic, and cultural achievements of the past in a cohesive pattern. Nigel Starck argues in *Life after Death* that obituaries, which he likens to an "instant exercise in biography," have, more than other forms of journalism, the "power to deliver an account of what it was like to be a citizen of communities past."

Reportage on celebrity and the "journalism of death," as American pundit Elaine Showalter calls newspaper obituaries, became a much more solemn and sombre business after Queen Victoria began her long reign in 1837. By then the *Times* had been publishing for more than fifty years. Launched by John Walter on January 1, 1785, as the *Daily Universal Register*, the newspaper officially changed its name to the *Times* on its third anniversary. From the beginning, the *Times* was interested in bringing news from Europe and especially France to its readers, and in publishing contributions from experts in the scientific, political, literary, and artistic realms.

Two inventions helped achieve those goals and to transform the *Times* into the most influential news source of its time. James Watt's steam engine went into production in 1775, a decade before the *Times* was founded, giving rise to steam-driven railways and steamships, which made it possible to ship goods, including newspapers, around the country and the world. Then in 1811, Friedrich Koenig, a German-born printer living in London, applied steam technology to the printing press and invented a single-cylinder steam-driven rotary press. Koenig and his British investor, Thomas Bensley, sold an improved, double-cylinder model of the press (capable of printing 1,100 sheets an hour) to John Walter II, son of the founder of the *Times* and, by 1814, its publisher. The press so improved the speed of production and therefore the dissemination of news that the *Times* was soon selling more than seven thousand copies a day.

Obituary coverage was spotty until John Thaddeus Delane (1817–79), who had trained as a lawyer but never practised, became editor in 1841. He encouraged the writing of long and eloquent essays on the lives of great men because he believed that would boost the paper's circulation and its authority. By 1850 the practice of writing major obituaries for the great and the good was well established, although the daily obituary page did not become an integral part of the paper until the twentieth century. When the Duke of Wellington died in 1852, his massive obituary, containing more than forty thousand words, ran over several dense pages on two successive days. "The Duke of Wellington had exhausted nature and exhausted glory. His career was one un-clouded longest day" was one of the milder tributes.

By the end of the century — Delane retired in 1877 and died two years later — truly maudlin deathbed scenes were creeping in because of the Victorian preoccupation with death. For example, when art critic and social thinker John Ruskin died at age eighty in January 1900, his obituary in the *Times* dwelt extravagantly on the bedside recollections of his cousin Mrs. Severn. Beginning with the onset of a throat irritation on a Thursday, Ruskin takes to his bed; Mrs. Severn sings him a favourite song, "Summer Slumber," perhaps to take his mind off the fact that it is winter. He has a temperature of 102 degrees Fahrenheit but manages to eat a dinner of sole and pheasant washed down with champagne. On Friday he feels better, but on

Saturday he fades away, attended by a doctor and a manservant "now and then feathering the lips with brandy and spraying the head with eau de cologne," with the faithful Mrs. Severn holding his hand. Afterwards she notices the time of day when she looks out the window and observes, "The brilliant, gorgeous light illumined the hill with splendour; and the spectators felt as if Heaven's gate itself had been flung open to receive the teacher into everlasting peace."

The fascination with noble and gentle death was blasted to bits in the trenches of northern France and Flanders during the First World War. Consequently the obituary as a popular entertainment and literary form declined in the 1920s. The most widely held theory is that readers were so dispirited by the wanton sacrifice of a promising generation of young men — in a war that was supposed to put an end to war itself — they didn't want to read about death in the newspapers.

Establishment papers carried on with windy accounts of military and political achievements of the great and the good — almost inevitably male — but most people paid little notice. Across the Atlantic, obituaries had been part of regional newspapers such as *Niles' Weekly Register* and the influential Washington-based *National Intelligencer* since at least 1800. Niles was the victim of an obituary hoax in 1818, according to Janice Hume in her book *Obituaries in American Culture*. Editors reported the death of Daniel Boone, who had allegedly "breathed out his last" in a deer lick with "gun in his hand just in the act of firing," allowing the writer to conclude that "as he lived, so he died." The paper later printed a retraction for the "fabrication," suggesting that the hoax was an attempt to mythologize the frontiersman's already dramatic life. Boone actually died of natural causes two years later at the age of eighty-five, after uttering his final words, "I'm going now. My time has come."

As much as the American Revolution dominated eighteenth-century life in the United States, the Civil War was the watershed that marked the nineteenth century. After four years of bloody carnage, the United States emerged with a strong central government, a nation that was well rooted in the industrial age, and one that was beginning to recognize the concepts of national citizenship and equal rights for men.

The *New York Times*, which was founded in September 1851 as the *New York Daily Times*, took advantage of an improved lithographic rotary printing press manufactured by Richard M. Hoe. He put the type on a revolving cylinder that made it possible to print much faster than on the traditional flatbed printing press. By 1860 the *New York Times*, as it was called by then, had doubled its original size to eight pages a day and had become one of the top newspapers in the city.

Along with industrial advances and the invention of the telegraph, which allowed news dispatches to be delivered rapidly, newspapers began hiring reporters and sending them out to gather news from battlefields, the Western frontier, and the gold rush. All of these measures gave rise to a more news-oriented and egalitarian journalism that was aimed at a mass audience, in obituaries as well as elsewhere. In the same way that the gruesome death tolls in the trenches of northern Europe would have a numbing effect on British obituaries in the 1920s, the post–Civil War era in the U.S. saw a dashing of sentimentality about noble or romantic death. "Obituaries no longer dwelled on the act of dying or its religious implications — death had become far too familiar," Hume writes about the *New York Times* in 1870 in *Obituaries in American Culture*.

Although the NYT did not set out to romanticize death and rarely gave prolonged descriptions of the cause of death, service to country was celebrated. Major General Joseph E. Hamblin was described as one of the "most gallant soldiers that fought for the union in the late war...and only sheathed his sword when his country had no further need of his services." As the country recovered, long lists of young men killed in battle were replaced with obituaries of men working as lawyers, merchants, and manufacturers as wealth and social status took a more prominent role than personal valour.

Hume argues that nineteenth-century obituary writers, who were more concerned with virtuous character traits such as courage, honesty, and gallantry for men and piety for women, were succeeded in the twentieth century by writers who downplayed individual character in their preoccupation with the work ethic and the reflected glory that came from being linked to business and social institutions and associations. Consequently the "ideal American," at least as represented in newspaper obituaries, changes with the times and meets a specific social need depending on the historical era — for example, the rugged individual in the frontier era, the entrepreneur in the industrial era, the compassionate citizen during the Depression, the hero during wartime. In other words, "Virtue is not stagnant, but adapts to the new cultural demands of a changing society," as Hume states in *Obituaries in American Culture*.

By the mid-twentieth century, American obituaries tended to be factual news stories that concentrated on the fact of somebody's death rather than the virtues and accomplishments of the deceased's life. All of that changed, at least at the NYT, when the Canadian-born editor and writer Alden Whitman (October 27, 1913 – September 4, 1990) was appointed chief obituary writer in 1965 by A. M. (Abe) Rosenthal (May 2, 1922 – May 10, 2006), another Canadian-born journalist who eventually became executive editor of the paper.

Here's how Whitman himself, in *The Obituary Book,* describes the situation at the NYT before he arrived on the dead beat: "Previously, it had been the *Times's* practice to print a matter-of-fact and rather brief account of a person's life. Containing few quotes or flashes of perception, these obits were as dreary to read as an entry in *Who's Who.* In this respect they were not much different from obits that appeared — and still do — in most American newspapers, where the practice was — and still is — to hand out obits to young reporters (to teach them a sense of discipline in writing), to rewrite men for knocking out in an idle moment, or to older reporters spinning out the days to retirement... The result has been dull writing, or, even worse, puffery."

Lacking any sense of false modesty, Whitman set out to change all that. He specialized in advances, writing long biographical sketches on statesman, aged worthies, and people whose health appeared to be failing, although even he admitted it was "impossible to anticipate every big death." Whitman's true innovation was interviewing subjects about their lives for their advance obituary. "From these conversations — all the more frank and open because the person knows that what he says is not for immediate quotation — emerges some of the best material. The task is to distill it and integrate it with information from other sources into a finished article. It is never, for me at least, an easy job ..."

Not everybody agrees with interviewing subjects. "I tend not to encourage it, though I leave it to the author," Ian Brunskill, obituaries editor of the *Times* of London, said in a 2008 interview with Adam Bernstein, obituaries editor of the *Washington Post.* "What's the effect likely to be? Either the subject will be horrified or delighted and tell you stories you have to spend hours checking. It's a minefield."

I'm of two minds. Interviewing a subject in advance gives you a physical sense of the personality behind the achievements, but I have learned that the encounter is useful only if I've done all the research and honed my queries into a few salient points. Sitting there with a tape recorder running is not the occasion to troll for biographical details, because most times the person can't remember specific dates or the conversation gets bogged down in myriad details. On the other hand I have had such memorable conversations with some of my subjects — actor William Hutt, *Chatelaine* editor Doris Anderson, and poet P. K. Page come to mind — that I have never forgotten them. Believe me, that is not what usually happens to a journalist who has interviewed thousands of people in the course of her job.

I interviewed only one of the ten builders in this chapter — Celia Franca — specifically to write her obituary. When the time came, I found I had little room for the descriptive passages I had written two years earlier, and my own perspective had become more nuanced with time. And that is true of these lives as well. I wrote obituaries of each of them in a hurry under the space and time constraints of newspaper deadlines.

For this book I re-researched and rewrote them all because I had continued to think about them in the intervening years in terms of how they related to the world and each other. That's why, for example, I have combined artist and writer James Houston and Kananginak Pootoogook in the same essay. Kananginak was one of four apprentices in Houston's printmaking studio, but he stayed in the Arctic, built the Co-op after Houston went south, and became both an internationally collected artist and a revered elder in his community. Their lives are both linked and yet very different. The same is true of Duff Roblin and Louis Robichaud. They were premiers — from different political parties — at about the same time. Each transformed his province. That connected them, even though they came from very different circumstances.

And that is the final thing I want to say about obituaries as biographical building blocks: they give you a way of seeing the past and recognizing how previous lives have enriched our times. That is what each of these builders represents to me.

FRANK CALDER

Politician and Nisga'a Chief

AUGUST 3, 1915 – NOVEMBER 4, 2006

S HORT OF STATURE and towering of vision, Frank Calder, who called himself the "little chief," was an inspirational leader of the Nisga'a Nation in British Columbia. He was the first status Indian admitted to a post-secondary institution in Canada and the first aboriginal cabinet minister. Most of all, though, he will be remembered as the driving force behind the Nisga'a land treaty, a monumental piece of legislation that has been emulated across the country and as far away as New Zealand.

After more than a century of negotiations and disputes between the Nisga'a and provincial and federal governments, Calder took the Nisga'a people's claim to own and govern their ancestral lands all the way to the Supreme Court of Canada. Although they lost in a 4–3 ruling, which determined that their ancestral rights had been extinguished, the 1973 decision caused then prime minister Pierre Trudeau — the man who had long argued that "you can't right historical wrongs" — to consider reversing his government's policy and putting aboriginal rights on the national agenda. He opened negotiations with the Nisga'a and enshrined aboriginal rights in the 1982 Charter of Rights and Freedoms (they were later increased). The Nisga'a Treaty, which was finally signed in 2000, gave the Nisga'a ownership of about two thousand square kilo-metres in the Nass Valley of northern B.C. Every modern First Nations land claim, from the Cree of James Bay to Delgamuukw in B.C. to the Inuit in Nunavut, is built upon the legal rights that Calder fought so hard to establish.

FRANK CALDER'S DESTINY as a leader of his people was set even before he was born. In 1913 Arthur Calder, or Na-qua-oon, the traditional chief of the Nisga'a Wolf clan, and his wife, Louisa, were paddling down the Nass River to seek jobs at the newly opened salmon cannery. Their small son fell out of the canoe and drowned. The tragedy was both personal and political: the Calders had lost their son, but the Nisga'a Wolf clan had also lost its next chief.

About eighteen months later, an old woman in the village of Gingolx (Kincolith) had a powerful dream in which she envisioned Louisa Calder's younger sister, Emily Clark, conceiving a son who would carry the "chiefly spirit" of Na-qua-oon's dead child. The dream, reminiscent of the biblical account of Elizabeth's foretelling of the Immaculate Conception, came to fruition after a third son was born to Job and Emily Clark on August 3, 1915, in Nass Harbour, north of Terrace, B.C. In a traditional adoption ceremony, the Clarks gave their baby, Frank, to Arthur and Louisa Calder to raise as their own child.

When the Nisga'a clans met four years later to discuss their ongoing struggle to claim title to their traditional lands, a task some chiefs felt was akin to shifting "an immovable mountain," Na-qua-oon presented the "dream child" and said: "I'm going to send this boy to school where the *K'umsiiwan* [white people] live. And I'm going to make him learn how the white man eats, how the white man talks, how the white man thinks, and when he comes back, he's going to move that mountain."

Frank Calder, as he was now called, spent several years in the Anglican Church's Coqualeetza residential school in Sardis, near Chilliwack, B.C. Although these institutions have been widely reviled — Calder himself received $8,000 in 2006 under the federal redress program for survivors of the residential school system — his experience was not completely negative. He learned networking and negotiating skills that he would need in leading the legal challenge, and he made connections with other children who grew up to be aboriginal leaders.

In the summers, Calder, who had been welcomed onto the Nisga'a land committee by the tribal elders when he was only nine, went back home to work with his father in the fish cannery at Nass Harbour. That's where he received a different kind of instruction: the ways of a future chief.

The summer Calder was twelve, Na-qua-oon, who was unable to write or read English, gave his adopted son a copy of the federal "blue book." These were the bound documents that recorded Ottawa's arbitrary decision to end discussions about land claims and threatened jail terms for Natives who gathered in groups numbering more than five people. "Start reading," Na-qua-oon ordered.

After residential school, Calder went to Chilliwack High School and the Anglican Theological College (now affiliated with UBC), the first status Indian ever admitted to that institution. By the time he graduated in 1946, he had become involved with a group of Native activists who were lobbying the B.C. government for the right to vote in provincial elections (at the time Manitoba was the only jurisdiction in Canada that allowed Natives to vote without relinquishing treaty rights). Politics had become his new religion, so he decided against ordination as an Anglican minister.

Calder and his fellow activists realized a victory when the franchise was extended to Natives in British Columbia in 1947. Two years later, Calder ran successfully for the CCF (the precursor to the New Democratic Party) in the provincial riding of Atlin and became the first aboriginal elected to a Canadian legislature. Articulate, intelligent, and doggedly patient, he made his maiden speech in 1950, calling for, among other measures, a bill of rights — a decade before Progressive Conservative prime minister John Diefenbaker tabled similar legislation in the House of Commons.

The following year, the federal blue-book decrees — those same documents forbidding any discussion of land treaties that had been given to Calder as a boy of twelve — were finally abolished. That opened windows and put an end to what Calder called "a time of darkness and despair for all aboriginal people."

While Calder was pushing Native rights and issues in the provincial legislature, he was also encouraging the Nisga'a clans to work together on their land claims. By 1955 he had revitalized the old land-claims committee as the Nisga'a Tribal Council. Three years later, he became one of the most significant Nisga'a leaders when he inherited the title Chief Long Arm from Na-qua-oon.

It was in this capacity that he made the momentous decision to approach a young white lawyer named Thomas Berger. As a politician, Calder had the wisdom to know when he needed help and the persuasive powers to go out and acquire it. He wanted Berger because he was the lawyer who had argued successfully before the Supreme Court in *Regina v. White and Bob* in 1965. That ruling, which gave two aboriginal men the right to hunt on unoccupied land, based on the terms of the Royal Proclamation of 1763, also established that those rights had not been extinguished over the centuries.

"Pard'ner, we want you to represent us," was Calder's informal approach, as Berger later recalled. "We are going to bring a lawsuit to establish our aboriginal title." The Nisga'a launched their suit in September 1967, centennial year. The *Calder* case, as it was known, came to trial in April 1969. After losing at trial and on appeal, the Nisga'a applied to be heard by the Supreme Court of Canada.

In November 1971, chiefs and elders from the four villages in the Nass Valley travelled to Ottawa for the five-day hearing before seven Supreme Court judges. Both sides were wearing their traditional robes — a graphic display of aboriginal versus Anglo hierarchies. Fourteen months later, six of the judges agreed that the Nisga'a had had aboriginal title before the Europeans came; three of them, including Mr. Justice Wilfred Judson, felt those rights had been extinguished, and three, including Mr. Justice Emmett Hall, argued that their rights could still be asserted. The final judge dismissed the case on a technicality without considering the issue of aboriginal title. Consequently the appeal was denied in February 1973.

Even so, the timing was propitious for political change. Both Prime Minister Pierre Trudeau and his minister of Indian affairs, Jean Chrétien, were impressed by Judge Hall's arguments in the Calder case. As well, the minority Liberal government was being pressed by the Progressive Conservatives and the NDP to recognize its obligation to settle Native land claims, a combined leverage that exerted additional pressure if the Liberals wanted to avoid an election.

In August 1973, Chrétien officially opened the land claims negotiations. They were finally resolved provincially and federally more than twenty-five years later, when the Nisga'a Treaty passed second reading in the House of Commons in December 1999. By then Chrétien was prime minister and Calder, eighty-four, had survived several upheavals in his own life.

As the CCF transformed itself into the NDP, Calder had continued to represent his rural riding of Atlin. When Dave Barrett became NDP leader in B.C. and handily defeated W. A. C. Bennett's Social Credit Party in 1972, he named Calder a minister without portfolio in his first and only government. Calder's appointment to Cabinet — a first for an aboriginal in Canada — was both historic and problematic: he was a minister of the Crown in one of the very governments he was suing to secure aboriginal title for the Nisga'a.

But there were other issues. Calder, who enjoyed a drink and the company of women, was arrested in July 1973 (a few months after the Supreme Court decision) following a consensual situation involving a female companion, alcohol, and a car parked at an intersection. Although Calder was not charged with a crime, Barrett fired him from Cabinet. The Nisga'a, distressed by their leader's public humiliation, also responded negatively and voted for James Gosnell to replace Calder as president of the Nisga'a Tribal Council in 1974.

Calder quit the NDP and ran successfully the following year for Bill Bennett's Social Credit Party. He held his seat until 1979, when he lost the riding by one vote to the NDP candidate and retired from party politics. He was sixty.

A prolific reader and an intelligent public-policy thinker, Calder avidly followed the drawn-out Nisga'a treaty negotiations even though he was no longer officially involved in the deliberations. And he was not averse to making his feelings and opinions known. "Had I been the leader, I would have stuck to issues relating to the land question. I do not believe that self-government is an aboriginal right; it is a civic right for all Canadians," he said six months after the treaty was ratified. The Nisga'a never argued with him publicly, and they later named him Chief of Chiefs in tribute to his monumental efforts in shifting the "immovable mountain."

In 1975 he married Japanese-born Tamaki Koshibe (named "Bright Star" by the Nisga'a), with whom he later had a son, Erick. About the same time, he bought a family plot in the Ross Bay Cemetery in Victoria. He wanted to be buried near the provincial legislature rather than on his ancestral lands so his grave could remind visitors to Victoria of the Nisga'a and their hard-won land treaty.

In the late 1990s he moved into an assisted-living retirement home and in September 2006 he went into hospital for cancer-related surgery. From there to a convalescent hospital with palliative care facilities. That's where the man who changed the history of First Nations died on November 4, 2006, at age ninety-one.

DUFF ROBLIN
Premier of Manitoba

JUNE 17, 1917 – MAY 30, 2010

&

LOUIS ROBICHAUD
Premier of New Brunswick

OCTOBER 21, 1925 – JANUARY 6, 2005

A T A GLANCE, the connections seem spurious between Louis Robichaud, the Acadian from New Brunswick, and Duff Roblin, the Loyalist from Manitoba. One was a Liberal, the other a Progressive Conservative; one a Roman Catholic francophone who spoke English from necessity, the other an anglophone Anglican who learned to speak French adequately. One was short and scrappy-looking, the other patrician and reserved. Yet what the two men shared was much more significant than the incidentals that separated them. Each dreamt of being premier from an early age and each was a pragmatic visionary who transformed his province into a modern social, political, and economic entity.

Both were in power at roughly the same time — the expansionist 1960s, an era when federal monies were available to augment singular provincial initiatives. Both were premiers of "have-not" provinces, although Winnipeg, the capital of Manitoba, was the fourth-largest city in Canada and the biggest on the prairie. They also had significant populations of francophones, especially in New Brunswick, and First Nations, particularly in Manitoba. Each of these groups had historical grievances. Separately, in their very different political arenas, Roblin and Robichaud demonstrated what government can do when it is led by imaginative, progressive, and activist provincial premiers who understand the workings, the geography, the history, and the aspirations of their electorate. (There were other transformative premiers — Jean Lesage in Quebec and Tommy Douglas in Saskatchewan — but their deaths are outside my time frame.)

As Manitoba's fourteenth premier, from 1958 to 1967, Roblin put the *progressive* into Progressive Conservative, a party that was almost moribund before he became leader. He overhauled the archaic education system, including a controversial but pragmatic "shared services" program between public and "separate," or Catholic, schools that dampened a still smouldering constitutional crisis, the "Manitoba Schools Question," that dated back to 1890. He reintroduced French-language teaching, expanded and integrated government services, upgraded highways, created provincial parks, revamped hospitals, instituted community colleges and expanded universities, amalgamated Winnipeg's outlying municipalities into a single metropolitan area, and built the Red River Floodway — forever known as "Duff's Ditch" — to curb the errant river from overflowing its banks during spring runoff.

Half a continent away, Louis Robichaud, the twenty-fifth premier of New Brunswick, was also revamping provincial and municipal services with his pervasive and massive equal-opportunity program. "I brought democracy to New Brunswick," he liked to say, with little exaggeration. A small-town lawyer who became provincial premier before he was thirty-five, Robichaud used his decade in power, from 1960 to 1970, to modernize Prohibition-era liquor laws, abolish the Hospital Premium Tax, pass an Official Languages Act, establish the francophone Université de Moncton, increase Acadian administrative influence, and encourage the mining and forest industries. He made New Brunswick Canada's first and only officially bilingual province and turned a divided and backward society into a thriving bilingual and bicultural one. Business historian Joseph E. Martin says Robichaud left such a superior administrative legacy that for the next thirty or forty years New Brunswick was the best-managed province in Canada, regardless of premier or party.

Both men were touted as potential prime ministers. Although Robichaud seemed spent after his dynamic decade in New Brunswick, Roblin had aspirations, however ambivalent, to succeed John Diefenbaker as leader of the Progressive Conservative Party. A loyalist to the West, the party, and the Chief, Roblin played down ambition with decorum; he waited so long to declare himself that he lost delegates and organization to his primary rival, Robert Stanfield, the popular premier of Nova Scotia. Had he won the leadership in September 1967, could Roblin have defeated Liberal Pierre Trudeau or would he, like Stanfield, have led the party to three successive defeats? Nobody will ever know.

CHARLES DUFFERIN ROBLIN was born in Winnipeg on June 17, 1917, one of four children of businessman Charles Dufferin and Sophie (née Murdoch) Roblin. The Roblins came from a mixture of Italian and Dutch stock who had settled in what is now New York State. When American rebels confronted his ancestor Elizabeth Roblin, demanding to know where her loyalties lay after the Declaration of Independence in 1776, she replied, in reference to George III, "My king yesterday. Why not my king today?"

That attitude compelled the Roblins to move north in 1783, along with thousands of other displaced persons, to the Bay of Quinte in eastern Ontario. They built and operated Roblin's Mill (which poet Al Purdy later immortalized). Three of Roblin's Loyalist forebears were active in the political affairs of what is now Ontario. John Roblin sat in the Upper Canada Assembly from 1808–10, and two later Roblins — John P. and David — were in the Union Parliaments of the 1840s and '50s.

His grandfather Rodmond Palen Roblin moved to the roaring West in the 1870s and was premier of Manitoba from 1900 to 1915. He is best known for building the massive limestone Manitoba legislative building, exchanging barbs with suffragist Nellie McClung, and fending off scandals surrounding the cost overruns on the legislature and allegations that he had appropriated some of the building materials to erect his own showcase stone farmhouse near Carman, Manitoba.

By contrast, his grandson was progressive, public-spirited, pragmatic, and slightly oddball. He loved to wear a kilt and to play the bagpipes as he wandered through the empty halls of the massive Manitoba Legislature, the keening sound reverberating off the stone walls. For him it was a way to alleviate stress, but it tended to alarm the cleaning staff and gave rise to his characterization as an eccentric.

He had an undeserved reputation as a non-drinker, stemming from his early days on the hustings. "When I started beating the bushes for candidates," he once told a journalist, "a typical morning would start with wine at the priest's house, home-brew beer at the first farm, straight whisky in a town merchant's office. I'd be tiddly by noon and dopey all afternoon....I knew I'd never finish the course that way, so I assumed the role of a strict teetotaller."

As a child of privilege, Roblin was educated at St. John's College School, an elite private institution. Family finances suffered during the Depression and he eventually went to Kelvin Technical High School for grades ten and eleven. There he became involved in the rough-and-tumble of student politics, serving as a conservative on the communist-dominated Winnipeg Youth Council.

He dropped out of the University of Manitoba after a year and enrolled in a local business college before heading south to take courses at the business school of the University of Chicago. Eventually he moved back to Winnipeg to study for a diploma in agriculture at U of M. Equipped with this motley assortment of courses and qualifications, he made an appointment with the president of the university and proposed that he had fulfilled the requirements for a degree. The president begged to differ and quickly showed him the door.

When the Second World War erupted in 1939, he enlisted in the Canadian Army as a private. Longing to become a pilot, he took private flying lessons; he achieved a transfer in the spring of 1940 to the fledgling Royal Canadian Air Force. His eyesight was poor, so he was shipped overseas in 1942 as a junior officer in a tactical and operations unit attached to the Royal Air Force. He landed in Normandy on June 30, 1944, and helped chase the retreating Axis forces all the way to Hamburg, Germany. By the time he was demobilized in 1946, his organizing skills in helping to plan the Normandy invasion had seen him promoted to the rank of wing commander, although he had never been behind the controls of a military plane.

He returned to the Prairies and a job in a Roblin family business. Although Roblin later wrote in his memoirs, *Speaking for Myself: Politics and Other Pursuits*, that he had planned to be premier from childhood, he showed little interest in running for political office, preferring to complain instead about the coalition government formed by the Progressive Conservatives and the Liberal Progressives. When friends challenged him to quit whining and put his name on the ballot in the upcoming 1949 election, he ran successfully as an independent anti-coalition Progressive Conservative, winning a seat in the provincial legislature as the member for Winnipeg South. He was re-elected six times, played a major role in getting the Conservatives out of the coalition, which had ruled since the early 1920s, and became leader of the Manitoba Progressive Conservative Party in 1954, defeating leader Errick Willis at a leadership convention.

As a politician, Roblin not only knew his statutes and the inner workings of government departments, he also understood the electorate and the province. He believed in using government to serve the needs of the people which, ideologically, made him a Red Tory and positioned him further left on social issues than the premier of the day, Douglas Campbell, and his Liberal Progressives.

Four years after becoming leader, Roblin led the Progressive Conservatives to a minority government on June 16, 1958, the day before his forty-first birthday. It was the first PC government in Manitoba since his grandfather's defeat at the polls in 1915. Roblin augmented his electoral success three months later by marrying Mary MacKay, a journalist who had worked as a reporter for the *Winnipeg Free Press* and produced children's programs for the CBC. They subsequently had a son, Andrew, and a daughter, Jennifer.

After winning a resounding majority in 1959, Roblin set about transforming Manitoba. Although he himself believed that education was his biggest priority and his most significant achievement, he is best known for building the controversial multi-million-dollar floodway to tame and divert the raging annual spring runoff from the Red River, which often threatened to drown low-lying parts of Winnipeg.

Having hefted his share of sandbags in his youth, Roblin held his ground against local opposition and finally won the day when he succeeded in persuading the federal government to share the costs. "Duff's Ditch" more than earned its keep during the "flood of the century" in 1997, when it was estimated that the floodway prevented billions of dollars in damage and incalculable disruption to hundreds of thousands of residents.

Meanwhile, another pivotal leader was entering provincial politics in the Maritimes.

LOUIS JOSEPH "P'TIT Louis" Robichaud was born on October 21, 1925, in the small lumbering and farming community of Saint-Antoine, New Brunswick. That same year, the government of Pierre Veniot, the first Acadian to become premier, was defeated at the ballot box.

Robichaud was one of six sons and four daughters of sawmill operator, village postmaster, and Liberal organizer Amédée Robichaud and his wife, Eugénie "Annie" Robichaud (née Richard). Like his siblings, Robichaud went to a two-room schoolhouse where all the instruction was in English and history lessons adhered to the glorious achievements of the British Empire. The ignominious *grand dérangement* of 1755 — the expulsion of the Acadians from their homeland during the Seven Years' War between the British and the French for control of what is now Canada — was barely covered in the curriculum. Looking back from adulthood, Robichaud believed that being forced to learn in English was another attempt to assimilate the Acadians.

As a boy, his great interests were sports, politics, and woodworking: the walls of his bedroom were covered with sports pictures in frames that he had made. Decades later, his Senate office in Ottawa was filled with tables and wooden sculptures that indicated the hours he had spent at the lathe, the saw, and the sander.

Destined for the priesthood, Robichaud entered a seminary in Bathurst at fourteen but had a change of heart and vocation three years later. By then resolved on a political career, he attended Collège Sacré-Coeur (now part of the Université de Moncton), graduating in 1947 with a bachelor of arts degree. After the ceremony, he handed prophetic notes to his classmates signed *Louis J. Robichaud, Premier of New Brunswick.*

He studied economics and political science for a year at Laval University (a petri dish for the Quiet Revolution, which would transform Quebec after the death of Premier Maurice Duplessis in 1959) before heading back to New Brunswick to article for three years with a law firm in Bathurst. He hung out his shingle — which he had made himself on his lathe — in 1952 in Richibucto, a small town on the coast about an hour north of Saint-Antoine, and a well-considered choice for building a law practice and securing the Liberal nomination in the upcoming elections. The year before, he had married Lorraine Savoie, a teacher he'd met through friends in Bathurst. They eventually had four children.

He was elected handily for the first time in 1952, although the Liberals, including party leader John McNair, were defeated. The party needed to rebuild, and the dynamic and energetic rookie was keen to assist. Within four years he was financial critic in the legislature, within six he had won the leadership of the party, and within eight he had become premier, when his Liberals defeated the Conservative government of Hugh John Flemming by winning

31 of the 52 seats on June 27, 1960 — less than a week after Jean Lesage won his upset victory in neighbouring Quebec and began implementing the framework for the Quiet Revolution.

During his ten years as premier, Robichaud gained national stature by turning New Brunswick into a socio-political laboratory, hoping to create a climate that would keep young people from seeking career opportunities in other parts of the country. At the time, the significantly francophone and Roman Catholic province was a rural backwater fraught with poverty and illiteracy, especially in the French-speaking north. There were more than 1,100 taxing authorities throughout the province. Even cows and chickens were taxed, and at widely differing rates. There were 422 school districts, each with its own educational standards and pay scale for teachers. Social welfare systems, based on eighteenth-century poor laws, varied so much that a single mother in Chatham might receive $45 a month while a mother in nearby Neguac got only $7.

On January 1, 1967, Robichaud, who had campaigned to abolish a "discriminatory" premium tax on hospital services, introduced sweeping reform legislation. The program involved a massive shift of public services from local governments to the province, which took over services to the people while municipalities kept control of services to property. Thirty-four school districts replaced 422 feuding, ill-equipped bodies, centralized taxation assessments were instituted, and the government took control of essential services.

Municipal tax concessions to industry were wiped out, incurring the wrath of New Brunswick billionaire K. C. Irving. His newspapers campaigned against the reforms, coining the phrase "robbing Peter to pay Pierre": a reference to the more prosperous English-speaking areas having to share their wealth with the mostly French-speaking poorer areas. The reforms required 131 bills and two years of sometimes bitter debate before they were passed into law. The rich-versus-poor and English-versus-French rancour, fanned by the Irving newspapers, led to such alarming threats against the premier and his family that armed guards were employed to protect them.

Besides the economic reforms, Robichaud also introduced fundamental language and educational changes, taking special pride in founding the French-language Université de Moncton in June 1963, adopting a provincial flag in 1965, and declaring New Brunswick a bilingual province in 1969. "Language rights are more than legal rights," he said in 1969 when he introduced the legislation. "They are precious cultural rights, going deep into the revered past and touching the historic traditions of all our people."

Both Robichaud and Roblin were touted as federal leaders. While he was still premier, Robichaud was regarded in some Liberal circles as the "little Laurier," a reference not only to his small stature but to his outsize reputation as a successor to Sir Wilfrid Laurier, one of the legends of the Liberal Party. Many thought of him as heir apparent to Prime Minister Lester Pearson. Indeed, Pearson had offered him a choice of portfolios if he would run for the federal Liberals, but Robichaud wasn't interested in leaving New Brunswick just as his equal-opportunity program was netting results.

After Pierre Trudeau became Liberal prime minister in 1968, Robichaud hoped for an appointment to the judiciary to offer him a graceful way to step down as premier after a frenetic decade of political change. When it didn't materialize, he reluctantly called a provincial election for October 26, 1970. The timing was disastrous, not least because of the terrorist actions of two independent cells of the Front de libération du Québec in the midst of the campaign: the kidnapping of British trade commissioner James Cross and the abduction and murder of Quebec labour minister Pierre Laporte. Even though Robichaud quickly endorsed Trudeau's invocation of the War Measures Act, the electorate wasn't about to give a mandate to a francophone premier in those seemingly treacherous days. Robichaud's Liberals lost to Richard Hatfield's Progressive Conservatives, 32 seats to 26.

Robichaud seemed exhausted. Years later he acknowledged that he hadn't campaigned hard enough. "I didn't fight the way I had fought previous elections," he told the *Globe and Mail* in 1992. "I had reached my ambitions when I was too young and I was fed up. When I was fed up, people [my age, forty-five] were just starting in politics."

Trudeau offered him an ambassadorship, which he declined because his son Jean-Claude had serious kidney disease and had to be close to a dialysis unit (Jean-Claude died of kidney failure in 1976, and Robichaud's wife, Lorraine, in 1980.) Instead he accepted an appointment as chair of the International Joint Commission in 1971 and a Senate seat in 1973. He was not yet fifty.

UNLIKE ROBICHAUD, ROBLIN tippy-toed into federal politics while he was still premier of Manitoba. Proficiently bilingual, a believer in "many cultures, two languages, One Nation," and Diefenbaker's preferred successor, he belatedly became a candidate when Diefenbaker, having refused to step down quietly, forced a publicly humiliating leadership contest at a party convention in September 1967.

Politicos still argue about Roblin's candidacy. Did he let his loyalty to Diefenbaker, whose electoral sweep in 1958 had bolstered Roblin's own success at the polls in Manitoba the following year, make him wait too long to enter the fray? Some say he was all set to declare on July 25, 1967, but was preempted by the political fallout and media scramble following Charles de Gaulle's reckless exhortation *"Vive le Québec libre"* to roaring *séparatiste* crowds from a balcony at City Hall in Montreal the day before.

Political organizer and Diefenbaker foe Dalton Camp, who had courted both Roblin and Stanfield as leadership candidates, had grown impatient with Roblin's dilly-dallying. "Duff wanted to wait until all the presents were under the tree," he confided to cronies. By the time Roblin finally declared, Stanfield had already entered the contest with the backing, organizational commitment, and razzmatazz of the Camp organization. Although Stanfield's French was poor and his provincial accomplishments lacklustre, the Nova Scotia premier defeated Roblin on the fifth ballot at the leadership convention in Toronto in September 1967.

Having lost his bid for leadership of the federal party, Roblin resigned as Manitoba premier in November 1967. He ran federally in Winnipeg South, supposedly a PC stronghold, which included part of his old provincial riding of Wolseley, in June 1968. "He was the wrong man in the wrong party at the wrong time," said victorious Liberal E. B. Osler on election night. In fact, Roblin was done in by the tsunami of Trudeaumania and local displeasure at a provincial sales tax his government had instituted the year before.

In 1970 Roblin joined the corporate world as director, executive vice-president, and then president of Canadian Pacific Investments Ltd. in Montreal. Four years later he again made a run for political office, winning the PC nomination for the federal riding in Peterborough, Ontario. As a popular and distinguished former premier of Manitoba, Roblin failed to anticipate the opposition he would encounter, not only from the local Liberal candidate, Hugh Faulkner, but also from the *Peterborough Examiner*, the town newspaper, which took editorial exception to what it considered parachute tactics by the Progressive Conservatives.

As Roblin admitted in his memoirs, running in an Ontario riding was a huge mistake. He was roundly defeated, but he returned to public life when

Prime Minister Pierre Trudeau appointed him to the Senate in 1978. Brian Mulroney named him leader of the government in the Senate in 1984, which gave him a seat at the Cabinet table.

A progressive to the core, Roblin was a vocal supporter of Senate reform even while sitting as a member of the upper chamber. In 1987 he wrote a letter to the *Globe and Mail* arguing in favour of an elected Senate because "the present body is responsible in no parliamentary sense and representative in no democratic sense." He stepped down from the Senate in 1992 when he reached seventy-five, the mandatory retirement age.

Among the tributes was one from Robichaud, who rose in the Senate chamber and said: "I want to tell Duff Roblin...how proud I was of him, and I want to tell [his family] that Duff Roblin is a great Canadian...He consistently talked about the Metis, because they were of special interest to him. He was an honest, dedicated, sincere politician, but above all he was a great Canadian and still is."

Robichaud, who was eight years younger than Roblin, continued to serve in the Senate, but he admitted in the late 1990s that he had grown "bored with the shenanigans." After twenty years' service, he stepped down in 2000, when he turned seventy-five. He moved to a modest house on the Acadian shore of the Northumberland Strait near Bouctouche, N.B., with his second wife, Jacqueline Grignon, whom he had married in 1998.

As Frank McKenna, another visionary premier of New Brunswick, said after Robichaud died at seventy-nine of cancer, on January 6, 2005, "Diminutive in appearance, [he] was a giant in action....He set a fire under New Brunswick that continues to rage....He made us believe in ourselves. He firmly established us as a province that could punch above its weight at the national level."

After retiring from the Senate, in 1993 Roblin accepted an appointment as chairman of a provincial commission into post-secondary education in Manitoba. After that he largely retired from public life, although he continued to play squash, play the bagpipes, and enjoy vigorous but not partisan discussions about politics, history, and contemporary events. He lived in good health into old age and had the pleasure of seeing himself proclaimed the "greatest Manitoban of all time" by the *Winnipeg Free Press* in 2008. He died, aged ninety-two, on May 30, 2010.

J. M. S. Careless

Historian

FEBRUARY 17, 1919 – APRIL 6, 2009

I F EVER A person soared above the inherent liabilities of his name, it was historian J. M. S. (Maurice) Careless. As a scholar, writer, teacher, and family man he was the antithesis of negligence. Of course, that didn't mean that his moniker escaped titters and jokes, some of them made by the man himself. He liked to tell his students at the University of Toronto that having a professor named Careless shouldn't alarm them, because an earlier generation had been taught by a man named Wrong.

Careless was a triple-hitter as a historian: he was a diligent scholar who delved deeply into primary documents, he was a visionary who could discern patterns and develop theories to explain the past, and he was a compelling writer and an engaging stylist who could communicate his historical passions both in the seminar room and beyond to people who were curious about their country and how it had developed. Such was his prowess that he spawned a generation of enterprising scholars who built on his pioneering ideas in intellectual, urban, and regional history and went on to teach these emerging scholarly fields at universities across the country.

An undergraduate student of Harold Innis, Donald Creighton, and Frank Underhill, Careless taught at U of T for nearly four decades, attaining the rarefied rank of university professor and helping to build the history department into a pre-eminent centre of Canadian studies. He taught survey courses and undergraduate seminars, supervised doctoral students, and served as chairman of the department from 1959 to 1967. The Careless era represented an enormous expansion in hiring, a broadening of subject areas, and a democratization of the curriculum, including the controversial abandonment of the four-year honours program.

He was not as well known outside the profession as the previous chair, Donald Creighton, an early biographer of John A. Macdonald and proponent of the Laurentian thesis, which argues that Canada, a supplier of staples to European economies, developed economically and politically along the St. Lawrence River and other transportation routes. Among historians and students, however, Careless was every bit as revered as a teacher, researcher, theorist, literary stylist, and scholar.

In a way, Careless is the affable yin to Creighton's crusty yang. His metropolitan thesis — that cities grow as regional nodules because they harness, dominate, and then service the commercial, political, and cultural activities in their hinterlands — is both the counterpoint to and a refinement of Creighton's Laurentian thesis and Innis's staples theory. In an era when nationalist history dominated, Careless demonstrated that the study of local and regional history was key to understanding Canada and how it developed into a modern nation.

Like Creighton, Careless wrote a pioneering monograph on an icon of Canadian history; both studies are foundation blocks for scholars and buffs. However, Careless's monumental two-volume biography of George Brown — reformer, founding editor of the Toronto *Globe* (now the *Globe and Mail*), and father of Confederation — is a more complete picture of the human being behind the politician than is Creighton's magisterial biography of Brown's political rival Macdonald, the first prime minister of Canada. Partly that's because Careless uncovered a trove of family letters and papers in Scotland that predated Brown's arrival in this country in 1843. They now reside at Library and Archives Canada for others to consult.

Compared to the often imperious Creighton, he was more approachable as a colleague and supervisor, although no less demanding of his students. He had trained as an intellectual historian by working on mid-Victorian values and beliefs, picking up on theories developed by his predecessor, the great political historian Frank Underhill. But his approach was different. Instead of looking at attitudes and political movements as rationalizations emerging from economic interests, Careless looked at ideas and intellectual history in social and cultural contexts, arguing that it was important to understand what people believed at a particular time, even though those ideas might be dismissed as irrelevant or nonsensical by subsequent generations.

He twice won the Governor General's Literary Award, for *Canada: A Story of Challenge* in 1953 and a decade later for the second volume of *Brown of the Globe*, titled *Statesman of Confederation*. He wrote at least half a dozen other pivotal works, including *The Union of the Canadas*; *The Rise of Cities in Canada before 1914*; *Toronto to 1918: An Illustrated History*, which won the City of Toronto Book Award in 1985; and *Frontier and Metropolis*. Careless also co-edited the *Canadian Historical Review* and served as historical consultant on several films and television shows. He was duly honoured for these achievements, receiving, among other awards, the Order of Canada, the J. B. Tyrrell medal, membership in the Royal Society of Canada, and at least six honorary degrees.

Careless's life was not without stress. When he was twelve, he collided with a bus while riding his bicycle; after the accident, doctors had to amputate his right arm. Within the year he was writing so smoothly with his left hand that a teacher observed that his penmanship, then a highly prized skill, was now equally as bad as it had been before the accident. He didn't dwell on his infirmity. Instead, he coped by keeping his shoelaces done up, his neckties knotted, and his empty right sleeve tucked into his jacket pocket.

He disarmed strangers with his deft left-handed greeting and impressed his good friend Freeman Tovell with his one-handed typing when they were graduate students at Harvard in the early 1940s. As for his children, they later attested to their father's capacity to spank, build model trains, and carve a turkey single-handed. He also worked prodigiously. While everybody else would go to bed, he typically stayed up until three a.m. writing. Early the next morning he was off to the university to teach his courses, run his seminars, and conduct the business of the department and the university — just another day in a busy life.

JAMES MAURICE STOCKFORD Careless was born in Toronto on February 17, 1919, three months after the end of the First World War. The younger son by nearly a decade of William Roy Careless, an electrical engineer, and his wife, Ada de Rees, he was essentially an only child. After elementary school he attended North Toronto Collegiate and then transferred to University of Toronto Schools, an academically elite boys' school. That's where he became interested in cultural history, according to a biographical article by Frederick H. Armstrong in *Old Ontario: Essays in Honour of J. M. S. Careless*.

In 1936 he entered Trinity College at the University of Toronto. By the time he graduated with a history degree in 1940, Canada and Britain were at war. The Armed Forces weren't interested in sending a one-armed combatant overseas, so he enrolled at Harvard to do graduate work in medieval British intellectual history. Fascinated by ideas — the way they germinate in dense and diverse populations, how cities and regions develop independently of major centres, and how newspapers can disseminate political attitudes and theories — he settled on the convergence of Victorian liberalism and the proliferation of daily newspapers as a thesis topic.

Thwarted from doing primary research in English repositories because of the war, he pondered the problem with Underhill when he was back in Toronto for Christmas. Underhill directed him to the plentiful newspaper documentation on George Brown in Toronto. Fortuitously, Careless's Harvard professor, David Owen, agreed to supervise his thesis on Victorian liberalism in the Canadian colonial environment, even though the subject was technically outside Owen's own field of expertise. Later Careless showed the same leniency and openness to his own graduate students, never expecting them to "write footnotes to his work," according to intellectual historian Carl Berger. "He was one of those people for whom you could do virtually anything you wanted as long as you had a lot of evidence and you were pursuing a serious line of enquiry."

In the summer of 1939 Careless had met Betty Robinson, the daughter of industrialist Gordon Robinson, at Jackson's Point on Lake Simcoe. They were married on New Year's Eve 1941 in the chapel of Hart House at the University of Toronto. Careless's Harvard roommate Tovell acted as best man while the Robinson family chauffeur waited outside to rush the newlyweds to the registry office to obtain a visa for the new Mrs. Careless so that she could return to Boston with her husband.

Careless was seconded to the Naval History Office in Ottawa in 1943 and then to External Affairs, where he often worked with Hume Wrong, son of historian George M. Wrong, preparing briefings for the Parliamentary press gallery. The official reports, which were always released under the heading "Wrong and Careless," gave wartime information bulletins an unlikely twist.

Near the end of the war Careless became an assistant to diplomat Saul Rae, dealing with prisoner exchanges with the enemy as the war approached its inevitable conclusion. A Swedish liner, the *Gripsholm*, transported Axis and Allied exchange candidates under a safe-conduct agreement, with the result that Careless was nicknamed "the Cruise Kid" because of his frequent sailings across the Atlantic.

After the German and Japanese capitulations in 1945, Careless was hired as a lecturer in the history department of the University of Toronto, simultaneously writing lectures and completing his dissertation. He was promoted to assistant professor in 1949, the year before he was granted his doctorate from Harvard. The next two decades were an incredibly busy time as the Careless family grew to include five children and he embarked on a bruising teaching and writing schedule. In the early years his wife typed manuscript pages for him after she put the children down for naps.

Careless succeeded Creighton as chair of the history department in 1959. He broadened, deepened, and expanded the department, which nearly doubled in the early 1960s and introduced Asian and immigration history, among other new fields. Those were the years when the baby boomers entered university, creating a huge demand for space and for academics to teach them.

When Careless retired in 1984, he was appointed professor emeritus. Of course, *retirement* was merely a word. He continued to write prolifically, to sit on committees, to serve the profession, and to expand the idea of history by serving as an advisor to regional history groups and documentary film units. He died on April 6, 2009, two days after suffering a stroke. He was ninety.

JAMES HOUSTON
Artist, Adventurer, Writer

JUNE 12, 1921 – APRIL 17, 2005

&

KANANGINAK POOTOOGOOK
Inuit Elder and Artist

JANUARY 1, 1935 – NOVEMBER 23, 2010

CARVERS AND PRINTMAKERS put down their tools and closed up their studios in Cape Dorset when they heard the news that Saumik, "the Left-Handed One," had died. That's the name the Inuit at Cape Dorset had given the artist and dealer James Houston when he arrived on Baffin Island half a century earlier, seeking a simpler, more elemental life. He stayed just over a dozen years, but in that time he helped the Inuit create a new art form and launched an international craze for the carvings that Inuit had been making for centuries. In so doing he changed their way of life and his own.

Five years later, the community shut down again to honour Kananginak Pootoogook, the internationally recognized Inuit artist and community leader in the Arctic after Houston returned to the south. Kananginak helped his people develop their own artist-run studios and manage the transition from a nomadic life of hunting and fishing through cycles of plenty and starvation on the land to a modern one in permanent settlements. After

Kananginak died in an Ottawa hospital of lung cancer on November 23, 2010, all of Cape Dorset waited for his body to be flown home.

Then, despite a snowstorm that had made many roads impassable, three hundred people crowded into the community centre for an emotional Anglican service in Inuktitut, the language of the Inuit. Because darkness comes early in the arctic winter, the mourners used flashlights to wend their way to the cemetery, where they placed Kananginak's coffin in a shallow grave, covered it with a blanket of gravel, rocks, and snow, and marked the mound with a handmade cross.

These two men, one white, one Inuit, are forever linked through family ties and the sunburst of Inuit carving and printmaking. Kananginak's father, Joseph Pootoogook, ancestral leader of the Ikerrasak camp, adopted Houston into his clan in the 1950s, thus making it easier for the southerner to live and work among the Inuit. In his turn, Kananginak adopted Houston's son John, carrying on a tradition and a relationship with the younger Houston that lasted as long as Kananginak lived.

With his artist's eye, Houston was the first white man to recognize the beauty and integrity of the carvings the Inuit had been making since before time was recorded; with his entrepreneurial muscle he found a market for the best pieces in the south; with his creative vision he helped them learn print-making, a gender-neutral artistic and income-generating activity. A charismatic figure, an artist, and a storyteller, Houston was a modern man at odds with his own civilization. His dual role in the Arctic – as a paid servant of the Canadian government and an art dealer who profited from the marketing of Inuit art — made him a controversial figure, but in the end the markers pile much higher on the positive side.

Houston wasn't responsible for contact and commercialization. That was as inevitable as the long polar night following the midnight sun. Transportation and communications systems — especially television and air travel — became more pervasive and sophisticated in the 1950s and 1960s, just as life on the land became less sustainable with the depletion of trapping and hunting.

Kananginak, one of the original four Inuit who learned printmaking techniques from Houston, became the artistic hand and guiding voice of Cape Dorset after Houston traded the ice flows of Baffin Island for the sky-scrapers of Manhattan in the early 1960s. Cherishing the old customs and beliefs, Kananginak embraced the future with a strategic intelligence that

honoured traditional culture while enabling the Inuit to chart an independent and self-sufficient destiny.

A founding member of the Inuit-organized West Baffin Eskimo
Co-operative, Kananginak served as the inaugural president of its board of
directors from 1959 to 1964. He was instrumental in developing its graphic
arts and stonecutting centre, the Kinngait Studios, and in transforming the
original shop for hunters and trappers — an alternative to the Hudson's Bay
Company store — into a multi-million-dollar community-owned business.

Today the co-op sells everything from milk to snowmobiles and manages
and builds infrastructure and housing projects in the community. There are
dozens of artists' co-ops across the North, and Inuit art is world-famous and
the only Canadian art form that has spawned galleries outside Canada. It is
hard to imagine how that could have happened without Houston to strike the
entrepreneurial spark and Kananginak to nurture and sustain the flame.

JAMES ARCHIBALD HOUSTON was born in Toronto on June 12, 1921, one of
two children of James Donald Houston, a clothing importer, and his wife,
Gladys (née Barbour). He went to local schools and, because he loved to draw,
began taking lessons at age eleven with Group of Seven artist Arthur Lismer
at the Art Gallery of Toronto (now the Art Gallery of Ontario).

He spent a year at the Ontario College of Art before enlisting with the
Toronto Scottish Regiment in 1940, the day after his nineteenth birthday.
After serving in British Columbia, Labrador, and overseas, he remained in
France to study drawing at the Académie de la Grande Chaumière in Paris.

When he returned to Canada, he became a successful commercial artist
in Grand-mère, Quebec. His restlessness and his itch to experience the northern wilderness spurred him to ride the railroad to its terminus, a Hudson's
Bay Company post in Moose Factory, at the southern tip of James Bay. It still
isn't easy or cheap to reach the Arctic, but back then there were no regular
flights. Houston hitched a ride with a bush pilot flying a doctor into Baffin
Island to treat an Inuit child who had been savaged by a dog. Even then,
Houston found a seat on the small plane only because he agreed to help load
and unload the gasoline drums on their stops to refuel.

Once in the Arctic, Houston refused to climb back on the plane. He was
enchanted. "I looked around at the barren rocks and tundra with the few
tents greying with age and weighted down against the wind," he said later,

"and I took in the steel-blue sea and the biggest ice that I had ever seen and then the tanned smiling people. I could scarcely breathe."

Equipped with a sketch pad, a toothbrush, a can of peaches, and two words of Inuktitut — *iglu* and *kayak* — Houston survived on his charm, the generosity of the local Inuit, and his ability to rough it on the tundra. The Inuit, fascinated by Houston's sketching implements, grabbed them and began making their own, insouciant drawings. Later some shyly offered their carvings in exchange. Houston was astonished by the elemental nature of their art, which was as timeless as it was modern, as simple as it was profound.

When the bush pilot flew in again, Houston went back south determined to find a way to return. He took some Inuit carvings with him, which he showed to the Canadian Handicrafts Guild in Montreal. They hired him as a consultant, advanced him a thousand dollars, and gave him institutional status to work through the Hudson's Bay Company and the federal government to export and promote Inuit sculpture in stone, bone, and ivory to the rest of the world.

The carvings he brought back from his next expedition north sold out in three days. In 1950 he went to the east coast of Hudson Bay, stayed for more than a year, and brought back more than three thousand carvings. Avid collectors, both private and institutional, camped out overnight and elbowed each other for the chance to pay the rapidly escalating prices the guild was charging for this new sensation in the international art market.

One of those early buyers was Budd Feheley. He was making an advertising call in Montreal in 1950 when he saw the commotion outside the Canadian Handicrafts Guild on Peel Street and joined the queue. He was entranced from his first glimpse because, as he said later, "it was the last primitive art available in the world, and it was being produced just north of us." Feheley amassed his own collection, went north in 1961 on the first of several trips to serve as a founding member of the original Canadian Eskimo Arts Committee (later Council), and eventually opened his own art gallery, Feheley Fine Arts, to represent Inuit artists internationally.

From the beginning, Houston lived as a fellow hunter in Inuit society, using dog teams and eating raw seal meat. He lived in the Arctic for fourteen years (from 1948 to 1962), working most of that time as a northern service officer and civil administrator for the federal government. In 1950 he married Alma Bardon, a reporter for the *Montreal Star* who had been sent to interview him. On their honeymoon she climbed a twelve-metre frozen waterfall and became the second white woman to cross Baffin Island by dogsled. They settled in Cape Dorset and had two sons, John and Sam, to whom they spoke only Inuktitut.

Carving was something the Inuit had always done, and so was embroidery. The urge to make a mark and to decorate tools, clothing, and packs arises from a universal and primordial human impulse. Printmaking, which became a huge cultural enterprise, was new to the Inuit, and it came about by chance.

In the late 1950s Houston and carver Osuitok Ipeelee were having a companionable smoke when Osuitok, noticing the illustration on Houston's tin of Player's tobacco, remarked that it must be tedious to paint the sailor's head individually on each tin. Realizing that Osuitok had no clue about lithography, Houston set about demonstrating the process in a culture where paper was scarce, if not alien. He put some frozen ink on an image that Osuitok had carved into a walrus tusk, pressed a piece of toilet paper on top, took it off, and got a semblance of a reverse image. "We could do that," Osuitok said, with a hunter's decisiveness. And so they did. Houston travelled to Japan to learn printmaking techniques, which he then introduced to the Inuit.

"The whole question of printmaking hung in limbo, no one knowing whether the idea would be accepted by West Baffin Islanders," Houston wrote in *Confessions of an Igloo Dweller*. "We worked to gain the support of Pootoogook and Kiaksuk, those two important elders of the Kingaimiut. I got up my nerve and went and asked Pootoogook to make me an illustration of something he had been trying to explain to me. He did this and sent the results next morning. I asked his son, Kananginak, to help print his father's drawing of two caribou.... Pootoogook greatly admired the result, and after that the whole stone block and stencil printing project was off to a powerful start." That is when Kananginak, age twenty-two, began working for Houston, doing odd jobs and some carving in the art studio and learning the technical aspects of printmaking.

KANANGINAK POOTOOGOOK WAS born on January 1, 1935, in Ikerrasak, a camp located about eighty-five kilometres east of Cape Dorset on Baffin Island. He was the ninth son of more than a dozen children born to Joseph Pootoogook and his wife, Sarah Ningeokuluk.

In winter the Pootoogooks lived in an igloo, but as soon as the snow started to melt, they moved into a canvas tent or a sod house while they trapped foxes to sell the pelts to the Hudson's Bay Company. At its height, Pootoogook's trapline had close to four hundred traps and extended over a long stretch of land from one side of Baffin Island to the other.

When Kananginak was seven, his family moved into its first wooden house, but they still went out on the land every summer. That is the way he imagined his life would be. "All I thought about was growing up to be a man, having a team of fast dogs and being able to get all the game I needed," he recounted in a biographical essay published by the Museum of Inuit Art in 2010. He was still living on the land when he married his wife, Shooyoo, in 1957, but he soon moved his family into Cape Dorset to help care for his father, who by then was old and ill.

At first Kananginak was nervous about drawing. He spent his time making prints and then lithographs of the work of other artists and working to establish the co-op store with Terry Ryan, a newly arrived southerner. Ryan, like Houston, had studied at the Ontario College of Art. He arrived in Cape Dorset aboard the icebreaker *C. D. Howe* in 1960 to take up a summer job working for Houston. Kananginak and Shooyoo provided his accommodation — their own house — while they joined a group of hunters on the land for the season.

Ryan decided to stay in Cape Dorset, accepting the position of general manager of the West Baffin Eskimo Co-operative and its nascent marketing arm, Dorset Fine Arts. He was the first white person ever hired by the Inuit to manage the co-op store. Later he said about Houston in an interview in 2005: "He'd established the nucleus of the co-op. There was one studio, a few drawers of drawings and a group of four men who had the ability to cut and print a stone-cut. But more than anything, he had instilled an enthusiasm in people to put pencil to paper, and prior to that had encouraged people to expand on their carving skills."

Houston, charismatic and dashing in the mode of rakish movie star Errol Flynn, was enormously appealing to women. By 1962 his marriage was foundering. He left Cape Dorset to become a senior designer for Steuben Glass Works, in a move that many found bewildering for a man who had always wanted to escape contemporary urban life.

His wife, Alma, moved south with their sons to Montreal and then to London, England, before returning to Canada and settling in Ottawa in 1965.

There she helped start Canadian Arctic Producers, an Inuit-owned marketing co-operative. Like Ryan, Alma Houston was inspired to carry on and expand the work that Houston had started.

Although the Houstons divorced in 1967 and he subsequently married editor Alice Watson, the duo remained colleagues. In 1981 they opened an Inuit gallery and bookstore in Lunenburg, Nova Scotia, which she operated for many years. She died in 1997 of lung cancer. At the time, their older son, John, told the *Globe* that his father was the spark that had created interest in Inuit art, but his mother was the one who tended the flame.

Although Houston had left the Arctic, it never left him. He returned on visits many times and he often used Arctic animals and landscapes in his own designs. In his more than four decades with Steuben Glass, he created over 120 sculptures and became the first designer the company honoured with a major retrospective exhibit, in 1992. Among his best-known works were *Arctic Fisherman*, a sculpture showing an Inuit fisherman preparing to spear a fish in the water, and *Trout and Fly*, in which a crystal fish leaps to catch a gold fly. He was the first person to introduce the use of gold, silver, and other precious metals to Steuben's glass sculptures. His creation *Aurora Borealis*, a twenty-one-metre work of polished prismatic spears, is on permanent display at the Glenbow Museum in Calgary.

At the same time as Houston was turning images of the North into paintings, drawings, and glass sculptures, he was rising every morning at six to spin his life experience into stories for young people, most of which he also illustrated. A prolific and dramatic storyteller, he wrote screenplays, produced documentary films and animated shorts, and wrote some thirty books, of which the most famous is *The White Dawn*. It was published in eleven languages and later made into a film. The royalties enabled him to cut back on his design work for Steuben, spend more time at his country house in Connecticut, and concentrate on his own projects, especially his burgeoning preoccupation with West Coast Native art. Beginning in the late 1970s, the Houstons spent summers in Haida Gwaii and winters in Stonington, Connecticut. That's where he died from heart disease in a nearby hospital on April 17, 2005, at age eighty-four.

WHILE HOUSTON WAS popularizing the North in stories, films, and glass sculptures, Kananginak was living in the North and finding his way as an artist. Although he had been represented in almost every print release from Cape Dorset since 1959, it wasn't until the early 1970s, when he was in his mid-thirties, that he had the confidence to give up his job in the studio and work full-time on his own art. Once unleashed, he was prolific, making carvings, drawings, and prints and showing his work in museums and commercial galleries.

Unlike other early Cape Dorset artists, such as Kenojuak Ashevak, who are more imaginative and overtly spiritual, Kananginak belongs to a naturalistic and narrative style. He inherited his father's love of drawing and the documentary skills of his paternal uncle, the photographer and historian Peter Pitseolak. He recorded the material culture of the past in detailed drawings of weapons, clothing, and tools, and he chronicled the transition from ancient to modern and the effect of southern communications, travel modes, and social influences on the traditional Inuit way of life. Using a narrative form, he told stories in images of Inuit hunting and fishing, watching television, surfing the Internet, riding snowmobiles, and consuming drugs and alcohol.

As a hunter and a butcher, he understood the anatomy of the creatures that he killed to feed his family; as an artist, he had the ability to transform that appreciation of sinew and muscle into drawings and carvings that captured an animal's essence. Often called the "Audubon of the North," he was particularly good at birds and owls, depicting them so realistically and yet so intuitively that they seem to be staring back at the viewer with a knowing if wary regard. Like the wildlife artist Fenwick Lansdowne, Kananginak captured the essence as well as the form of the creatures he depicted.

From his earliest work, in the initial 1959 release of Cape Dorset prints, to the mural-sized coloured drawings of caribou that he made in the last few years of his life, Kananginak was inspired by both the world around him and the one he carried inside his head. In 1977 the World Wildlife Commission released a limited-edition portfolio of works that included four of his images, and in 1980 he was elected a member of the Royal Canadian Academy of Arts. Governor General Roméo LeBlanc commissioned him to build a nearly six-foot-tall inukshuk in Cape Dorset in 1997, which was then disassembled and shipped to Ottawa, where Kananginak and his son Johnny put it back together again on the grounds of Rideau Hall. He travelled to Vancouver for the Olympics in February 2010, attended the opening of a solo exhibition of his drawings at the Marion Scott Gallery, received the National Aboriginal Achievement Award for the Arts later in the spring, and had another solo exhibition at the Museum of Inuit Art in Toronto from February through May 2010.

Usually Kananginak worked at home, but after he turned seventy he began finding it more physically difficult to carve and decided to work in the Kinngait Studios, where he had toiled as an apprentice more than half a century earlier. Studio manager Bill Ritchie thought he also wanted to spend more time with the art community in town because he had things to say to them. "He was a real gentle soul, always settling disputes, just one of those guys who was always there to help out." The younger artists flocked around him in the studio when he took a break from his own work, according to Ritchie. "Even then he was teaching people how to get along and how to work in groups and not to be isolated and sit by yourself, as so many drawers do," said Ritchie. "It was a real communal experience when he was around."

Much as he gave to the younger artists, he also gained something: the impulse to work on large-scale drawings, as they were doing. These huge pieces represent Kananginak's final artistic flowering. His last, unfinished drawing was a huge depiction of his father's diesel-powered Peterhead, a wooden boat with two masts that was used for hauling soapstone and walrus and whale carcasses. While he was working on it, he was so racked by coughing spells that he often had to stop and hold his chest. He guessed he had lung cancer, and he was correct.

Even when Kananginak was old and sick, he was not only moving in new artistic directions, he was trying to help his people prepare for a future without him. In his most fervent messages he beseeched the Inuit to preserve the Inuktitut language and to keep working together in the co-op. He also warned that if the market for Inuit art looked as though it was going to collapse, they needed to look ahead at what else was out there and plan for the future.

In 2010 he and his wife, Shooyoo, went to Ottawa and moved into Larga Baffin, a facility that houses Inuit people who have come south for medical treatment. He underwent surgery in October, but he never recovered from the operation and he died on November 23, 2010. He was seventy-five.

Celia Franca

Dancer and Founder of the National Ballet of Canada

June 25, 1921 – February 19, 2007

FEBRUARY IS A cruel month, especially in Canada, but neither the howling winds nor the icy snowbanks dissuaded Celia Franca from mounting the biggest performance of her life: the National Ballet of Canada. In February 1951, when Franca stepped onto the tarmac at Toronto's Malton Airport in her Persian lamb coat, she was a twenty-nine-year-old raven-haired British ballerina and choreographer. Along with a suitcase or two she had a reputation as a powerful personality, a dramatic dancer, and a demanding teacher.

What really mattered was less obvious: the delicate, aquiline-nosed, 110-pound, five-foot-four Franca was a risk-taker with steely determination and stratospheric standards. At the time there were only two ballet companies in Canada, the flamboyant and Russian-influenced Volkoff Canadian Ballet and the still largely amateur Winnipeg Ballet. Franca was not impressed by either and chose to model her company on the ones she knew best, Ballet Rambert and the Sadler's Wells Ballet in London.

Luckily for Franca, she arrived at a propitious time. The shoots of a cultural spring were germinating across the country. Canada had helped win the war, our cities had not been bombed, and the men and women who had survived the conflagration overseas had come home buoyed by exposure to European cultural institutions. Many veterans returned with sophisticated ideas to a country that was confident about itself and the future and eager to nurture homegrown talent. Besides the National Ballet, which premiered in

1951, CBC Television launched in 1952, the Stratford Festival and the National Library in 1953, and the Canada Council in 1957.

Franca had barely unpacked before beginning an arduous regimen of recruiting and training dancers, staging promotional promenade concerts, organizing a summer school, and setting off on a national audition tour. All that activity was essential if she was going to whip her uneven but enthusiastic new company into shape for its opening a scant nine months later, on November 12, 1951, at Toronto's Eaton Auditorium.

Word of Franca and the fledgling ballet company spread quickly; there were news reports of four Yugoslavian dancers who had defected with their ballet shoes from behind the recently hung Iron Curtain and stories of British ballerinas who had come here as war brides, wanting to audition for Franca. Her principal male dancer was David Adams, a Canadian whose work she knew from London. He insisted that his wife, Lois Smith, be part of the package. Together Adams and Smith became the stars of the new company — until his roving feet and wandering eye broke up the marriage and he left the company to dance again in England.

The company's debut program at the Eaton Auditorium featured an abundance of Franca, as dancer, choreographer, and artistic director. Writing in the *Globe and Mail*, an ecstatic Herbert Whittaker concluded: "A rousing stamping performance of Kokine's Prince Igor brought to a conclusion the first full-fledged Canadian National Ballet and one left Eaton's auditorium with a happy feeling that Celia Franca had got her dancers off to a strong start." He went on to extol the "quality of the music" that she "had managed to instill in the young dancers from Winnipeg, Edmonton, London, Vancouver, Toronto, and elsewhere west and east. This is a national ballet in those points of origin, and it behaved itself like one last night."

CELIA FRANKS WAS born on June 25, 1921, in the East End of London, England, the second child and only daughter of two Jewish Polish immigrants, Solomon Frankelstein and his wife, Gertrude (née Morris). Her father, who anglicized his name to Franks, made his living as a shoe salesman and then a tailor. His daughter also changed her name — to the more Italian-sounding Franca — shortly after Germany and Britain went to war in 1939.

Even as a small child, Celia wanted to dance, gripping her mother's hand at the cinema when she was "just a tiny tot" and pleading to go on the stage.

At a reception for her aunt's wedding, four-year-old Celia made such a nuisance of herself dancing around the tables that the bandleader told her mother to organize ballet lessons — the first time, Franca said later, she had heard the word that would encompass her life's work.

Her mother followed the bandleader's advice and took Celia to the Guildhall School of Music in London's East End, where she was admitted to study music, dance, theatre, and elocution. As well she absorbed heavy doses of self-discipline and a respect for excellence. She won a scholarship in dancing at six and another in piano when she was eleven, the same year she was awarded a fellowship at the Royal Academy of Dance.

Her father despaired that she would never be able to support herself through dancing, a skepticism that brought out the Franca steel — the same determination she would call upon so many times during her tenure with the National Ballet of Canada. Having heard about *Spread It Abroad*, a musical starring Dorothy Dickson, Hermione Gingold, and Michael Wilding, she showed up at the auditions for chorus girls. She scarcely looked the part, with her straight, dark hair cut in a bob with bangs across her forehead, dressed in her school uniform, her ballet bag slung over her shoulder.

The directors were looking for tap dancers, a skill she had never been taught. Undaunted, she told the pianist to play the same music that the previous applicant had requested — Jerome Kern's "I Won't Dance," from the 1933 musical *Roberta* — and "I just improvised." She got the job, mainly because the choreographer, bored by all the dyed blondes he'd auditioned, looked at her feet instead of her face.

Spread It Abroad, which marked her first appearance at the Saville Theatre, also let her hone her teaching skills by coaching one of the principal actors, who'd been given a little dance number to execute. Her doubting father changed his tune when he learned that his dancing daughter was adding three pounds a week to the family coffers.

She joined the corps de ballet of Ballet Rambert (now the Rambert Dance Company) in early 1937. Founded in 1926, it is the oldest dance company in Britain. She was a soloist and the company's leading dramatic dancer when she joined the Three Arts Ballet in 1939, although she continued to dance for Rambert in their lunchtime ballets during the Blitz. When German planes were spotted over London, the management would hold air-raid warning signs above the orchestra pit. "It was always so satisfying to find that nobody in that audience ever got up to go to the shelter," she said in a CBC interview in

1974. "I can remember saying at that time that I am so glad to have chosen this profession because all you can do is give pleasure to people. You can't kill anybody by dancing on the stage."

In 1941 she became a member of Ninette de Valois's Sadler's Wells Ballet (now the Royal Ballet), where she excelled as a dramatic ballerina in roles such as the Queen in *Hamlet*, the prostitute in *Miracle in the Gorbals*, the Queen of the Wilis in *Giselle*, the spider in *The Spider's Banquet*, and the Prelude in *Les Sylphides*.

After the war she joined Sadler's Wells Theatre Ballet as a choreographer and achieved acclaim by creating the ballet *Khadra*, with an Oriental setting to music by Jean Sibelius. The next year she presented *Bailemos*, with a Spanish motif, and joined Ballets Jooss for its last tour of the European continent, teaching ballet in exchange for training in modern dance. Then she joined the short-lived Metropolitan Ballet Company as a soloist and ballet mistress. It was there that she began choreographing for television, creating the first two ballets — *Eve of St. Agnes* and *Dance of Salomé* — that were ever commissioned by the BBC.

Chance intervened in 1950 when a trio of Canadian balletomanes — Eileen Woods, Sydney Mulqueen, and Pearl Whitehead — sent an envoy to England to ask de Valois's advice on starting a Canadian classical company. She urged them to speak with Franca, describing her as "probably the finest dramatic dancer the 'Wells' ever had." Although some have suggested that de Valois was hoping to rid herself of a potential rival, Franca snapped up the all-expenses-paid invitation to attend the Third Annual Canadian Ballet Festival in November 1950. Three months later she was back in Canada, having left behind a career, a former husband — the dancer and choreographer Leo Kersley — and a devastated postwar Britain. In a leap worthy of a prima ballerina's jeté she embraced the unknown and the chance to create something new in a barren cultural landscape.

Franca got a job as a file clerk at Eaton's to support herself and briefly married Bert Anderson, a keyboard musician and manager of the box office at the Eaton Auditorium. She also forged an alliance with Betty Oliphant, a British war bride, who was the proprietor of a small dance school and a founding member of the Canadian Dance Teachers' Association.

In the company's second season, Franca hired Oliphant as ballet mistress, the beginning of a long and often fractious association. Franca trained her dancers by her own example and in annual summer-school sessions, but she longed for a more intensive training program and argued for the creation of a permanent ballet school at the 1958 annual general meeting. She was supported by the late Eddie Goodman, who had been dragooned onto the board and had chaired the management committee (which usually meant staving off creditors and hitting up his friends for financial contributions) since the ballet's founding. "Without Eddie Goodman, there would be no National Ballet [Company]," Franca said in a 2005 interview.

Even before the school opened its doors in 1959 in a former Quaker meeting house, Goodman recognized that the school and the company should be separate entities, although they were linked through the working relationship between Oliphant, the school's principal, and Franca as the founding director of the school and founder of the company. Today there are still debates about which was the more significant achievement, the school that trained the likes of Karen Kain and Veronica Tennant or the company that cultivated and showcased their talent across the country and in international venues. "Celia Franca had a dream, but I made it a reality," Oliphant sniffed in an interview in 1984, on the twenty-fifth anniversary of the school's founding.

During her twenty-three-year tenure as artistic director, Franca danced leading roles herself and brought in guest artists including Lynn Seymour, Erik Bruhn, and Rudolf Nureyev. Nureyev's lavish $400,000 *The Sleeping Beauty* in 1972 threatened to bankrupt the company, but it attracted international attention, made a star of Karen Kain, the young dancer Nureyev picked to be one of his Auroras, and eventually put the company in the black.

Franca relied on the classics she had learned during her dance career in England, and called up on the choreographic talents of her English friends, such as John Cranko and Antony Tudor. She presented his *Offenbach in the Underworld*, calculating that the racy cancan dance would draw in men who wouldn't normally attend the ballet. She even created ballets herself (*Cinderella* and *The Nutcracker*). In 1973, she and Bruhn collaborated on the National Ballet's classic production of *Les Sylphides*.

The National Ballet nabbed international headlines in the news rather than the arts pages in June 1974, when Mikhail Baryshnikov, the star of the Kirov Ballet, defected in Toronto while on a North American tour. After receiving political asylum, he came out of seclusion to dance *La Sylphide* with Veronica Tenant for the National Ballet. He then moved to the United States, where he joined the American Ballet Theatre.

By then Franca was worrying about defections of a different sort. She had leapt from one financial crisis to another and admitted that she could be a "tyrant." But throughout her time as artistic director, she stressed the importance of developing Canadian choreography, taking more than thirty Canadian ballets into the repertoire and starting the National Ballet's choreographic workshops. She served on the jury of the Fifth International Ballet Competition in Varna, Bulgaria, in 1970 and in the same capacity at the Second International Ballet Competition in Moscow three years later.

Franca also took the company across Canada and the United States and to Mexico, Japan, and Europe, simultaneously creating a strong international reputation and seeing that the company remained worthy of its fame. Performing in the 1970s in London, her old jeté ground, was the highlight of her travels with the company, because it meant that "we have been accepted as an established ballet company and we don't have to run around proving it."

While she had built a company of stellar dancers, she had not created a choreographer of equal merit — a point U.S. critic Clive Barnes made pointedly in 1971 when he opined that the company lacked a "genuine creative spark" and needed "a choreographer as badly as the Sahara needs rain." In retrospect it was obvious that the spark was there in James Kudelka, who arrived at the ballet school as an eleven-year-old boy, danced as a member of the company, left to expand his choreographic opportunities, and then returned as artistic director from 1996 to 2005 — a tenure that saw him mount several of his own ballets, including *The Contract, An Italian Straw Hat, The Actress,* and *The Firebird,* as well as new interpretations of *Swan Lake, The Nutcracker,* and *Cinderella.*

After more than twenty years at the helm, Franca decided to share the artistic directorship with arts administrator David Haber for the 1973–74 season and then to step down, although she insisted later that she had merely wanted a sabbatical. With Franca gone, Oliphant quarrelled with Haber and resigned her position as associate director, which led the board to fire Haber after only a year as artistic director. Franca stepped back into the breach temporarily as artistic director and then stayed on as a teacher and coach until Alexander Grant was appointed to the position in 1976.

By then Franca had moved to Ottawa with her third husband, James Morton, a clarinettist with the National Arts Centre Orchestra, and announced plans to write her memoirs. She returned to the NBC to dance Lady Capulet in *Romeo and Juliet* with Karen Kain and Frank Augustyn, a gala performance of John Cranko's version set to music by Sergei Prokofiev. In 1978 the People's Republic of China invited her to teach and give lectures in Guangzhou, Shanghai, and Beijing, in a tour so successful she was asked back again two years later. Although she continued to live in Ottawa, where she was in demand as a coach and teacher and as co-artistic director of the School of Dance, she returned to the National Ballet to produce a thirty-fifth anniversary gala performance at Toronto's O'Keefe Centre in 1986, and to stage *Judgment of Paris* in 2002.

The "Haber business," as Franca called it, and public bickering over dancer Kimberley Glasco's forced retirement during James Kudelka's era as artistic director caused a major rift between the two prima donnas of Canadian ballet. Oliphant and Franca ceased speaking and publicly traded insults until Franca was able to enjoy the ultimate revenge: outliving Oliphant, who died in July 2004. "Betty became jealous of my position," she said in a 2006 documentary. "She wanted to be the big queen bee and I had made her as big a queen bee as I possibly could. I made her director of the National Ballet School and that was as much as I was prepared to do for Betty."

Her many honours included the Molson Prize and being made a Companion of the Order of Canada. The National Arts Centre organized a gala performance for her eightieth birthday in Ottawa in 2001. The National Ballet School named part of its new facility the Celia Franca Ballet Centre in 2004. Karen Kain, who had succeeded Kudelka as artistic director of the NBC, dedicated the 2005–06 season — the company's first as a principal tenant of the Four Seasons Centre for the Performing Arts — to her mentor.

In August 2006 Franca made an elegant final appearance in Toronto for a screening of *Celia Franca: Tour de Force*, a documentary made by her former dancer Veronica Tennant. Already bedridden after a series of falls and in chronic pain, she arrived — elegant as ever, sitting in a wheelchair as though it were merely a stage prop — at the Carlu, the contemporary update of the Eaton Auditorium, where she had staged the National Ballet's first performance half a century earlier. That was the swan song of the woman who had trained and exhorted generations of young dancers and created an internationally renowned ballet company out of hope, tenacity, and ambition. Back home in Ottawa, her dancer's body was painfully wearing out. Finally she was admitted to hospital, where, after visits with some of her favourite dancers, she quietly died on February 19, 2007. She was eighty-five.

KEN THOMSON

Business Magnate and Art Collector

SEPTEMBER 1, 1923 – JUNE 12, 2006

A MAN OF small economies and grand generosities, media magnate and art collector Kenneth Thomson was Canada's richest man and ninth-wealthiest in the world. When he inherited the Thomson media empire in 1976, many thought that he was merely a pallid version of his father, Roy Thomson, first Lord Thomson of Fleet. In fact, the two men were very different, a fact that the senior Thomson acknowledged to colleagues when he said about his son, "He is so full of goodness he will be successful" in managing the company and looking after the family.

Roy Thomson was a gambler and an opportunist who loved making deals, an extrovert with an ego to match. A barber's son, he started out poor and was in his forties before he achieved financial success. He was almost eighty when he joined the North Sea oil and gas consortium that made him fabulously wealthy in the 1970s.

By contrast, his son was shy, private, extremely modest, and much more focused. Although he was keenly interested in business, Ken Thomson's job, as he saw it, was to serve as steward of the empire on behalf of his family and the shareholders of the Thomson Corporation. "Roy was more the entrepreneur, the tycoon, the guy who saw opportunities and propelled the business beyond anything else. Ken truly was a builder," according to Geoff Beattie, deputy chairman of Thomson and president of the Woodbridge Company Ltd., the Thomson family's private holding company. "In business, people are either traders or builders. Traders are looking for things and trying to move from opportunity to opportunity, whereas Ken was someone who saw opportunities, but more in the context of wanting to stay the course. He was not an impatient guy, because he had tremendous confidence that if you keep doing good things, more good things will happen."

What father and son shared, according to the late John Tory, the lawyer who worked for them both for half a century, was shrewdness and an ability to distinguish between owning a company and running one. Neither Thomson was a micro-manager; both encouraged consensus and risk-taking and were loyal and committed to the professional managers in their employ. "They both realized that you couldn't do everything yourself, so you had to have good people and to provide them with really strong support and to trust them."

After his father's death from a stroke in London in August 1976, Thomson inherited vast holdings and a hereditary title — Baron Thomson of Fleet, of Northbridge in the City of Edinburgh — for which his father had happily renounced his Canadian citizenship a dozen years earlier. Typically, the younger Thomson found a way to remain himself and to accede to his father's wishes. "In London, I'm Lord Thomson. In Toronto, I'm Ken," he told writer David Macfarlane in a profile in *Saturday Night* magazine in 1980. Although Thomson never sat in the House of Lords, he did allow to having two sets of Christmas cards and two sets of stationery, one for each country. Bizarrely, considering Thomson's significance in Canadian life, he was never inducted into the Order of Canada or the Business Hall of Fame.

Thomson moved the crux of the family's operations back across the Atlantic to North America and transformed the corporation from a print-based media conglomerate to a Web-based provider of information and services. In the process, he increased the company's value exponentially, from about US$500 million in 1976 to roughly $29 billion by 2006, with a personal fortune of about $20 billion.

During his tenure, Thomson sold off most of the company's newspaper holdings, including the *Times* and the *Sunday Times*, prestigious but tempestuous and money-losing British newspapers, and acquired FP Publications, which included the *Globe and Mail*, a local flagship with a national reach that had always eluded his father. Thomson's ownership of the *Globe* was diluted in a corporate merger in 2001 with CTV and Bell and their subsidiaries and partners. That changed nine years later, when the Thomson family bought back a majority interest in the *Globe and Mail* in September 2010. Observers could sense the friendly if ghostly presence of Ken Thomson on the day of the announcement as Thomson's widow, Marilyn, his son David, the current chair of the global company, and his closest colleagues, Beattie and Tory, trooped into a crowded meeting room at the newspaper. "It was a dream," David Thomson said later about the repurchase of the media company that had been intrinsic to three generations of his family.

Thomson the Collector

Stories of Thomson's frugality abound, from watching the parking meter run out before feeding it more coins to sorting through the bargain bins for socks and pushing a cart up and down the aisles checking the cost of produce in his local grocery store. Although he seemed unwilling to spend money on himself — his suits were serviceable rather than elegant — he was willing to dig deep to indulge his passion for Canadian and European art.

In the same way that he refined his family's business holdings, he pruned and buffed his collection of paintings by Cornelius Krieghoff, the Group of Seven, and David Milne, among other landscape artists, and his assemblage of European ceramics, ivory miniatures, and other artifacts. In building this art collection he created his personal legacy. "I like business," he once said, "but I feel the same way about art that my father felt about business."

What propelled Thomson as a collector was a visceral reaction to something that pleased him aesthetically. He set about learning more about the artists he admired, studying their techniques and acquiring paintings that complemented each other. Collecting for him was more than a hobby; it was a process of discovery and self-education that he loved to share with friends such as John Band.

"I wish I knew the first time I shook his hand," Thomson said in an interview after Band's death in 2005. "I think it was in the mid-fifties and it must have been about art." For half a century the two men discussed upcoming auction sales, although their friendship meant they never bid against each other. "He was always around the corner from my house and up here," Thomson said, tapping his forehead with his finger. "I never got along with anybody better."

These were also the years when Thomson made his first forays into collecting by scouring shops in Chinatown for carvings and curios. He moved on to genre paintings, buying his first Krieghoff in 1950, only realizing several years and many acquisitions later that he had developed a passion for the artist. Whenever Band was "adamant" about a picture, such as *Steamship Quebec*, painted by Cornelius Krieghoff in 1853, "I jolly well bought it. There wasn't going to be any doubt about that," Thomson admitted. In 1966, the same year his father bought the *Times*, he "made a decision to go strongly for Krieghoffs. I changed from a casual acquirer to an aggressive collector."

But it was not until he met Hermann Baer, an antique dealer in London, that Thomson became a serious as well as a passionate collector. A seventeenth-century ivory and ebony crucifix in the window of Baer's store drew him inside one day in 1959. "He showed me some things, beautiful things," Thomson told the *Globe* in 2003, "but he told me I was not yet ready for them. He was showing them, he said, to the Ashmolean Museum in Oxford."

Baer helped Thomson refine his tastes, encouraging him to move boldly in pursuit of ivory and boxwood carvings, Baroque goblets, enamels, miniature portraits, and mementos mori. When Baer died in 1977, Thomson made some of his most significant acquisitions from the dealer's estate. Two of the objects Thomson cradled in his hands back in 1959 — a boxwood Madonna and Child and a carved ivory depiction of Saint George slaying the dragon, are now in the Thomson collection. So is the ivory and ebony crucifix that Baer wanted the Ashmolean to have.

In 2005 Thomson gave his friend Band a small J. E. H. MacDonald painting of his family's island in Georgian Bay as a ninetieth-birthday gift. Knowing the value of the painting, Band refused to accept it, although he delighted in pointing out familiar landmarks. Finally he agreed to "borrow" the painting after attaching a note to the back saying it belonged to Thomson. When Band died shortly afterwards, the painting went back to Thomson, now layered with "priceless" sentimental value. Thomson hung it in his office and arranged for it to become part of his planned gift to the Art Gallery of Ontario.

Others have given away a greater percentage of their fortunes, but the size of Thomson's personal gift to the art gallery — more than three thousand works of art, valued in 2012 at approximately US$500 million, plus C$100 million in cash — is without precedent in Canadian history. He died two years before the acclaimed addition designed by Toronto-born architect Frank Gehry opened in 2008. The loss of such a dedicated and involved partner was devastating to AGO director Matthew Teitelbaum, who missed Thomson's "incredible focus" and the "sparkle" of his conversation as the project progressed to completion. Once he had made the commitment to share his treasures, Thomson changed his approach to collecting, according to Teitelbaum. "I don't want to acquire things that I just happen to like. I am going to acquire things that make the collection better," he remembered Thomson saying.

As in business, when Thomson increased expenditures to enhance well-developed initiatives, he bumped up his donations to the AGO. In 2002 he bought Peter Paul Rubens's *Massacre of the Innocents* at a Sotheby's auction in London for close to C$120 million. "I call it an electrifying painting," he told the *Globe* at the time about the work. "How do you paint a painting like that — with such a gruesome subject — without it being totally off-putting? Its horror is obscured by its aesthetics. I find that extraordinary." Today the painting is prominently displayed in the AGO, attracting visitors to the gallery and giving ordinary people, who could never afford a Rubens, an insight into the painting, the artist, and the collector.

Early Days

KENNETH ROY THOMSON was born on Isabella Street in Toronto on September 1, 1923, the only son and youngest of Roy and Edna (née Irvine) Thomson's three children. He was descended from Archibald Thomson, a master carpenter, and David Thomson, a mason, two of three Scottish-born brothers who came with their families from Niagara to York, as Toronto was then called, in 1797. David Thomson built Upper Canada's first parliament buildings on Front Street, as well as the stone powder magazine at Fort York — probably his only surviving building.

For a man who ended up fabulously wealthy, Thomson's childhood was far from luxurious. His father was an itinerant salesman who struggled to make enough money to pay the rent and feed his family of five. The Thomsons moved to Ottawa in 1925 and to North Bay three years later, always in search of more lucrative employment.

When young Ken started school in North Bay, his father was away for days at a time, travelling by train to Cobalt, New Liskeard, Timmins, Cochrane, Sudbury, and Sault Ste. Marie to sell radios, auto parts, washing machines, and refrigerators. "He was always busy with various projects, travelling the North, selling, arranging things. He would often come home late at night," Thomson told *Saturday Night*. "My mother would try to keep his dinner warm. We all knew he was a big worker, but it was difficult sometimes."

But life wasn't all loneliness and watching his father read the newspaper ("every inch of it"). He was, and remained, very close to his two older sisters. When he talked about his childhood in an interview with the *Globe* in 2003, he described a life of riding bicycles, exploring the woods, and fishing for pickerel in the summers and skating on the frozen lake in winter. He credited those halcyon memories for his later fascination with Cornelius Krieghoff and the Group of Seven.

It was his mother who kindled his appreciation for music and painting. "Art almost bemused my father," he said. "With music, the most serious thing he liked were Strauss waltzes. He liked people like Irving Berlin. But even then, if you were driving in the car, he was always fishing for news on the dial, even though it was the same news on every station. You could say he was obsessed with it."

Selling radio parts was tough in an area where reception was so dismal that listening was a frustration rather than a pleasure. Undaunted, Roy Thomson paid one dollar for a broadcasting licence, bought a fifty-watt transmitter on three months' credit, and started CFCH, his first radio station, in North Bay in 1931. "I was eight years old and radios were still exciting things," his son recalled. "All I really knew was that something big was going on in town and that Dad was at the middle of it all." Soon his father had bought radio station CKGB in Timmins and followed up that purchase by moving into print, acquiring the Timmins *Daily Press* in 1934, in the depths of the Depression.

The family moved back to Toronto in 1937, when Ken was fourteen. By then he was aware that his father was "really rolling." He went to Upper Canada College, the elite private school, as a day boy. An average student and definitely not a jock, he was not part of the in-crowd. "I didn't give it much of a chance," he said later. "I was a little bit different from the other guys." When he was sixteen, he worked as a disc jockey at CFCH for a summer.

He graduated from UCC in 1942 and registered that fall at the University of Toronto, but dropped out in December to join the RCAF. He was nineteen when he was shipped overseas. After working as an instrument mechanic he was posted to London, where he rewrote news articles for an Air Force magazine called *Wings Abroad*.

After the war, Thomson took a degree in economics and law at St. John's

College, Cambridge University. Back in Canada, he began learning his father's business from the bottom up, working as a cub reporter for the Timmins *Daily Press* in 1947. A year later he went to Galt (now Cambridge, Ontario) as an advertising salesman for the *Daily Reporter* before serving as general manager of the newspaper from 1950 to 1953.

Transatlantic Dynamics

Two years after Thomson's mother died in 1952, his father packed up and moved to Scotland. By then he had begun making acquisitions that would include the *Scotsman*, Scottish Television (a franchise he would later equate with "a licence to print money"), the *Times* of London (a debt-ridden colossus that was rife with labour unrest), the *Sunday Times*, and an interest in North Sea oil and gas. When he joined the consortium along with J. Paul Getty and Armand Hammer in 1971, oil sold for less than a dollar (US) a barrel; at his death five years later, it was close to thirty dollars.

While his father was buying and selling abroad, Ken Thomson stayed in Toronto as president and chairman of Thomson Newspapers, which became a public company in 1965. He had married Marilyn Lavis, a model whose picture he had seen in an Eaton's catalogue in 1956. Together they raised two sons — David, born in 1957, and Peter, in 1965 — and a daughter, Lesley (now known as Taylor), born in 1959.

By the time Roy Thomson died in 1976, the company was worth about $500 million and was publishing 110 daily newspapers in North America. "Ken immediately identified that the future was going to be about trust and stewardship and patience and it wasn't about Ken being able to go off with the assets and fulfill his own dream of being an entrepreneur," said Beattie. "These were his dad's assets. 'Everything we have today,' Ken would say, 'was because of my father.'"

Immediately after his succession, Thomson wrote to shareholders to reassure them that their investment was safe because of the quality and dedication of the people running the myriad Thomson companies. "Successful businesses are sustained by people — men and women who contribute their time, their skill, their energy and their ideas to the development of a living, breathing, expanding enterprise.... Without them, no business amounts to more than a collection of buildings, machines and paper assets."

Within two years of his father's death he formed the International Thomson Organization, with its headquarters in Toronto and two main operating subsidiaries in the United Kingdom and the United States. John Tory became deputy chairman. Now, instead of acquiring newspapers as he had done under Roy Thomson, Tory was seeking out specialized information companies.

Tory, who had worked closely with Roy Thomson since the mid-1950s, made a seamless transition to working with his former boss's son. The relationship was different but it was equally close. They were more of an age and they established a great rapport, which David Thomson compared to the prolific scoring duo of Wayne Gretzky and Jari Kurri with the Edmonton Oilers in the 1980s. "They knew where each other was, where the puck was, and where the opposition would be," he said. "My father was able to do pretty much what he was consummate at, which was leading people; but he needed John's support to précis and present ideas and possibilities."

The Newspaper Wars

LABOUR DISPUTES AND wildcat strikes at the Times newspapers in London provoked Thomson into suspending publication of both the *Times* and the *Sunday Times* in December 1978. The lockout lasted nearly a year and cost the company nearly £70 million. Later admitting that the ploy was a "disaster," Thomson said, "You don't go into something unless you can see how it's going to come out. We did, when we couldn't. Our problem was that we paid the journalists throughout and so nobody believed us when we said we would close the papers for good...There was no realism about our handling of the dispute."

In October 1980 the company put the newspapers up for sale and Australian media magnate Rupert Murdoch made a low but successful offer of £14 million on February 13, 1981. Thomson insisted that he never regretted selling the *Times*. "We had to get on with our own lives, and we did, and rebuilt the company. I'm sure if my father came back today, he would understand."

The bruising from the sale of the *Times* was soothed by the acquisition of FP Publications in Canada in 1980, with its flagship newspaper the *Globe and Mail* as well as the *Winnipeg Free Press* and the *Ottawa Journal*, among other titles, for C$165 million. The purchase brought the company's share of

English-language daily newspaper circulation in Canada to about 26 percent, with daily sales topping a million.

The Thomsons may have been happy with their new newspapers, but many Canadians were afraid that the country had been split between two rival newspaper chains, owned by the Thomson and the Southam families. This fear became even more acute on August 27, 1980, when Thomson Newspapers closed the *Ottawa Journal* and the Southam family simultaneously shut down the *Winnipeg Tribune*, leaving both of those cities with only one daily newspaper.

Radio and television had been eroding print's share of the marketplace for decades. In the early part of the twentieth century, at least five hundred towns in North America had at least two rival newspapers. By 1978 only thirty-five towns could make that boast. Pierre Trudeau's Liberal government appointed the Royal Commission on Newspapers in 1980, under the chairmanship of Tom Kent, a British-born journalist, former editor of the *Winnipeg Free Press*, and policy adviser to former prime minister Lester Pearson. It recommended that chain ownership in the future should be limited to twenty percent of national circulation, but a bill to that effect died on the order paper in 1983.

Nevertheless, both Thomson Newspapers and Southam were charged with two counts of criminal conspiracy to reduce competition and with criminal merger. John Tory and Southam head Gordon Fisher were named as co-conspirators under the federal Combines Investigation Act. They were eventually acquitted when Mr. Justice William Anderson accepted defence arguments that the closings of the *Ottawa Journal* and the *Winnipeg Tribune* were the result of independent decisions based on the state of the marketplace, and not the consequence of collusion.

Thomson never again purchased a major Canadian newspaper. Instead he looked south of the border for new print acquisitions, eventually becoming the owner of more dailies in the United States than any other corporate entity. By 1989 Thomson Newspapers had annual revenues in excess of US$1 billion. To make its financial resources available to the wider Thomson group of companies, Thomson Newspapers was merged with its sister company, the International Thomson Organization Ltd., to form the Thomson Corporation, with Thomson continuing as chairman of the new company and Tory as deputy chairman.

The 1990s were a decade of refocusing and restructuring the corporation into strategic marketing groups. The U.K. newspapers were sold, and the move into the professional and reference fields — which had begun in 1987 with the purchase of legal publishers in the U.K., Canada, and Australia — continued with the acquisition of West Publishing in 1996, a company best known for its Westlaw online research services and databases.

This trend — to be global in scope, electronic in nature, and aimed primarily at the business and professional marketplace — accelerated after Richard Harrington became president and CEO of the Thomson Corporation in 1997. By the turn of the century Thomson Travel had been sold, and so had all of the community newspapers that had been the original source of the company's wealth.

Canada was a battlefield in the late 1990s in a huge and acrimonious national newspaper war between the *Globe and Mail* and the *National Post*, which had been launched in October 1998 by Conrad Black. By 2001, Black, faced with mounting legal and financial woes, had sold the *Post* to the Winnipeg-based Asper family. The *Globe* had triumphed in the war, in the view of rival John Honderich, then publisher of the *Toronto Star*, because "Conrad Black underestimated Ken Thomson's resolve." He once suggested this to Thomson over a drink at the SkyDome in Toronto, and Thomson's face lit up with a gentle smile. "I rather thought so myself," said the magnate, in a rare moment of self-satisfaction.

RETIREMENT

IN 2002 THOMSON, by then in his late seventies, stepped down as head of the Thomson Corporation, the conglomerate he had run for forty years, in favour of his elder son, David. He kept his position as chair of Woodbridge, the family holding company, and continued to work with Teitelbaum on the expansion of the AGO and the massive gift he was planning to make to the art gallery. He also strategically expanded his collection, acquiring Paul Kane's *Scene in the Northwest: Portrait of John Henry Lefroy* and Rubens's *Massacre of the Innocents*.

Even though he was retired, he stuck to his routine of heading to the office on weekdays. That's what he did on June 12, an ordinary early summer morning in 2006. He completed his exercise routine at his downtown club and then, along with one of his beloved dogs, took the elevator to the fifth floor of the Thomson Building, at Queen and Bay Streets in Toronto. He went into his office, which looks west towards Osgoode Hall and north over Finnish architect Viljo Revell's mushroom-shaped city hall, and sat, as usual, at his modern glass desk. Perhaps he fondled a few of the small ivory carvings that rested there, glanced at a picture of himself on a see-saw with one of his granddaughters, or looked around the room at some of his favourite paintings hanging on the walls — an Emily Carr, a small Lawren Harris, the J. E. H. MacDonald that he had tried to give to his friend John Band, a large William Kurelek, and a Jean-Paul Riopelle.

Then he got up and headed towards the hall to speak to his assistant. On the way he suffered a heart attack and collapsed. It was about 7:45 a.m. In a year when he had lost two of his closest friends — Steve Stavro, former owner of Knob Hill Farms and the Toronto Maple Leafs, and Band, his art-collecting pal — Thomson died as he had lived, quietly and without fuss. He was eighty-two.

BERTHA WILSON

Lawyer and Supreme Court Judge

SEPTEMBER 18, 1923 – APRIL 28, 2007

H AD BERTHA WILSON meekly followed the patriarchal advice handed down to her when she inquired about doing a law degree in the mid-1950s, the Canadian judicial system might have looked very different today. "Madam, we have no room here for dilettantes. Why don't you just go home and take up crocheting," Horace E. Read, the dean of the law school at Dalhousie University barked at her when the minister's wife and former schoolteacher appeared before him, seeking admission to the school in the fall of 1954. He finally relented, according to Madam Justice Wilson, who recounted the story in a rare interview with journalist Sandra Gwyn in *Saturday Night* magazine in 1985. "From my very first day of classes, I knew the law was my thing," she said. "I just soaked it up like a sponge."

Wilson was the first woman appointed a judge of the Ontario Court of Appeal, in 1975, and the first woman to sit on the Supreme Court of Canada. Like most professions, the law was slow to welcome women into its ranks. There were no female barristers in Ontario until Clara Brett Martin was called to the bar in 1897, three decades after Confederation. By the time Wilson was named a Queen's Counsel, almost two centuries later, there were still fewer than three hundred female lawyers in the province; it would be another decade before the Law Society of Upper Canada, the self-governing body for lawyers in Ontario, elected Laura Legge as its first female treasurer (head), in 1983. A new century would have to dawn before one of Wilson's younger colleagues, Beverley McLachlin, became the first woman appointed Chief Justice of the Supreme Court.

In Wilson's day, women had to find not only their own bathrooms but their own niches within corporate firms. She did it by becoming a lawyer's lawyer and establishing a sub-specialty in estate planning, especially in drawing up wills for the wives of wealthy clients at Osler, Hoskin & Harcourt in Toronto. Her forte was research, preparing legal documents, analyzing judgements and statutes, and setting up a nimble information-retrieval system in the days before Quicklaw and LexisNexis. Her diligence and organizing skills enabled her to solve tangled legal questions so adroitly that her billable hours diminished alarmingly, much to the distress of some senior partners.

Her ascendancy as a jurist owes something to circumstance: she had an enlightened husband and no children. John Wilson did the shopping and the cooking and he was proud of his wife's intellect and her ambition. The intensely private Bertha Wilson never revealed if her lack of offspring was a deliberate choice or a personal sorrow, but it gave her the opportunity to pursue legal studies and to work diligently at a career outside the home.

Timing also played an auspicious role for Wilson. She was appointed to the Ontario Court of Appeal in 1975 in a dynamic era of family law reform. Marriage and parenting were being redefined as economic partnerships in which both parties had rights as well as responsibilities. Patriarchal and prejudicial relationships in the workplace and in the home, which had been immutable for centuries, were suddenly open to interpretations based on new readings of legal arguments and current definitions of social, sexual, and racial discrimination.

The same was true of her appointment to the Supreme Court of Canada. She was sworn in on March 30, 1982, less than three weeks before the Queen arrived in Canada to sign into law the Charter of Rights and Freedoms. Consequently, her period on the bench was a pivotal time during which the definitions of individual and collective rights and freedoms were tested, from a woman's right to abortion to spousal battering as a defence for murder to a refugee claimant's right to be heard.

Her stance as a triple outsider — as a woman, an immigrant, and the child of a lower-middle-class family — gave her a different perspective from many of her legally and socially connected male colleagues. An independent thinker and a socialist, she was highly principled, with a ramrod integrity. "It's her sense and her sensibility," Gwyn explained, "a kind of practical sensitivity tinged with Scottish asperity, enriched but by no means defined by her genes."

Wilson had the courage to avoid consensus and to speak her mind. Although she didn't consider herself a feminist, she believed in equality and fairness. Known as the "Great Dissenter," she was a prolific writer who wielded an eloquent pen and frequently took minority positions on the Court when it would have been much easier to conform to the views expressed by colleagues. "Bertha was very often out in left field" and "she was stubborn as a mule," her fellow judge Antonio Lamer told *Globe and Mail* reporter Kirk Makin in 2002.

"It was not just her brilliant mind, which was remarkable in its rigour, it was the serendipitous presence of Bertha Wilson and Brian Dickson on the Supreme Court of Canada," Madam Justice Rosalie Abella said after Wilson's death on April 28, 2007. "I call them the Fred and Ginger of the Charter. They gave it the muscular interpretation that launched the Charter in its first decade," especially in contrast to the legalistically anemic Bill of Rights that preceded it. Speaking of the jurisprudence that Judge Wilson developed, Abella said that her commitment to fairness was "unshakeable" and her legacy was "profound" in many areas.

That's not to suggest that Wilson's appointment to the bench by Prime Minister Pierre Trudeau was met with enthusiasm or even equanimity. "The 'establishment' in the Ontario legal community was shameless in making the case that she wasn't 'ready,'" Eddie Goldenberg, then special constitutional advisor to justice minister Jean Chrétien, wrote in his memoir *The Way It Works: Inside Ottawa*. "Even Chief Justice Bora Laskin, who had his own preferred candidate at the time, made that argument very vociferously to Prime Minister Trudeau."

From the beginning, it was the study, not the practice of law that intrigued Wilson. Even so, she brought a quotidian rather than an abstract focus to legal issues that enabled her to see the practical consequences of legal decisions. Her logical mind would have made her stand out at any time, but it made her especially significant in an era of landmark rulings that reshaped Canadian society. She led the way for all Canadians — and that included women and First Nations — to be equal in private and professional life.

BERTHA WILSON WAS the only daughter and the youngest of Archibald and Christina (née Noble) Wernham's three children. She was born on September

18, 1923, in Kirkcaldy, Scotland, an industrial town on the north side of the Firth of Forth. Although her patriotic parents, who had served as a soldier and a nurse in the First World War, never finished high school, they valued education and had high academic expectations for their children. Her father, a commercial traveller for a stationery firm, was rarely home during the week, so her ambitious mother was the prime disciplinarian.

The Wernhams moved to Aberdeen when Bertha was three. After primary school she went to Aberdeen Central Secondary School and then followed her two older brothers, Archibald and James, to the University of Aberdeen. After graduating with a master's degree in 1944, she went to the local teachers' training college, earning her certificate in 1945. Despite her mother's objections, she married John Wilson, a Presbyterian minister, a pacifist, a socialist, and a close friend of her brother Jim, on December 14, 1945. She was twenty-one; he was twenty-five.

After four years of ministering to the community of Macduff, a fishing village on the northern coast of Aberdeenshire, the Wilsons both wanted to escape the ingrained attitudes of their parishioners. Canada, with its postwar opportunities, beckoned, not least because her brother Jim and his family had settled there. In 1949 the Wilsons sailed across the Atlantic on a converted troop carrier to take up a "call" from a Presbyterian congregation in Renfrew, in the Ottawa Valley.

Yet more waves of change were about to buffet them. John Wilson had come to regret his vocal pacifism during the Second World War and his refusal to serve in the Armed Forces. After forging a close friendship with the Presbyterian Chaplain of the Fleet for the Royal Canadian Navy, Wilson agreed to enlist late in 1951 to serve as an RCN chaplain in the Korean War. His six-year stint meant separation for the Wilsons and an opportunity for her to move to Ottawa, where she found a job working for two dentists — the first time she had worked independently of her husband's vocation — and then to settle in Halifax, her husband's home base, where once again she had no official duties related to his work.

Having convinced Dean Horace Read that she was not a dilettante, Wilson, along with five other female students, enrolled in first-year law in 1954. He was so pleased with her response to an exam question at the end of the first term that he read it aloud, adding the comment "I think I'll make a lawyer of you yet," according to Ellen Anderson's biography, *Judging Bertha Wilson: Law as Large as Life*.

Wilson graduated three years later, ranking seventh out of fifty-eight students, tying for the Smith Shield in legal argument, earning the respect of her professors for the intensity of her scholarly curiosity, and winning a graduate scholarship to Harvard. Once again the crusty Read dissuaded her. "There will never be women academics teaching in law schools, not in your day," he insisted.

Despite her stellar grades, Wilson's age and the paucity of her local contacts made it difficult for her to win an articling position. She finally found a place with a local criminal lawyer after her corporate law professor interceded on her behalf. When her husband's naval appointment expired in 1958, the couple, who by then had left the Presbyterian Church for the more liberal United Church, moved to Toronto. That's where John Wilson had accepted, almost on a whim, a job as an interdenominational fundraiser.

Wilson, who had been called to the Nova Scotia bar but had not yet practised as a full-fledged lawyer, had to article again in Ontario and write the examinations for bar admission. First, though, she had to find a firm willing to take her on as a student. After looking up law firms in the Yellow Pages, she cold-called Osler, Hoskin & Harcourt. They grudgingly took her on after a stern admonishment that there was no possibility she would be hired after her call to the bar. She was thirty-five, a decade older than most articling students.

Once again, intelligence, hard work, and superior organizing abilities won the day. By the time she was called to the bar in May 1959, she had become indispensible for the depth and breadth of her legal research and her cross-referencing of client files and government statutes. Osler's offered her a permanent position, the first female lawyer they had ever hired. She was made a partner in 1968 and a Queen's Counsel in 1973, but she never became a senior partner or a member of the management committee.

Just before Christmas of 1975, Ron Basford, then the Liberal minister of justice, surprised Wilson — and many of her colleagues — by inviting her to become the first woman justice on the Ontario Court of Appeal. At her swearing in a month later, she said: "I hope you will forgive me if I confess an element of unreality," going on to explain that she had never argued a case in court or "practised law in the way most solicitors practise." She was not apologizing for her lack of litigation experience. On the contrary, she pointed out that the nature of her experience had helped her to remember that "people and the law are inextricably intertwined, and that the role of the profession is essentially to serve the needs of the people." True to her word, she made a fact-finding tour of Ontario prisons so that she could see for herself "exactly where we were sending people."

In an era of huge advances in family law, her rulings on the Court of Appeal soon attracted the attention of lawyers and judges across the country, especially those who advanced the rights of women. She never pictured herself as a feminist lawyer and shied away from minority groups attempting to cling to her legal gown. Nevertheless, she ruled in favour of the divorced common-law wife of a beekeeper, arguing that she was entitled to a half-share in the business they had built up and run together; she wrote a minority opinion in favour of a girl who was denied a place on a boys' softball team simply because she was a girl; she found in favour of an East Indian mathematician who claimed she had been discriminated against in job interviews because of her race and wanted to sue in a civil action and claim damages. In all of these cases Wilson found intriguing and innovative legal arguments, no doubt the product of all those years in the research department of Osler's.

From the beginning of her term on the Supreme Court of Canada in 1982, she wielded a persuasive pen. When the Court widened the legal meaning of self-defence, Wilson was the author of the court's unanimous decision restoring the jury acquittal of a battered woman who had shot her boyfriend in the back of the head after she had been subjected to years of physical abuse. In rejecting out of hand a man's historically sanctioned right to own and discipline a woman, she wrote: "A man's home may be his castle, but it is also a woman's home — even if it seems more like a prison in the circumstances."

In the case of Dr. Henry Morgentaler, while other judges ruled on procedural grounds, she wrote in favour of a woman's constitutional right to choose to have an abortion. "It is not just a medical decision. It is a profound social and ethical one as well. It asserts that the woman's capacity to reproduce is to be subject not to her control, but to that of the state." In her written opinion in *Regina v. Singh*, a case in which she argued that refugee claimants had the right to oral hearings, she wrote: "The guarantees of the Charter would be illusory if they could be ignored because it was administratively inconvenient." The ramifications of that decision, which have led to its own inconveniences in appeals and administrative costs, are still hotly debated.

Wilson retired from the Supreme Court on January 4, 1991, at the age of sixty-seven, eight years before the mandatory retirement age of seventy-five. She cited "diminished energy" as her main reason and said she was looking forward to living a more normal domestic life. In fact she had suffered from high blood pressure for thirty years and had been plagued with arthritis and a series of other health issues. There were other reasons that weren't publicized at the time. Her great colleague Brian Dickson had retired six months earlier, and she was troubled by what she later described as the cliquish behaviour of some of her male colleagues. "People would spend long periods in each other's rooms, arguing about changes and amendments, and so on and so forth," she told her biographer Ellen Anderson. "You might not know anything about this, of course...So there was never any kind of opportunity to explain why you didn't think that was a sound addition, or a sound subtraction. The first thing you knew was that a group had now formed."

Wilson had been an assiduous judge, having signed her name to more than 160 decisions, including at least fifty rulings under the Charter, and delivered some sixty-odd major speeches. The Royal Society of Canada elected her a fellow in 1991, she was appointed a Companion of the Order of Canada the following year, and she continued to add to her collection of honorary degrees — nearly fifty in total.

She may have stepped down from the Supreme Court, but she was certainly not ready "to sip Campari on the Riviera," as she herself ruefully admitted. She had become enmeshed in two contentious and unwieldy projects, one within the legal profession and the other without. She agreed to chair the Canadian Bar Association's Task Force on Women in the Legal Profession. The report, which was called *Touchstones*, let the legal profession know that women faced the same inequities before the bar as they did in other professions.

Many more women were graduating from law schools, but alarming numbers were leaving the profession. Conclusions about discrimination both before the bar and on the bench and recommendations that changes be made in the brutal system of billable hours to accommodate female lawyers with young children caused a furor within the profession. The stress of raising funds and staffing the commission, researching and writing the report, and then dealing with the acrimonious backlash caused Wilson considerable anguish.

Almost simultaneously with the Task Force, she accepted an appointment from Prime Minister Brian Mulroney to the Royal Commission on Aboriginal Peoples. The three-year mandate was to work with "Canada's aboriginal peoples," conducting hearings into their grievances and their social and economic problems, and to find a way forward "so that they can control their own lives, contribute to Canadian prosperity and can share fully in it." This was a thornier issue than any she had encountered on the bench. The Commission took five years to complete its report, years of extensive travel, gruelling hearings, eye-opening horror at the sufferings indigenous people had endured, cost overruns, internal staffing issues, and despair that much could be changed.

By the time the report was delivered, Mulroney had retired from active politics and Jean Chrétien's Liberals were in power. For many it seemed too little, too late, but Jane Stewart, the minister of Indian affairs, did offer the First Nations a statement of reconciliation — not apology — in a ceremony on Parliament Hill in January 1998. Stewart also presented an action plan amounting to $600 million over four years, much less than the $2 billion a year the commissioners had recommended.

Frustrating and depleting as it had been to wrestle the final report into submission and to withstand the fractiousness of the deliberations, Wilson found the process illuminating and reaffirming, especially in the way it nurtured the ongoing negotiations for the Nisga'a and Delgamuukw Treaties and the establishment of Nunavut. In many ways the royal commission was the culmination of her judicial activism on behalf of fairness and justice.

As the century turned, Wilson retreated more and more from public life as the fogginess of Alzheimer's disease gradually destroyed her virtuosity. With her faithful husband of sixty-one years by her side, she died at Rideau Place on-the-River in Ottawa on April 28, 2007. She was eighty-three.

ROBERT SALTER

Orthopedic Surgeon

DECEMBER 15, 1924 – MAY 10, 2010

A S A BOY, Robert Salter dreamed of becoming a medical missionary in China, Africa, or India, healing the sick and spreading his practical Christian faith, patient by patient and soul by soul. Instead he followed a different path to the same vocation — as a surgeon, innovator, and teacher. Instead of working as a solitary doctor in the field, he changed the nature and practice of pediatric orthopedic surgery around the world. Besides treating his own small patients at Toronto's Hospital for Sick Children, he invented surgical methods and equipment that revolutionized orthopedic surgery, travelled extensively to impart his medical know-how in more than thirty countries, and trained hundreds of doctors from abroad who came specifically to study under him so that they could take his mentoring, his procedures, and his practices home with them.

Salter grew up in an era when polio was a prevalent childhood illness. Dealing with its ravages was a major preoccupation of pediatric surgeons. Salter realized early on that the correct intervention at the appropriate moment — while a child was still growing and developing — could make a lifelong difference between permanent disability and mobility, between dependence and independence.

During a more than fifty-year career as a pediatric orthopedic surgeon, he developed a surgical procedure to fix congenital deformities of the hip. It was called the Salter innominate osteotomy for hip dysplasia (although he preferred to call it the "no name, no fame" operation). Salter overrode centuries of medical theory that said broken limbs needed to be immobilized in rigid casts for prolonged periods; he invented a post-operative apparatus called the continuous passive motion (CPM) machine, which has improved post-surgery recovery for at least nine million patients. Besides the Salter-Harris classification of growth plate injuries, he wrote the authoritative orthopedic *Textbook of Disorders and Injuries of the Musculoskeletal System*, which is used throughout the world. Salter was making revisions for the fifth edition when he died, aged eighty-five, from complications of Parkinson's disease in Toronto on May 10, 2010.

But Salter wasn't all theory and medical practice. He loved to paint with oils and had such an obsessive interest in heraldry that he designed coats of arms for most of the institutions and clubs to which he belonged, including the Hospital for Sick Children. He liked to wear a Sherlock Holmes–style deerstalker cap and a holster under his suit jacket for his pipe while he drove around town in a 1949 Allard sports car — with his foot to the floor and the top down, no matter the weather. The car was so sleek and so low-slung that he could drive under parking barriers, and he kept it up until he reluctantly pulled the key out of the ignition in the mid-1980s because spare parts had become scarce.

Famous for treating poor kids for free and for dealing with his young patients as equals, Salter always ended his consultations with the mantra "friends for life." That included Garth Drabinsky, the disgraced impresario, who had contracted polio in 1953, when he was three years old. Drabinsky went under Salter's knife six times — "my entire childhood," he writes in his memoir, *Closer to the Sun*. Although he hated walking into Salter's office because he knew it meant "another procedure, another operation, another summer in hell" of surgery, recovery, and physiotherapy, Drabinsky never forgot the kindly doctor who did his best to help him walk like other kids. Forty years later, Salter wrote a personal letter on Drabinsky's behalf before the former head of Livent and convicted felon came up for sentencing in August 2009. For once the good doctor couldn't perform a miracle: Drabinsky was handed a seven-year prison term.

Another of Salter's patients was Colleen Beanish, later a special-education consultant with the Ottawa Catholic School Board. Born in 1961 in Ottawa with a congenital dislocated hip, she was confined in a body cast from eighteen months until she turned three. By the time she was ten she was limping and in pain. After a failed procedure she was sent to Salter. "I trusted him completely from the first," she said of the surgeon, who operated on her several times over the ensuing years, including a hip replacement at age thirty. "He always spoke to the child before the parents," she said. "He explained everything, he never lied and he always held my hand while the anesthetic was taking effect." As an adult, she gave him "credit for being able to walk unassisted," but what she remembered more than anything was the way he always made time for her and eventually her children, so he could reassure Beanish that they had not inherited her congenital hip problems. "Friends for life" was a promise he upheld through the generations.

ROBERT BRUCE SALTER came from Loyalist stock on both sides of his family. His father, Lewis Salter, from Chatham, New Brunswick, was manager of the Bank of Nova Scotia in Liverpool, Nova Scotia, the hometown of a young woman named Katherine Cowie. After he wooed and wed her, they moved to Stratford, Ontario, where he headed up the local BNS branch. There the Salters had three sons, Douglas Campbell (who died in 1993) and fraternal twins Robert Bruce and Andrew Jack, who were born on December 15, 1924.

Almost from birth, Bob Salter seemed destined to care for others, an ambition nurtured by his mother, a woman he once described as shy, loyal, kind, and "deeply religious." Another huge influence was David Smith, the family physician. At age six Bob told his twin brother that he wanted to be a doctor, but only "if he could be as good, or better than Dr. Smith," recalled Jack Salter. "He worshipped him."

When the boys were nine, Jack became seriously ill with rheumatic fever; in those pre-antibiotic days the treatment was complete bedrest for a year. "Bob taught me all during the summer holidays and I wrote the exams so that when I was well and able to go back to school I could stay in the same room with him," Jack said. "That was very important to us."

In the mid-1930s Lewis Salter embarked on a serious career change when he quit the bank to launch an orange-juice business. The family moved to North Toronto and the three boys transferred from Romeo Public School in Stratford to Lawrence Park Collegiate. Even then Bob was interested in research. When he was sixteen, he brought home a dead monkey from the Connaught Medical Labs. "I went into the basement and there was Dr. Bob dissecting the poor little monkey, which was staring up at the ceiling," said his brother. "I honestly believe that is how he became fascinated with bone surgery, because he ended up with the skeleton of the monkey and he could see how the various joints functioned."

After high school, Jack went into the navy and Bob entered a six-year medical program at the University of Toronto, the first time in their lives that the twins had taken divergent paths. Bob was about five-foot-ten and of average build, but he was very strong, athletic, competitive and driven. "When he played football and hockey, if he tackled or body-checked you, you would beg to live for another day," said his brother. "He played to win."

During school breaks, Bob worked as a labourer and truck driver to earn his tuition, but in his last two years of medical school he combined his religious and medical vocations by spending his summers at the Grenfell Mission, an organization that had been established by medical missionary Wilfred Grenfell in the 1890s to bring medical and social services to remote communities in northern Newfoundland and Labrador. The Grenfell Mission was a testing ground for Salter's dream of becoming a missionary doctor.

Back in Toronto in 1947 for his final year at U of T, he met Robina McGee, a community health student. She had done fieldwork on a scholarship in Copper Cliff, a community near Sudbury, in northern Ontario, and was hoping to work for the Grenfell Mission, so "we united our paths," she said, after he completed his internship year. "I didn't know whether it was a proposal or a job description he was offering me," she joked about what turned out to be more than sixty years of marriage, community service, and the rearing of five children.

The day after their wedding on July 3, 1948, the Salters left for the Grenfell Medical Mission at St. Anthony, on the northern peninsula of Newfoundland, doing "whatever needed to be done" in what "Bob always called 'our two-year honeymoon,'" she said. Then, with a baby on the way, revolution in China, and partition in India, the Salters agreed to put aside his dream of working in a missionary field. Instead he enrolled in postgraduate training under W. E. Gallie, the legendary surgeon and educator who radically overhauled surgical education at U of T. Gallie believed students should be exposed to a variety of disciplines before specializing and that the coveted position of chief resident should rotate so that each of them would have the experience of being "in charge" in a supervised setting before heading off into the "real" world.

Salter then spent a year as a McLaughlin Fellow in orthopedic surgery at the Royal London Hospital. That's where the trainee from Canada took on Sir Reginald Watson-Jones, the world's reigning orthopedic guru. Listening to

Watson-Jones deliver his dictum that the only treatment for fractured limbs was complete, rigid, enforced, and prolonged immobilization, Salter realized intuitively that this was precisely the wrong thing to do. What's more, he said so, to the rising ire of Sir Reginald. Over the next thirty years Salter delighted in proving he was right and relating that confrontation to generations of his own graduate students.

Salter began working at Toronto's Hospital for Sick Children in 1955, when Alfred Farmer was head of surgery. At that time pediatric surgeons were generalists. But Farmer believed that doctors needed to specialize if they were going to grow in expertise, and so he insisted that all of the doctors reporting to him had to pick a specialty. William Mustard, who excelled in both cardiac and orthopedic surgery, decided to concentrate on the former, which allowed room for Salter to become chief of orthopedic surgery at Sick Kids and a professor of surgery at U of T in 1957, at the incredibly young age of thirty-two.

Forcing doctors to specialize put Sick Kids ahead of everybody else in pediatric surgery and turned the hospital into a mecca for young doctors seeking advanced training. Salter, with his combination of ingenuity, research, and clinical expertise, led the way in orthopedics. He became surgeon-in-chief in 1966 and a "university professor" at U of T in 1984, a position held by only fifteen scholars at a time. In a life filled with accolades and honours, Salter's curriculum vitae included president of the Canadian Orthopaedic Association and the Royal College of Physicians and Surgeons of Canada; fellow of the Royal Society of Canada; member of the Canadian Medical Hall of Fame; Companion of the Order of Canada; and winner of the Gairdner Award for Medical Science, the FNG Starr Medal of the Canadian Medical Association, and the Bristol-Myers Squibb/Zimmer Award for Distinguished Achievement in Orthopaedic Research.

He remained a practising Christian who found a comfortable balance between science and religion. "Some things in life are not measurable — faith, hope, and love — and therefore not amenable to scientific investigation," he told the *Globe* in an interview in the mid-1980s. As for his own soul, he said he tried every day to become a better Christian. And when pressed, he admitted: "I am not a humble man. It's one of my real frailties."

Although he stopped doing surgery at seventy, he continued to research, write, attend conferences, and see patients even after he was diagnosed with Parkinson's disease. By 2010 the disease was accelerating and he was having increasing difficulty with his balance. After a fall at home early that May, he was taken to hospital, where he died a few days later, on May 10, 2010. He was eighty-five. "I always referred to him as my pal and twin," said his brother sadly. "There is no living person who has known and loved him as long as I have."

ROGUES,
RASCALS, AND
ROMANTICS

OBITUARIES AS ENTERTAINMENT
AND THE RISE OF DEAD-BEAT
GROUPIES

ECCENTRICITY COURSES LIKE a river through the lives of the ten people I have written about in "Rogues, Rascals, and Romantics." They are all large personalities who in various ways made their mark on Canadian society.

They include a hapless spy, a self-promoting saxophonist, an ingenious crook whose disguises duped police on both sides of the border, an inspired graphic designer who was felled by his addiction to cocaine, the establishment scourge and author of Canada's first significant gay novel, and the inventor of Trivial Pursuit, one of the most successful board games of all time. Some, such as actor Jackie Burroughs, poet Irving Layton, writer Lindalee Tracey, and singer Denny Doherty, had talents that will guarantee their cultural legacies, but all of them will be remembered as characters who lived at full tilt, whatever the consequences.

I used to be stunned when grieving friends and family were outraged that I would write about peccadilloes as well as triumphs. Over the years I came to realize that blaming me — the messenger — was really an indication of their mixed emotions about the departed. They couldn't get mad at their loved one for having the effrontery to die or for exhibiting embarrassing character traits, so they transferred their anger to me instead.

In October 2008 I wrote the obituary of Connie Rooke, a woman I had known and admired. She was a friend, but that is not why I wrote about her.

She was a well-published literary critic, a former editor of the *Malahat Review*, a co-founder of the Eden Mills Writers' Festival, a former president of the University of Winnipeg, and a champion of Canadian writers and writing — among other coups she was the first person to publish short stories by Yann Martel and Rohinton Mistry. She also had a dramatic life, as the wife of writer Leon Rooke and as a well-connected literary force. Besides, she had turned her own dying into a "best practices" lesson about how to grab hold of every moment that remained.

There's nothing uplifting about a terminal cancer diagnosis. For most people it is the beginning of an increasingly solitary journey into the unknown. But Rooke approached her own death at sixty-five with such an openness (and that did include railing against the fading light) and an intellectual curiosity that her hospital bed — set up in a bright, sunny room in the front of her downtown Toronto house with an "Obama for President" poster on the footboard — became a salon where family, friends, neighbours, and colleagues gathered to gossip, debate, and share the company of an always stimulating and generous woman.

Some of Rooke's friends wanted me to ignore her blustery tenure at the University of Winnipeg, which ended abruptly when in 2002 the Board of Regents bought out the remaining two years of her contract. That was impossible, for it was on the public record. Even more contentious, apparently, was a rupture in her long marriage. That too was well-known in literary and academic communities, and it had a significant impact on her decision to leave the University of Victoria and relocate to the University of Guelph, where she and her husband co-founded the Eden Mills Writers' Festival.

After checking the details with Rooke's widower, I wrote: "The Rookes' marriage, which had always been a volatile mix of hard work, partying, and the occasional indiscretion — on his part — burst its seams in the eighties after she became passionately involved with poet George Bowering, although he now denies that they had an affair. As for [Leon] Rooke, he admits that he strong-armed the king-sized marital mattress down the stairs and threw it on to the front lawn — although he refutes reports that he set it on fire. 'Everything eventually settled down and returned to the way it should have been,' he said. 'Friends said things would never be the same, but that wasn't true. They were better. Maybe it is necessary sometimes for marriages to go through those brittle break-up things. It was always an exciting marriage, but after that, it just got better.'"

Those details, amounting to one paragraph in an almost 2,500-word obit, caused me to be whispered about, shunned at social gatherings, and publicly criticized for telling the truth. More than fifteen months later, in the question period following a public lecture I had given in Victoria, a freelance documentary filmmaker demanded to know why I hadn't sought the permission and approval of Rooke's husband and grown son before publishing the obituary — a breach of fundamental journalistic ethics. The furor eventually passed, but it was an ugly example of how mourners can try to hijack obituaries.

In the fall of 2011 I reluctantly wrote about another friend, Richard Landon, the director of the Thomas Fisher Rare Book Library at the University of Toronto. I wasn't prepared to sanitize the facts of his personal life while paying tribute to his professional accomplishments. "Even in his younger years, Landon had the appearance of a man who had been up far too late the night before, doing things that were probably best forgotten," I wrote. "His sartorial style was ramshackle, but his conversation was discursive and replete with fascinating tales of his exploits as a collector of literary treasures. He loved to smoke and drink, especially at the same time, although he rarely had a drink before noon. His capacity, which was prodigious, was exceeded only by the strength of his friendship with colleagues, competitors, collectors, patrons, researchers, and booksellers.

"On the personal front, he was uncommonly successful with women, even to the surprise of his own mother. He was married twice and had a long-time relationship with a British antiquarian bookseller that was as good as a marriage. His soulmate, however, both romantically and intellectually, was Marie Korey, the rare books librarian he met at a conference in Ann Arbor, Michigan, in 1976, and married in 1990. They shared a passion for books and a mutual appreciation that extended to completing each other's sentences."

This time, though, friends and family recognized the man they knew in the portrait I had drawn in the obituary. How to explain the radically different reactions five years apart? Time and gender are insufficient. It all comes down, I think, to grief and how it affects different mourners. I can empathize with their outrage, but I can't muffle what I write in anticipation of hurt feelings. I'm writing for readers, not the family.

The trend to unfettered obituaries can be attributed to yet another Canadian, Conrad Black, back in his media baron days. In 1985 Black bought the *Daily Telegraph*, among other papers. His main newspaper rival was

Rupert Murdoch, who had acquired the *Times* in 1981 from another Canadian mogul, Ken Thomson, second Lord Thomson of Fleet. Thomson had put the paper up for sale after a disastrous strike that saw the *Times* shut down for nearly a calendar year — from December 1978 to November 1979.

During the strike, a deeply eccentric man named Hugh Massingberd, an editor at *Burke's Peerage*, the publication that keeps track of who has what title and has been awarded which gong — sort of like a manual for champion dog breeders — approached Bill Deedes, editor of the *Daily Telegraph*, and suggested he should hire him to improve its "cenotaph" obituaries while the *Times* was shut down. Massingberd's proposal was rejected on the grounds that it was "rather bad form" to exploit the absence of "Another Newspaper" in that way. Let me tell you, those old-boy rules no longer apply in today's cutthroat journalism.

So Massingberd stayed at *Burke's Peerage*, doing valuable genealogical research for the job that would eventually make him famous. After Black appointed the war correspondent and historian Max Hastings editor of the *Daily Telegraph*, he in turn hired Massingberd — or "Massivesnob," as he was called in the satirical magazine *Private Eye* — as obituaries editor.

From his arrival in July 1986 until he had to resign the post in 1994 after a heart attack and a quadruple bypass, Massingberd "dedicated myself to the chronicling of what people were *really* like through informal anecdote, description and character sketch rather than merely trot[ting] out the bald *curriculum vitae*," as he explained in the introduction to *The Daily Telegraph Book of Obituaries: A Celebration of Eccentric Lives*. In the process, Massingberd revolutionized the obituarist's craft.

Besides having worked at *Burke's Peerage*, Massingberd was an expert on country houses and a huge fan of John Aubrey, the gossipy seventeenth-century chronicler of the rich, the capricious, and the devious whom I talked about earlier in the "Builders" chapter. Aubrey's twentieth-century biographer and editor Anthony Powell aptly described his *Brief Lives* as "that extraordinary jumble of biography from which later historians have plundered so much of their picturesque detail."

Unweighted by the cenotaph tradition so beloved by the *Times*, Massingberd was able to start afresh at the *Daily Telegraph*. He made the new obituary page much more egalitarian, eccentric, and lively. One of my favourites, from January 1987, was for a former car salesman named Charles Gordon, who had become the twelfth Marquess of Huntly on the death of his great-uncle in 1937. After the failure of his first marriage in 1965, Lord Huntly, then sixty-nine, married a nurse more than forty years his junior. When asked about his choice of a bride, he apparently replied: "I'm a very fit man. I walk my dog every day. I don't have to wear spectacles. I still have my own teeth. Why should I marry some dried-up old bag?"

Before the advent of blogs and online newspapers, Massingberd made obituaries interactive because he encouraged his contributors to write about a subject's less salubrious traits and escapades in a thinly veiled code that discerning readers could decipher to their private delectation. And since the obituaries were unsigned, obituarists could unsheathe their literary knives on friends, rivals, and foes without public accountability — although readers delighted in guessing who had written what.

Early on, Massingberd began gathering the best obituaries from the newspaper and publishing them in book form. That gave them a second life and a much wider readership. The series, which has carried on under Massingberd's successors, includes *A Celebration of Eccentric Lives: Rogues, Entertainers, Sports Figures* and even *Canada from Afar: The Telegraph Book of Canadian Obituaries*, edited by David Twiston Davies, with an introduction by Conrad Black.

The same month that Massingberd arrived at the *Daily Telegraph*, an Oxford antiquarian bookseller named James Fergusson was hired to be the obituaries editor of an about-to-be-launched newspaper called the *Independent*. Fergusson took his inspiration, or so he wrote in "Last Words" in the *London Library Magazine* in 2010, from the *Gentleman's Magazine,* which "with its monthly lists of the interesting dead" was "a democratic calendar of curious anecdotes," and from the "timeless authority" of *The Dictionary of National Biography*. Founded in 1882 by Sir Leslie Stephen, father of Vanessa Bell and Virginia Woolf, the DNB was "a monument of original scholarship" and "one of the great achievements of the Victorian age."

Fergusson insisted that all obituaries in the *Independent* must carry bylines. Even now the argument rages between the "accountability" of signed obituaries in the *Independent* and the *Guardian* and the "objectivity" of anonymous ones in the *Times*, the *Daily Telegraph*, and the *Economist*. Unlike Massingberd, who loved military types — "the moustaches," as he called them — eccentrics, and scoundrels, Fergusson wanted the obscure and the overlooked on his pages: "We relished difficult academics, untranslated poets, untranslatable graffiti artists, Aboriginal dream-painters, Scotland's greatest potato collector, Britain's oldest working ploughman; and we led the field in commemorating a generation scythed down by the AIDS epidemic of the late 1980s." In a barely veiled swipe at Massingberd, Fergusson pointed out: "We aimed our obituaries not at the readership of clubby coevals, speakers of code, and partners in euphemism, but at a larger, younger audience."

Besides bylines, Fergusson introduced two other innovations during his tenure (1986–2007) that are now standard on obituary pages: the use of archival and news photographs that illustrated the personality of the subject rather than the airbrushed head-and-shoulders coffin shots that were typical of the time, and a sidebar summarizing vital statistics, including birth and death dates.

The obituary upheavals of 1986 remain legendary. At the *Times*, acting obituaries editor John Grigg — noted historian, author of a celebrated three-volume biography of David Lloyd George, former Lord Altrincham, and failed Conservative candidate — emphatically put paid to the tradition of *de mortuis nil nisi bonum* in a sexually explicit beyond-the-grave condemnation of Sir Robert Helpmann, the Australian dancer, choreographer, and director who played the child-catcher in the film *Chitty Chitty Bang Bang*. After Helpmann died at age seventy-seven on September 28, 1986, the *Times* ran an unsigned obituary that described him as "a homosexual of the proselytising kind, [who] could turn young men on the borderline his way."

The *Daily Telegraph* topped that less than five months later when they published a derisive (if hilarious) obituary of Liberace, the flamboyant American pianist and entertainer, who died at sixty-seven in February 1987, after a precipitous weight loss. His long-time manager, Seymour Heller, blamed a watermelon-only diet for Liberace's alarmingly gaunt appearance before he disappeared from public view. But other sources, including the pianist's biographer, Darden Asbury Pyron, say he died of complications from HIV/AIDS. (Incidentally, one of the big differences between British and North American obits is cause of death. The Brits often ignore it; the Americans dwell on it. It is said that when Massingberd, who resisted putting death details in obits — including Liberace's — was finally forced to comply, he retaliated with the tale of a man who died when his penile implant exploded.)

The *Daily Telegraph* obituary quotes liberally from a "particularly venomous" review of a performance Liberace gave in 1956 at the London Palladium.

"He reeks with emetic language that can only make grown men long for a quiet corner, an aspidistra, a handkerchief, and the old heave-ho," was one of the milder comments. "He is the summit of sex, the pinnacle of masculine, feminine, and neuter, and everything that he, she, and it can ever want." After denying his homosexuality in the High Court in London — at a time when consensual sex between adult males was a crime — Liberace won damages in a libel suit in 1959.

By the time Liberace died, three decades later, the law and sexual mores had changed. Besides, Liberace and his beloved mother were no longer around to be offended, so repeating the once libellous review, although hardly respectful, was fair game. The final line of the obituary was a typically coded message to readers of the *Daily Telegraph*. It consisted of a one-sentence paragraph: "He was unmarried."

Massingberd was inordinately fond of rogues. Here is a passage from the obituary for Ronnie Kray, who with his twin brother, Reggie, "formed one of the most notorious criminal partnerships of modern times." Describing them as "criminal entrepreneurs," the obituarist wrote: "Amateur boxing champions, they eschewed the traditional razor as ineffective and, besides employing the knife, cutlass, and broken bottle, developed an early affection for guns."

Ronnie Kray, a "paranoid schizophrenic" and "compulsive fantasist" who loved his nickname "the Colonel" and behaved as if he "were directing a film of his own life," was "in thrall to his twin, who was drawn to violence and saw killing as the ultimate proof of manhood." As Kray himself once said, "We never hurt innocent people. The men we killed were other villains," as though that made it all right. The obituary recounts a long list of blood-curdling crimes before concluding: "While in Broadmoor, Ronnie Kray married twice; neither marriage was consummated."

Of course, obituarists were in anecdote heaven when Massingberd himself died from cancer at age sixty on Christmas Day 2007. The *Guardian* quoted him as saying that the best remedy for depression was the thought of singing "patriotic songs in drag before an appreciative audience." The *New York Times* offered a short lexicon of his prize euphemisms, such as "gave colourful accounts of his exploits" for a habitual liar, and included quotes from pet obituaries, including the 1988 notice for London restaurateur Peter Langan. "Often he would pass out amid the cutlery before doing any damage, but occasionally he would cruise menacingly beneath the tables, biting unwary customers' ankles."

True to the style Massingberd had made famous, the *Daily Telegraph* described its "invariably strapped for cash" former obituaries editor as "a valiant trencherman." Over the years this "tall, slim and notably handsome youth with hollowed-out cheeks" had transmogrified into an "impressively corpulent presence whose moon face lit up with Pickwickian benevolence." Along with the biographical details about his several books on subjects ranging from country houses to the genealogy of the landed gentry to his self-effacing memoir, *Daydream Believer*, the obituary incorporated several oft-repeated gems from the half-dozen anthologies that Massingberd had edited, including a reference to the sixth Earl of Carnarvon as a "relentless raconteur and most uncompromisingly direct ladies' man."

Massingberd deserves full credit for turning obituaries into entertainment. The competition that ensued among obit editors in the quality British papers was a bonanza for readers, who delighted in comparing notes about the meanings of coy or barbed references and in guessing which anonymous friend was sending up a recently departed worthy. The best obituaries had always been informative and thought-provoking, but suddenly they had become fun, even outrageous reading, especially if it wasn't your loved one who was being skewered.

Irreverent send-offs created a new audience: obituary groupies. American journalist Marilyn Johnson wrote a bestselling book in 2006 called *The Dead Beat: Lost Souls, Lucky Stiffs, and the Perverse Pleasures of Obituaries,* not as a writer of obits but as a fan. In a chapter titled "I Walk the Dead Beat," she describes the thrill she felt when she read obituaries on two successive days of Paul Winchell, the voice of Tigger, and John Fiedler, the voice of Piglet, in the Disney cartoon *Winnie the Pooh*, noting as she clipped that "the two had gone silent a day apart." It reminded her of John Adams and Thomas Jefferson: "the second and third presidents of the United States died in harmony on July 4, exactly fifty years after they adopted the Declaration of Independence." I don't know what you do with curious coincidences like these, but people have collected much stranger things than obituaries, so go for it, I say.

Bismarck supposedly said people should never watch the making of laws or of sausages. Believe me, the same is true of conferences. A few years ago I joined the Society of Professional Obituary Writers (SPOW) and went to its founding workshop in Portland, Oregon. The first time I googled the society's acronym, I came up with "Sex Position of the Week," but the back story of SPOW is almost as spicy; it is a tale of rivalry, power struggles, and journalistic standards that began in the late 1990s in a north Dallas bar.

Carolyn Gilbert, a high school English teacher turned consultant, was tossing back a few with a group of friends who, like her, were obit junkies, when it suddenly occurred to her that she should convene the first Great Obituary Writers' Conference. ("I just said it as a lark," she later told the *New Yorker*. "I'm not even sure what I meant — whether I meant great obituaries, great writers, or great conference.")

The inaugural conference was held in Archer City, the hometown of Texas writer Larry McMurtry and the setting for his novel *The Last Picture Show*. Two years later, Gilbert expanded the group, forming the International Association of Obituarists and soliciting dues to support www.obitpage.com, a compendium of memorable obituaries, book reviews, and blurbs about upcoming conferences. She also found a new venue for the third GOWC: the Plaza Hotel in Las Vegas — New Mexico, not Nevada — a restored Wild West saloon and hostelry that has provided locations for many films, including *No Country for Old Men*.

After that she attracted the weird, the wannabes, the professionals, and the curious to gatherings in places as diverse as Bath, England, and tiny Arthur, New York. In the early years, Australian obituary expert Nigel Starck was a mainstay, and American writer Marilyn Johnson came to conduct research for *The Dead Beat*. But there were also some arcane participants, such as EllynAnne Geisel, an "apron archeologist" and the author of *Apronisms: Pocket Wisdom for Every Day*, who talked — a lot — about the more than four hundred aprons she had collected.

Conference events featured gatherings in cemeteries, appearances by creatures dressed as the Grim Reaper, much quaffing of martinis, ritualized recitals of obit highlights, and even some transatlantic rivalry between Americans, who love to celebrate the quirks of ordinary people, and Brits, who specialize in mocking the foibles of outlandish aristocrats. The fourth conference ended with a metaphorical drum roll. The news flash that Ronald Reagan had died of Alzheimer's disease had obituary writers scrambling for their cellphones and laptops.

Zany and eccentric began to pale when the closing speaker at the conference in Alfred, in June 2007, was somebody Gilbert had met at the bar the night before. Tensions between professional journalists and obit junkies led to such radical notions as inviting celebrity speakers rather than oddballs, producing an agenda in advance of the gathering and sending out a call for papers. In other words, more like an academic conference than a backroom chat.

In the end, plans to hold the tenth GOWC in Toronto fell apart following a clash of wills and standards between Gilbert and the local convener, Colin Haskin, then obituaries editor of the *Globe and Mail*. The contretemps got so heated it actually became fodder for a column by journalist Alex Beam in the *Boston Globe* — a first for scribes on the dead beat.

"You must take a backseat entirely and allow us to run everything," Haskin wrote to Gilbert. "You must give up all control, including the website, finances, attendance, fees, list of speakers," he continued. "The tenth anniversary conference cannot proceed in the same manner as those in the past." To which Gilbert retorted: "I am gobsmacked with your comments and innuendo...I am bewildered by your repeated demand for 'control.'" As in a marriage gone sour, the two eventually began haggling over money and possessions, with Gilbert offering to sell Haskin the rights to the conference and its website for $200,000, an offer she later told Alex Beam was not "serious." For his part, Haskin concluded that he "just didn't trust Gilbert."

Personally, as a lover of eccentrics, I'm all for letting scribes and fans share the same conference. By concentrating on credentials, especially in recessionary times, the professional obituary writers in SPOW tolled their own death knell. After a hiatus, some stalwarts are planning a conference in Toronto for 2013.

As for the ten rogues, rascals, and romantics I have gathered here, their lives can't be separated from their achievements or, in some cases, their notoriety. To say they were colourful is too pallid a descriptor: they were cosmic singularities, in good ways and bad. That's why I've written about them in all their livid outrageousness. They deserve nothing less.

IRVING LAYTON

Poet

MARCH 12, 1912 – JANUARY 4, 2006

S TOCKY, WITH AN unruly mane and a ferocious glare, Irving Layton was fond of referring to himself in the same breath as Shakespeare, Wordsworth, and Keats. Despite his bombast, he was a grand and glorious poet. In March 2012, celebrations were held across the country on the centenary of his birth to remember the man and to read from his work. Tales of his hyperbolic self-importance abounded, of course, but the poems themselves reminded listeners of Layton's discerning eye, lyrical ear, and, above all, the virtuosity with which he used the English language. Nominated for the Nobel Prize for literature in 1981 — he lost out to Gabriel García Márquez — he was also a mentor to generations of younger poets, including Leonard Cohen and Al Purdy, and a proselytizer who brought urgency and passion to Canadian life and letters.

"There was Irving Layton, and then there was the rest of us. He is our greatest poet, our greatest champion of poetry. Alzheimer's could not silence him, and neither will death," a grieving Leonard Cohen said after Layton died in Montreal, at age ninety-three, on January 4, 2006. "I taught him how to dress. He taught me how to live forever," Cohen once said of his mentor and father figure.

Years earlier, the late Al Purdy had described Layton's personality as a fusion of opposites, saying he "was the Montreal magnet for me...I felt about him as I had not about any other Canadian writer, a kind of awe and surprise that such magical things should pour from an egotistical clown, a charismatic poseur. And I forgive myself for saying these things, which are both true and untrue."

Whenever he could afford it, and often when he couldn't, Layton lived the overblown life of a poet, producing more than forty books. He made poetry important, wrenching it from pretty verse into raw, sensual, visual, and aural imagery. Believing he was one of the elect, Layton felt his poems would, "like the severed head of Orpheus, sing for all eternity," as his son David Layton wrote in a biographical essay, "Irving Layton, Leonard Cohen and Other Recurring Nightmares" in *Saturday Night* magazine.

He delighted in furious debate, defying authority, undermining conservatism, and ridiculing cant. He prided himself on his classical sensibility, and his writing was more orderly and rhythmical than his savage personal style suggested. But he hated to be tied down, in poetry or in marriage: "I am a Romantic with a sense of irony," he once told a student.

He loved women — their pursuit, their bodies, and their company. He had three wives and two partners, including Aviva Cantor Layton, who lived with him for more than twenty years and bore his second son, David. Describing the poet's death as a "body blow," she said his real wife was his muse.

The stories about Layton, beginning with his claim that he was born circumcised, are legendary. "Who knows," Aviva Layton responded when the question was put to her directly. "It is like asking whether Achilles or Zeus ever existed." Everybody mythologizes his or her life to a certain extent, she said, adding that his mother certainly believed he had been born without a foreskin, the sign of the Messiah.

In the early 1960s, the couple was in Rome and wanted to visit St. Peter's Basilica. The guards barred her because she was wearing a mini-dress. Without pause, Layton opened his wallet, pulled out all his lira, pinned some to the bottom of her skirt to make a hem, then slipped the rest under the straps of her dress to fashion sleeves. "Now," he demanded, "is she respectable?" The guards, seemingly oblivious to the poet's eloquent deriding of mammon, made no objection as the couple swept past the barrier and into the holiest of Catholic churches.

Editing Layton was a fraught experience because "he did not believe he had ever written a bad poem," said Anna Porter, who worked with him at McClelland and Stewart beginning in the late 1960s. "He was brilliant," Porter said, "and when he viewed himself in the pantheon of great poets, he wasn't saying it lightly, he was saying it with some foreknowledge of the precedents."

She edited his *Collected Poems*, which was to be his magnum opus. The problem was that it kept growing. They had a temporary falling out over the number of poems. He was so angry with her that he went to another publisher, who released the "uncollected" Irving Layton.

What made Layton special as a mentor and a teacher, according to Sam Solecki, who wrote the introduction to a selected edition of Layton's poetry, *A Wild Peculiar Joy*, in 1982, was the way he nurtured younger poets without trying to turn them into models of himself. He was like Nietzsche, who said the best student is the one who goes beyond the master. And he left behind stellar poems such as "A Tall Man Executes a Jig," "The Swimmer," "The Birth of Tragedy," "Song for Naomi," "The Cold Green Element," "On Seeing the Statute of Ezekiel and Jeremiah in the Church of Notre Dame," "Keine Lazarovitch 1870–1959," "The Tightrope Dancer," and "A Wild Peculiar Joy."

IRVING LAYTON WAS born Israel Lazarovitch in Târgu Neamț, Romania, on March 12, 1912, two years before the onset of the war that would change the map of Europe. His father, Moses, was shy and religiously observant and his mother, Keine, was domineering, ferocious, and besotted with Layton, the youngest of her several children — he slept in her bed until long past childhood. After his mother's death, Layton wrote an elegy to her, "Keine Lazarovitch 1870–1959": "O fierce she was, mean and unaccommodating; / But I think now of the toss of her gold earrings, / Their proud carnal assertion, and her youngest sings / While all the rivers of her red veins move into the sea."

When Layton was about a year old, the family left Romania for Montreal, settling in the Jewish ghetto in Montreal's east end, later made famous by Mordecai Richler. He was a scrappy kid who learned to suppress his whimpering and keep on pounding in fistfights with local kids. His father died in 1925, the same year that Layton graduated from Alexandra Elementary School. He went to work as a peddler, selling dry goods on the streets of Montreal. But he longed for more, and he turned away from commerce and went to high school.

He discovered literature from his teachers at Baron Byng High School, political and social theory from his older friend David Lewis (future leader of the NDP), and poetic cadence from Lewis's friend A. M. Klein. Listening to Klein the poet read Virgil's *Aeneid* made him realize, as he said later, "how very lovely and very moving the sound of poetry could be."

It was Lewis, then a student at McGill, who signed Layton up as a member of the Young People's Socialist League, an association that administrators at Baron Byng found so threatening they expelled Layton in his final year of high school. Klein became Layton's tutor, Lewis provided the ten-dollar examination fee, and Layton supplied the intellect and effort to pass his high school matriculation.

Layton's older friend A. M. Klein had already published his first poem, in an underground campus journal called *The McGilliad*. However, McGill University rejected Layton, perhaps because of its infamous Jewish quota, perhaps because of his reputation as a rabble-rouser. The alternatives were few. In 1934 he went to Macdonald College, a McGill affiliate, to study agriculture, graduating in 1939.

By then he had met and married a woman named Faye Lynch. They moved to Halifax, where Layton worked as a door-to-door salesman for the Fuller Brush Company. Discouraged by his occupation and aware that he felt more pity than love for his wife, Layton returned to Montreal. He resumed his literary friendships with poets Louis Dudek, Raymond Souster, and John Sutherland (the editor of two early and prestigious magazines, *Preview* and *First Statement*, which later merged to become *Northern Journey*) and earned a meagre living teaching English to recent Jewish immigrants at the public library.

Appalled by Hitler's warmongering, he enlisted in the Canadian Army in 1942 but got no further than training camp in Petawawa before being granted a discharge. Back in Montreal, he published his first book of poetry, *Here and Now*, in 1945. Having divorced Faye Lynch, he married Sutherland's sister, the painter and poet Betty Sutherland. They had two children, Max, who was born in 1946 — the same year Layton completed his MA thesis on Harold Laski, the English political theorist and politician — and Naomi, in 1950.

Writing poetry and the occasional manifesto was not lucrative. Layton self-published his poetry and took work teaching wherever he could find it, including lecturing part-time at Sir George Williams (now Concordia) University while he dreamt of finishing a PhD and becoming a professor. This workload didn't keep him from writing, or from getting noticed, though his self-assertive style earned equal blame and praise. In 1951 Northrop Frye wrote of *The Black Huntsmen* that "the successes are quiet and the faults raucous.... One can get as tired of buttocks in Layton as buttercups in *Canadian Poetry Magazine*."

Even so, Frye drew a line between Layton's "serious" poetry and his "stage personality." In his seminal work, *The Bush Garden: Essays on the Canadian Imagination*, Frye called Layton "the most considerable poet of his generation." Robert Weaver and William Toye praised him even more lavishly in *The Oxford Anthology of Canadian Literature*, saying that he was "perhaps the best poet we have in Canada."

By the late 1950s he had made the leap from small literary presses to McClelland & Stewart, which published his selected poems, *A Red Carpet for the Sun*, in 1959. The volume, which was the only one of his books to win a Governor General's Literary Award, included poems from a dozen previous collections. Showcasing some of his best work, the collection was packaged with a brooding photograph of the author on the cover and a polemical essay, disguised as a foreword, in which Layton dismissed his contemporaries as "insufferable blabbermouths" while extolling his own "impeccable ear for rhythm." With this book, Layton the swaggering and defiant poet came down from the garret and stomped into mainstream society.

By then he had met Aviva Cantor, the partner of his most prolific and celebrated years. She had arrived in Montreal from her native Australia in 1955 with a list of names and addresses of people to look up in Montreal, including the poets Frank Scott, A. M. Klein, and Irving Layton. For some reason she phoned Layton. He invited her to a party at the house he shared with Betty and their children in Côte Saint-Luc — and that was that.

They never wed, although they came close. One day in the early 1960s Layton announced he was going to marry her; he summoned his metaphorical son Leonard Cohen, and the three of them trooped down to a jewellery shop in Old Montreal. There the poet became distracted and, instead of buying his lover a ring, he purchased a silver clasp for his estranged wife Betty and sauntered out of the store. The ever-debonair Cohen bought the ring that Aviva desired, slipped it on her finger, and pronounced her married.

Aviva Cantor changed her name to Layton after their son, David, was born in 1964. They moved to Toronto at the end of the decade after the poet Eli Mandel engineered a teaching job for Layton at York University. These were the years of his greatest literary and public success. He published a volume of poetry almost every year into the 1980s, and began winning over enough doubters to get Canada Council grants that allowed him to roam the world, spending several summers in Greece, Italy, India, and Marrakesh.

As his fame and his vanity grew, he liked to pretend that there was some sort of conspiracy against him in Canada. But he was a successful poet and a household name from his appearances on a CBC debate show that could have been named for him: *Fighting Words*. The late Hugh MacLennan declared him to be the best poet in Canada, a compliment that soothed Layton's ego but did nothing to rein in his embattled nature or make him more self-critical.

He objected strenuously to a biography written by Elspeth Cameron in the mid-1970s, igniting a high-octane vendetta against the literary biographer, and later wrote his own, self-serving memoirs, *Waiting for the Messiah*. After Aviva Layton left him for the writer Leon Whiteson in the late 1970s, he became captivated by Harriet Bernstein, one of his students at York University. They married after he finally divorced Betty Sutherland, and had a daughter, Samantha, in 1981, when Layton was almost seventy. Like so many of his closest relationships, this one ended badly. Bernstein took custody of the child and charged him with harassment when he unleashed his verbal dexterity to deride her.

Layton the poet started to slow down at this point, but Layton the lover was still going strong. He soon took up with twenty-two-year-old Annette Pottier, changing her name to Anna. She left him in 1995 after his creeping Alzheimer's was finally diagnosed. When his money ran out in 2000, leaving him as impoverished as he had been in his immigrant childhood, he was moved to the Maimonides Geriatric Centre in Montreal's Côte Saint-Luc district, the same area where he was living when he met Aviva Cantor in the 1950s.

Among his visitors was his former protegé and brother-in-arms Leonard Cohen. Cohen's early poem "Last Dance at the Four Penny," from *The Spice-Box of Earth* (1961), was written as a tribute to his mentor. It begins "Layton, when we dance our freilach / under the ghostly handkerchief," and ends "I say no Jew was ever lost / while we weave and billow the handkerchief / into a burning cloud, / measuring all of heaven / with our stitching thumbs."

When combined with another poem, "Irving and Me at the Hospital," from *Book of Longing* (2006), that early poem forms one of a set of elegiac bookends to their long friendship and love of poetry.

He stood up for Nietzsche
I stood up for Christ
He stood up for victory

I stood up for less
I loved to read his verses
He loved to hear my song
We never had much interest
In who was right or wrong
His boxer's hands were shaking
He struggled with his pipe
Imperial tobacco
Which I helped him light.

GORDON LUNAN

Spy

DECEMBER 31, 1914 – OCTOBER 3, 2005

G ORDON LUNAN WOULD probably have ended his days in obscurity if
Igor Gouzenko, a cipher clerk at the Soviet embassy in Ottawa, had not
defected in September 1945 and offered him up as a trophy in what came to be
called the Cold War.

Compared with spies such as Kim Philby and Guy Burgess, Lunan, a left-
leaning advertising copywriter, hardly rated as a threat to national security or
the safety of the free world, as it was called then. His story is significant
because of the lives he damaged, what it reveals about the times, and how
Canadians responded to the news that we harboured Soviet spy rings during
the Second World War.

The Soviet Union was our ally against Nazi Germany in the war, but after
the D-Day landings in Normandy in June 1944, the ground shifted under that
carapace of loyalty. The Germans had lost the war; it was only a matter of time
and resources before the British, Canadian, and American forces who were
marching on the Fatherland from the west and the south met up with the
Soviets, who were pushing towards the same target through the occupied territories of Eastern Europe.

When the tanks rolled to a halt and the guns stopped blazing, the map of
Europe would be redrawn, but how the spoils would be divided depended
on who reached Berlin — or beyond — first. The balance shifted again after
the Americans dropped atomic bombs on Hiroshima and Nagasaki in

August 1945. Suddenly the U.S. had the power to destroy not only a sovereign enemy but the world. Fear of nuclear annihilation turned the Soviet Union and the United States, the two most powerful nations on earth, into enemies, despite the handshaking and speechifying at peace conferences. That abrupt shift in *realpolitik* put hapless fellow-travellers like Lunan on the wrong side of history.

DAVID GORDON LUNAN was born in Kirkcaldy, Scotland, on December 31, 1914, one of four sons of a commercial traveller. When Lunan was nine, the family moved to London, where his father was put in charge of persuading the public to buy Congoleum, a cheap substitute for linoleum. He did so well that the company tried to renegotiate his contract to give him a smaller commission, a cheat that was not lost on his son, who tended even then to side with the underdog.

His father's earnings made it possible to send Lunan to Belmont, a feeder for Mill Hill, a non-conformist public school on the outskirts of London. A boarder from the age of ten, he liked school and did well, ending up as one of two head boys at Belmont. At Mill Hill he was taught music, theatre, and officer training along with standard school subjects. He graduated at seventeen in 1932 and immediately began an apprenticeship with the S. H. Benson advertising agency. It took him two years to secure a place in the copy department (where Dorothy Sayers had once toiled), becoming, at twenty, the agency's youngest copywriter.

Meanwhile, fascism was on the rise in Germany, where Adolf Hitler had become chancellor in 1933. The Soviet Union, ruled by Joseph Stalin, had joined the League of Nations in 1934 and become an active player in fascist/anti-fascist political machinations. In 1935 Mussolini invaded Abyssinia from the adjacent Italian territory of Somaliland.

A year later, Lunan visited Spain and saw the anti-democratic and repressive effects of General Francisco Franco's crusade to destroy the republican government. After returning to England, where Sir Oswald Mosley was gathering momentum for his British Union of Fascists, Lunan took a stand by joining the anti-appeasement movement. He was convinced that another war was inevitable. After British prime minister Neville Chamberlain capitulated to Hitler's demands in Munich in September 1938, Lunan decided to immigrate to Canada and leave behind the politics that he found so cowardly.

He soon found a job with the A. McKim advertising agency in Montreal, took a lease on a large flat with friends on what is now Aylmer Avenue, and immersed himself in the city's left-wing artistic community. The Quebec of Premier Maurice Duplessis was rigidly authoritarian, overtly Catholic, and rampantly anti-Semitic. This was the era of the infamous "padlock law" that allowed authorities to shutter the premises of suspected communist sympathizers.

Lunan quickly turned from a left-leaning sympathizer into an activist with communist connections. He was part of a welcoming committee at Windsor Station for a trainload of veterans of the Mackenzie-Papineau Battalion when they returned in 1938 from the Spanish Civil War. Anticipating that the reception might get out of hand, the RCMP and the local press were out in force, and Lunan was snapped giving a clenched-fist salute.

In the spring of 1939 he met Phyllis Newman, a Polish émigré. Their family backgrounds could not have been more different, but they espoused similar political causes. They married right after Britain declared war on Germany in September 1939.

In January 1943, Lunan enlisted in the Canadian Army as a private. He earned a commission as a lieutenant in November 1944 and was seconded to the Wartime Information Board (later the Canadian Information Service). He was posted to Ottawa, where he edited a military journal, *Canadian Affairs*, which supplied a summary of Canadian news and editorials for troops stationed abroad and in Canada.

While in Ottawa he met frequently with Fred Rose, a union organizer, politician, and Communist Party member. The two men had known each other since the late 1930s in Montreal. While Lunan never joined the Communist Party, which had been banned early in the war, he was a member of its close affiliate the Labour Progressive Party. He also hung around with known Communists such as Rose and offered them space in his apartment for meetings. Lunan's sympathies for the Soviets were well known, and Rose persuaded him to keep up the good work by befriending Soviets working at the embassy in Ottawa.

As Lunan wrote in his 1995 autobiography, *The Making of a Spy: A Political Odyssey*, "I admired the Soviet Union for what I believed then to be its enlightened world view...but like most of my comrades, I suspect, I would not have wanted to live there or to make Canada over in its likeness...the real glue that bound me to my comrades and them to me was the shared desire for a more humane society, a fairer distribution of wealth."

One morning, as Lunan later testified to the Kellock-Taschereau Royal Commission on Espionage, he arrived at his office on Sparks Street and found an anonymous note on his desk inviting him to an assignation with an unidentified person. The mystery date turned out to be Vasili Rogov, an assistant to Nikolai Zabotin, the Soviet military attaché to Canada.

Rogov recruited Lunan as a spy with the code name Back. His quasi-journalistic career was the perfect cover for organizing a coterie of informants, several of whom thought they were legitimately chatting to him in his capacity as editor of *Canadian Affairs*. Lunan passed along whatever information he was able to glean, even about the most inconsequential matters, and tried to enlist others in the cause. "Far from damaging Canada," he wrote fifty years later in his self-serving memoirs, "my motive — and I assumed it must have been theirs also — was to help Canada by helping our most powerful and effective ally and thereby shortening the war."

Indeed, the Canadian Army thought Lunan was doing such a good job he was promoted to acting captain in June 1945 and sent to London by the Canadian Information Service. One of his supervisors described him as "a very ordinary, likeable chap with not too much imagination but very industrious."

The war was over in Europe and the first meeting of the General Assembly of the United Nations was about to take place in Westminster Central Hall in London. Lunan was supposed to be helping with the publicity but ended up working as a pinch-hitting speechwriter for Paul Martin Sr., then secretary of state in Prime Minister William Lyon Mackenzie King's Cabinet.

Back home, his world had begun to collapse with Igor Gouzenko's defection in September 1945. The Soviet cipher clerk brought documentation with him about an extensive Soviet espionage network linking Canada, the United States, and Britain that was directed at finding information about the U.S. atomic bomb program. Gouzenko implicated Lunan as a "recruiting agent" and the leader of a cell of three informants who were passing information to Soviet intelligence on trends in Canadian politics and military weapons.

The alleged informants were Israel Halperin (for a fuller account of his life, please see Service), a mathematician on military leave from Queen's University to work at the Canadian Army's research and development establishment in Ottawa; Durnford Smith, an electrical engineer at the Canadian National Research Council; and Edward Mazerall, also an engineer at the NRC. None of them produced anything that was either secret or innovative, but everything, including Halperin's personal address book, took on sinister overtones in the overheated atmosphere of the Cold War.

Five months after Gouzenko's defection, in February 1946, Lunan was summoned back to Ottawa for an "important assignment." After his plane landed in Montreal, he was surrounded and restrained by three men in plain clothes, frisked, and taken to the RCMP barracks in Rockcliffe, a suburb of Ottawa. Two days later he was read a detailed surveillance record dating back to 1939 and a list of his alleged co-conspirators.

Civil liberties were legally trampled in the roundups and detentions that followed, even though the War Measures Act had expired at the end of the Second World War. The Mackenzie King government had secretly extended one of its provisions a month after Gouzenko's defection through special order-in-council PC 6444. It gave the prime minister and the justice minister the power to arrest and detain people suspected of passing secrets to the enemy.

King was so twitchy about this potential national and international crisis that he didn't tell his full Cabinet about Gouzenko's defection until February 5, 1946, according to historian Amy Knight in her book *How the Cold War Began: The Gouzenko Affair and the Hunt for Soviet Spies*. That was five months after the fact and, more important, two days after American journalist Drew Pearson had broken the news on a national radio broadcast of a "gigantic espionage network inside the United States and Canada." At the same time, King appointed the Royal Commission on Espionage, headed by two Supreme Court justices, R. L. Kellock and Robert Taschereau. Within days the RCMP had started rounding up suspects and detaining them without access to legal counsel or to their families.

Under heavy interrogation, and fearing that as a member of the Armed Forces he might be shot as a traitor, Lunan crumpled and agreed to co-operate with the espionage commission on February 20, 1946. Lunan implicated Smith, Mazerall, and Halperin, although not his pal Fred Rose, the Communist MP who had recruited him as a spy in the first place. Late in March 1946, he was jailed for contempt after refusing to answer questions at Rose's preliminary hearing.

At trial, Lunan was brought before Judge James McRuer, whose outrageous rulings set the precedents for later accused. McRuer allowed transcripts of the espionage commission to be admitted into court, even though the accused had been interrogated without benefit of counsel. Ignorance of the law was not a defence, he argued, and the accused should have demanded protection under the Canada Evidence Act to avoid incriminating themselves.

Lunan was convicted of conspiracy to violate the Official Secrets Act in November 1946. Before his sentence was handed down, he told the judge: "I do not consider myself guilty of the charge either in law or in fact." Nevertheless, he spent the next five years in Kingston Penitentiary, with extra time tacked on for refusing to testify in court about some of the colleagues he had implicated earlier.

His marriage with Newman, the mother of his daughter, held together while he was in prison but fell apart quickly thereafter. He met his second wife, Miriam Magee, at a party thrown to celebrate his release. They were married in Montreal, where Lunan was again working in the advertising business.

He eventually opened his own agency and retired with his wife to the countryside near Ottawa in 1975. He spent the rest of his life growing strawberries, cooking gourmet meals, espousing social justice principles to his step-grandchildren, and writing two memoirs, *The Making of a Spy* and, a decade later, *Redhanded: Inside the Spy Ring That Changed the World* (2005). The major difference between the two books is an epilogue in the second one in which Lunan explains, more explicitly than ever before, that he acted "naively, stupidly and admittedly outside the law" in the "best interests of winning the war against Nazism." He also acknowledged that the Gouzenko affair helped trigger the Cold War and expressed regret that he "played a part in making it happen so soon." By that time the Soviet Union had collapsed and all most Canadians could remember about Gouzenko were his bizarre appearances with a paper bag or a pillowcase over his head on the popular current affairs show, *Front Page Challenge*.

Not a huge *mea culpa*, by most definitions. Still, Lunan did serve his time for betraying his country, however ineffectually and naively. In researching his second memoir, he made a freedom-of-information request for his RCMP dossier and learned that the security force had been keeping tabs on him until the mid-1970s — when he was in his sixties.

Shortly after finishing the manuscript, he suffered a bad fall and died two weeks later in hospital in Hawkesbury, Ontario, on October 3, 2005. He was ninety.

SCOTT SYMONS

Writer

JULY 13, 1933 – FEBRUARY 23, 2009

S HORT, WITH A dark complexion, smouldering brown eyes, and a thick helmet of black hair, Scott Symons had a chunky wrestler's body and a magnetic but quixotic personality. He could energize a gathering simply by being there; just as easily, though, his voracious narcissism could suck all the oxygen out of a room.

Born into a prosperous, well-connected Toronto family, he had all the pre-sumed attributes for a charmed life, along with a fierce intelligence, a passion-ate curiosity, and the literary ambition to write the great Canadian novel. He was driven by a messianic vision, one that hearkened back to the homoerotic and whacky beliefs of Aleister Crowley, the early twentieth century oculist, mystic, alleged spy, and founder of the religious cult of Thelema.

Symons wrote three novels, including *Place d'Armes*, arguably CanLit's first openly gay novel, but he will be remembered most for his outrageous life-style, which began in scandal and ended in poverty and illness. After several years of declining health, he died in a publicly subsidized Toronto nursing home at seventy-five, on February 23, 2009.

In his zeal to destroy the puritanical establishment that had cradled him, Symons affronted family, alienated friends and lovers, and destroyed rela-tionships. He wantonly inflicted pain in the most flagrant and public ways without any semblance of remorse. At thirty-four he abandoned his wife and small son to run away with a seventeen-year-old boy at a time when

224

homosexual acts between consenting adults were a criminal offence. Vicious in print, he attacked the character and writings of a coterie of friends that included Margaret Atwood, Graeme Gibson, Bill Glassco, and Robertson Davies.

His closest and oldest friend, the late journalist and essayist Charles Taylor, supported him emotionally, intellectually, and financially. Back in 1977, in *Six Journeys: A Canadian Pattern*, Taylor wrote what remains the most perceptive profile of Symons, a biographical essay that is empathetic, knowing, and revealing.

Taylor was not his only champion. The late Jack McClelland, his publisher, believed Symons was "one of Canada's most important writers." And he was — as a non-fiction writer. His political and cultural journalism in *La Presse* about post-Duplessis Quebec and the stirrings of the Quiet Revolution in the early 1960s was lucid and perceptive, while his lavishly illustrated book *Heritage: A Romantic Look at Early Canadian Furniture* was an imaginative and culturally provocative treatise with photographs by John de Visser and a preface by George Grant.

Turning his back on what he did best, Symons wrote fiction that was over-blown and rambling. As literature it was forgettable; as sexual polemic it was revolutionary. His goal was to empower readers to embrace hedonistic experience and shrug off the complacent shackles of postwar Canadian society.

He could craft visually charged scenes as though he were wielding a paint-brush instead of a pen, but he had profound difficulties in stepping back from his material and establishing a distance between himself — the author — and the characters he manipulated to espouse his homoerotic views about the "lived life." As for absorbed experience, the bedrock of all fiction, he paraded it raw. Perhaps his biggest mistake as a writer was his obsessive journal-keeping, an addiction that began in his mid-twenties. He recorded everything in his "combat journal," as he called his diary, which then became, seemingly without transformative editing, the sprawling stuff of his fiction. His life was his art. Alas, it was not a masterpiece.

HUGH BRENNAN SCOTT Symons was born on July 13, 1933, in Toronto, the fifth of seven children of Major Harry and Dorothy (née Bull) Symons. (One of his older brothers, Tom Symons, was the founding president of Trent University and author of the Symons Report on Canadian studies.)

His father, a fighter pilot in the First World War, made his living in real estate and won the inaugural Stephen Leacock Award in 1947. His British-born grandfather, William Limberry Symons, designed the Old Union Station and many of the houses in the exclusive Rosedale enclave where the Symons family lived; he was also a president of the Ontario Society of Architects. On his mother's side, the Bulls were United Empire Loyalists. His maternal grandfather was William Perkins Bull, a lawyer, financier, art patron, and writer who was known as the "Duke of Rosedale."

Symons grew up surrounded by books, traditions, and culture and "thinking highly of himself," according to his youngest brother, Bart Symons. After attending Rosedale Elementary School, he was, according to his friend Charles Taylor's profile, "already showing signs of a moody truculence," a rebelliousness that his parents hoped to curb by sending him to board at Trinity College School, a private boys' school in Port Hope, Ontario. That's where the two met, the shy and diffident son of industrialist E. P. Taylor and the self-assured and authoritative scion of old money. Despite their disparate personalities, they were equally dismissive about an inherited life of privilege and social status.

Although Symons hated everything about the school—except his pal Charles—he was an excellent student. At TCS he fell in love with another student, a love he repressed by becoming a gymnast, "a form of athletics which suited him because it was solitary and ritualistic, with a touch of grace," Taylor wrote. He practised obsessively, and one night, alone in the gym, he fell off the high bar and broke his back. He was immobilized in a body cast for several months.

While it is tempting to speculate that being trapped in a body cast is symbolic of the way Symons felt encased by society, what we know for certain is that he moved back into the cocoon of his parents' home after the accident and spent his final year of high school at the University of Toronto Schools, an academically elite boys' school in the centre of the city. That fall he entered Trinity College at the University of Toronto, where he enlisted as a naval cadet, served in the student government, and excelled academically, earning a slew of scholarships and medals along with a bachelor's degree in modern history in 1955.

Instead of revelling in his triumph, he skipped the ceremony and spent the day working at a part-time job at Woodbine Racetrack—perhaps a sign that he wouldn't be going easily into the dark establishment night.

Nevertheless, he went up to Cambridge that fall as a student of F. R. Leavis at King's College, although later he said he received his real education at evensong and in the Fitzwilliam Museum. About this time he became engaged to Judith Morrow, a childhood friend and a bank president's daughter, and returned to Toronto to take up a short-lived job on the editorial page of the *Telegram*. After being asked to write a report surveying the paper's editorial policy over the previous fifty years, he said it had deteriorated miserably, and he was soon shown the door.

He and Morrow were married on March 1, 1958. At the reception, both the groom and his best man, Charles Taylor, made well-lubricated speeches denigrating the guests and everything they represented. Two months later the newlyweds settled in Quebec City. Symons took a job with the *Chronicle-Telegraph*, improved his French, and moved so easily in Québécois intellectual circles — then dominated by André Laurendeau and Jean-Louis Gagnon — that he was invited to join the Saint-Jean-Baptiste Society, becoming the first non-francophone and non-Catholic member, as he liked to boast.

By the autumn of 1959 Symons and his wife were in Paris, studying French literature and grammar at the Sorbonne, exploring the countryside, and helping to harvest grapes in a Bordeaux vineyard. They returned to Canada a year later with their newborn son, Graham, because Symons had been offered a reporting job at *La Presse*. The end of the Duplessis era — the autocratic premier had died the previous year — was a propitious time for a bilingual outsider to sniff out political and intellectual ferment, and Symons made the most of it with a National Newspaper Award–winning series of twenty-five articles in 1960–61 that presaged the coming Quiet Revolution. Indeed, he said later that he had coined the term.

Although his family and his wife's had frowned upon his career choice, Symons had considerable prowess as a journalist. But success frightened him. With his customary restlessness he "backed into what seemed more respectable," as he later wrote. He quit *La Presse*, moved back to Toronto with his family, and took a job as an assistant curator in the Canadiana department of the Royal Ontario Museum.

Again he seemed to have found his métier. Within three years he had been appointed curator and assistant professor of fine arts at the University of Toronto and granted a sabbatical, which he spent as a visiting curator at several august institutions in the United States. He gave a memorable public lecture, complete with slides, at the Smithsonian Institution, in which he compared the "full-bodied and orotund" Quebec weathervane roosters with the flat and one-dimensional American "cocks" as his stunned audience slowly grasped that they were on the losing side in a discussion of comparative cultural eroticism.

Symons was intent on kicking against the pricks, a defiance that he tried once too often with his superior at the ROM, who fired him for insubordination. Unable to quit the field of battle, he turned down the offer of a permanent job at the Smithsonian so that he could pursue his self-styled vocation as "a kind of priest of the chapel of Canadiana." Living on a fifty-acre farm east of Toronto that his wife had bought from her husband's family, he began and abandoned a book on Canadian history, wrote a play in which a symbolically unfulfilled English Canadian achieved a beatific state when sodomized by a French-Canadian chair, and, perhaps deliberately, messed up an audition for *This Hour Has Seven Days*, a provocative television show that seemed suited to his talents and tastes. The Symons universe was unravelling.

He fled the farm and holed up in a small hotel in Montreal. In an obsessive twenty-one-day outpouring, he produced his first novel, *Place d'Armes*, an autobiographical torrent about Hugh Anderson, an English Canadian, who wants nothing more than "the right to love my country, my wife, my people, my world," a goal that he can achieve only by reclaiming his emasculated soul through sexual intercourse with male Québécois prostitutes in the square adjoining the Église de Notre-Dame. Anderson celebrates his deliverance by taking Holy Communion in the church, eating the Host in the Place d'Armes, and embracing bemused passersby.

Critical reaction was not mixed when *Place d'Armes* — Symons's centennial project — was published in 1967. Writing in the *Toronto Star* under the headline "A Monster from Toronto," cultural critic Robert Fulford castigated Symons's gauzily veiled protagonist as "the most repellent single figure in the recent history of Canadian writing" and criticized the author for being incapable of writing with or about love. A savaged Symons licked his wounds in Yorkville, which was enjoying its sexually liberated heyday, by cavorting with all manner of libertines, including two statuesque and begowned black transvestites whom he invited to a family party hosted by his in-laws.

He was also creating his second novel, *Civic Square*, an even more unwieldy manuscript that was the English-Canadian counterpart to *Place d'Armes*. A massive collection of polemical letters addressed "Dear Reader," it was printed as a nearly 900-page unbound manuscript and packaged in a blue box, symbolic reminder of a gift package from Birks, the tony establishment jeweller. As a final flourish, Symons drew birds, flowers, and a red phallus on each page as it came off the Gestetner machine. He then delivered a copy to St. James Cathedral, his family's church, depositing the nearly four-kilogram offering on the collection plate after Communion.

By now Symons had more serious preoccupations than rampaging book critics. The year before, at thirty-four, he had run off with John McConnell, the underage son of a prominent Canadian family. The lovers fled to Mexico with the police in hot and fruitless pursuit and then lived for a time in lumber camps in northern British Columbia. Coincidentally, Symons received a minor literary prize — the Beta Sigma Phi Best First Canadian Novel Award — while he was on the lam. He returned to Toronto to pick up his laurels and his thousand-dollar cheque and to have a formal meeting with his disaffected wife, who, not surprisingly, had begun divorce proceedings.

And so Symons began the long nomadic phase of his life. He lived variously in Trout River, a west-coast Newfoundland village, where he wrote much of the text for *Heritage*, his furniture book (which would eventually be published by M&S in 1971); in the Mexican expatriate artists' colony San Miguel de Allende, where he began writing *Helmet of Flesh*; and mainly in Morocco, where he lived and loved and wrote for more than two decades in Essaouira, a walled medieval town. That's where he seemed most in harmony with himself, his new lover, Aaron Klokeid, and his cultural and physical environment.

Periodically he returned to Canada: in 1970 on "a personal odyssey into the heart of early Canadian belief" as he researched his furniture book; in 1986 for the launch of *Helmet of Flesh* at a lavish party hosted by Charles Taylor at Windfields, his family estate (now the home of the Canadian Film Centre); and in 1998 to attend the International Festival of Authors at Harbourfront, where Nik Sheehan's documentary film about him, *God's Fool*, was being screened and Christopher Elson's anthology *Dear Reader: Selected Scott Symons* was being launched by Gutter Press.

Symons always claimed that he was homosexual, not gay, by which he probably meant that he didn't embrace the gay liberation movement as a defining political and social cause. He wasn't seeking equality, he was railing against the real foe: the Blandmen — the establishment types who he felt had betrayed Canada's British and French heritage. Frequently lonely and depressed, often suicidal, perpetually broke, he was dependent on the indulgence of friends as his job prospects dwindled and his health deteriorated. He smoked, drank, and ate prodigiously at their expense and suffered over the years from diabetes and kidney problems.

In 2000 he returned permanently to Toronto. Taylor had died three years earlier and his final bequest had long since been spent; Symons was on his uppers and "a postscript to his own life," according to one friend. He spent his last years at Leisure World, where a few of the faithful continued to stop by to take him out for a meal or celebrate his birthday. He often got into rows with other residents, accusing one of sexual harassment after the man objected to the cavalier way that Symons appropriated his newspaper every day.

Although Symons had long since divorced himself from his family, his youngest brother, Bart, attempted a reconciliation in the summer of 2008. "Almost in fear" of a confrontation, he made the train trip from his home in Stratford to visit his older brother, who was in St. Michael's Hospital suffering from respiratory problems. "He was an absolute sweetie," Bart Symons said later about a five-minute duty call that turned into a lengthy and emotional visit several months before his brother died. "It was an incredible event and he was so glad I had come and in hindsight so am I."

In the end, blood and family proved stronger than kicking against the pricks.

PAUL BRODIE

Saxophonist

APRIL 10, 1934 – NOVEMBER 19, 2007

O N AN ORDINARY day in 1978, musician Paul Brodie was playing the saxophone in his Toronto studio when the phone rang. Warren Beatty, the actor, was on the other end of the line. A fan of Brodie's musicianship, Beatty wanted permission to use a recording of Brodie playing the fourth movement of Handel's Sonata no. 3 in Beatty's new movie, *Heaven Can Wait*. In the film, Beatty was cast as a wealthy football hero who played the soprano saxophone as a hobby; he wanted to use Brodie's solo as background music for the scene in which Beatty's character and his servants, all dressed in tuxedos, toss around a football in the garden of his mansion.

Brodie quickly agreed to terms with Beatty, put down the phone, and set to work parlaying a less-than-three-minute part in composer Dave Grusin's film score into something akin to a Command Performance at the Royal Albert Hall in London, England. Before long "the Canadian media somehow got the idea that a Canadian saxophonist was being featured throughout the film," Brodie wrote disingenuously in *Ambassador of the Saxophone,* his self-published autobiography.

When *Heaven Can Wait* was nominated for several Academy Awards, Brodie, whose chutzpah was surpassed only by his musicianship, flew to Los Angeles. He wangled tickets to the awards, sent 250 postcards to Canadian media pumping his connection with the film, and arranged to do a live telephone interview with CBC Television the day after the ceremonies.

Brash, dynamic, and entrepreneurial, Brodie had precisely the right combination of talent and salesmanship to promote himself and his instrument at home and abroad. The saxophone is a relative newcomer as a musical instrument, so it did not have a role in traditional orchestras or in the music of the great classical composers. Invented by Belgian Adolphe Sax in Paris in the 1840s, the saxophone is a hybrid that combines the volume and carrying power of brass with the intricate key work and technical finesse of woodwinds. Although some modern classical composers have written for the saxophone, it is still mainly played in military and blues bands and jazz combos. Brodie tried to change that.

He was the first person to teach saxophone at the Royal Conservatory of Music in Toronto. Although not himself a composer, he persuaded composers such as Srul Irving Glick, John Weinzweig, Bruce Mather, and Violet Archer to write music for his instrument. In his quest to promote the saxophone he co-founded the World Saxophone Congress with Eugene Rousseau in Chicago in 1969. The organization brings players, critics, composers, and audiences together in a different city every three years.

Early on, as a struggling performer and teacher, he invented a fictitious character, Ronald Joy, to be his front man for booking and promoting concerts to impresarios throughout North America. When potential sponsors responded to Brodie's mass mailings by telephoning and asking to speak to Joy, Brodie would lower his voice by a couple of octaves and start bargaining performance fees, hotel rates, and dates. The fake manager arranged nearly eight hundred concerts for his "client" in the 1960s and '70s.

During his fifty-year career as a professional musician, Brodie, the self-styled "ambassador of the saxophone," probably played more concerts, recorded more albums, toured more countries, and taught more private students than any classical saxophonist of his or any other day. He was a champion not only of his own virtuosity as a player but of the saxophone as a musical instrument.

PAUL ZION BRODIE was born in Montreal on April 10, 1934, the younger son of Sam and Florence (née Schiller) Brodie. When Paul was ten months old, his father, who ran a dry goods store, shifted his family to the north end of Winnipeg, where he found work selling radios in an appliance store. The family moved again when Paul was eleven, to Regina, in neighbouring Saskatchewan.

He went to Strathcona School and sang in the junior choir at his synagogue. His father gave him a clarinet for his bar mitzvah and taught him to play "Alexander's Ragtime Band." In high school, the only subject that interested him was music. Sick in bed with a cold one day, Brodie was listening to the radio and heard Freddy Gardner play "I'm in the Mood for Love" on the saxophone. He was besotted with the sound and immediately decided to switch instruments. Goodbye, clarinet. Hello, saxophone.

He earned money to buy a saxophone by working at a local deli, but he couldn't find a teacher and so transferred what he knew about playing the clarinet to the saxophone. After graduating from high school in 1952, he packed his sax and his clarinet and headed to Winnipeg. He enrolled in a pre-law program at United College (now the University of Winnipeg) but failed so miserably he switched programs and schools, ending up at the University of Michigan, where Larry Teal taught the saxophone. Unable even to play scales, he was stunned by the virtuosity of the other applicants. When the university accepted him on probation for six months, he "practiced like a nut, ten hours a day," and still barely passed the audition. But he'd learned discipline and how to set a goal.

In one of his first classes in the history of music he heard a recording of French classical saxophone virtuoso Marcel Mule playing the alto sax. His ambitions changed: whereas he had once hoped to be good enough to play in a band led by a musician of the calibre of Tommy Dorsey or Les Brown, he now considered the possibilities of becoming a classical saxophonist.

He joined the university band under conductor William Revelli and played the bass saxophone when they performed at Carnegie Hall in April 1954. He also formed a dance combo called the Stardusters, which helped earn tuition money and taught him a great deal about the business of promoting and organizing a group.

After graduating with a bachelor's degree in music education and a master's degree in performance in December 1957, he went to Paris to study with Maestro Mule. Back in Canada, he moved to Toronto and looked for a job teaching saxophone.

"The Royal Conservatory of Music is now in its seventy-second year and we have never allowed a saxophone in the building," protested Ettore Mazzoleni, director of the RCM, but the ever-persuasive and persistent Brodie succeeded in getting an audition. He played so well he broke the embargo and was hired as a woodwind instructor. Soon he was also playing on an occasional basis for the Toronto Symphony Orchestra and doing regional tours with Jeunesses Musicales, first with pianist George Brough and then with Colombe Pelletier as his accompanist.

He made his debut as a soloist with the TSO at a Sunday afternoon concert on December 27, 1959, with Walter Susskind conducting, and his New York debut at the Town Hall on November 18, 1960, with George Brough accompanying him on the piano and Rima Goodman, a modern dancer from Toronto whom he'd married eight months earlier, turning the pages. There were only about forty-five people in the audience, but one of them was Raymond Erickson, the music critic for the *New York Times*. "Mr. Brodie's skill made everything he played sound fluent and easy although the music was studded with technical difficulties... producing a lovely soft tone when he wanted to... in his splendidly vital performance," he wrote. A jubilant Brodie phoned the Canadian Wire Service and begged them to pick up Erickson's review, which they obligingly did, flashing the news about the Canadian native's success in the Big Apple. Brodie carried that tattered clipping in his wallet for the rest of his life.

Two performance careers in one family meant too much travelling for a couple who wanted to stay married, so the following year, the Brodies settled in Toronto, added teaching to their repertoires, and established the Brodie School of Music and Modern Dance in a former furniture store. The dance studio was on the ground floor, six music studios were in the basement, and the second floor had two apartments. They lived in one and turned the other into an additional five music studios.

The Brodies ran their school for nearly twenty years, employing about twenty music and dance teachers and training about 650 students a season, among them Willem Moolenbeek, Lawrence Sereda, Robert Pusching, John Price, Robert Bauer, and Jean-Guy Brault, who went on to a long and successful career as a flautist with the National Arts Centre Orchestra. Brodie also taught woodwinds at the University of Toronto from 1968 to 1973; he formed a quartet in 1972 to showcase his own playing and the work of a revolving group of three students. The Paul Brodie Saxophone Quartet played at the World Saxophone Congress in London in 1976 and in the 1981 film *Circle of Two*.

After his "international" success with the film *Heaven Can Wait*, Brodie shuttered the school and wound up the quartet. The lease was up, he was in "phone ringing off the hook" demand, and she was "wildly busy" with commissions for her work as a fibre artist. He never stopped teaching, however, either privately in a smaller studio or at York University, where he taught from 1982 until the late 1990s.

Concert saxophonist and composer Daniel Rubinoff was one of his last students. "I needed a mentor and I found one," he said about his relationship with Brodie. After studying in Europe, Rubinoff worked with Brodie for eighteen months beginning in 1995 and won the gold medal for the 1997 ARCT (Associate of the Royal Conservatory) exams.

"One of the things about Paul's legacy is that he realized that you had to practise the saxophone to become as good a performer as you could possibly be, but you also had to be a tireless promoter," Rubinoff said. "He was a wonderful businessperson and he passed that on." How to have a career as a concert saxophonist, how to talk to an audience, how to be tough about criticism, how to cold-call a concert promoter, and how to set up a teaching studio were among Brodie's synergistic "life lessons."

In his mid-sixties Brodie, who had high blood pressure and diabetes, almost died from an aortic dissection — a tear in the wall of the aorta. Even that nearly fatal condition didn't persuade him to pack away his saxophone. When an MRI revealed an enormous aneurysm in his aorta in 2007, he insisted on postponing surgery until after he had finished recording a CD of his favourite pieces with harpist Erica Goodman. Once again the man and his instrument prevailed, but at a perilous cost. Near the end of the long operation, his heart finally gave out. He died, aged seventy-three, on November 19, 2007.

JACKIE BURROUGHS

Actor

FEBRUARY 2, 1939 – SEPTEMBER 22, 2010

A S SKINNY AS a praying mantis, tottering on platform shoes, sucking on a cigarette, her hair a cumulus of auburn curls, Jackie Burroughs — all of five feet, three inches — showed up for an audition at the Stratford Festival in 1975, clutching a handmade male doll so large it threatened to topple her.

"If you don't mind, I thought we would do it together. It's so boring doing it by yourself," she explained to artistic director Robin Phillips in the first of a litany of deadpan comments larded with double entendres. "She was absolutely hysterical," he remembered thirty-five years later. "Everything she said was so provocative that it was almost impossible not to give him [the doll] a contract too, because she was able to make him look so good. That is one of the most extraordinary things about her: she has always made the rest of us look better than we are."

Burroughs, a classically trained dancer, had a body that she could twist like a corkscrew and a quicksilver imagination that could morph from sexy to farcical to tragic. Along with the great actor William Hutt, she shared an ability to find humour in the tragic roles and tragedy in the humorous ones, according to Phillips, who directed them both.

Best known for her triple-Gemini-winning role as the twitchy and eccentric schoolteacher Hetty King in the long-running television series *Road to Avonlea*, Burroughs appeared in more than seventy-five films, often in a cameo that stole the viewer's heart, beginning with a role as a factory worker in Don Owen's 1966 National Film Board classic *Notes for a Film about Donna & Gail*. She luminously played Kate Flynn, with her toothy, sensual smile, opposite Richard Farnsworth in *The Grey Fox*, the Missus with Gordon Pinsent in *John and the Missus*, and the narcissistic and obsessive Maryse Holder in *A Winter Tan*, a film she also co-wrote and co-directed.

Beginning as a stage actress at Hart House at the University of Toronto, she played contemporary and classical roles in Canada and abroad, including Portia opposite Hume Cronyn's Shylock in *The Merchant of Venice* at Stratford. She appeared with Peter O'Toole in *Uncle Vanya* at the Royal Alexandra Theatre and as part of the original cast of *Ten Lost Years* at Toronto Workshop Productions.

A bohemian by inclination, Burroughs, who died at age seventy-one of gastric cancer at home in Toronto on September 22, 2010, was an unconventional celebrity in the tiny world of Canadian entertainment. Despite her many Genie and Gemini Awards, including an Earl Grey Lifetime Achievement Award from the Academy of Canadian Cinema and Television (2001) and the Governor General's Performing Arts Award for lifetime achievement in 2005, she rarely, if ever, displayed the hauteur of a *"grande actrice"* deigning to grace a stage or set.

Instead she had intense friendships with men and especially young women, including actress and director Sarah Polley. She took an eager but not avid interest in their careers and their creative lives. She was "an artist in the most true, pure, brutal sense of the word," said Polley, who first met Burroughs as an eleven-year-old on the set of *Road to Avonlea*. She was "passionate, fierce, uncompromising, honest."

JACQUELINE WEST BURROUGHS was born in Southport, Lancashire, England, on February 2, 1939, during the treacherous diplomatic preamble to the Second World War. Her mother, Edna Berry, had been a silent screen actress before marrying salesman Harry Burroughs, who worked for the company that made True Temper golf-club shafts. He spent the war flying missions as a pilot in the Royal Air Force. After suffering through the bombs and the casualty lists with a small child, the Burroughses waited for the advent of peace to have a second one. Their son, Gary, was a "peace baby," born in December 1945.

When Burroughs was twelve, her father moved the family to Toronto because he had business opportunities there: importing True Temper golf shafts into Canada and running a tool-manufacturing company called Brades Nash Tyzack Ltd. The family settled on Chestnut Park Road in Rosedale after a romantic spell on Centre Island, a ferry ride across the Toronto harbour. A decade later, the effervescent Edna Burroughs persuaded her husband to buy the historic Oban Inn in Niagara-on-the-Lake, a hostelry that was later owned and operated by their son.

At home, Burroughs was a rebel, often clashing with her mother at the dinner table; but at school she was a conformist. Head girl in her final year at Branksome Hall, a tony private girls' school, she carried a hefty 165 pounds and strutted around in her uniform of knee socks and a kilt, eager to please the headmistress. "I was a horrible suck," she confessed later.

After Branksome she went to Trinity College at the University of Toronto (1958–61), where she shed her extra schoolgirl weight, "discovered literature and was full of angst about Virginia Woolf," and began acting at Hart House and in summer stock theatre in the Muskoka region.

About this time she opened a front-loading dryer at her local laundromat and out tumbled a "seventeen-year-old Jewish boy with green teeth and acne," according to a *Toronto Life* profile by journalist Martin Knelman. That's how she met Zal Yanovsky. Five years her junior and a self-taught musician, Yanovsky was playing guitar in coffee houses; later he teamed up with Denny Doherty in the Halifax Three and still later joined Cass Elliot to form the Mugwumps in Greenwich Village. (For more about Denny Doherty, please see page 242.)

Doherty and Elliot went on to form the Mamas and the Papas and Yanovsky collaborated with John Sebastian in the short-lived but hugely influential pop-rock group the Lovin' Spoonful. One friend described Yanovsky in those days as "the guy...in the striped shirt with the sheepdog bangs and a world-eating grin" who played the "classy, joyful, percolating guitar solo in 'Do You Believe in Magic.'"

While Yanovsky was playing in coffee houses, Burroughs, who had spent years in ballet classes, went to England to study drama, mime, and interpretive dance and ended up joining the Chesterfield Civic Theatre in Derbyshire. "It was a bleak little northern town, but the people there came to our plays just the way they'd go bowling or play bingo on other nights," she recounted years later. "It was terrific experience — you'd play a lead one week, an extra the next and a character part after that."

That's what Burroughs loved: the process of creating character, using every gram of her being—intellectual, emotional, and physical—to react to the script, her fellow actors, and the audience. After returning to Canada in 1963, she acted in theatre companies in Toronto and Winnipeg and in a couple of small parts at the Stratford Festival before moving to Greenwich Village in New York City, where she resumed her tempestuous relationship with Yanovsky.

While he was busy becoming rich and famous as a rock star, travelling back and forth between Los Angeles and New York, she lived mostly in Greenwich Village with her pet iguanas and frogs and studied theatre with Uta Hagen and dance with Merce Cunningham and Martha Graham. Pressured by her parents, she and Yanovsky married in 1967, shortly before their daughter, Zoe, was born on October 17, 1967.

The following summer, after a drug bust that had turned acidic, Yanovsky quit the Lovin' Spoonful and turned his back on the music business. He and Burroughs moved back to Toronto with their daughter. Within a couple of years they had split; in the early 1970s he moved with Zoe to a farm outside Kingston to live with restaurateur Rose Richardson. Together they created the landmark Kingston eateries Chez Piggy and Pan Chancho Bakery. "My mother was an actress and my father a musician, and I was carted around to all sorts of adult situations," Zoe Yanofsky said in an interview after her mother died. They "were fiercely in love with each other" and had an "intense" although atypical mother-daughter relationship, including hanging around backstage while Burroughs was acting at the Stratford Festival.

As artistic director, Phillips had lured Burroughs away from contemporary theatre in Toronto and back to Stratford in the mid-1970s. "A lot of people spend a lot of time acting for the audience," he said. "Jackie is so compelling and so bizarre and so penetrating that she demands your full attention. And God help you if you don't pay attention to her [on stage as an actor] because you will find yourself walking straight through a laugh where you least expect it... [or in rehearsal as a director] because she will go from the text to asking you a question and unless you are very alert, you will never know the difference."

Incessantly in search of the fresh and the immediate, Burroughs was passionate about getting it right rather than delivering what a director demanded, a perfectionism that often led to tears and arguments in rehearsal halls, at television studios, and on film sets. Polley remembers Burroughs "constantly sticking up for the crew" and "confronting" the production bosses on the set of *Road to Avonlea*. "She put herself on the line constantly for other people, for their rights as workers on a set."

Performing a defined role in a continuing series — *Avonlea* ran for six seasons, from 1990 to 1996, on CBC and the Disney Channel in the U.S. — was artistically wearing, but the show gave Burroughs a comfortable financial cushion and made it possible for her to create a winter respite and an artistic oasis in Mexico.

She "loved the people, the language and the culture" of Mexico, said Yanovsky, who can remember her mother drawing pictures of her dream house after acquiring a piece of land in a tiny village in Oaxaca. Eventually, with help from locals, she built an adobe house opening onto a courtyard, in keeping with the landscape. And then she added a twist: painting it a bubble-gum-pink colour. With another local friend, a gardener named Julio, she dug a multi-level series of gardens connected with intricate walkways and planted masses of flowers and blossoming shrubs.

Her love of Mexico melded with another creative project, her obsession with the life and letters of Maryse Holder, a feminist author and sexual hedonist who had published the book *Give Sorrow Words: Maryse Holder's Letters from Mexico* in 1979. It is hard to understand Burroughs's fascination with Holder, but it is certainly true that she delivered a virtuoso (and Genie Award–winning) performance as the self-destructive and doomed drug- and sex-addicted tourist in the 1987 film *A Winter Tan*. "It would never have been a film without her," Yanovsky said of the project, which began as a monologue written by Burroughs.

A vigorous smoker and reformed drinker who loved partying, dancing, and talking late into the night, Burroughs was diagnosed with gastric cancer in 2009. As the disease rampaged, she made a final visit to her beloved home in Mexico. Then, sustained by family and dear friends, she began the serious business of dying, holding court in her Yorkville apartment in Toronto, making her own funeral arrangements, and sharing final thoughts and wishes with friends and family.

She approached death with the same intensity, honesty, and creative impulse that she had done everything else in her life. "I never knew it was possible to die so eloquently," said Polley. "She's redefining what it means... breaking down boundaries and rules and storming the gates of experience, refusing ever to deny what is real and honest in her work and her life. It's kind of amazing to see her do that to the end."

But it wasn't the end. Burroughs had planned a curtain call. Mourners sitting in the pews at St. James Cathedral in Toronto, a week after her death, knew from the order of service that there was going to be a reading of the Twenty-Third Psalm. What they didn't expect was to hear that husky, alluring voice intoning "The Lord is my Shepherd; I shall not want . . ." from across the ultimate threshold, in a performance that was simultaneously haunting and comforting. Burroughs was gone but the voice lived on, in the silence of the cathedral and the memories of the bereaved.

DENNY DOHERTY

Musician and Actor

NOVEMBER 29, 1940 – JANUARY 19, 2007

F OR A SHINING moment in the mid-1960s, the Mamas and the Papas were an American counterpoint to the Beatles. In three short years — 1965 through 1968 — they produced five albums and sold an estimated twenty million records. Their ten hits included "California Dreamin'", "Dedicated to the One I Love," "Dream a Little Dream of Me," and "Monday, Monday."

Unlike the well-tailored mop-tops, this hippie group had as many women as men — and a Canadian. Michelle Phillips was blonde and beautiful and could carry a tune; Cass Elliot garbed her obesity in caftans but she had a magnetic charisma and a haunting alto voice. The leader and Michelle's husband was John Phillips, a lanky songwriting guru who sported a funny chinchilla hat. Haligonian Denny Doherty was the fourth. A cherubic, sweet-voiced tenor, he co-wrote the hits "I Saw Her Again Last Night" and "Got a Feelin'."

Behind the scenes the group was wasting its talent and energy because they were all in thrall to sex, drugs, and alcohol in those sexually liberated and naive post-Pill, pre-AIDS times. Cass Elliot (whose real name was Ellen Naomi Cohen) was in love with Doherty; he was besotted with Michelle Phillips; and John Phillips, not surprisingly, was jealous, especially since the threesome all lived in the same house.

"He came downstairs and caught us...flagrante delicto," according to Doherty in *Go Where You Wanna Go: The Oral History of The Mamas & the Papas*, by Matthew Greenwald. Michelle and John attempted a reconciliation so the band could keep on playing, but the following year, in June of 1966, the band signed a statement, with the backing of their record label, that temporarily kicked Michelle, the most beautiful but least talented member, out of the group.

"I'll bury you all," she screamed at them in a rage. And she did. Mama Cass died of a heart attack in 1974, when she was only thirty-two, and John Phillips succumbed to heart disease after decades of drug and alcohol abuse, in March 2001, at sixty-five. Doherty turned his life around with the help of his wife, Jeannette, but even he didn't reach his three score years and ten. Doherty died of complications following abdominal surgery on January 19, 2007. He was sixty-six.

BORN IN HALIFAX, Nova Scotia, on November 29, 1940, Dennis Gerrard Stephen Doherty was one of five children of a hard-drinking Halifax pipe-fitter. He began singing publicly on a dare, performing "Love Letters in the Sand" in a skating-rink-turned-dancehall with Peter Power's dance band. He was fifteen. After high school he began working in a pawn shop and singing after hours with a local rock band, the Hepsters.

He formed his first folk trio, the Colonials, in 1959. The group changed its name to the Halifax Three and signed a recording contract with Columbia Records in New York. They had a minor hit, "The Man Who Wouldn't Sing Along with Mitch"; released an album, *San Francisco Bay Blues*, in 1963 on the Epic label; and performed in eastern Canada and in the United States.

Separately he also became friends with Cass Elliot, a singer with a band called the Big Three that also featured Tim Rose. A few months later Doherty's band broke up, ironically in a hotel called the Colonial, the original name of his ill-fated group. He and his accompanist, Toronto musician Zal Yanovsky, were destitute in New York City.

After hearing about their troubles, Cass Elliot convinced her manager to hire them. So Doherty and Yanovsky joined the Big Three and enjoyed some success in Greenwich Village. More players were added and the group changed its name to the Mugwumps. They also broke up, as so many groups did in those fluid times, and for the usual reasons: insolvency and bickering.

About this time, John Phillips's band the New Journeymen needed a replacement for tenor Marshall Brickman, who had left, after an affair with Michelle, to pursue a career as a television and screenwriter. That band also broke up — those were tempestuous times. Two powerful new groups emerged from the wreckage: Sebastian and Yanofsky formed The Lovin' Spoonful and Elliot and Doherty joined voices with the Phillipses in 1965.

Finding a name was more difficult than forming the group. John Phillips fancied The Magic Cyrcle, which was too arcane for the rest of them. Then, "lying around vegging out watching TV" and doing the usual — drinking — the foursome saw a Hells Angels member on a talk show refer to his girlfriend as a "mama." Elliot decided that's what she wanted to be, and Michelle agreed. "We're the Mamas," she declared, which left the men little choice but to become the Papas.

Six months later, in September of 1965, the group signed a recording contract with ABC/Dunhill Records and began to record their debut album, *If You Can Believe Your Eyes and Ears.* That's when Doherty and Michelle Phillips began their tumultuous affair. After the band stripped Michelle of her Mama status the following year, she was quickly replaced by Jill Gibson, girlfriend of the band's producer, Lou Adler. Her tenure as a Mama lasted ten weeks, a period during which Doherty drank heavily to console himself over the loss of the beautiful Michelle. In an effort to put things back together, Michelle was allowed to rejoin the Mamas and the Papas, but things were no longer copacetic.

"The first thing I did in the morning, and the last thing I did at night, was have a blast of rum," Doherty, by then a recovering alcoholic, told a reporter for the *New York Times* in January 2000. The band seemed to have lost its focus. In the middle of making another album, Elliot left to go out on her own. With the loss of her outsize presence and distinctive singing voice, the group fell apart in the summer of 1968, although it did re-form briefly in 1971.

Elliot, who had embarked on a successful solo career, remained friends with Doherty, even though he continued to drown his romantic sorrows about Phillips. Later he admitted he had ignored a marriage proposal from Elliot because he'd been too stoned at the time to respond. Like most of the pop music world, he was devastated when she suffered a fatal heart attack in July 1974, after two sold-out performances at the Palladium in London, England.

On his own, Doherty released *Whatcha Gonna Do* in 1972 with ABC/Dunhill. He acted on Broadway in Andy Warhol's 1974 production of *Man on the Moon*, with a script written by John Phillips. It closed after five performances. Three years later he headed back home to Halifax. He performed at the Atlantic Folk Festival for the next two summers, was host of the regional CBC TV program *Denny's Sho'* in 1978, and took on several acting roles at the Neptune Theatre in Halifax under artistic director John Neville. Among other plays, he appeared in *The Taming of the Shrew*, *Much Ado about Nothing*, and *Cabaret*.

Unwilling to bury his halcyon memories of pop success, he re-formed the Mamas and the Papas in 1980, with John Phillips and his daughter Mackenzie and Elaine "Spanky" McFarlane. They toured internationally until 1986, when Doherty moved to Toronto.

In the late 1980s Doherty appeared in *Fire*, a gospel-rock musical written by Paul Ledoux and David Young. In his most enduring role as an actor, in 1993 he began playing the Harbour Master in *Theodore Tugboat*, a children's television show chronicling the "lives" of vessels in a busy port loosely based on Halifax Harbour. By then he was married to Jeannette, and was the father of three children. Often credited with saving Doherty's life, Jeannette was the one who insisted he had to leave Hollywood in the 1970s and make Halifax and then Toronto home base. She died of ovarian cancer in 1998.

That same year he launched an autobiographical musical, *Dream a Little Dream: The Nearly True Story of the Mamas and the Papas*, which opened in Halifax and went on to Toronto and then Santa Barbara, California. He opened the show by saying: "My name is Dennis Gerrard Stephen Doherty... In the sixties, I was in a group called the Mamas and the Papas, and this, among other things, is the story of that group and those times. But, as Grace Slick said, 'If you remember the Sixties, you weren't there.'"

Doherty was inducted into the Canadian Music Hall of Fame in 1996 and nominated for a Gemini for best performance in a children's or youth program or series for *Theodore Tugboat* in 1997.

Just before Christmas 2006, Doherty had surgery for an abdominal aneurysm. He subsequently suffered kidney problems and was put on dialysis, but his earlier life had caught up with him. He collapsed at home in Mississauga, Ontario, and died before he could receive medical attention.

ROBERT BURNS

Graphic Designer

APRIL 16, 1942 – MAY 14, 2005

ROBERT BURNS WAS many things: a graphic artist, a creative thinker, a brander—he and partner Heather Cooper created the beaver logo for Roots—but most of all he was a drug addict. That fact obscured his talents and darkened his life, from the collapse of the high-flying design firm Burns Cooper Hynes in the early eighties to the ruin of personal relationships and his own early death in 2005. He had been abusing drugs for nearly half his life.

"Addiction isn't a flaw. It's a disease," communications consultant Bob Ramsay said in a eulogy at Burns's funeral, lamenting the waste of such brilliance. Himself a recovered cocaine addict and winner of a Courage to Come Back Award from the Centre for Addiction and Mental Health Foundation, Ramsay had intervened several times to get Burns into treatment, but the addiction's hold was too tenacious.

As a designer, Burns was the equivalent of a bandleader, said his former partner, copywriter Jim Hynes. "He was like Glenn Miller. He knew the sound he wanted to create and he was a genius at putting together the right ingredients to get that result." Other people did most of the work, of course. "He used to call me the donkey," said Hynes, "because I did a little work every day, keeping the cart moving at all times while he would run, run, run and then crash because he would be running at a pace that nobody could sustain."

At his best, Burns was a virtuoso of the big idea—the central phrase or image that you could build a product or an advertising campaign around. "He

had heart, wit and intelligence," said Eric (Ric) Young, a social and environmental communications consultant. "That is a rare combination and it was
invested in all of his work, which was strategic and conceptual. He had real
passion and ambition and he brought fantastic energy and an aspiration for
greatness to every project."

Like Svengali, he "could plug into another person and tune himself onto
that wavelength so perfectly that it was mesmerizing," said Hynes. "That was
his greatest talent when he was building a very successful organization, but it
was also the talent that enabled him to survive on the street and carry on with
a lifestyle that most people can only manage for a few years before they end up
in the graveyard."

ROBERT BURNS WAS born on April 16, 1942, in London, England, less than a
year after the Blitz ended. His early childhood was spent in a war-racked
working-class neighbourhood on the outskirts of London.

He was hard to handle as a teenager and once made headlines in a local
newspaper after he and a couple of friends were arrested for urinating on
somebody's front lawn. His parents, fearing he was headed for trouble, made
him enlist in the Royal Air Force after he left school at sixteen. The RAF tried
to train him as an armaments technician working on nuclear weapons, but he
couldn't tolerate the routines and regulations. The quintessential free spirit,
he frequently butted heads with his superiors, although he did find success as
a bugler and a fencer. Finally, having joined the Campaign for Nuclear
Disarmament, he persuaded the RAF that he was a conscientious objector and
won a discharge.

He put together a portfolio and won a grant to go to art school to study
painting and sculpture. Later he confessed that he had spent his grant money
on Savile Row suits and handmade shoes to "make up for lost time" before
dropping out. Like so many creative types in the early 1960s, he fancied himself a folksinger. As well as strumming a guitar, he ran an artists' booking
agency called Folksounds in Lewisham.

He met Canadian Ellen Anderson (later an artist and social activist) in
1965 as she "stepped off the plane" from Toronto. One of her high school
friends, who was working at Folksounds, had asked Burns for a ride to the
airport. They were together from that moment, according to Anderson.
They married and made plans to move to Canada because she thought

they would both have a greater chance of making a living in the arts in Toronto.

Burns, then twenty-two, needed a passport. At the registry office he made a casual joke about his parentage and then learned that he'd been adopted as a baby. He felt betrayed, according to Anderson, who believes that confronting the truth about his birth was one of the demons that Burns wrestled with for the rest of his life.

In Toronto, Burns and Anderson shared a house with a number of artists, including the photographer Bert Bell. Burns found work as a graphic artist for CFTO, the Toronto flagship station of the CTV television network, and then formed his own company, Robert Burns Designs. The Canadian market was too small for him to specialize in, say, exhibit design or annual reports, so he had to learn to be a generalist, which became an advantage because he could "cross-pollinate" ideas from one aspect of the business to another and combine images, type, and metaphors in fresh ways that caught the attention of some big American clients.

Burns, who had grown up with rationing and deprivation, was so bewitched by the wealth of North America that he wrote a letter to a friend back in England saying, "The streets are filled with cars as big as houses." Soft drugs and easy money were big parts of the advertising world in the late 1960s, and few were more attracted to both than Burns.

He left Anderson in 1969, when she was pregnant with their son, Gabe. The breakup was cruel and acrimonious. By then he was working on a freelance basis with Heather Cooper, an illustrator and graphic designer whom he'd met through photographer Bert Bell. They began a professional and personal relationship that lasted eleven years, a creative partnership that brought them a stellar list of clients, a lavish lifestyle, and a daughter, Sarah.

Either separately or together, as the graphic design firm Burns Cooper, the duo seemed to be involved in everything that was hip and innovative, from David Crombie's mayoralty campaign in Toronto to the Canadian Brass, Roots, and Citytv. "Being intensely creative was what we were about," said Cooper in an interview after Burns died. "Work was our passion and probably the original reason for us being together."

Jim Hynes arrived in Toronto from Montreal in 1972 to work as corporate communications chief for the Industrial Acceptance Corporation, which was about to become the Continental Bank of Canada. He hired Burns Cooper to develop a new graphic identity and design an annual report for the transformed company. Over the next three years the two men became such close friends and colleagues that Burns persuaded Hynes to quit his job in 1975 and join him and Cooper in a partnership that became Burns Cooper Hynes.

Within five years they became one of the biggest, best known, and most prestigious graphic design companies in the country. They produced corporate identities, annual reports, and sales materials for clients such as Northern Telecom, Alcan, Imperial Oil, Cadillac Fairview, and Canadian Pacific Air Lines.

"He loved luxury. When he had money, it vanished instantly on the most expensive things he could find," said Hynes. In those days it was not uncommon to end a meeting with an advertising agency by doing a "mile-long line" of cocaine on the boardroom table. "Everybody snorted coke," said Hynes. "It was considered completely harmless fun." But Burns, who had become a serious addict by the end of the decade, moved on to injecting, quickly draining the company to feed his rapacious habit.

"He changed our lives in a big way, first for the better and then for the worse," said Hynes. "I needed to get out of the corporate world and I still remember that decade as the happiest of my working life. Heather is a very reclusive person and for her to sell herself as an illustrator was very difficult, but Robert made her into a superstar. The first requirement of one of Robert's big ideas was a great big poster by Heather Cooper. He created an unending market for her work that she could never have created for herself."

After the collapse of Burns Cooper Hynes in the early 1980s — Cooper said it took her years to wind up dealings with creditors and contractors — Burns started a couple of other design firms and collaborative ventures, but he never really recovered his momentum or his sobriety. By the mid-1990s he was calling himself a communications designer and a "cartographer of new realities" and had a business card advertising his services as "Making Values Visible." He declared: "Design is at least as important, maybe more important than art in contemporary society," in an April 1993 talk sponsored by the Advertising and Design Club of Canada.

That was probably the highlight of his post–Burns Cooper Hynes career. He couldn't control his addictions and ended up on the streets for close to a decade. In 2004 he learned that he had at least two types of hepatitis and terminal liver damage. The following year he moved into a group home run by the Homes First Society and connected with outreach and religious workers at St. James Cathedral in Toronto and a neighbourhood centre called 6 St. Joseph Street. There is a photograph of him looking happy and peaceful standing with the rest of the crew on a break from a renovation project. Not long after that picture was snapped, he collapsed at his group home. He was taken to hospital, where he died of complications of hepatitis on May 14, 2005. He had turned sixty-three the month before.

PADDY MITCHELL
Bank Robber

JUNE 26, 1942 – JANUARY 14, 2007

A s a crook, Paddy Mitchell was charming, manipulative, and flamboyant. One of Canada's most successful armed bank robbers, he was a master of disguise and a diabolically clever escape artist. He considered himself a gentleman thief and took pride in never harming anyone — at least physically. In that nicety, he was the consummate Canadian. His signature was a ticking stopwatch dangling from a chain around his neck, a graphic reminder to keep moving in order to get in and out of a bank in ninety seconds.

During an eleven-year crime spree, his Stopwatch Gang, which included Lionel "The Ghost" Wright and Stephen Reid, stole $15 million from banks across North America. The only casualty was Reid, who once shot himself in the foot during a holdup.

Mitchell was the mastermind. Impossible to imagine what he might have become if he'd parlayed his wits and his chutzpah in a more conventional career. Instead, the kid who grew up poor and rough in a working-class district of Ottawa graduated from pinching money from his mother's purse to planning bank heists to underwrite his lavish drug-and-booze-soaked lifestyle.

He once boasted that there wasn't a bank in the world that couldn't be robbed. "No matter how careful they are, they always seem to miss at least one little chink in their security. And that was where I came in," he wrote in a letter to a journalist friend in 2000 from his final home, an American prison. "I could always find that little chink."

A strategic and tactical whiz, he'd often plan diversions such as calling in a bomb threat at one end of town to preoccupy the police while his Stopwatch Gang was pulling a bank heist in another. Even when apprehended, he could slip through prison walls. He faked a heart attack to break out of the Joyceville prison, east of Kingston, and later strolled out of a maximum-security institution in Arizona after crawling through an air-conditioning duct located in the ceiling of the warden's office. Mitchell was also a master of disguise who dyed his hair, wore wigs, and even submitted to plastic surgery when his face, plastered on wanted posters throughout the U.S., became dangerously familiar to law enforcement officials.

He estimated that he had taken part in more than a hundred robberies in his three-decade-long career as a bank robber. At the peak of his notoriety he was at the top of the FBI's Most Wanted list. His gang's exploits were the subject of a film, television documentaries, and a 1992 book, *The Stopwatch Gang*, by Greg Weston.

"Stealing was not something any of us wanted to make a career of," Mitchell confided from his final prison cell. What he couldn't resist, though, and what he described as "the greatest thrill in the world," was being "back in the apartment after a successful job, counting the money." That's why he and the rest of the gang kept going back to the till, hoping to make "that one BIG score so we could all retire and never have to rob or steal again."

Instead he died alone, more than two thousand kilometres from his family, of metastasized lung cancer in a prison hospital in Butner, North Carolina, on January 14, 2007. He was sixty-four.

PATRICK MICHAEL (PADDY) Mitchell was born on Preston Street in Ottawa on June 26, 1942, in the middle of the Second World War. He grew up in what was then a scrappy neighbourhood with his two older brothers: boxer Fred, known as "Pinky," and Bobby, also a thief, who died of cancer in 2002.

He was only twelve and in Grade 6 in Our Lady of Perpetual Help School when he pulled his first scam. The nuns had organized a campaign to send food to the starving children in China. It was the aftermath of the Mao Zedong–led revolution, and the nuns promised that every ten-cent donation would help move a soul out of purgatory and to the first rung of the ladder towards heaven. By his own admission, Mitchell embarked on a two-month crime wave, pilfering money from purses, helping himself to loose change in his older brothers' pockets, and grabbing money from the cash drawers in local shops. "I was the biggest donor in the school," he later bragged.

Nobody caught him that time, but as a teenager he was frequently in trouble with the local police for fighting, drinking under age, loitering, or petty vandalism. His high school years were spent behind bars, learning a life of crime rather than the usual academic skills. When he was fourteen, he got into a brawl with another boy. During the fight, the other kid hit his head on a cement sidewalk and died. Mitchell was convicted of manslaughter and sent to a reformatory in Guelph for two years. Only two months after his release, he got into trouble again and was sent back to Guelph, where he was detained until his eighteenth birthday.

While he was honing his larcenous craft throughout the 1960s, he married, had a son, and held a number of low-level jobs. But parenting and punching a clock didn't have the lure of carousing and thievery. He had hooked up with Lionel Wright, the night clerk for a large trucking company that had a warehouse the size of a football field crammed with property belonging to customers. The two thieves systematically removed the goods and sold them on the black market.

By 1973 Mitchell was a thirty-one-year-old aluminum-siding salesman by day and the after-hours boss of a burgeoning criminal empire that he operated mostly from a table in the tavern of Ottawa's Belle Claire Hotel. That's when he met convicted bank robber Stephen Reid, "just turned three times seven" and holed up in a basement suite in Ottawa, "fresh off a prison break," as Reid recounted in "The Art of Dying in Prison," an essay in *The Heart Does Break*, a collection edited by George Bowering and Jean Baird. The two meshed. "Pat's strong suit was charm and he carried it off with the smile of a little boy and the manicured look of a Las Vegas pit boss."

Initially Mitchell planned the robberies and Reid carried them out in what he later described as a relationship like that of Jack Sprat and his wife: "We licked a lot of platters clean." With Mitchell's felonious sidekick Lionel Wright, they formed what came to be called the Stopwatch Gang. They pulled their first big job — the "Great Gold Heist," a robbery at Uplands Airport in Ottawa — in April 1974. Mitchell, the mastermind, and his cohorts, Reid and Wright, stole seven gold bars destined for the Canadian mint that were worth more than $750,000.

He got away with that one, but he was charged, tried, and convicted for another crime, although he always claimed he was innocent. The Ottawa Police and the RCMP connected him to a suitcase filled with cocaine at the same airport. Mitchell said he abided by the criminal's honour code of not snitching on a fellow thief, but police linked the suitcase to Christopher John Clarkson, a nephew of Stephen Clarkson, a University of Toronto professor. (Clarkson jumped bail in 1976, while awaiting trial on charges of conspiring to import cocaine from Curaçao. He was extradited back to Canada in late December 2006 to begin the twenty-year prison sentence he had been given in absentia thirty years earlier.)

Meanwhile, Mitchell had been given a seventeen-year prison sentence on the cocaine charges, to be served at a Kingston-area penitentiary. The prison walls couldn't contain him, though, because he was prepared to risk his life for freedom. In November 1979 he soaked a pack of cigarettes in a cup of water, filtered the resulting mixture, and then swallowed the massive dose of nicotine. It simulated the symptoms of a heart attack. Prison guards rushed him by ambulance to a Kingston hospital, where Stopwatch Gang members Wright and Reid were waiting with Mitchell's brother Bobby, all of them garbed as paramedics.

They wheeled him inside the hospital on a gurney and then came back outside a short time later, claiming the prisoner had fled. When the guards rushed inside to track down Mitchell, the fake paramedics wheeled the gurney to a parked ambulance and spirited the crook away to freedom. Later Mitchell reported that his heart was beating double-time for days, but whether that was solely the result of the nicotine rush was never clear.

After his heart calmed down, the trio took a train across the border into the United States, where they kept right on thieving for nearly five years, including holding up two armoured cars that were delivering US$283,000 to a San Diego bank. He was finally arrested in the Phoenix, Arizona, area for another robbery in December 1981, but he walked away after giving the police a false name.

He disappeared until 1983, when the FBI found him living with a girlfriend in a suburban bungalow near Orlando, Florida. He was tried and sentenced to seventeen years in the Arizona State Prison system. After serving only two years, he and two inmates escaped by slithering to freedom through overhead air ducts. They pulled a robbery, brandishing a .22 revolver that one of the three had bought in a bar for a hundred dollars. Apparently the gun was in such poor condition they had to twist an elastic band around the barrel to keep the bullets from falling out.

Mitchell's luck held for more than a decade. He fled to the Philippines, where he married a local woman named Imelda who believed the tale he had spun about being a wealthy American named Gary Weber. Together they had a son, Richard.

All was sweet until the television show *America's Most Wanted* began flashing Mitchell's mug on the small screen in the early 1990s. That's when his Filipina wife knew she had been had. Neighbours reported him to the FBI and he fled the country, bizarrely going back to the U.S. for one more score that he hoped would set him up for the rest of his days.

He stole $160,000 from a bank in Southaven, Mississippi, several weeks later, but the small-town sheriff took him down. He was again convicted and sentenced, this time to sixty-five years in Leavenworth prison in Kansas, with no possibility of parole. Escaping from Leavenworth was not an option. The 1906 prison has walls that go twelve metres below grade and tower equally high above the ground. This was where Robert Stroud, the Birdman of Alcatraz, spent thirty years enhancing his knowledge of ornithology.

Mitchell tried three times to get a transfer to a Canadian prison, writing appeals every two years. After the final rejection he settled down to follow the model established by his friend Reid, who had written an autobiographical novel, *Jackrabbit Parole*, while in prison. After taking a creative writing course, Mitchell eventually produced and self-published his own autobiography, *The Bank Robber's Life: The Life and Fast Times of Patrick Mitchell*.

In the final chapter of the book he admitted that he had allowed another thief, Ron C. Gaskins, to take the rap for a 1980 robbery of $65,000 in cash and cheques from a Sears store in St. Petersburg, Florida. Mitchell said he confessed to the crime in 1994 but it took prison authorities at least a decade to process the information. By then Gaskins had died of cancer, handcuffed to a hospital bed in Jacksonville, Florida. Right up to his dying breaths in 2004, Gaskins was desperately trying to clear his name of the one crime he hadn't committed.

In a series published in the *Ottawa Citizen* in June 2000, Mitchell described his life as a bank robber. "Our number one rule was: nobody gets hurt," he wrote. He also confessed his fear of dying in prison. "I think about it constantly," he said. "It's a horrible fate." And it turned out to be his destiny. In 2006 he felt a lump under his ribcage. Tests indicated that he had a large malignant tumour in his lungs that had already metastasized to his brain. Nobody ever determined whether it had any connection to the nicotine cocktail he had imbibed back in 1979 to escape from the Joyceville Institution.

He was airlifted to the Federal Medical Center, a high-security hospital for convicts in Butner, North Carolina, where the brain tumour was surgically removed, although with some impairment to his cognitive abilities. The doctors decided that the illness had progressed too far for any further chemotherapy or radiation to be effective. "He just wanted to be near his family, near us," his older brother Pinky Mitchell told the *Ottawa Sun*. "We did everything to try and get him back here."

As he was dying, Mitchell continued to write letters to his pal Reid, "but every passing month the envelopes grew thinner" and the letters less frequent. The last one, on a scrap of yellow paper, was delivered from Mitchell's U.S. prison to the institution where Reid was then doing time in Canada. "We've had a life, haven't we," Mitchell wrote. "God bless…"

CHRIS HANEY

Inventor of Trivial Pursuit

AUGUST 9, 1950 – MAY 31, 2010

O N A BITTER December day in 1983, journalist David Cobb was strolling down Yonge Street in Toronto when he stumbled into a queue of people stretching back from a Toys "R" Us store to around the corner of a midtown cross street.

"What are you guys lining up for?" he inquired idly.

"We're waiting to buy a copy of that new game, Trivial Pursuit," somebody replied.

Ah, thought Cobb, with the equivalent of that dumbfounded look that appears on the faces of lottery hopefuls the moment they realize that the numbers on their ticket might actually be worth something.

For once Christmas had come early, not only for Cobb but for the rest of a circle of small investors. About eighteen months earlier they had ponied up some not-so-ready cash to take a flyer on a board game invented by Chris Haney and Scott Abbott, a couple of unheralded Montreal journalists. Cobb won't say how much he has made in the ensuing decades, but he does allow that it was "one of the very few investments where I have ever made my money back." And then some.

That was the beginning of the Trivial Pursuit phenomenon, one of the most successful board games in history — ranking up there with Scrabble and Monopoly. Consumers have bought more than 100 million games in its myriad editions, generating sales of more than a billion dollars. In 2008, multinational toy company Hasbro bought the rights to TP for US$80 million.

Why Trivial Pursuit was such a hit is the stuff of pop-culture theses, but its popularity probably has a lot to do with the times and the people who played it so avidly. By the 1980s the early boomers were in their late twenties and beginning to settle down with steady partners and jobs. The recession had curbed free spending, but boomers had delayed child-rearing, so they had lots of leisure time. They had grown up with sassy educations, so their memory banks were stuffed with general and arcane knowledge that they delighted in spouting — this was the era when *The Book of Lists* by Irving Wallace and his offspring became a bestseller. The Internet existed, but Google was not yet either a noun or a verb, so it was not possible to look up everything, anywhere, all the time. Testing one another's information base was a pleasurable and time-consuming pastime. Throw in chance and a set of dice, and bingo! — Trivial Pursuit was the next big thing.

If TP was good for its investors, it should have been a fairy tale for the founders and the small coterie of friends and family who helped to develop and market the game. And it was for all of them, except Chris Haney, the driven creative visionary who grew up poor and was a millionaire by the time he was thirty-two.

"He spent most of his life, even when he was young, being a good buddy and a friend, and once the game got going, helping and looking after everybody," said his younger sister, Shaw Festival actress Mary Haney. "But he forgot to look after and love himself. That is what saddens me more than anything."

Somebody once asked Haney how Trivial Pursuit had changed his life and he replied that he now had the opportunity to choose his own miseries. "He just didn't enjoy his good fortune like I have and the other partners have. It was the oddest thing and a very sad waste," said his older brother, John Haney.

"He was the most charming person to be around, constantly telling stories and surrounded by a group of people," but he also had a "very dark" streak. "He didn't tolerate fools much, he drank too much and he smoked too much and it wore him down. As Chris once said about himself, 'His best friend was a bar stool.'"

CHRISTOPHER FREDERICK HANEY, the middle of three children of broadcaster Jack Haney and his wife, Stratford Festival actress Sheila Haney (née

Woollatt), was born in Welland, Ontario, on August 9, 1950. His parents had met at a dance in England during the Second World War; Jack Haney was serving overseas as a sergeant in the Canadian Army and Sheila Woollatt had the corresponding rank in the British forces. They married early in 1945. At war's end he was shipped home to be demobilized, and she arrived late the following year on the *Queen Mary*, as a war bride with a babe in arms, the Haney's eldest child, John.

The Haneys lived a peripatetic life because Jack Haney's career as a news editor took him to radio stations in Welland, Cornwall, Saint John, and Hamilton before he ended his working life at the Canadian Press's Broadcast News Division in Toronto. Although Chris was smart, curious, and well-read, he was also bored by school and quit in Grade 12. His father helped get him a job at CP in Toronto as a "gofer," running errands and delivering copy from reporters to editors. Within a few months he was an assistant editor and by his late teens he was a photo editor.

Journalism was a natural choice for a boy who had grown up hearing his father lead discussions around the kitchen table about breaking news and world events. The senior Haney was a wit and a jokester, but he was also a heavy drinker and a "hard liver," traits his son inherited along with the family tendency to heart disease. Jack Haney died of a stroke in 1972, at age fifty-three, leaving his widow $32,000 in insurance money. Encouraged by an actor friend, she spent $30,000 of her inheritance on a small villa in Nerja, Spain, near Malaga on the Costa del Sol, planning to recoup the purchase price by renting it to tourists. That never happened, but the house did nurture her younger son's love affair with Spain.

A year before his father died, Haney met a nurse named Sarah Crandall. "He was the handsomest, most intelligent and funniest man I have ever met, bar none. The party began when Chris entered the room," she said. Together they moved to Ottawa in 1972, where she nursed and he worked in the CP bureau earning money to go travelling. He left for Europe in the fall of 1973, she met him up with him the following February, and they set off in a Volkswagen to travel "from Stockholm to the Sahara Desert."

They returned to Ottawa in the spring of 1975, recouped their resources, and drove across the country, eventually pitching a tent at the Robert Service Campground in Whitehorse. That summer he picked up a job from the Canadian government, setting up darkrooms to process photographs from Prince Charles's royal tour of the Northwest Territories.

Haney had an acute fear of flying that dated back to his teenage years, when the plane carrying his junior hockey team to a game in Quebec City suddenly plunged five thousand feet. But for this government job in the Arctic, he quelled his nerves and flew aboard a Hercules. That was one of the very few times he travelled by any means other than train, ship, or automobile.

After the trip to the Arctic, he worked for CP on photo coverage of the 1976 Summer Olympics in Montreal. Haney and Sarah Crandall married in September 1977. Chronically short of funds — especially after their first child was born, in November 1978 — they used his mother's place in Spain as their home base until they returned to Montreal in 1979, where Haney took a job as a photo editor with the *Gazette*. To reduce expenses, the Haneys began sharing a place with Scott Abbott, another journalist at the newspaper.

On a sleepy, wet December day — the fifteenth, to be exact — the three of them and baby John were hanging around the house when the two men decided to have a competition to crown the best Scrabble player of all time. Alas, six tiles were missing from the set. Haney ran out to buy a new game and returned bemoaning what he had spent on Scrabble over the years and suggested there was money to be made in board games. Abbott said they should invent one about trivia. A few beers later, Scrabble forgotten, they had sketched out the idea for what would become Trivial Pursuit.

The next morning Haney came downstairs brimming with ideas, found a cardboard box and some construction paper, and within forty-five minutes had produced a skeleton of the board, with its design based on the six spokes of a ship's wheel — even then Haney must have been thinking of cruise ships. Players moved around the game board by rolling the die and winning different-coloured pie pieces for correct answers to trivia questions in each of six categories. When players had filled their tokens with all six colours, they moved to the centre of the ship's wheel and answered a final question to win the game.

Designing the folding board and the ingenious player tokens, which eliminated scoring pads and pencils, was the easy part. Coming up with the questions and the seed money to manufacture the game was something else. Haney quit the *Gazette* in the spring of 1980 and moved to his mother's place in Spain, with every reference book he and his wife could cram into their suitcases. The next two years were an arduous slog of writing questions — they needed ten thousand from which to select six thousand keepers — making prototypes, and finding investors. Some of the questions were hard, some easy, and some quirky. What is the biggest diamond in the world? Answer: a baseball diamond.

The banks weren't interested in lending money for a start-up board game invented by a couple of journalists, so Abbott's father offered to mortgage his own house. Working full-time on the game and with no money coming in, Haney began suffering from anxiety attacks. His older brother remembers sitting in bars that winter and reading the backs of gin and vodka bottles to come up with arcane facts that could be turned into questions. His sister, who also dreamed up questions, remembers getting the princely sum of twenty-five cents for every question that her brothers accepted.

The first 1,200 games were put together in Niagara-on-the-Lake in 1981, just as the recession that had begun in the U.S. hit hard north of the undefended border. The manufacturing cost was about sixty dollars per game because of the heft of the box and the quality of the board and the cards, but the inventors could wholesale it for only about fifteen dollars. Money was so tight that Sarah Haney, who recalls cashing in beer bottles to buy food, went back to work as a nurse after their second child, Tom, was born in November 1982.

Eventually they sold shares at $1,000 each to thirty-two small-time investors, including the copy boy at the *Gazette*, journalists in Toronto and Montreal, and childhood friends — although not Haney's widowed mother. He refused to let her risk her meagre savings. And so it went until they had enough money to produce twenty thousand games, which they began shipping to stores early in 1983. Everybody was tense, especially Chris Haney.

And then suddenly, Trivial Pursuit took off. Sarah Haney can remember receiving the first welcome returns in the form of a cheque for $5,000 in April 1983. The lineups began in the pre-Christmas rush that year. The following year, twenty million TP games were sold, "one every second, twenty-four hours a day, we used to say," recalls John Haney, who along with lawyer Ed Werner was a partner with his brother and Abbott in a company they had formed in January 1980, called Horn Abbott Ltd.

The annual general meeting, which had always been a drab, low-key affair, was shifted to the upscale Deerhurst Resort, just outside Huntsville, Ontario. From the surroundings alone, shareholders must have been thinking that prospects were improving, but the four partners appeared grim-faced as they handed out envelopes and announced that one of them contained a winning ticket for a custom-made Trivial Pursuit gaming table. Instead the envelopes held dividend cheques: $50,000 for each lot of five shares. One of the shareholders, an actor, who had two lots of shares, was sitting in the front row. He expressed the general mood in the room by yelling, "Holy fuck!"

Life should have been golden for Chris Haney. Instead he was as driven as ever. After the sale of TP to Hasbro in 1988, he needed a new challenge. He built a palatial home in Caledon, Ontario, sailed on a luxury cruiser to Spain every winter, and helped several friends build dream houses. With Abbott he built two magnificent golf courses, Devil's Pulpit and Devil's Paintbrush, on the Niagara Escarpment in Caledon. He began working on new electronic board games and studied photography, creating some stunning images and reaching Level 8 in Photoshop expertise.

By 2007, Haney's genetic predisposition to heart disease, along with his chronic drinking and smoking, had caught up with him. He suffered from serious circulation problems that culminated in crippling pain in his legs and eventually kidney failure. In late May 2010 Haney decided he wanted to come home from Spain, but he was too ill to travel by anything but air ambulance. His sailing days were over. Even then, he didn't think he was going to die. "He was always an optimist that way," said his brother. "Every time he survived a medical crisis he would say, 'I just dodged another bullet,' with his typically black sense of humour."

On landing, he and his second wife, Hiam, were taken immediately to St. Michael's Hospital in Toronto as his children and siblings rushed to his bedside. "Over the years, he suffered anxiety attacks, but he chose that self-destructive lifestyle, and that is what eventually killed him," said John Haney, who added the plea "May he finally rest in peace" as the final line in the death notice he wrote after his younger brother died on May 31, 2010, of heart disease and kidney failure. He was fifty-nine.

LINDALEE TRACEY
Filmmaker and Writer

MAY 14, 1957 – OCTOBER 19, 2006

THE CHILD OF an alcoholic father and a chronically poor mother, Lindalee Tracey ran away from home as a young teenager, made a living as a stripper and an exotic dancer, and then forged an award-winning international career as a writer and filmmaker. Driven to make her mark, almost as though she had a presentiment that her time would be short, Tracey had an uncanny ability to document her own life in print and on film.

She could turn her gaze outwards as well as inwards, by connecting with her interview subjects on a visceral level in hardcore journalism that was as controversial as it was memorable. This approach — working at a story from the inside, from the perspective of a participant rather than the viewpoint of a detached, "objective" observer — is the signature of her work.

At first she was a willing contributor to the controversial film *Not a Love Story: A Film about Pornography*, made in 1981 by Bonnie Sherr Klein and Dorothy Henault for Studio D, the women's unit of the National Film Board. When she saw the finished version, she felt betrayed and exploited.

"I'm reduced to porn queen, me, the softest thing in the film, the stripper who doesn't spread, immortalized as a cheap cliché and the 'articulate' voice of all the live sex girls," she wrote in her autobiography, *Growing Up Naked*. "Being moral, being decent, being honourable," whether "you are in front or behind the camera," were lessons, Tracey said, that she had derived from her experience with *Not a Love Story*.

Mischievous, determined, difficult, and passionate, Tracey was both the-atrical — a trait she used to advantage as a burlesque dancer — and irrepress-ibly interested in other people, especially the poor and disadvantaged. Instead of averting her eyes or tossing a loonie into a plastic cup when she saw a pan-handler, she would sit down on the curb and start a conversation that often ended in an invitation to a meal at the nearest eatery.

When her son, Liam, started asking questions about his dead grandfather, Tracey decided to make a documentary about the father who had abandoned her as a baby. *Abby, I Hardly Knew Ya* (1995) was a cinematic journey that took her through flophouses and long-term care facilities as she sought out her father's drinking buddies, and ended in the cemetery beside his grave. Although she had intended to mouth conventional bromides about absent fathers, she found invective pouring out of her mouth in torrents of rage as the cameras rolled. Another filmmaker would have yelled, "Cut!" and com-posed herself and started again. That might have been professional but it wouldn't have been authentic — and authentic was what Tracey was all about, as a filmmaker, a writer, and a person.

LINDALEE TRACEY WAS born in Ottawa on May 14, 1957. Of Irish and Québécois ancestry, she was the elder child of Abby Tracey, a small-time criminal, and Yolande Tremblay, a government clerk. Her father took off when she was a few months old, reappeared briefly, and left again before her brother, Paul, was born a year later.

Home was an apartment above a diner in the west end of Ottawa. "There were no trees, no parks, just the incessant rattle and dark belching of ware-houses, factories and rag plants," she wrote in her first book, *On the Edge: A Journey into the Heart of Canada* (1993), "I remember a sweet unknowing before awareness and shame. The cheesy clumps of Kraft dinner and ketchup in the roof of my mouth. The gummy front-yard tar melting to my shoes in summer." Her father was "a deadbeat, a man I didn't know," while her mother "lived for years without her own room, without new clothes, with constant worry that lined her face early."

Although proud of her mother's frugality and strength, Tracey was a rebellious teenager who ran away from home when she was fifteen. She rode the rails until she was picked up in Kamloops, British Columbia, and sent home. A year later she quit high school and moved to Montreal, where she began appearing in clubs as a stripper and an exotic dancer. She was sixteen.

"I just loved stripping; those were grown-up girls with real boobs, and I wanted to do that, too! It was the express lane into adulthood," she explained to Marc Glassman in an interview in the fall 2006 issue of *POV* magazine. "We paraded our imperfections. We enjoyed them...The people who came to the clubs were often sorrowful folk; and we talked to them."

She wrote a book, *Growing Up Naked: My Years in Bump and Grind* (1997), about her life as a peeler, working at a club called Eden under the stage name "Fonda Peters." She was a runner-up in the Miss Nude Canada contest and was billed as "Canada's Top Young Show Exotic" on a tour of the United States before going back to Montreal in 1967 to work in an upscale club called SexOHrama. That's where, a few years later, she began organizing an annual striptease fundraiser for the Montreal Children's Hospital called "Tits for Tots." "Certainly the mid-seventies was the last good time to be a stripper," she wrote in *Growing Up Naked*, "before television swallowed our imagination, before the corporate agenda made us homogeneous and hard-core pornography spread its numbing venom."

The publicity from *Not A Love Story*—the film was variously banned and lauded—helped her to find on-air work with a Montreal television show. "I wasn't supposed to do anything but wear tight clothes, but I brought on people like [abortionist Dr. Henry] Morgentaler," she said in *POV* magazine. She began writing stories and columns for print, including articles about street people, notably a piece about homeless women—largely unexplored territory in the early 1980s—and worked in radio, hosting and co-producing *Montreal Tonight* on CJAD.

Tracey "went down the road" to Toronto to work for CBC's *As It Happens* and *Sunday Morning* in the mid-1980s. "She was very street wise, incredibly brash and an amazing thinker—very curious and very smart—and she could connect with almost anybody. I could send her into the most improbable places and she would find a way to get them to open up and bring back great tape," according to Norm Bolen, then the executive producer of *Sunday Morning*. "She was a real word master," said Bolen. At the same time, she had no deference for authority or experience, which could irritate her colleagues even as they were "dazzled" by her talent.

She met her husband, filmmaker Peter Raymont, in a documentary workshop at the old CBC Radio building on Jarvis Street in 1986. Like Tracey, he had been born in Ottawa, but on the right side of the tracks. His father, a colonel in the Canadian Army who had been awarded an MBE for his war service, was a senior staff officer and historian for the Department of National Defence.

Their similarities were bigger than their differences. They shared a deep commitment to social justice, human rights, and making the world a better place. When Raymont travelled to Nicaragua to make *The World Is Watching* in 1987, Tracey went with him. They were married in Ottawa in 1989 and their son, Liam Tracey-Raymont, was born the following year.

They conjoined their professional relationship as well when she became a partner in White Pine Pictures, his film, video, and television production company, in 1993. Its credits include *Shake Hands with the Devil: The Journey of Roméo Dallaire* and *A Scattering of Seeds: The Creation of Canada,* for which Tracey also wrote the book.

An unregenerate multi-tasker, Tracey, who had been writing poetry since her days as a stripper in Montreal, was also producing magazine articles, mainly for *Toronto Life.* "The Uncounted Canadians" — about the thousands of illegal migrants who work in our fields and kitchens, hotels, and restaurants — won a National Magazine Award in 1991 and later became the spur for a 1997 documentary, *Invisible Nation,* about the underground illegal immigrant community in Toronto. In collaboration with Raymont, she produced the 2002 documentary *The Undefended Border,* which later became the backbone of a dramatic series, *The Border,* that ran on CBC TV for three seasons, beginning in January 2008.

Although Tracey was a very active partner in White Pine Pictures, she formed Magnolia Movies as a "boutique production company" in 2003. She did it partly because she wanted her own identity and partly because she wanted to make films that either didn't fit the profile of White Pine or came at similar subjects from a different slant.

Her first film for Magnolia was *An Anatomy of Burlesque,* tracing the bawdy business as far back as Chaucer's *Canterbury Tales* and linking revolutionary fervour to naughty dancing. When it ran on the History Channel early in 2004, the *Globe's* television critic John Doyle deemed it "smart and entertaining" and a "cheerfully informative jaunt."

Bhopal: The Search for Justice — a scathing indictment of what happened after the massive chemical leak at the Union Carbide plant in Bhopal, India, on December 2, 1984 — aired on CBC's *The Nature of Things* in 2004 to mark the twentieth anniversary of the disaster. Initial reports said that three thousand people died, but later estimates put the number much higher, suggesting that at least fifteen thousand died and many thousands more suffered long-term effects. Bhopal is Tracey at her insistent, social democratic best.

In 2001 Tracey was diagnosed with HER2/neu-positive breast cancer, a very aggressive form of the disease. She was forty-four. After a mastectomy and chemotherapy, the disease went into remission for about two years. In fact it was only gearing up for another attack, on her bones, her lungs, and her liver.

She sought out an alternative cure in Tijuana, Mexico, in the late fall of 2004 and returned looking devastated. Desperately ill with metastatic cancer, she was eligible to receive Herceptin, which was then only available as a last-hope treatment. The drug gave her another year of life, in which she continued her frenetic work schedule and found time to help lobby the Ontario government in a campaign that eventually made Herceptin available to non-metastatic HER2 breast cancer patients.

By January 2006 the cancer had invaded her brain. Late that September, her family took her to the palliative care unit at Toronto's Princess Margaret Hospital, expecting that she would last two or three days. In the end she defied death for almost a month, as she had always confounded authority, even asking her loved ones to sing Gordon Lightfoot songs around her bed. She died on October 19, 2006, at age forty-nine. At her funeral, Raymont picked up his guitar and led the congregation in singing Ed McCurdy's "Last night I had the strangest dream...to put an end to war," as he followed her coffin out of the church.

PRIVATE LIVES, PUBLIC IMPACT

There Is No Such Thing as an Uninteresting Life

There's an old adage that a lady's name should appear in the newspaper only three times in her life: to announce her birth, her marriage, and her demise. Death notices in newspapers and online obituary sites may seem archaic in an era when social media sites trumpet even the most insignificant personal details, but their discreet announcements can be rich repositories of information about fascinating lives that have been lived outside the glitter of celebrity. That's why I'm addicted to scouring family-placed notices about people whose passing will never make headlines or whose fame has diminished with the decades. Something about them awakens my curiosity about their lives and the times in which they lived.

For example, I learned about Kenneth Cambon in a newspaper death announcement. The notice was unusual in that it was witty and full of delicious biographical details that most people leave out because of the solemnity of the occasion. Here's the sentence that first caught my eye: "After graduating from Commissioner's High School in 1939, Ken joined the Royal Rifles of Canada, ostensibly to flee his job at a soda fountain where two broken coffee carafes were about to cost him a week's wages."

I glanced back to his birthdate — July 29, 1923 — and realized that he had been only sixteen when he enlisted. He must have lied about his age, but what a price he paid for those broken coffee pots, I thought, as I read on: "Towards the end of 1941, having been initially trained to fight on the snowy slopes of

Finland, the Royal Rifles were sent to semi-tropical Hong Kong to defend the then British colony." Somehow he had survived the debacle of Hong Kong and four years as a prisoner of the Japanese and had trained as an ear, nose, and throat doctor after the war. What's more, in 1990 he had written a memoir, *Guest of Hirohito.*

I was hooked. I got hold of the book, contacted the funeral parlour with a request to speak with the family, and began the reading, researching, and interviewing that uncovered a life of sacrifice and resilience that continues to haunt me. Fortunately for me, Cambon's widow, Eileen, and his younger brother, Austen, were sharp, articulate, and willing to talk frankly about Cambon's life and career.

He grew up in a distinguished military family in Quebec City. A lacklustre high school student, he found a job as a soda jerk after completing Grade 11, earning ten dollars a week plus the occasional tip. Miserable and frustrated by the coffee pot incident, he was trudging home when he passed a recruiting sign for the Royal Rifles of Canada. The advertised pay was $1.30 a day.

What did he know about risk, the watchword of the old and timid? He was after adventure and escape from a tedious job. He got more than he bargained for when the Royal Rifles were sent to Hong Kong in an ill-fated stand against swift and brutal military aggression by the Japanese. After the Canadian, British, and Hong Kong regiments surrendered on Christmas Day 1941, Cambon was taken prisoner by the Imperial Japanese Army. He spent the next forty-four months in execrable conditions in diabolical POW camps.

Japan finally surrendered in August 1945, after the Americans had dropped atomic bombs on Hiroshima and Nagasaki. Cambon's last forced act was to help dig a deep pit in front of the POW camp in Niigata, Japan. The prisoners were told they were preparing the foundations for an air-raid shelter, but in fact the hole was meant to be a mass grave for their executed remains if the Americans invaded.

After his release from Niigata, Cambon made the long journey home by ship and train, arriving in Quebec City more dead than alive. He weighed less than ninety pounds and was suffering from hideous gastrointestinal complaints and nightmares that plagued him for decades. That fall he enrolled at McGill University on a veteran's allowance. After excelling academically, he was eventually accepted into medical school. There he met another student, Eileen Sinclair Nason, from New Brunswick. She remembered that every time he took her out for dinner he would vomit outside the restaurant. His stomach still couldn't tolerate too much rich food at one sitting, coupled with his anxiety about being in university after such a long absence from studying. They were the first McGill medical students to marry — in 1949, at the end of their second year — and to graduate together, in 1951.

A man with an expansive personality who loved conversation, socializing, and playing tennis, Cambon was adamant about one thing: he wouldn't go back to Japan, not even to attend medical conferences. When one of his grown daughters visited Japan in the mid-1980s, she tried to find the POW camp where her father had been imprisoned and was told that it didn't exist. Outraged, Cambon fired off a letter to the mayor of Niigata, who wrote an apologetic reply along with a promise to search out the campsite if the former POW ever made a visit to Japan.

That invitation prompted Cambon to put aside forty years of hatred and fear and revisit the scenes of his capture and imprisonment. "The tears that had been held back so many years finally fell freely," he wrote later in *Guest of Hirohito*. "I had come filled with doubts, fears, and prepared for catastrophe. I left with renewed hope and warmth, happy to have come back."

In researching his life, which to me emphasized the human capacity for forgiveness, I came across a newspaper photograph that captured the scene at the train station in Quebec City after Cambon was finally reunited with his family. It showed a skeletal Cambon flanked by his parents — his mother holding on to his arm as if she were never going to let go — his two older sisters, both of them in uniform, and his kid brother, bounding in front like a rambunctious Labrador pup. What a sacrifice that showed: three young adult children in uniform, a commitment that was not unusual for a Canadian family during the Second World War.

So when I saw a second death notice headed "Cambon" a year later, I recognized the subject as Ken Cambon's older sister Margery Quail. After completing nurse's training at the Jeffrey Hale Hospital in Quebec City in 1939, she enlisted in the nursing service of the Royal Canadian Army Medical Corps and went overseas late in 1940, during the most treacherous days of the Battle of the Atlantic.

Along with head nurse Dorothy Macham (who was later awarded the Royal Red Cross Medal by King George VI), Margery Cambon worked in a pioneering plastic surgery unit, treating burn victims at a Canadian hospital in Basingstoke, southwest England. She survived the war, returned to Canada with her British husband, John Quail, and raised a family, only to succumb to the same illness that had claimed her brother — Alzheimer's disease — at age eighty-six in 2008. She spent her final days in a special hospital unit for veterans with dementia, named after her old mentor Dorothy Macham.

The Cambon siblings were ordinary Canadians who lived lives of sacrifice and duty without fanfare or glory, but that doesn't mean their lives aren't worth remembering or chronicling. Or that our lives aren't enriched by reading about them and their times.

I felt the same way when I learned that Betty Fox was dying. The mother of Canadian hero Terry Fox was certainly famous, even beyond our shores, but she was known mainly as a mother and not in her own right as a woman who had faced the unimaginable — the death of one of her children — and responded with extraordinary courage and endurance.

After a right-wing media outlet made headlines by declaring that she was dying of cancer in June 2011 — the same disease that had killed her twenty-two-year-old son in 1981 — her family posted a press release on the Terry Fox Foundation website. They denied that she had cancer, admitted that she was seriously ill, asked for privacy, and said they would make no further comment. Having faced Terry's death in the midst of television crews and media scrums, they wanted to share the last moments of Betty Fox's life as a family and to mourn away from the spotlight.

I appreciated that request and didn't try to contact the family, but I still wanted to know how a grieving mother had found the strength and the acumen to front the annual Terry Fox Run, protect her son's memory for thirty years, fight off the commercialization of his name, and raise more than $500 million for cancer research.

Born Betty Lou Wark in Boissevain, Manitoba, on November 15, 1937, she was a working mother living with her husband, Rolly Fox, and their four children when her second son, Terry, was diagnosed with osteogenic sarcoma. A keen athlete, he had his right leg amputated above the knee in March 1977.

After reading everything I could find in newspaper files, on the Internet, and in biographies of Terry Fox's short life, I wanted to talk with somebody who knew her. That led me to Isadore Sharp, the founder of the Four Seasons hotel chain. Sharp's own teenage son Chris had died of melanoma two years before Terry Fox began his run. That was an obvious connection, but what really intrigued Sharp was the "impossible" challenge that Terry Fox had set himself. He had befriended Terry in the early days of the run, before the public had become enamoured of the skinny kid in T-shirt and shorts awkwardly running with a hop-skip-hop on his prosthetic device.

The hardest lesson you have to learn as a journalist is to shut up and listen. Fortunately I had my wits about me when Sharp called me early one morning in response to my interview request. "You look at these people who set goals that are beyond our ability to imagine and it attracts you to them," he said of the early days of the run, when motorists were laughing at Fox and he was drawing sneers instead of contributions. Sharp ran ads in newspapers and magazines saying that the Four Seasons would contribute two dollars a mile, amounting to $10,000 if Fox got as far as Vancouver. Then he invited 999 other companies to join him in order to make it a $10-million run and organized a huge reception for Fox when he reached Toronto.

"He took cancer out of the closet. He always presented himself with his leg exposed," said Sharp. "It is never the outspoken, out-front, macho characters who become heroes; it is the kids in the crowd who live and die by their principles and become extraordinary in circumstances that call upon people to live by what they believe in. He was a remarkable man, wise beyond his years." Before he died, Fox knew he had raised more than $24 million for cancer research, one dollar for every person living in Canada at the time.

After Fox had to stop running in Thunder Bay, slightly more than halfway through his run, Sharp contacted Betty Fox. He talked to her about holding an annual non-competitive fundraising run for cancer research in her son's name and persuaded her to be the public face of the event. "I told her if she wanted the run to really have meaning, and to have longevity, she would have to become the spokesperson, be out there, travel, and try to keep Terry's image alive, because people's memories are short."

He knew he was demanding an enormous effort from her, but he also knew the run would give her a purpose. "The pain was always going to be there, but this was an opportunity that I sensed would be good for her for the rest of her life," he said. Terry "gave her a cause that made her life better, having suffered that loss. You think you can't do something from the grave, but he did."

Because of space and balance, I used almost nothing from that interview in the obituary I wrote about Betty Fox after she died of complications from diabetes and arthritis on June 17, 2011. I was trying to tell the story of her life, not her son's or the reason for Sharp's ongoing support and philanthropy. But it offered such a revealing and inspiring insight into the making of a hero and a legacy that we ran it as a separate story. That's one of the enduring private rewards of writing obituaries: the chance to learn what moves people and spurs them to make superhuman acts of generosity.

Some of the ten people I have written about in this chapter were famous, some were known only to friends, family, and colleagues, but all of them had an impact beyond the intriguing details of their private lives. Ralph Lung Kee Lee, for example, one of the oldest surviving head-tax payers, was long retired from his Chinese restaurant when he made a special trip to Ottawa in June 2006. He sat in the visitors' gallery of the House of Commons and listened to Prime Minister Steven Harper apologize for the racist policy that had separated families and caused such hardship for the Chinese who came here to work on the railroad and to help build this country.

Mabel Grosvenor, the last grandchild of Alexander Graham Bell, was one of the first women to graduate in medicine from Johns Hopkins University, but she was also a tiny witness to the first attempts at manned flight in this country, at her grandparents' estate in Baddeck, Nova Scotia, in 1907. Sculptor Dora de Pédery Hunt, who became the first Canadian to mould the likeness of the Queen on the coins that jangle in our pockets, came here as a penniless refugee from Hungary and championed the ancient art of medal-making.

Others had public profiles in sharp contrast with their humble beginnings. Who knew that Simon Reisman — the tough-talking, cigar-chomping market capitalist chosen by Prime Minister Brian Mulroney to negotiate a free trade deal with the Americans in the mid-1980s — had flirted with communism as a student at McGill University?

"Honest Ed" Mirvish made a fortune as a bargain-basement retailer by claiming to be the cheapest guy around. But he was a big-hearted benefactor of the arts and his community. Giving away free turkeys at Christmas was only one of his many generosities. Broadcaster Peter Jennings, the eloquent voice and cultured face of ABC News, was in fact a high school dropout who had educated himself by reading voraciously and roaming the world as an international correspondent.

Dorothy Joudrie wanted nothing more than to be a housewife and a mother, but she became infamous as "Six-Shot Dot" when she emptied a gun into her husband, corporate titan Earl Joudrie, after he tried to terminate their tempestuous marriage. Ted Rogers, a relentless entrepreneur, was actually driven to build his communications empire to avenge and honour his father, who had died when he was a boy. The senior Rogers had been an inventor who developed a radio that could operate without batteries and had founded the Toronto radio station CFRB. He died suddenly in 1939, when he was thirty-eight and his only son was six. His devastated widow was pressured into selling the radio station. For the rest of his life, Ted Rogers, in a roller-coaster career that culminated in his being one of the richest men in Canada, was propelled by and thwarted in his drive to regain control of his father's radio station.

Jane Rule was an American writer who fled her country in the repressive McCarthy era and found a refuge in Canada, where she was instrumental in the development of two movements: the blossoming of cultural nationalism, and gay literature. Finally, Doris Anderson, the child of an unwed mother, was a pioneer feminist who bludgeoned male opposition in order to become the first female editor of *Chatelaine* and turned the magazine into a vocal vehicle for women's rights.

Everybody has a private life. What unites these people is the impact they made on the public agenda.

Ralph Lung Kee Lee

Chinese Head-Tax Survivor

March 10, 1900 – March 15, 2007

C ANADIANS CONFRONTED AN ugly part of our collective past in June 2006, when Prime Minister Stephen Harper rose in the House of Commons to offer a formal apology to the remaining payers of the Chinese head tax and their families. His contrition and the symbolic $20,000 payment for "racist actions" had been such a long time coming that there were only six survivors, including Ralph Lung Kee Lee, who were well enough to sit in the visitors' gallery that day to hear Harper speak.

"We acknowledge the high cost of the head tax meant that many family members were left behind in China, never to be reunited, or that families lived apart and in some cases in extreme poverty for years," he said. "We also recognize that our failure to truly acknowledge these historical injustices has prevented many in the community from seeing themselves as fully Canadian."

At 106, Lee was the eldest of the fewer than two dozen surviving payers of the infamous tax. His story mirrors the hardship and prejudice that so many Chinese endured when they came here as foreign workers. We tend to assume that the Chinese arrived with the building of the railroad, but they have actually been here since 1788. That's when Captain John Meares sailed from China with a crew that included some fifty Cantonese and landed in Nootka Sound, in present-day British Columbia. He bought some land from a First Nations chief and, with the help of his Chinese carpenters, built a trading post and a ship — the *Northwest America*, the first European vessel launched in B.C.

Some of the Chinese jumped ship and "intermingled" with aboriginal women, according to historian Anthony Chan, author of *Gold Mountain: The Chinese in the New World*.

The second wave of Cantonese Chinese was prospectors. They moved north from California in 1858 during the gold rush in the Fraser River Valley. Because they were seeking gold and because B.C. was mountainous, they began referring to what is now Canada as Gum Shan, or Gold Mountain. There were soon about five thousand Chinese living in B.C., some of them taking over abandoned mines and forming their own companies, and others providing food and laundry services in mining towns.

After Confederation there was a great push to link the West Coast to the rest of Canada by completing the Canadian Pacific Railway, and that meant that cheap Chinese labour was in demand. Prime Minister Sir John A. Macdonald put it bluntly: "The choice is only between Chinese labourers or no railway; there is no alternative." More than fifteen thousand Chinese immigrants worked laying track and at other jobs to build the CPR. More than a thousand of them died during construction. When the railway was finally completed in 1885, the prime minister acknowledged their contribution in the House of Commons by saying, "Without the great effort of Chinese labourers, the CPR could not have been finished on schedule, and the resources of Western Canada could not also be explored."

The public mood about the Chinese turned sour after the railway was finished and manual and service jobs dried up. Many laid-off Chinese sojourners became destitute and faced social and racial discrimination. Unable to return to China, some moved east into the Prairies and Ontario. To curb immigration, the government passed the infamous Head Tax Act in 1885, which levied a fifty-dollar entrance fee on all Chinese immigrants coming into Canada. The tax increased to $100 in 1900 and was raised again, to $500 (the equivalent of about $10,000 today), in 1903. Newfoundland began charging a similar tax in 1906, which was repealed only after the province entered Confederation in 1949. About 81,000 Chinese immigrants paid a total of $23 million in head tax to enter Canada.

And yet, despite the costs and the prejudice, Chinese people like Ralph Lung Kee Lee continued to come to Gold Mountain. He was born on March 10, 1900, in Toisan, Guangdong province, the middle of three children. Because he was "number two," his parents decided to send him to Canada, hoping he would prosper and send money back home.

He was only twelve when, with two younger cousins aged nine and five, he boarded a ship in Hong Kong for the long voyage to British Columbia. All three boys had identification tags hanging around their necks. An uncle met the ship in Vancouver, claimed the three tagged boys, and took them to Fort William (now Thunder Bay).

Lee was indentured for five years, washing dishes (standing on an apple box to reach the sink), peeling potatoes, and doing whatever else was asked of him, until he had paid back the debt his uncle had incurred for his head tax. Then he began working maintenance on the railroad tracks — hard physical labour from morning to night.

Lee finally got a break when a white engineer offered him a job working in the train kitchen, helping the cook prepare meals for passengers and crew. For the first time in his life he was making enough money to set some aside. When he was twenty-two, a decade after he had landed in Vancouver with a tag around his neck, he sailed back to China. His parents had found him a bride, Kem Lun Lee. They married in 1922 and had a son, Ming, a year later. By then Lee was running out of time: if he remained out of Canada for more than two years, he would forfeit his immigration status.

Once again he made the long voyage, leaving his family behind in China. By now, though, he had marketable skills. He found a job in a restaurant in Windsor, Ontario, and began saving money to bring over his wife and child. Politics again intervened. The onerous head tax was repealed, but the Liberal government of William Lyon Mackenzie King replaced it with something even more draconian: the Exclusion Act of July 1, 1923.

The law curtailed immigration from China and prohibited family reunification. Between 1923 and 1947, when the Chinese Exclusion Act was repealed, fewer than fifty Chinese were allowed to enter Canada. As a result, many Chinese Canadians called Dominion Day (now Canada Day) "Humiliation Day" and refused to celebrate.

By the mid-1930s Lee had saved his passage back to China. By then his son, Ming, was a teenager, older than Lee had been when his parents had sent him to Canada in 1912. Lee stayed for two years, the maximum time he was allowed to be out of the country without losing his status. His wife gave birth to a daughter, Faye, in 1937 and became pregnant with a second daughter, Linda, before Lee had to return to Canada.

In China, Lee's elderly parents found the money to send Ming to school in Hong Kong. There the boy fell ill, and with no family to organize medical care, he died in 1939, when he was seventeen. Lee, who had known his son for only two brief periods in his short life, never discovered where Ming was buried, a trauma that haunted him for the rest of his life.

The Exclusion Act was lifted in 1947, two years after the Second World War ended. Lee applied in 1949 to have his wife and two daughters join him in Canada, but they weren't granted permission until 1952 — three decades after Lee and his wife had married.

His younger daughter, Linda, saw her father for the first time when he met their boat in Vancouver. She was an adolescent, about the same age as Lee had been when he arrived in Canada for the first time with his two younger cousins. The adjustment was hard — neither the children nor their mother spoke English — and they had to learn each other's ways. They settled in a small town near Windsor, where Lee ran a restaurant and later operated a small import-export business in Chinese herbs and dry goods.

In the late 1970s, his daughters grown and independent, Lee and his wife moved to Mississauga, a city to the west of Toronto. She died in 1981 at the age of seventy-nine, but he continued to live on his own until 1991, when he moved in with his daughter Linda. When she and her husband relocated to Vancouver in the mid-1990s, he moved into a nursing home close to one of his granddaughters. He continued to drive his car until he was ninety-five and, a robust walker, agreed to use a wheelchair only when he was past a hundred.

All this while the political movement to lobby for compensation for those who had suffered under the head tax was gaining momentum in the Chinese community. Beginning in the mid-1980s, more than four thousand head-tax payers and their families, including Lee, registered with the Chinese Canadian National Council, seeking redress. Compensation was one thing — it was only money, after all — but a formal apology was one concession too far for many politicians, who feared it would set a precedent for other groups seeking public remediation of historical wrongs.

The debate ramped up when Stephen Harper, leader of the Conservative Party, made redress and an apology part of his platform in the 2006 election campaign. Negotiations began in earnest after the Conservatives won the January election and formed a minority government. Six months later the stage was set for the Ottawa ceremony.

A train dubbed the "Redress Express" left Vancouver, stopping en route to pick up several of the fewer than two dozen survivors, the roughly two hundred widowed spouses of head-tax payers, and other family members at stops along the way. Passengers settled into complimentary seats provided by Via Rail.

Lee, accompanied by his daughter Linda and a grandson, climbed aboard at Union Station in Toronto. As the eldest of the surviving head-tax payers, he was asked to carry a ceremonial last spike. After Harper's statement in the Commons, Lee asked the prime minister to hang the spike on the wall of the Railway Committee Room, the very room where the decision had been made to build the national railway more than 150 years earlier. No Chinese had been invited to the ceremony at Craigellachie in 1885, when railway baron Donald Smith had pounded in the last spike linking the eastern and western tracks of the transcontinental railroad.

Lee had a very special celebration on his 107th birthday the following year, when his local MP presented him with his $20,000 redress cheque. Later his daughter Linda offered to use some of the money to take her father back to China to look for her brother's grave, but he declined, saying he was too old to make the journey. Although nobody realized it at the time, he had suffered a small stroke, and he went into hospital the next day. He died on March 15, 2007, five days after turning 107.

Mabel Grosvenor

Pediatrician

July 28, 1905 – October 30, 2006

THE LAST SURVIVING granddaughter of Alexander Graham Bell and one of the first women to graduate from Johns Hopkins School of Medicine, Mabel Grosvenor began working as a pediatrician in Washington, D.C., in the 1930s, an era when the likely outcome of most childhood illnesses was death. More than sixty years later, when she was asked to name the greatest medical advance during her career, she promptly replied: "Antibiotics." Although she lived most of her life in the United States, she began and ended her life at her grandparents' estate in Baddeck, in the rugged highlands of Cape Breton overlooking Bras d'Or Lake in Nova Scotia.

Why she decided to become a pediatrician is lost. She never married and had no children of her own, which may have been a factor. Then, too, she probably absorbed the idea of nurturing and caring for other people's children from her own grandparents. Grosvenor's grandmother, Mabel Hubbard Bell, after whom she was named, was deaf. She had lost her hearing as a child, as a complication of scarlet fever in the days before antibiotics made it a serious but not deadly disease. Her grandfather, Alexander Graham Bell, began his working life as an elocution teacher specializing in deaf students. That's how he met both his wife, Mabel, and Helen Keller, the blind, deaf, and mute child who, largely thanks to his interventions, graduated cum laude from Radcliffe. In 1913, when Grosvenor was eight, her grandparents, who were dedicated to children and teaching, hosted a huge reception for Maria

Montessori, the Italian early childhood education advocate and pioneering female doctor, and founded an American branch of her movement in their Washington home. If her grandparents were not the models for her, she was a keeper of their legacy.

As the last person to have a close relationship with the inventor of the telephone, Grosvenor was a precious conduit to the past for journalists wanting to know more about her grandfather's work and personality. "People were always bringing children to Grampie," she told her nephew Edwin S. Grosvenor for his 1997 biography, *Alexander Graham Bell: The Life and Times of the Inventor of the Telephone*. "If they called on him or wrote that they had a deaf child, whom they wanted him to see, he would always make time to see them."

She also described doing experiments with her grandfather, including demonstrations of how sound carried better underwater than through the air. "When we were swimming at the shore, he would go away from us and have us duck our heads under water," she told her nephew. "He would then clap stones under water and we could hear it. Then we would raise our heads out of the water and he'd clap stones in the air and you couldn't hear it."

Grosvenor depicted Bell as "a very theatrical person," in a 1994 interview with Baddeck journalist Jocelyn Bethune, remembering that when he told a story, "you were on the edge to hear it." She described him as "six feet — which was tall in those days. He had sparkling hazel eyes and great expressions. His hair stood up — but it was flat when he was not feeling well."

While researching *Reluctant Genius: The Passionate Life and Inventive Mind of Alexander Graham Bell*, biographer Charlotte Gray went to visit Grosvenor in 2003 at her retirement home in Washington. By then ninety-eight, Grosvenor was nearly blind and quite deaf and "had terrific mobility problems," but "she had *all* her marbles." Happy to talk about her grandparents, she told Gray that she was ten years old before she realized that her grandmother was deaf. "We all knew that we had to look her in the face when we spoke to her, and we could never call to her from another room, but we thought this was just good manners."

As for her Edinburgh-born grandfather, she described him as speaking an educated English without a Scottish or regional accent. This was a key detail, because there is no known recording of Alexander Graham Bell speaking. "His father Melville was a speech teacher, and he would never allow his sons to speak with an Edinburgh brogue," Grosvenor said. "The only times I heard him use a Scottish accent were when he was reciting 'A man's a man for a' that' by Robbie Burns, or when we visited Edinburgh together in 1920."

In a long life stretching the length of the past bloody century and well into this one, Grosvenor embraced electricity, the telephone, cars, airplanes, female suffrage, television, men on the moon — everything but the computer, which she resolutely resisted. Self-effacing, private, and forward-looking, Grosvenor was cherished by several generations of nieces and nephews in the extended Bell-Grosvenor family, as a confidante, a mentor, and the embodiment of love and caring.

MABEL HARLAKENDEN GROSVENOR was born on July 28, 1905, at The Lodge, Beinn Bhreagh (which is Gaelic for "beautiful mountain"), in Baddeck, Nova Scotia, her grandparents' summer home. The property included not only "The Lodge" — the thirty-seven-room mansion built by her grandparents in the 1890s — but several other houses and buildings dating from the same era. She was the third of seven children of Elsie (neé Bell) and Gilbert Grosvenor, the man who transformed *National Geographic* from a dry journal into a glossy, heavily illustrated monthly magazine.

She grew up in Washington, D.C., in the family home near Dupont Circle, but she spent extended periods of time, including most summers, in Baddeck because her parents travelled extensively as what we now call photojournalists. "He was the centre of her life, but she was the centre of ours," she said about her grandparents to biographer Charlotte Gray.

By all accounts the Bells doted on their ten grandchildren. In *Alexander Graham Bell and the Conquest of Solitude*, Robert V. Bruce described the inventor as having "the majesty of Moses and the benevolence of Santa Claus." Grosvenor's older brother Melville told Bruce that his earliest memory was "sitting on his grandfather's lap and, on instructions, tweaking the nose of Alexander Graham Bell to produce a dog's bark, pulling his hair for a sheep's bleat, and by way of climax, tugging his Santa Claus beard for the deliciously fierce growl of a bear."

Grosvenor was in Baddeck when her grandfather's red silk kite, *Cygnet*, soared 150 feet above Bras d'Or Lake with a young man named Tom Selfridge clinging to its structure. The apparatus hovered for a breathtaking seven minutes and then sank gently into the water after the wind dropped. Bell, who was obsessed with the idea of manned flight, later wrote about this experiment: "I almost forgot to mention the witness who will probably live the longest after this event (and remember least about it) — my little granddaughter Miss Mabel Grosvenor — two years of age."

He was right about that. She didn't remember the *Cygnet's* brief flight in 1907, and she was not even there — being at home in Washington — when the *Silver Dart* achieved the first controlled powered flight in Canada, on February 23, 1909. Even so, in a 1994 interview with journalist Jocelyn Bethune, she said: "I swear I remember being there with Grandma — being very cold, being frozen, but everyone was excited. I didn't see why everyone should be so excited — if Douglas [pilot J.A. D. McCurdy] wanted to fly, why shouldn't he? Being brought up on wonders, they seemed commonplace."

Four years later, on March 3, 1913, the day before Woodrow Wilson's inauguration, Grosvenor, then eight years old, rode in an open carriage up Pennsylvania Avenue to the Capitol building in Washington with her mother, grandmother, aunt Daisy Fairchild (neé Bell), and two of her own four sisters. They were part of a suffragist march at least five thousand strong, demonstrating in favour of giving women the vote. The march drew an estimated half-million onlookers; many of them were violently opposed to the female franchise and hurled abuse and lit cigar butts at the marchers while the police looked away. According to Grosvenor, her grandfather was the original suffragist in the family. "He persuaded my grandmother. I think he felt that women had just as much right [to vote] as men."

She described her early school days to journalist Jim Morrow in an interview for the Baddeck *Victoria Standard* in 2005. "We got out of school at lunchtime. And then in the afternoon two days a week we had horseback riding and one day a week we had dancing class," and all of this in addition to art classes on Saturday. All the great adventurers of the day probably passed through the Grosvenor home, but the only one she could remember was the Canadian Arctic explorer Vilhjalmur Stefansson, because he stayed with them and "he put sugar on everything."

An intelligent, studious girl, Mabel at the age of fourteen served as an unofficial secretary to her grandfather, taking dictation from him on a variety of subjects ranging from genetics to genealogy to the mechanics of hydrofoil boats. She'd had a bad bout of whooping cough in the spring of 1919. Her parents, wanting to "toughen her up" because the deadly influenza epidemic (which had spread through returning soldiers of the Great War to civilian populations around the world), was still raging, agreed to let her extend her usual summer sojourn at Beinn Bhreagh. She was in residence on September

9, 1919, when her grandfather's hydrofoil boat the *HD-4* set a world marine speed record of 114 kilometres per hour, a record that stood for a decade. "As I remember, the speed of the *HD-4* was measured on land," she told Morrow. "There was a mark on the shore and when the *HD-4* reached another mark further up the shore, they measured the time it took to get there."

At Beinn Bhreagh she slept in a sleeping porch off one of the balconies, a habit that persisted until her last five years. "I slept out there all winter. We had a child's play broom and we'd brush the snow to get to the floor. And I had a cold bath every morning to strengthen me," she told Morrow. That winter she took up skiing, ice skating, and snowshoeing, but mostly she was being "tutored" by her grandfather in his new hobby, genealogy.

The following year she accompanied her grandparents on a sentimental trip back to Bell's native Scotland, partly in search of his roots. "He didn't really get interested in genealogy until his father died," she remembered decades later. "We went to parish offices to look through records and visited cemeteries. He found several cousins he didn't know existed."

While they were in the U.K., Bell, who had never flown in any form of aircraft himself despite his fascination with manned flight, arranged for his granddaughter and his wife to fly from London to Paris, but, as she told journalist Allen Abel in 2003, "at the last moment, he chickened out and wouldn't let us go. He said it was too dangerous."

Back in the U.S., Grosvenor enrolled in Mount Holyoke College, South Hadley, Massachusetts, a liberal arts college for women and the eldest of the academically elite "Seven Sisters." After graduating Phi Beta Kappa in 1927, she entered the medical school of Johns Hopkins University in Baltimore, Maryland, choosing that institution over Harvard because of its smaller classes.

Grosvenor was one of only seven female medical students (one dropped out after contracting tuberculosis) in her graduating class in 1931. After doing an internship at the New York Hospital in New York City, she moved back to Washington, where she worked as a pediatrician in private practice and in clinics for disadvantaged children at the Children's Hospital.

After practising medicine for thirty-five years, Grosvenor retired early, in the mid-1960s, to care for her own parents, who were both frail and in poor health by then. As well, she took over stewardship of the Beinn Bhreagh estate. She loved to sail on the lake in her dinghy, the *Carola*, or on the yawl *Elsie*. A well-known figure in Baddeck, she spent her time driving her silver convertible, gardening, presiding as honorary president over meetings of the Alexander Bell Club — one of the longest continuing women's clubs in Canada — and taking care of others.

She was an ongoing source of awe for family and local residents for her ability to recall names, events, and people. As she grew older, she was granted the first conservation easement in Nova Scotia to help ensure that the property and its gardens would continue as a heritage site.

As she had done almost every year for more than a century, she travelled from Washington to Baddeck in June 2006. As the days grew shorter and cooler she stayed on because her health problems, including congestive heart failure, were accelerating and she thought she would receive better medical care there than in Washington, according to her great-nephew Grosvenor Blair. "That's what she said, but I think she also loved Baddeck and the people, and she was very much at home here," he said. Grosvenor died quietly of respiratory failure on October 30, 2006, in the place where she had been born more than a century earlier. She was 101.

Dora de Pédery-Hunt

Artist

November 16, 1913 – September 29, 2008

A FTER CONQUERING GAZA, Alexander the Great and his troops headed for Jerusalem in 332 BCE. The news of the brutal siege and the raping and pillaging that had ensued preceded him. So instead of resisting, the high priest Jaddus and a multitude of inhabitants welcomed the invader on the outskirts of the city. In gratitude, Alexander declined to sack Jerusalem and is said to have given a "golden button" — the world's first medal — to Jaddus before pushing south into Egypt in his quest to conquer the known world.

The Italian artist Antonio Pisano, or Pisanello, made the earliest modern medal in 1438–39. It was small enough to be held in the hand and depicted the Byzantine emperor John VIII Palaeologus on one side and an allegorical scene on the other. From Italy, medal-making spread throughout Europe, but it was slow to cross the Atlantic and take root in Canada.

The earliest Canada-related medal was the "Kebeca Liberata," which was cast in France in 1690 to mark the defeat of a British attack on Quebec. After the fall of Quebec in 1763, the British cast medals to commemorate military victories and other significant events, including the signing of treaties with First Nations chiefs. It wasn't until the early twentieth century, however, that local artists Louis-Philippe Hébert and Alfred Laliberté began creating medals here, having learned the technique in France.

These were isolated examples. Medallic art barely existed until an influx of skilled European artisans arrived in the middle of the twentieth century.

Sculptor Dora de Pédery-Hunt was the first woman to make an international reputation as a medallic artist in this country, but even she had to use a commercial iron foundry to cast her first medals. She arrived in 1948 as an indentured servant from Hungary, having survived both World Wars: the one that destroyed the Austro-Hungarian Empire and the one that had turned Europe into an inferno.

Her name may not trip off the tongue, but her work is as familiar as the change that jingles in your pocket. She is the artist who sculpted the effigy of a "mature" Queen Elizabeth that appeared on all our coins minted between 1990 and 2003. It was the first time a Canadian artist had ever been given such a commission.

Beginning with the Canada Council Medal in 1961, de Pédery-Hunt designed and moulded hundreds of commemorative decorations. She created medals for Canada's centennial in 1967, Expo 70 in Osaka, the Montreal Olympics in 1976, the 300th anniversary of the Hudson's Bay Company, and the portrait medallion of Dr. Norman Bethune that Prime Minister Pierre Trudeau presented to Mao Zedong during Canada's first official visit to the People's Republic of China in 1973. A founding member of the Medallic Art Society of Canada (MASC), she was also the first and for many years the only Canadian delegate to the Fédération internationale de la médaille d'art (FIDEM), the International Art Medal Federation.

Although she worked on larger secular and especially religious sculptures, including altarpieces, stations of the cross, candlesticks, and crucifixes, medals were her "favourite form of expression," as de Pédery-Hunt said later. "They are like short poems."

In a passage that appeared in *Medals*, a trilingual book about her work with photographs by Elizabeth Frey, she said: "I have to accept the challenges of working inside the limits of a small disc and obeying the strict rules of the striking, casting and finishing processes. But the clay is soft and it yields pleasantly, almost too easily to the touch of my fingers. Maybe, after all, these limitations are necessary. I welcome these odds — my medals are the result of a good fight against them — and at the end at least I can look back on a bravely fought battle."

There were other, less lyrical impulses to make medals. They are small, so they don't require a huge financial outlay for materials or a large studio in which to fashion them. Indeed, medals can be moulded in bed, a key consideration if you are as poor as de Pédery-Hunt was in the early years, when pulling the covers up was one of the best ways to stay warm.

DOROTHEA DE PÉDERY, the middle of three daughters, was born prematurely on Sunday, November 16, 1913, in Budapest, Hungary. Her mother, Emilia Festl, was out with friends; her father, physicist Attila de Pédery, was at the opera. The tiny baby, who weighed less than a kilogram, was wrapped in cotton wool and placed in the only available bassinet — a shoebox.

Her hastily summoned father took one look and quickly baptized his daughter, naming her "Dorothea — gift of the Gods," because in Hungarian folklore a Sunday child will understand birdsong and commune with flowers. That makeshift incubator saw Dorothea (Dora) through the night and launched the beginning of a long, adventurous life that transformed her from the "shoebox baby" into, as she herself liked to say, "the mother of Canadian medals."

After graduating from the State Lyceum in 1932, she vacillated between her artistic ambitions and pleasing her father by becoming a scientist. By her mid-twenties she had found her vocation, and despite her father's disappointment, she entered the Royal Hungarian School of Applied Art. Besides fine art, she studied bronze and plaster casting and wood and stone carving — crafts that later helped her support her family. After four years of basic studies for her honours diploma, she earned a master's degree in sculpture and design in 1943. For her graduation project, she sculpted a thirty-centimetre solid bronze elephant.

Life in Hungary carried on in a twitchy fashion during the early years of the Second World War. The country had formed an uneasy alliance with Germany, so it wasn't occupied like many of its neighbours. De Pédery found work designing clothes and accessories, did some private teaching, eventually sold some drawings to international fashion magazines and even had a bust and a life-sized plastic sculpture exhibited by the National Gallery of Hungary.

All of that changed in March 1944, when Germany occupied Hungary, imposed martial law, and began mass deportations of Jews to death camps. The de Péderys, who were Catholic, were spared that horror, but they knew that the Germans were losing the war and they were afraid of the Soviets marching towards them from the east.

On Christmas Eve 1944, the family, including her two sisters and two small children, fled Budapest by foot and then train, with the frail Attila de Pédery lugging his daughter's bronze elephant. The journey to Dresden took them twenty-three days on a barely functioning rail system. Fortuitously the de Péderys left the city the day before the Allies launched their intensive bombing sorties in February 1945, and so they escaped the firestorms that destroyed much of the city. They headed northwest until they reached Hanover, which by then was occupied by the Allies, becoming part of the British Occupied Zone.

Father and daughter both found work with the British Admiralty — he designed anti-sonar devices from 1945 to 1948 — and were befriended by a British officer in the occupation forces named Chutter and his Canadian-born wife. The Chutters offered to sponsor de Pédery as a Canadian immigrant. To increase her chances she posed as an unmarried woman, although she had recently married Hungarian journalist Béla Hunt, and agreed to work as an indentured servant for two years for a family in Toronto in return for her passage.

After flying to Montreal on a Canadair North Star — the pride of Trans-Canada Air Lines — she told immigration officials that she was a sculptor. "How do you spell that?" was the response from the immigration clerk dealing with "displaced persons." He wasn't impressed when she explained that she carved small animals in wood, but when she allowed that she could also carve lamps, he brightened, stood up, shook her hand, and welcomed her to Canada.

The Chutters' son Donald, who was waiting in the airport, took her home to Ottawa with him and introduced her to Harry Orr McCurry, the director of the National Gallery. After looking approvingly at photographs of de Pédery's work, McCurry suggested she contact his friends "the Girls" in Toronto — the sculptors Frances Loring and Florence Wyle.

First, though, she had to meet her sponsoring employers and get to work as their housekeeper. The Olsons turned out to be warm and hospitable, opening their home to her parents and her "fiancé" when the trio arrived (with her prized bronze elephant) several months later. Shortly thereafter de Pédery (re) married her husband and added his last name to hers. Then she and her reconstituted family — two parents, two sisters, and their children — moved into a small apartment above a store. Her siblings quickly moved on, but she remained the financial mainstay for four adults.

In addition to her housekeeping duties, she started a small business making Christmas cards, tree ornaments, and centrepieces for tables and combined it with a variety of other modestly paying endeavours: art classes, making decorative cushions and window treatments for restaurants, painting lampshades, repairing and restoring an antique metal rooster, and creating

murals for schools. Life was hard but satisfying, except for her depressive husband, who never adjusted to the loss of his former journalistic career.

"My husband was impossible," she told Elspeth Cameron, author of *And
Beauty Answers: The Life of Frances Loring and Florence Wyle*, complaining
that he refused to take on the menial painting jobs that she accepted with relish. By 1958 her parents had immigrated to Argentina to join one of her two
sisters, and de Pédery-Hunt and her husband had separated, although they
didn't divorce until the early 1960s.

Finally on her own, and aided by the stalwart and influential support of
Wyle and Loring, she was able to concentrate on her abiding passion — art.
"The Girls" fed her Sunday dinners at their studio in a former church in the
Moore Park area of Toronto, encouraged her artistic aspirations, and arranged
for her to take over A. Y. Jackson's room in the Studio Building (an artist's
facility in the Rosedale Valley, designed by Eden Smith and financed by
Lawren Harris) while he was away on a sketching trip.

"The Girls" also helped her get a job teaching sculpture beginning in 1950,
supported her for election to the Sculpture Society of Canada in 1953, and
introduced her to critics and curators. "We like her very much — and think
she will be a great acquisition to Canada," Loring had written to McCurry at
the National Gallery in August 1948. They also encouraged their friend Alan
Jarvis, who became the third director of the National Gallery in 1955, to support her work.

Jarvis saw de Pédery-Hunt's bust of Loring at an exhibition in Toronto in
1957. Because she couldn't afford to have it cast in bronze, she had concocted a
mixture of plaster, sawdust, and white glue that hardened to the point where
she had to carve rather than model it like clay. Intrigued, Jarvis asked to meet
the artist, who wasn't there because she was teaching. He persisted and not
only met de Pédery-Hunt but bought the carved bust of Loring and its
maquette for the National Gallery. He also recommended her for a $700 trav-
elling grant to visit European museums and galleries and meet sculptors —
including Henry Moore in England.

While in Europe, she found her vocation as a medallic artist. She didn't go
to Soviet-controlled Hungary, where revolution had been brutally suppressed
two years earlier, but she did go to Belgium, which was hosting Expo 58 in
Brussels. Nostalgia (and hunger) drew her to the Hungarian pavilion to sam-
ple goose-liver sandwiches, but what captured her imagination was a display
of exquisitely crafted art medals. From that moment she knew that she wanted

to make medals, and she wanted to do it in Canada. "I studied medal-designing for some years in my art school," she said in a speech at her ninetieth birthday party in 2003. "This art-form was unknown in Canada. So I will introduce it! This might become my contribution to my country."

And so it did. While she was in Europe she used her travels as a primer: every country she visited, including Italy, France, and England, had a strong medal-making tradition. Back in Canada she spoke with her friend Alan Jarvis about medal-making; he proposed that the fledgling Canada Council should commission a medal from her. It did, and she made the design in plaster, but there was no bronze foundry for artistic work in Canada at the time. Sending the medal abroad to be cast would be prohibitively expensive, so she searched around for an alternative and found a small commercial firm operated by Eric Knoespel that used similar methods for machine parts. Enterprising and innovative, Knoespel took on de Pédery-Hunt and her project and eventually created a company, Artcast Foundry, that still works with artists.

Besides being an artist, de Pédery-Hunt was a passionate advocate for her art form. In this role she described the "magic" of owning a medal. "Clasp it in your fist, let your warmth enter the cold metal and then take it to the window. Watch it: The light hits some edges, hidden crevices appear, there are some mounds you had not even seen before. Feel the tension of the surface. There is life underneath. It is not a cold piece of metal any more: Trees grow here, bodies leap high, faces emerge. All of this is brought about by you, and only you can arrest this magic moment or change it at any time with a light flick of your fingers."

After an extremely long and celebrated life, de Pédery-Hunt died of colorectal cancer in the palliative care unit of St. Michael's Hospital in Toronto on September 29, 2008. She was ninety-four. A few days later her family lovingly placed the ashes of the "shoebox baby" in another cardboard box — this one brandishing the name of the designer Ferragamo — and buried her in her adopted city of Toronto.

Ed Mirvish

Entrepreneur and Impresario

July 24, 1914 – July 11, 2007

L ONG BEFORE BIG-BOX stores existed, with their sky-high warehouse shelves crammed with outsize containers of everything from soup to nuts, "Honest Ed" Mirvish invented the discount store in Canada. His bargain emporium at Bloor and Bathurst Streets in midtown Toronto was a model of entrepreneurial chutzpah.

Mirvish developed his marketing philosophy early and he never changed it: fulfill a need; go against the trend; keep it simple. That's why he opened Honest Ed's in the downtown core instead of a suburban shopping mall, and he never developed a branch-store system. What he lost in savings on bulk purchases he gained in having only one store to stock, staff, and oversee.

Among the marketing tips Mirvish lived by were "bright lights lure customers like moths" and "the bigger the display of merchandise, the more people buy." To show he meant business, he illuminated the store's exterior with a mammoth sign implanted with 23,000 light bulbs and plastered the walls with luridly painted signs such as HONEST ED'S A FAT SLOB, BUT HIS PRICES KEEP A SLIM FIGURE and DON'T JUST STAND THERE, BUY SOMETHING.

As a young man he joked that when he died, he wanted to be cremated and have his ashes sealed in a large hourglass prominently mounted in the store. That way, somebody could turn the hourglass upside down every hour so that his employees and his customers could say "There's good old Ed... still running."

Despite his brash approach to business, Mirvish was soft-spoken, with a courtly manner. A dapper dresser, even down to patent-leather black shoes, he loved to go ballroom dancing with his wife, the artist Anne Mirvish.

He opened the doors of Honest Ed's in 1948, financed by the proceeds from cashing in his wife's insurance policy. Five years later he was pulling in an annual gross of some $2 million. His privately held, strictly cash business took him from poverty to wealth, especially as the city expanded in the post-war boom and turned his rock-bottom property acquisitions into prime real estate. His empire included a city block running south from Honest Ed's, a residential street of brightly painted Victorian houses that he rented to artisans and book dealers and dubbed Mirvish Village.

Mirvish's entrepreneurship was revered, but it was his zany antics, generosity to immigrants, and open-armed embrace of the arts that earned him an affectionate place far beyond the commercial reach of his store. He revitalized King Street West by opening restaurants, buying and building theatres, and importing blockbuster theatrical productions to Toronto such as *The Lion King*, *Mamma Mia*, and *Miss Saigon*. He rescued the Royal Alexandra Theatre in Toronto and the Old Vic in London and built (with his son, David) the lavish Princess of Wales Theatre, projects that enabled him to rub shoulders with both royalty and theatrical stars, including the Queen Mother, Peter O'Toole, and Sir John Gielgud.

He never had a secretary, never accepted government subsidies for his theatrical productions, never took his operations public, and never — well, hardly ever — went into hock.

YEHUDA EDWIN MIRVISH was born on July 24, 1914, in Colonial Beach, Virginia. He was the eldest of three children of David and Anna (née Kornhauser) Mirvish. By the early 1920s the Mirvishes, who had both immigrated to the U.S. as teenagers fleeing pogroms, had moved north to Toronto with their three children. They lived above the small grocery store they operated in the west end.

His father "loved to sit in the store and read up to six newspapers a day," Mirvish told Jack Batten in *Honest Ed's Story: The Crazy Rags to Riches Story of Ed Mirvish*. "He also gave credit to customers who couldn't pay. Which is why the store was always insolvent — and why, after school, I worked."

After his father died in 1930, Mirvish quit school to become "the proprietor of a completely bankrupt store." He was fifteen. "Somehow, I ran it for the next nine years. Or it ran me," he told Batten. His day began at four a.m., when he climbed on his bicycle and rode to the local markets to buy fruit and vegetables, racing back to open the store at seven a.m. His mother clerked while he stocked the shelves and set the prices. His brother, Robert, quit school at thirteen to help out.

The family kept the business open during the long years of the Depression before calling it quits in 1938. Mirvish went to work for Leon Weinstein, a local kid who had started a chain called Power Supermarkets. By then he had met Anne Macklin, a painter and singer from Hamilton. They married in 1941 and lived in the family duplex while she worked a variety of jobs, including the Sports Bar, a clothing store they opened with money they received as wedding gifts and a loan from the bank.

Unlike his father's store, the Sports Bar began making money because of Anne's winning way with customers, Ed's canny deal-making with suppliers in the rag trade on Spadina Avenue, and the spending power of style-conscious young women working in wartime munitions factories. Their real break came at the end of the war, however, when Mirvish struck a deal with the University of Toronto to buy a property the institution had been bequeathed but didn't want: the stretch of small shops on Bloor Street running west from Bathurst to Markham Street. He paid $5,000 down and carried a $20,000 mortgage for what turned out to be a prime real estate asset.

By now the Mirvishes were parents. Their only child, David, was born on August 29, 1945. With Anne Mirvish at home taking care of the baby, Mirvish gave up the dress business and went back into dry goods. In the spring of 1948 he bought up the entire stock of a burned-out Woolworth's store in Hamilton, evicted the shopkeepers on his strip of Bloor Street, and piled up his merchandise on orange crates on the sidewalk. Over the entrance he hung a sign: NAME YOUR OWN PRICE! NO REASONABLE OFFER REFUSED! The store, which at first was open only on Saturdays, was mobbed. "Finally, I'd found my true forte," he said later. The name Honest Ed's was a spoof on what he hated about hypocritical advertising. As the persona of Honest Ed, he enlisted Dick MacDougal, a local drunk, who slept in the store's basement and shovelled the sidewalks when he could stand upright. Known as Dirty Dick, MacDougal was "skinny, totally toothless, perpetually filthy, with stubbled chin, cauliflower ears, and a corkscrew nose," according to Mirvish. For years most people believed that the photograph of Dirty Dick hanging under the sign reading HONEST ED WELCOMES YOU was a likeness of the proprietor.

Even though consumer credit ballooned with postwar optimism and prosperity, Mirvish, having learned a painful credit lesson from his father, stuck to his cash-only policy. He also introduced daily door-crashers, taking a loss by selling spectacles or bloomers for nine cents a pair but more than recouping his investment by selling additional merchandise to the customers he had lured into the store.

Mirvish's penchant for buying low and selling cheap got him into trouble with brand-name manufacturers, who tried but failed to organize a boycott of his store in the 1950s. His location proved a boon when the east–west Bloor-Danforth line of the subway opened in 1966; the stop at Bloor and Bathurst was only steps away from his emporium.

By the late 1950s, Mirvish felt secure enough to buy his family a home in affluent Forest Hill and to snap up the Victorian-era houses on the street behind his store. Although he had to fight city hall because the street was zoned residential, he finally won the day.

Accompanied by clowns and brass bands, he opened his expanded four-storey, 6,000-square-metre store on October 23, 1958. Four months later, Nathan Phillips, then mayor of Toronto, pushed the button to illuminate the "World's Largest Readograph," a six-by-forty-one-metre sign containing 1,500 metres of neon tubing and 1,500 copy panels. The energy surge caused local blackouts. Today Honest Ed's still has one of the biggest electric signs in the world.

Of all his crazy promotion stunts, including Noah's Ark and Pink Elephant sales, the Marathon Sale and Dance in February of 1958 was the wackiest. A "wilderness girl" named Janet Benson made the 1,500-kilometre trek from a village west of Fort William (Thunder Bay) to Toronto on a dog-sled to publicize spot sales in the store, including a washing machine for $1.89 and a mink stole for $1.98.

The big draw was the dance, in which couples shuffled around trying to last seventy-two hours and win the thousand-dollar first prize. Some eighty thousand customers crowded into the store during the three days and nights of the marathon, spending $75,000 — six times more than Mirvish had ever made in a single week in February, the slowest sales month on the calendar.

Because the event ran continuously for three days, Mirvish violated a local bylaw that said retail establishments had to close by seven p.m. Sixteen

Toronto police officers were sent in the middle of the night to check out his dance marathon, and they laid four charges. Mirvish paid the fine without arguing, calculating that it was small potatoes compared to his gross from the marathon. But by flouting the embargo against staying open late, he'd drawn press and public attention to the silly bylaw, and before long it was changed.

He had a much more serious contretemps with the legal system in 1959, after he rented space to pharmacist Norman Englander to set up a discount drugstore. The Ontario College of Pharmacists refused to register Englander and the wholesale drug companies refused to deal with him, on the spurious grounds that selling bargain-priced drugs didn't serve the common good.

Riled, Mirvish went to the press, a favourite tactic that invariably resulted in megawatt headlines. "Abject persecution," one columnist complained. The case ended up in the Supreme Court of Ontario, which ruled that the college had no right to refuse to register a qualified pharmacist. Englander was back in business, filling 6,500 prescriptions in his first year at Honest Ed's.

By the early 1960s, with the success of Honest Ed's assured, Mirvish began looking for new ventures. He bought up the rest of the late-Victorian-era houses on the west side of Markham Street below Bloor, intending to knock them down to create a parking lot. The residents protested and the city refused the application.

Instead of fighting city hall, he surprisingly acquiesced, for reasons that were personal rather than commercial. His wife, Anne, was restless. Stories circulated that she was thinking of leaving Toronto to study art in New York City. She changed her mind after her husband bought up the houses on the other side of Markham Street, painted them pastel colours (following her suggestion), and leased the premises on both sides of the street to art dealers, artisans, and restaurateurs. Their own son operated an art gallery and bookstore on the street for several years. Eventually Toronto renamed the street Mirvish Village and designated it and Honest Ed's store as tourist sites.

Mirvish also toyed with the idea of buying the Victory Burlesque Theatre, a vaudeville house on Spadina Avenue that had been turned into a striptease venue, and transforming it into a legitimate theatre. Experts advised him that the Royal Alexandra, on nearby King Street, would be a much better investment. The theatre, which was architecturally and historically significant, had been built by Cawthra Mulock in 1907. Orson Welles, Paul Robeson, the Marx Brothers, Jessica Tandy, Raymond Massey, and Mary Pickford were among the greats who had appeared on its stage.

Time had not served the grand old theatre well, and it came up for sale at a bargain-basement price in 1962. Egged on by his wife and his son, Mirvish acquired the Royal Alex for $200,000 cash and a promise that he would run it as a legitimate theatre for the next five years; after that, he could convert the building and property to another use if the theatre couldn't sustain itself.

He spent twice the purchase price on renovating the theatre, replacing the original tearoom with a bar, furnishing the lobby with his own Louis XV–style furniture, hanging framed photographs of famous performers in the lobbies, and mounting a marquee sign outside with 1,362 flashing light bulbs. Audiences and critics raved about the reopening on September 9, 1963, even though they panned the production of *Never Too Late*, starring William Bendix.

Having jumped into the precarious live theatre business, he embarked on another risky venture a few years later: opening a restaurant to feed his theatre patrons. He bought a six-storey dry-goods warehouse next door to the Royal Alex for $525,000 in cash, decorated it with antiques and stained glass that he had picked up for a song, hung out a blazing sign advertising ED'S WAREHOUSE, and opened for business on January 20, 1966. One critic described the decor as "Baroque bordello," but the food was simple — roast beef and Yorkshire pudding — and the prices were cheap.

Before long Mirvish had acquired more property along King Street and opened more restaurants. By the mid-1970s he had six eateries serving close to six thousand meals, from Italian to Chinese, on busy nights. They ran full tilt until the mid-1990s, when, faced with competition from a range of high-end restaurants and bars in the area, Mirvish began closing his places down. The last to shut was Old Ed's in 2000; it now houses an antiques market.

Two decades after buying and refurbishing the Royal Alex, Mirvish bought an even more famous theatre: the Old Vic in England. He'd never been inside — indeed, he'd never been to London — but he'd been warmed by tales of performing there by touring actors Sir Ralph Richardson, Sir John Gielgud, and Peter O'Toole. In June 1982 he offered £550,000 in a bidding war and was stunned to learn he'd bought the theatre.

There was a big fuss about a foreigner buying up a national treasure, but Mirvish flew to London and held a press conference to defuse fears that he might be intending to move the Old Vic to Toronto, the way London Bridge had been transplanted to Arizona. He won over the hostile media when he declared, "They're calling me a foreigner. But I'm really just a lad from the colonies." The Queen rewarded him with a CBE — Commander of the British Empire — a gong that Mirvish typically translated as "Creator of Bargains Everywhere."

After spending almost $4 million sprucing up the ageing theatre to reclaim its high-Victorian splendour, he personally welcomed the Queen Mother at the reopening on October 31, 1983. Even though the Old Vic was celebrated for winning awards, the Mirvishes could never break even, and in August 1997 they put it up for sale. The deal — for an undisclosed price to the Old Vic Theatre Trust — was concluded in September 1998.

His final foray into theatre-building was to turn the parking lot down the street from the Royal Alex into a new venue named the Princess of Wales, to accommodate *Miss Saigon* when it finished its West End run in London. The Mirvishes built a state-of-the-art facility with a huge stage and two thousand seats that cost $50 million, including the land and parking. The Princess of Wales, which opened on May 14, 1993, was the first privately built theatre in Toronto since the Royal Alex in 1907.

For somebody who billed himself as cheap, Mirvish was a generous soul. Beginning in the late 1980s, he hung a sign on his store every Christmas that read YOU'VE GOT A DATE WITH A TURKEY and gave away more than a thousand frozen birds to the needy, and he shipped enough food to a Salvation Army shelter to give another two thousand people a turkey dinner. On his birthday he threw an annual party for himself outside the store on Markham Street, giving out presents to customers and hiring clowns and jugglers to roam the street entertaining the huge crowds that showed up for free pizza and pasta.

Mirvish had a fixed rule that employees must retire at sixty-five — until he himself turned sixty-four. He immediately scrapped the rule and let people stay on the payroll as long as they remained productive. In 1986 he made a concession to his age — he was seventy-two — by bringing his son into the business. Nonetheless, he continued to spend mornings in the store, the noon hour at one of his restaurants, and the afternoon working on his theatre operations. Except on those nights when he was committed to ballroom dancing, he was in bed by ten p.m.

He missed his eighty-ninth birthday party in 2003 because of a bout of double pneumonia, but organizers still served 25,000 free hot dogs and 20,000 bags of potato chips and presented large cheques to local causes. In May 2004 he made his first public appearance in more than a year when, sitting in a wheelchair, he received the Jane Jacobs Lifetime Achievement Award from the Canadian Urban Institute. A month later the Mirvishes made it a family affair when father, mother, and son were granted honorary degrees by the University of Toronto for their contributions to arts and entertainment. In all, Mirvish received more than 250 awards, including the Order of Canada.

Friends and family gathered on June 29, 2007, to celebrate the Mirvishes' sixty-sixth wedding anniversary at a garden party at their home. Less than two weeks later he died, aged ninety-two, at St. Michael's Hospital, on July 11, 2007.

SIMON REISMAN

Free-Trade Negotiator

JUNE 19, 1919 – MARCH 9, 2008

T HE CLOCK WAS ticking on the free-trade deal with the Americans. Negotiations had dragged on for nearly two years and were set to expire. With only ten days to go, Simon Reisman, Canada's chief negotiator, still couldn't get key American politicians to focus on a primary issue: the dispute resolution clause. So he cooked up a piece of theatre with Prime Minister Brian Mulroney and Allan Gotlieb, Canadian ambassador to the United States.

He stomped out of a scheduled meeting in Washington on September 23, 1987, and barked to the reporters waiting outside: "I am suspending negotiations." Then he headed for the airport and a flight back to Ottawa, where his boss, Mulroney, was waiting to play his part in the drama.

Mulroney phoned U.S. Treasury secretary James Baker and threatened to call President Reagan — the very man with whom Mulroney had sung "When Irish Eyes Are Smiling" on a stage in Quebec City in March 1985. As Mulroney later recalled, he snapped at Baker: "You can do a deal on nuclear arms reduction with your worst enemies and you can't do a free-trade deal with your best friends." According to the prime minister, "Baker nearly jumped out of his skin, because he knew that Reagan would have raised holy hell on that issue immediately. That's why they came around."

Reisman, wavy-haired, bespectacled, pugnacious, and short, looked more like a wrestler than a diplomat. A veteran not only of the Second World War but of the hard-fought Auto Pact deal with the Americans, he wasn't afraid of a fight. Even when he wasn't putting on an intimidating act to cow an opponent, he was a hard-boiled customer. That's why Mulroney had picked him to make the case and hold the line in the free-trade talks. Having flirted with communism while growing up in the Jewish ghetto of Montreal in the Depression, he'd swung just as far to the right and was a fervent free-trade continentalist.

Reisman had gone eyeball to eyeball often enough with the Americans to know how they worked. It was widely rumoured that during a tense conversation with U.S. Treasury secretary John Connolly in the early 1970s, he had ground his cigar into the American politician's heirloom desk — a sacred piece of furniture that had once belonged to founding father Alexander Hamilton.

Even people on Reisman's side of the table called him abrasive and hardline. "He was one tough bird," Allan Gotlieb, ambassador to the United States throughout the free-trade talks, said after Reisman died of heart disease in 2008. "He was extremely direct and totally unfearful of the consequences of his comments. He was the diametric opposite of the namby-pamby civil servant."

Reisman had an ongoing conflict with Pat Carney, the minister of international trade. She took — and expressed — great umbrage that Reisman wasn't keeping her in the loop. More than twenty years later she was still riled. "He wasn't a team player. He was abrasive and difficult to work with because he didn't like political direction or involvement," she said in an interview. "Even though I was the minister responsible for the negotiations he would insist he wasn't reporting to me. He was exasperating," she said, while acknowledging that he "did know the file."

A former deputy minister of finance, Reisman had taken early retirement in 1975, at least partly because he himself was exasperated with the machinations of his political masters. Reisman was not going to kowtow to Carney, especially since he knew he had the ear of the prime minister. After hearing Reisman's complaints, Mulroney installed himself as chairman of that particular Cabinet committee, with the negotiating team reporting directly to him and not the minister.

Reisman's well-timed snit actually got the Americans' attention and moved the talks along. Both sides signed the FTA on October 4, 1987. As Gottlieb writes in The Washington Diaries, 1981–1989: "The deal was done and completed at ten minutes before midnight" the night before the deadline. But it still had to be ratified on both sides of the border. That prompted a blistering public debate in Canada, fuelled by the pro-free trade *Globe and Mail* and the anti-free trade *Toronto Star*, and led to a hotly contested election in November 1988.

Free trade with the U.S. had been a political hot potato since before Confederation. Lessening ties with Great Britain diminished the preferential trading relationships the colony (and then the dominion) had enjoyed with the mother country. Two national elections had been fought over the advantages (bolstering the economy) versus the disadvantages (loss of independence) of unfettered bilateral trade, or reciprocity, as it was often called.

Sir Wilfrid Laurier's Liberal Party had championed the pro side in 1891 and 1911 and had been roundly trounced by the Conservatives under Sir John A. Macdonald and then Sir Robert Borden. Those roles were reversed in the 1980s when Mulroney's Conservatives raised the banner of free trade against the Liberals, led by newly minted leader John Turner, and Ed Broadbent's New Democratic Party in 1988. This time the results were reversed as well, with the Conservatives winning the point — and the election — although with a reduced majority after Mulroney's landslide in 1984.

No matter how volatile, Reisman was a smart and shrewd negotiator who helped mould Canada into a modern economic player. He was a key figure in every significant Canadian trade deal from the General Agreement on Tariffs and Trade (GATT) in the late 1940s — the precursor to the World Trade Organization — the Auto Pact in the mid-1960s, and the Free Trade Agreement in the late 1980s. Before it was supplanted by the more problematic North American Free Trade Agreement, or NAFTA (which included Mexico), in January 1994, the FTA was heralded as an economic and political success for Canada (and Mulroney) because it eliminated many barriers and exponentially increased business with our largest trading partner.

SOL SIMON REISMAN was born in Montreal on June 19, 1919, the second of four children of Kolman and Manya Reisman. His father, a factory worker in the rag trade, had trouble supporting his family during the Depression. While working odd jobs, Reisman completed Baron Byng High School and made it into McGill University, despite its alleged Jewish quota. He graduated with an honours degree in economics and political science in 1941. He spent another year at McGill earning a master's degree (graduating summa cum laude) and then enlisted in the Royal Canadian Artillery. He went overseas in November 1942, a month after marrying Constance (Connie) Carin. They had met through friends.

Even his wife had problems with Reisman at first. "I disliked him immediately," she said. "I didn't like his forthright abrupt manner and I thought this was not the man for me, but it turned out I was wrong." She was "busy" the first several times he asked her out, but, undaunted by these rebuffs, he told her to name a date when she would be free. She did, and so she learned about the warm man beneath the brusque, self-confident exterior. "He always said what he thought, and he was not suited for diplomacy. He would have been a terrible failure in external affairs, but he was good where he was."

After landing in England in 1942, he served as a troop commander with the 11th, 15th, and 17th Field Artillery in the Italian campaign and finished out the war in the liberation of Holland. While waiting to be repatriated, he studied for several months at the London School of Economics. After four years overseas, he returned home in 1946 and went to Ottawa. He was hired by the Department of Labour but moved before the year was out to Finance, to work under Mitchell Sharp in the economic policy division.

Soon he was working closely with John Deutsch, director of the international economic relations division. Deutsch wanted to take him to Geneva as secretary to a twelve-man delegation working on preparations for an upcoming international trade conference. His wife had other ideas. "Either I go [with you] or we dissolve the marriage," she told him, having no desire for another long-distance separation. He acquiesced "and we went on from there, for 65 years" and three children, a son and two daughters.

Several months and many preparations later, delegates from nearly sixty countries met in Havana, Cuba, to establish what would become the General Agreement on Tariffs and Trade (GATT) in 1947. At the hearings Reisman noticed that Canadian prime minister William Lyon Mackenzie King was especially interested in Article 24, a provision that would permit groups of nations to establish free-trade areas. Canada was facing a foreign-exchange crisis that winter, and King wanted to secure a secret free-trade deal with the U.S. as a potential solution. As it turned out, the crisis passed, King lost interest, and the U.S. Congress refused to ratify the Havana Charter, so Canada — and Reisman — had to wait another forty years to complete a continental free-trade deal.

Back home, Reisman worked his way up through the civil service hierarchy. As deputy minister of finance from 1964 to 1968, he led the negotiations
that resulted in the Automotive Products Trade Agreement (APTA) being
signed by Prime Minister Pearson and U.S. president Lyndon Johnson in
January 1965. Called the Auto Pact, the agreement removed tariffs on cars,
trucks, buses, and automotive parts between the two countries, which greatly
encouraged trade. Essentially the Auto Pact was a free-trade deal in the automobile industry. It bolstered the bottom line of the big American car manufacturers, greatly increased assembly-line jobs in Canada, and lowered the
cost of purchasing automobiles.

By 1968 the percentage of cars that were manufactured in Canada and sold
in the United States had risen from seven to sixty percent, while forty percent
of cars bought in Canada were made in the U.S. There were downsides:
Canada didn't develop an indigenous car industry and it was restricted from
negotiating similar trade pacts with other countries, such as Japan. The Auto
Pact was abolished after the World Trade Organization declared it illegal in
2001, but by then the FTA, negotiated by Reisman, and the subsequent North
American Free Trade Agreement, which added Mexico to the mix, had made
it largely irrelevant.

Reisman gave up his job as deputy minister of finance in 1975 to take early
retirement. The timing was good, as the federal government had recently
decided to index civil service pensions to the consumer price index. But that
wasn't the only reason Reisman wanted to leave at the age of fifty-five.

Pierre Trudeau had been re-elected the year before with a majority after
having engineered the defeat of his minority Liberal government on a budget
vote. Back in power, Trudeau reversed direction on his economic policy, causing John Turner, the finance minister (and Reisman's political master), to
resign in September 1975. A month later Trudeau implemented wage and
price controls, although he had ridiculed Progressive Conservative leader
Robert Stanfield for proposing the very same measures — sneering, "You can't
say, 'Zap! You're frozen!' to the economy" — during the election campaign the
year before.

Reisman said he quit the government because he was fed up with a
diminishing scope for "people of energy and a certain independence of
mind" in the public service. Many believed that the real impetus had a lot to
do with his antipathy towards the prime minister's flip-flop on wage and
price controls and his own loyalty to John Turner. When Turner later ran for

leadership of the Liberal Party, Reisman acted as one of his unpaid economic advisors.

After leaving the civil service, Reisman formed a consulting firm with James Grandy, another deputy minister who had bolted the government bureaucracy in 1975 with his indexed pension. Reisman and Grandy signed up a roster of clients that included Bombardier Power Corporation and Lockheed. A ruckus erupted in the House of Commons over the firm's dealings with Lockheed, which was in the process of negotiating a huge contract to supply airplanes to the federal government. As former public servants, Reisman and Grandy were violating conflict-of-interest guidelines, according to some critics. We aren't lobbyists, Reisman insisted, explaining that there was a difference between peddling influence and peddling knowledge. Or, as he said to the *Globe and Mail*, "Some girls dance and some girls are whores... we just dance."

As a consultant, Reisman had a number of high-level assignments, including a commission investigating the auto industry in 1978 and serving as chief negotiator for aboriginal land claims in the western Arctic in 1983, one of the first pieces of legislation affecting aboriginals under the newly proclaimed Charter of Rights and Freedoms. But the biggest deal of his life materialized when Mulroney appointed him ambassador for trade negotiations and chief negotiator for Canada of the Canada–U.S. Free Trade Agreement in November 1985, at a per diem rate of $1,000.

The two men knew each other personally from salmon-fishing trips in Quebec with the likes of Paul Desmarais and John Rae of Power Corporation. "He was a natural for us," Mulroney said later, describing him as the "indispensable player" in the free-trade talks. "Simon was the star. He was the one who took the free-trade concept from infancy to maturity and made it whole."

Reisman slowed his pace somewhat in his eighties, but he was still salmon fishing in white water in July 2007 and attended a tribute dinner for Mulroney in Montreal to celebrate the twentieth anniversary of the Free Trade Agreement that October. "Free trade has created millions of jobs, raised our standard of living, and helped Canada balance our books and pay down the national debt," Mulroney bragged. He then recapped Reisman's career as a negotiator, ending with the FTA: "Not only was he our most experienced official, he was tough as nails and he succeeded brilliantly."

The following month Reisman fell at the Rideau Club in Ottawa, and then in January he collapsed at his condominium in Fort Lauderdale and had to be airlifted home. He was admitted to the Heart Institute in Ottawa, where he had a pacemaker installed. He seemed to be recovering from the operation — his family reported he was reading newspapers and talking on the telephone — but he slipped into cardiac arrest and died very early on the morning of March 9, 2008. He was eighty-eight.

Doris Anderson

Journalist and Political Activist

November 10, 1921 – March 2, 2007

Doris Anderson, the first female editor of *Chatelaine* magazine, was an early leader of the women's movement in Canada. She fostered feminist debate about abortion and spousal rights in divorce and custody disputes, and advocated for greater participation by women in public life and elected office — and she did all this before Betty Friedan published *The Feminine Mystique* in 1963.

Anderson made her own success in the sexist, *Mad Men* world of magazine publishing in the 1950s and '60s. As Floyd Chalmers, president of Maclean-Hunter, once said, "What I like about Doris is that she looks like a woman, acts like a lady, and works like a dog."

She acquired her feisty feminism in opposition to her belligerent, overbearing father. Originally a lodger in her mother's boarding house in Calgary, he threw his weight and his opinions around at the dinner table after marrying Anderson's mother when Doris was nearly eight. The girl's well-honed fury, nurtured from an early age, probably explains why, as a grown woman, Anderson found it so difficult to choose consensus over confrontation as a management style.

No matter how successful she became or how much she was celebrated for her tough, fearless stands on behalf of women's equality, Anderson was actually vulnerable underneath her bristly demeanour. One of her very few regrets in her eighty-five years was her inability to find more effective "tools" to deal with men in authoritative positions.

"I never learned to be subservient to men," she cheerfully admitted in an interview weeks before she died of pulmonary fibrosis on March 2, 2007, at the age of eight-five. "What I learned to do was to cope," she said, looking thin but stalwart, her beautiful hands with their sculpted nails as expressive as ever as she made her way down a corridor in a Toronto rehabilitation facility, using a walker for stability and attached to a portable oxygen tank.

HILDA DORIS BUCK, the only daughter of Rebecca Laycock Buck and her lover, Thomas McCubbin, was born on November 10, 1921, in Medicine Hat, Alberta. Her mother's first husband, a swindler named Alvin Buck, had remortgaged the house and skipped out with the funds, leaving his twenty-three-year-old wife with two young sons and a lot of debt. That's when Buck turned the family home into a boarding house.

When she became pregnant by her lodger, Thomas McCubbin, Buck did what "fallen" women did in those days: when she was visibly pregnant, she left town to give birth and then made discreet arrangements to place her "illegitimate" infant in a home for unwanted babies. After several months, she had a change of heart and reclaimed her daughter.

McCubbin, who was prone to drink and larcenous behaviour, married her mother when Anderson was already in grade school. Much to the little girl's dismay, he thrust himself into what had been, at least from her perspective, an ideal matriarchal world. He was a difficult and domineering man, and she resented his influence over her mother and his loud rebukes about her forward and unladylike behaviour.

"I fervently wanted my father to be hit by a streetcar," she wrote in her 1996 memoir, *Rebel Daughter*, "particularly when we were waiting for dinner and he reeled in late, three sheets to the wind, and sat pontificating at the head of the table." She softened somewhat towards him late in her life. "He was a rebel, and he had a good mind, read widely and challenged everything," she said in her final interview, but "I never felt any warmth toward him."

By contrast with her father, her mother was "terribly conservative" and wanted her only daughter to be demure, keep her head down, and conform to "respectable" expectations — as she had done in marrying and sticking with the obnoxious McCubbin. Unwilling to accept her mother's notion of marriage and child-rearing as the only desirable lifestyle for a woman, Anderson went to teacher's college — not because she wanted to teach but because it was a way to earn money for her real goal: a university education.

After graduating from the University of Alberta in Edmonton in 1945, she moved to Toronto at the age of twenty-three, intent on a career in journalism. From her first job, as an editorial assistant on *Star Weekly* magazine, she moved to radio as a scriptwriter on the Claire Wallace program. After a miserable six months clashing with her boss, Anderson quit to become an advertising copywriter for the T. Eaton Company department store chain.

When she had saved some money, she sailed for England in November 1949 to try her luck at writing fiction. In those days few thought it was possible to write fiction in such a cold and humdrum place as Canada. Literature — indeed, life itself — happened elsewhere, so, like Mavis Gallant and Mordecai Richler, Anderson went abroad to exercise her creative muscles.

She sold a few short stories to *Chatelaine* and *Maclean's* but soon realized it was almost impossible to earn a living as a fiction writer. She returned to Toronto and got a job at *Chatelaine* as an editorial assistant in the advertising promotion department, an inauspicious start to what would become a monumental career move, not only for her but also for Canadian women.

Six years after joining the magazine, she had risen through the ranks to become editor, a job she was given only after she had threatened to quit if management appointed another man to the position. Two weeks earlier she had married PEI-born lawyer and Liberal Party backroom organizer David Anderson. She wasn't desperately in love but she wanted children, and at thirty-five she felt her options were running out.

Her mother told the groom: "Now Doris has someone to look after her." But, as Anderson wrote in *Rebel Daughter*, "what I wanted more than anything was to be able to look after myself and make sure that every other woman in the world could do the same."

The Andersons had three sons, Peter (1958), Stephen (1961), and Mitchell (1963). Like most employers of the day, Maclean-Hunter had no maternity leave policy. Traditionally women resigned in their fifth month of pregnancy, then stayed home to raise their children. Anderson torpedoed that custom, but the downside was that she went back to work almost immediately after giving birth. She and Anderson divorced in 1972 after fifteen years of marriage. He died of cancer in 1986.

As editor of *Chatelaine,* Anderson gave readers not only what they expected in the way of recipes and beauty and parenting tips, but also something to "shake them up a bit," with hard-hitting investigative pieces on abortion, birth control, discriminatory divorce laws, and the wage gap. And she hired excellent journalists to write those articles, including June Callwood, Christina McCall (later Newman), Michele Landsberg, Barbara Frum, and Sylvia Fraser.

One of her first editorials was an appeal for more women in Parliament — there were only two female MPs in 1958 — and another early one called for reform of the draconian abortion laws. She quickly learned that effecting social change meant revisiting issues in editorials and articles, so she devoted lots of space over the years to push for a royal commission on the status of women and to expose horrors such as child battering, racism, and the plight of Canada's Native peoples. Although some readers felt she was turning "a nice wholesome Canadian magazine into a feminist rag," circulation had more than quadrupled by the late 1960s to 1.8 million readers.

She made Maclean-Hunter lots of money but she was never paid anything like the salary given to the editor of rival publication *Maclean's*. For example, when she was earning $23,000 annually at *Chatelaine*, Charles Templeton, editor of a very troubled *Maclean's* for only six months in 1969, was making $53,000. After Templeton was forced out, she campaigned for the job but was rejected in favour of Peter Gzowski. "I would have had that job in a flash if I had been a man," she said in her final interview. "I was the most successful editor all through that time. *Chatelaine* was sustaining the magazine division."

Anderson quit Maclean-Hunter in 1977, about five years after she had first thought of leaving, because she couldn't stand working any longer with Bruce Drane, then the publisher of *Chatelaine*, a job she had coveted. When asked in 2006 how she felt about being passed over for promotion three decades earlier, she replied bluntly, "Angry. Still." And then she added: "That wouldn't happen today."

A confirmed workaholic, she quickly thrust herself into work of a different sort by agreeing to run as a last-minute Liberal candidate in Toronto in a 1978 federal by-election. She lost (7,602 votes to 19,027) in an anti-Trudeau sweep, to Progressive Conservative Rob Parker, a former broadcast journalist. That one electoral experience convinced her that she did not have the appropriate personality for party politics. "Most successful backbenchers behaved like football players in a scrum — never any dissent or criticism," she wrote in *Rebel Daughter*. "If I won a seat, I knew I would chafe under that kind of strict party discipline."

In 1979 she accepted a federal appointment as chair of the Canadian Advisory Council on the Status of Women (CACSW). After Pierre Trudeau was re-elected the following year, he was determined to patriate the British North America Act, with a constitutional amending formula and a Charter of Rights and Freedoms. Anderson saw the constitutional talks as an opportunity to lobby for strong wording on women's equality. The advisory council planned a conference, but it was delayed by a translators' strike. The Charter, meanwhile, was drafted and an equality clause was formulated that prohibited discrimination on a number of grounds, including sex.

Anderson felt it didn't go far enough because it "was exactly the same wording as in the 1960 Canadian Bill of Rights," which she argued had "been tested ten times in the courts between 1970 and 1980, and had been found to be useless as a legal tool to help women." She criticized the wording publicly and sent a detailed critique to Lloyd Axworthy, then the minister responsible for the status of women. She also hired feminist lawyer Mary Eberts, a constitutional expert, to write a brief for a parliamentary committee hearing.

When the conference on women's equality and the constitution was peremptorily cancelled, in a move that Anderson felt had been orchestrated by Axworthy in tandem with some female members of her own board, she resigned in protest. The media played the fracas as a story about women fighting not only each other but the male minister in charge of the status of women. "Every time Lloyd Axworthy opens his mouth, a hundred more women become feminists," an angry Anderson retorted in a widely quoted comment.

A small group of self-organizing feminists decided to hold a conference anyway. Helped by Progressive Conservative MP Flora MacDonald, who booked a meeting room on Parliament Hill, more than 1,300 women arrived in Ottawa from across the country on February 14, 1981, to hold what became known as the "Ad Hoc Conference." Eventually a new clause was added to the Charter: Section 28, which states: "Notwithstanding anything in this Charter, the rights and freedoms referred to in it are guaranteed equally to male and female persons."

The fallout was bitter. Axworthy appointed Lucie Pépin, one of the women on the CACSW board who had voted against holding the conference, as Anderson's successor. Anderson then became head of the National Action Committee, a coalition of more than seven hundred women's organizations, serving as president from 1982 to 1984. She also sat on the Ontario Press

Council (from 1977 to 1984) and began writing a biweekly column for the *Toronto Star*, a podium she kept for the next decade. The University of Prince Edward Island appointed her chancellor in 1992 for a four-year term, after which she presided as chair of the Ontario Press Council from 1998 to 2006.

Besides her autobiography, Anderson published *Two Women, Rough Layout*, and *Affairs of State*, three readable but polemical feminist novels, and *The Unfinished Revolution*, an examination of the feminist movement and its effect on the lives of women in a dozen European and North American countries. Researching *The Unfinished Revolution* made Anderson realize that Canadian women were very unlikely to achieve electoral power unless the voting system switched from the first-past-the-post method favoured in North America to proportional representation, as practised in many European countries. In the last fifteen years of her life, Anderson supported Equal Voice, a women's political advocacy organization, and campaigned relentlessly for proportional representation.

Her health declined drastically in the first decade of this century. She had a heart attack in 2001 and began suffering gastrointestinal and kidney system failures five years later, followed by a second heart attack and ongoing problems with her breathing. A diagnosis of pulmonary fibrosis, a degenerative and incurable thickening and scarring of the lungs, was a slow but inevitable death sentence. She confronted the disease with her trademark feistiness while adding a new cause to her activist agenda: campaigning for the right of terminally ill patients, such as herself, to end their lives with dignity at a time of their own choosing. Others have had to take up that battle.

JANE RULE

Writer and Lesbian Role Model

MARCH 28, 1931 – NOVEMBER 27, 2007

J ANE RULE WAS a key player in two huge social and cultural revolutions: the decriminalization of homosexuality and the international ascendancy of Canadian literature. As a writer, teacher, cultural nationalist, and lesbian role model, Rule normalized the idea of women loving women through her writing and her personal life.

She lived openly with her partner, Helen Sonthoff, for nearly fifty years. That doesn't sound unusual now, but when Rule immigrated to Vancouver in 1956 from the United States by way of England, consenting adults could be charged under the Criminal Code and imprisoned for five years for engaging in homosexual activity. As for Canadian literature, it barely existed as a subject in schools, a discipline in universities, or a vocation for aspiring writers. If they had any ambition, Canadian novelists and poets lived elsewhere and offered their work to New York or London publishers.

Tall and lanky, she was a striking figure with her outsize owl-shaped, dark-rimmed glasses and her Louise Brooks bob. She smoked, drank, and partied with an enthusiasm that dwarfed ordinary hackers and tipplers. In her novels, short stories, and essays, Rule explored the conflict between desire and convention and the constriction that fear can bring to bear on intimacy, joyfulness, and freedom. As she grew older, her focus shifted to ageing and the social webs that single women form as an emotional and physical counterpoint to traditional family networks.

Although not overtly political, Rule believed ferociously in freedom of expression and the innate ability of readers to define their own literary tastes. She loathed censorship and hypocrisy. That's largely why she was such an active supporter of the Writers' Union of Canada and the gay liberation magazine *Body Politic*. She sat on committees for the former and wrote essays and a regular column, "So's Your Grandmother," for the latter from 1979 to 1985.

She also defended Little Sister's Book & Art Emporium in Vancouver during its fifteen-year legal dispute with Canadian customs officials, who took it upon themselves to impound shipments of gay and lesbian books (including some written by Rule) and other materials at the border. The case went all the way to the Supreme Court of Canada in 2000.

JANE VANCE RULE was born on March 28, 1931, in Plainfield, New Jersey, the middle child and oldest daughter of Carlotta Jane (née Hink) and Arthur Richards Rule. She was a tomboyish five before she discovered that being a girl had serious drawbacks, six before she realized that being left-handed indicated a behaviour problem in need of modification, and ten before her myopia was corrected with glasses. Gangly and awkward, she had grown to a full six feet by the time she was twelve, and she suffered in school for her husky voice and dyslexia. As well, she was the perpetual new kid because her parents moved frequently. At fifteen she read Radclyffe Hall's *The Well of Loneliness* and "suddenly discovered that I was a freak," as she wrote later in *Lesbian Images*.

She earned a bachelor of arts in English in 1952 from Mills College. That fall she followed a female lover to England, where she was an "occasional student" at University College London, reading seventeenth-century writers and working on her first novel. Through lectures and student events she became very close friends with literary critic John Hulcoop, who was doing a doctorate at UC.

After a year she went back to the United States and enrolled in the writing program at Stanford University, but she quit after a few months because she hated "the competitive, commercial atmosphere of the school, the condescending attitude toward women students." She "marked time" until the fall of 1954, when she began teaching at Concord Academy, a private girls' school in Massachusetts.

At Concord she met and fell in love with Helen Sonthoff, a creative-writing and literature teacher who was the wife of Herbert Sonthoff, a political dissident who had fled his native Germany in the middle of the Second World War. Rule's passion for Sonthoff and the uneasy times — the Cold War and Senator Joseph McCarthy's virulent anticommunist witch hunts of the early 1950s — made all sorts of people suspect, including gays and lesbians. That atmosphere made life at Concord Academy untenable.

Hulcoop, who had accepted a job in the English department at the University of British Columbia in Vancouver, offered her a refuge. Rule moved to Vancouver in the fall of 1956 and began sharing a four-room flat with him in the home of a B.C. longshoreman. She spent her days working on fiction at a rolltop oak desk in a room with a view of the sea and the mountains, and supplemented her "otherwise frugal fare" with bounty "from coffee and tea to caviar and rock lobster tails" that her landlord brought home from the docks.

Although originally just friends, Hulcoop says that he and Rule eventually became lovers, an ill-fated coupling that was complicated by the coincidental arrivals of Hulcoop's girlfriend and Rule's lover, Sonthoff. Initially Sonthoff came to Vancouver for a visit with Rule, but that trip extended into a lifelong commitment after an "amicable" divorce from her husband.

In 1957 Sonthoff was hired as a teaching assistant at UBC, the beginning of a long university career. Rule held a variety of jobs to buy herself time to write — she read scripts, did freelance broadcasting and temporary administrative jobs, and taught as a sessional lecturer in English literature and creative writing. Both women became Canadian citizens in the early 1960s.

As a couple, Jane and Helen, as they were invariably called, had their share of spats, infidelities, and illnesses, but they were bound by a deep and abiding love. They relished travel, conversation, food, friendship, and drinking and smoking — one friend said Rule "smoked like a furnace and drank like a fish and enjoyed every minute of it." Their lives incorporated an expansive circle of friends, including many poets who embraced the avant-garde Black Mountain and Tish poetry movements swirling around Warren and Ellen Tallman at UBC.

For decades they also operated an unofficial welcome-wagon service for newcomers to Vancouver. "They were the first people I met," recounted Margaret Atwood, who arrived at UBC as a sessional lecturer in 1964. "They helped me rent an apartment, they lent me a card table — I wrote *The Edible*

Woman on it — they lent me plates, they invited me to parties. They were just terrific and they were like that with tons of people."

Rule produced more than a dozen books, beginning with the novel *Desert of the Heart*. Set in Reno, Nevada, it juxtaposes the arid, empty, and starkly beautiful desert with the tawdry, commercial, and exploitative casino strip. Even after accepting the novel in 1961, her publisher, Macmillan, demanded many changes that included deleting dates to avoid libel suits from casino employees who might claim to have been implicated as lesbians. When the novel finally appeared three years later, it was received warily by Rule's academic colleagues. Rule liked to comment that her more liberal colleagues had defended her against charges of moral turpitude by comparing her to a writer of crime fiction, arguing that if writing about murders doesn't make you a murderer, then writing about lesbians... (leaving the listener to complete the illogical syllogism).

Despite a chilly official reception, the book generated a flood of "very unhappy, even desperate" letters from women who sensed that Rule was the only person in the world who might understand them and their lives. It wasn't only closeted lesbians who sought her out. Rule quickly became the "go-to" spokesperson for journalists writing or broadcasting on issues involving homosexuality.

"I became, for the media, the only lesbian in Canada," she wrote in an autobiographical essay, "a role I gradually and very reluctantly accepted and used to educate people as I could." She was not above editing her own life to suit the cause, according to her old friend and lover Hulcoop, who claimed after her death that he was "excised from all interviews" because "it didn't fit the picture, that she had come to Canada to live with me."

After director Donna Deitch made *Desert of the Heart* into the film *Desert Hearts* in 1985, it became a cult classic. Starring Helen Shaver and Patricia Charbonneau, the film is one of the first and most highly regarded works in which a lesbian relationship is depicted favourably. The film gave to the novel a new life, which sold thousands of copies and secured translation rights from several European countries.

In 1976, when Sonthoff retired at sixty from UBC, she and Rule moved to Galiano, one of the Gulf Islands, a fifty-minute ferry ride from Vancouver. Some weeks before the move, Rule suffered a severe attack of arthritis in her spine and neck. Told she would soon be in a wheelchair, she turned to self-help remedies, especially swimming, a physical activity she had loved since childhood. The couple built a lap pool for Rule's daily regimen in 1979. As a bonus, the children of Galiano enjoyed free swimming lessons in the summers, with Rule as the volunteer lifeguard. And many of their parents benefited from preferential mortgage rates from the "Bank of Galiano," as Rule was affectionately called because of her largesse with the money she had inherited from her parents, a legacy which had grown because of her canny investments in the stock market.

Arthritis meant that she had to change her writing habits. Instead of sitting hunched over a typewriter for hours at a time, she had to complete first drafts in longhand, lying on a couch with a board in her lap, before quickly typing up what she had written at the end of each day. In 1989 she began taking anti-inflammatory drugs. Two years later she announced that she "no longer felt driven to write," at least partly because of the dulling effects of the medication.

Sonthoff died in January 2000, five years before Canada legalized same-sex marriage. Rule, an icononclast to the core, insisted they had never wanted to marry anyway. "To be forced back into the heterosexual cage of coupledom is not a step forward but a step back into state-imposed definitions of relationship," she wrote in the spring 2001 issue of *BC Bookworld*. "With all that we have learned, we should be helping our heterosexual brothers and sisters out of their state-defined prisons, not volunteering to join them there."

When Rule was diagnosed with liver cancer in September 2007, she refused any radical treatment that would involve leaving her island home. Instead, in the middle of November, she retreated to her bed with a bottle of Queen Anne whisky and a bar of good chocolate on her bedside table, hundreds of love letters from friends and admirers, and a circle of friends and family who cared for her until her death, on November 27, at age seventy-six.

TED ROGERS
Communications Czar

MAY 27, 1933 – DECEMBER 2, 2008

IN THE FIRST week of May 1939, Batman made his inaugural appearance as a caped crusader in a comic book, and Lou Gehrig, the Yankee first baseman known as the "Iron Horse," quit baseball, hanging up his mitt because of amyotrophic lateral sclerosis, a degenerative motor neuron disease, and ending a record run of 2,130 consecutive games played. The following day there was a thunderstorm in Toronto. Of these three events, that is the one that Ted Rogers, who was only five years old at the time, remembered all his life.

His parents were having a dinner party that evening in their home on Glenayr Road in Forest Hill. From his bed he could hear laughter and voices wafting upstairs as he drifted off to sleep. His mother kept from him the details of what happened next until he was an adult, but the trauma was so vivid he could visualize the scene as though he had actually been present.

After the guests left, his mother got into bed and his father went downstairs to his basement workshop to tinker with one of his radio inventions. In the middle of the night his mother woke up to find her barely conscious husband hunched over the bathroom sink, blood spattering the wallpaper and the floor, according to Rogers's account in *Relentless: The True Story of the Man behind Rogers Communications*. He was raced to hospital by ambulance, underwent emergency abdominal surgery, and was given massive transfusions — his radio station, CFRB, broadcast an appeal for blood from listeners. He appeared to rally until a second aneurysm burst twenty-four hours later. He died on Saturday morning, May 6, 1939, at age thirty-eight.

Rogers left a sickly wife — she had suffered a heart attack four years earlier — and an even sicklier skinny and bespectacled red-haired son. He had no life insurance, and most of his money was invested in his companies. The widow took solace in drink and succumbed to the interfering advice of her in-laws. They persuaded her to sell her late husband's businesses, a wound that festered in the hearts and psyches of both mother and son. Forever after, Rogers attributed his own drive to succeed to the early loss of his father and what he believed was the denial of his birthright: radio station CFRB.

Throughout a roller-coaster life of vertiginous successes and several near-bankruptcies, Rogers was propelled by the fear of dying young as his father had done, and of losing control of Rogers Communications Inc., the conglomerate he had built in memory of the man known as an electronic genius. Rogers also had an obsession with regaining ownership of the radio station his father had founded. It didn't matter how many fortunes he made, how many cable companies, magazine empires, wireless networks, or sports franchises he owned, CFRB was the prize that eluded him. He couldn't let it go until his wife, Loretta, over a glass and a heart-to-heart, finally persuaded him to move on when Rogers was in his seventies.

The same was not true of his corporate baby, Rogers Communications Inc. A visionary who solved the convergence dilemma by packing content and delivery into one corporate entity, Rogers had a mercurial personality and a hair-trigger temper. He had his finger on every aspect of the company and his colleagues on speed dial 24/7. *Delegation* and *consensus* were not part of his administrative lexicon.

When Ryerson University acknowledged a $15-million donation by naming its business faculty the Ted Rogers School of Management, one of his senior executives quipped: "Shouldn't that be the Ted Rogers School of Micromanagement?" No matter how far the stock price plummeted, how egregious his demands, how insulting his tongue-lashings, or how risky his pitches, Rogers would offer the rainbow promise "The best is yet to come" and flash his boyish grin.

"If my dad had lived a normal lifespan, I am sure I would not have had that emotional drive... If your drive is simply to make money, it peters out after a while," he told biographer Robert Brehl in *Relentless*. "In Canada we've seen people come from abroad and want to prove themselves to their parents who are still back in the old country. They start by digging trenches and end up owning thousands of acres and are huge developers...We all know these stories. What drives them is that emotional need to prove to their parents, whether they are still alive or not, that they have achieved something in their name. The same applies to me."

By most accounts, Rogers left his company in good hands when he died of heart disease on December 2, 2008. He was seventy-five, nearly twice the age his father had achieved, the president and CEO of Rogers Communications Inc., and one of the richest people in Canada, with a net worth of approximately $5 billion.

Among its bundle of assets, RCI owned the country's largest wireless telecommunications and cable companies, the Toronto Blue Jays baseball team, the Rogers Centre, more than fifty radio stations, and more than a dozen television outlets — including five Citytv and as many Omni television stations, Sportsnet, and the Shopping Channel — as well as some seventy trade and consumer magazines, including *Maclean's*, *Chatelaine*, and *Canadian Business*.

Although not in charge of operations, his family is still deeply involved in Rogers Communications. Son Edward was made deputy chair of the board of RCI in 2009, and daughter Melinda, who is also a corporate director, is senior vice-president of strategy and development, while his widow, Loretta, also sits on the board of directors. Unlike in Rogers's lifetime, when he was both president and CEO of RCI, the executive reins were handed over to chartered accountant Nadir Mohamed on March 29, 2009.

Mohamed, who had worked under Rogers in several branches of the hydra-like conglomerate, has since turned arch-rival Bell Canada into at least a partial ally. The two telecom megaliths purchased a majority stake in Maple Leaf Sports and Entertainment in December 2011, giving them ownership of the Toronto Maple Leafs hockey team, the Toronto Raptors basketball team, the Air Canada Centre arena, the Toronto FC soccer team, and the Toronto Marlies of the American Hockey League. By letting an outsider in, Rogers ensured that his family's interests and his own legacy would be protected — two things he valued much more highly than mere money.

EDWARD SAMUEL (TED) Rogers Jr. was born on May 27, 1933, the only son of Edward S. Rogers Sr., an inventor, an entrepreneur, and founder of radio station CFRB, and his wife, Velma Melissa Taylor. His father's family were Quaker Loyalists and abolitionists who had come north in the 1780s. They had made their money in oil and coal and were part of establishment Toronto; his mother's family were Baptists who hailed from Woodstock, a small town in southwestern Ontario.

At twenty-one, Ted Rogers Sr. became one of the first ham radio operators to send a signal across the ocean to Europe. By twenty-five he had invented the alternating current (AC) radio tube — he called the result the Rogers Batteryless Radio. He displayed his invention at the Canadian National Exhibition that summer with the catchy slogan "Just plug in — then tune in."

By 1927, the same year the Toronto Maple Leafs hockey franchise was launched and two years before the stock market crash, Rogers had built the first radio station powered by electricity. Thanks to two powerful transmitters located north of Toronto, "Canada First Rogers Batteryless Radio," or CFRB, was capable of emitting a clear long-range signal. A canny entrepreneur, Rogers pumped content from the radio station to encourage listeners to buy his radios, a crossover marketing scheme that his son would later perfect. By 1931 he had been given an experimental television licence. Eight years later he was dead.

While he was still grief-stricken, seven-year-old Ted was sent to Sedbergh, a boarding school in Montebello, Quebec, to be toughened up. After he had run away a couple of times and his grandmother had intervened, he was allowed to go to Upper Canada College, again as a boarder, even though the school was within easy walking distance of the family home.

Two years after his father's death, his mother remarried, and this time she didn't consult her in-laws. The choice was hers and it was a good one. Lawyer John W. Graham, a kind, stable man, was a calming and nurturing influence on his bride, his stepson, and his daughter, Ann (Rooney), who was born in 1943. Graham got his wife off the bottle and his stepson through school. He used to say: "It's up to you to get out, but I'll get you in if I can." Graham — Rogers called him his second father — provided steadying counsel and support until he died in 1998.

After UCC, Rogers went to Trinity College at the University of Toronto and then Osgoode Hall Law School. To say he was an indifferent student would be flattering. He simply wasn't interested in attending lectures and slogging through case studies. When his mother and stepfather complained about his marks, he argued that "if you get 50 percent you'll get ahead just as fast as the person who gets 90 percent."

He always had a business on the side. At ucc he hooked up an antenna outside his dorm room to broadcast rudimentary television shows to an audience of other boarders; as a teenager he organized dance bands and supplied sound systems for social events to which he sold tickets to his classmates and then took Polaroid snapshots of them and their dates. In 1960, while he was still in law school, he bought FM station chfi, using an inheritance and a loan to come up with the price tag of more than $85,000.

Undaunted by the fact that fewer than 5 percent of listeners had FM receivers, he bought the new radios in bulk and offered them at bargain prices to increase the listening audience for his station — echoing the move his father had made decades earlier with cfrb. He also bought chfi-am, later changing its call letters to cftr in memory of his father. In the 1970s it morphed into a Top 40 station and in the early 1990s into 680 News, a twenty-four-hour all-news station that became the model for other news stations across the country.

Despite his dismal law-school marks — Rogers often sent an assistant to class to take notes for him — he found an articling position with J. S. D. Tory and Associates, the corporate law firm that later became Torys llp. When Rogers approached J. S. D. Tory in 1962, the lawyer initially thought the brash young man was looking for investors for his radio station. Eventually Tory's son Jim took him on as an articling student. He was so unimpressed by Rogers's aptitude for and dedication to the law that he agreed to sign his articles only after securing a promise that the brash young lawyer would never practise.

Two years later, Rogers asked Jim Tory's twin brother, John, also a lawyer, to sit on the board of his fledgling company. Tory, who later became a stalwart advisor to Roy and then Ken Thomson, agreed and remained as loyal and calming a force for Rogers as his second father, John Graham, had been when he was a boy. Rogers was far too risk-embracing to heed all of Tory's sage advice, but he trusted and respected him. A few months before Rogers died, he gave a $7.5-million donation to the Sunnybrook Health Sciences Centre in Tory's name, a gift Rogers knew that Tory couldn't refuse.

From radio, Rogers became interested in television and especially in cable, winning television licences for several stations in and around Toronto in the late 1960s. By 1974 Rogers Cable Television had more than a dozen channels, including several multicultural ones catering to an increasingly diverse immigrant population. Six years later, he had acquired enough other cable companies to lead the pack across the country. Rogers, who always wanted more, even if he didn't have the cash to pay for it, had a keen eye for the future direction of the communications business.

Early on he realized that the market for cable was finite because most people, especially younger ones, didn't want to be tethered to a stationary television that was plugged into a wall. They wanted mobility but they also wanted to be connected; that led him to mobile phones and wireless networks and nearly disastrous ventures on both sides of the undefended border. Others lost faith but Rogers never did, and he came out on top in the end — the only place that mattered to an entrepreneur like him.

His best personal investment was marrying his wife, Loretta. They met in Nassau in 1957, the year after he graduated from U of T. The daughter of British MP Jack Robinson and his wife, Maysie, Loretta was blonde, attractive, and six years his junior. He shared an affiliation for Conservative Party politics with her father. Rogers's early political hero was the populist Red Tory John Diefenbaker, and he later became close friends with Brian Mulroney. But he found it even more significant that Loretta had been born three weeks before his own father died.

They dated for six years, while she finished her bachelor's degree at the University of Miami, before marrying on September 25, 1963, in a lavish ceremony at St. Margaret's Church Westminster, adjacent to Westminster Abbey. Their honeymoon trip to Kenya was cut short so that he could attend a regulatory hearing back home about his AM licence. Eventually they had four children, Lisa, Edward, Melinda, and Martha.

Before the wedding, Robinson, who later became Lord Marton Mere and governor of Bermuda, had told his prospective son-in-law: "What's Loretta's is Loretta's, and what's yours is negotiable." In practice, the opposite was true. The Robinsons advanced money to the young couple to buy their first house from a trust fund in Loretta's name, albeit with the proviso that Rogers would never mortgage the house to finance his business interests. As Rogers himself has admitted, he was so desperate for money over the years that he and Loretta triple-mortgaged the house several times to meet payroll and other financial hemorrhages.

If she resented or worried about their precarious finances, she kept it to herself, appearing to be the most loyal and stalwart of spouses. "His wife Loretta has been his staunchest ally and sounding board," Caroline Van Hasselt wrote in *High Wire Act: Ted Rogers and the Empire That Debt Built.*

"Without her moral and financial support, especially in the early days, Ted Rogers might not be where he is today."

Rogers was always scrawny and sickly, suffering from celiac disease as a child and nearly going blind in one eye before he was a year old. His workaholic lifestyle didn't mesh with his genetic predisposition to heart disease, especially as the years passed. He survived skin cancer, a coronary aneurysm, a heart attack, and a quadruple bypass, and was so seriously ill in late October 2008 that he relinquished oversight of the $2-billion-plus company to Alan Horn, chair of the board of directors, before entering hospital — the first time he appeared to recognize his own mortality. He weathered that crisis, but his body was worn out. Less than two months later he died of congestive heart failure, at home surrounded by his family. Ted Rogers's big adventure was finally over.

Dorothy Joudrie

Housewife and Criminal

March 16, 1935 – February 14, 2002

Things happen in marriages that outsiders can never know or comprehend. The private life of businessman Earl Joudrie and his wife, Dorothy, went scandalously public after she shot him six times with a .25 calibre Beretta handgun in her Calgary condominium on January 21, 1995. Lying in a seeping pool of his own blood, promising not to testify against her, he finally persuaded his wife to put down her drink, pick up the telephone, and call 911. Joudrie recovered, but he walked with a limp and carried four bullets in his body until he died of non-Hodgkin's lymphoma in November 2006, having outlived his former wife by four years.

On trial for attempted murder in 1996, the elegantly dressed silver-haired woman, dubbed "Six-Shot Dot," pleaded not guilty, arguing that she was in a robotic state when she wielded the gun, a defence that was buttressed by her complaints of violent physical abuse in the early years of her nearly four-decade-long marriage. Although their marriage and her estranged husband's character were on trial, he was not officially a defendant, so he could not call character witnesses to refute his wife's testimony. But there was another, even more telling circumstance, according to his supporters. He wanted to protect his children from being caught in a vicious battle between their parents, and that meant doing whatever he could to keep his wife out of prison.

One fact was never disputed: Dorothy Joudrie shot her husband in the back, not because he was beating her but because he was divorcing her.

Nevertheless, the jury of eleven women and one man found her not criminally responsible by reason of a mental disorder. Joudrie's lawyers argued, and the jury agreed, that she was suffering from non-insane dissociative automatism and therefore not capable of murderous intent when she tried to kill her husband.

Several women have used variations of that argument since the Supreme Court ruled in 1990 (with Madame Justice Bertha Wilson writing the unanimous decision) that a severely battered woman doesn't have to be in "imminent" danger from her abusive partner to claim self-defence against a murder charge. Joudrie pushed the argument to the extreme and the judge didn't grant an outright acquittal. She was ordered to undergo a psychiatric assessment and was later confined to an Edmonton mental health facility for five months of treatment before being granted an absolute discharge in 1998.

How a supposedly successful couple like the Joudries had unravelled so disastrously was the stuff of gossip, newspaper and magazine articles, and even a book. A feminist account, *Be Good, Sweet Maid: The Trials of Dorothy Joudrie*, was written by a childhood friend, Audrey Andrews, who used her own life experience to paint Joudrie as the victim in her marriage to a powerful corporate executive.

If you were born in the 1930s and you were smart, capable, hardworking, ambitious, and male — and Earl Joudrie was all of those things — success and affluence were pretty much a given in the Canadian postwar economic boom. Before the shooting, Earl Joudrie had a reputation as a self-made Calgary businessman who was sought out by dysfunctional or financially troubled companies such as Canadian Tire, Algoma Steel, and Dome Petroleum as a corporate fixer, strategist, and restructuring guru. After the trial, his status in the business community remained intact. Although he was often publicly reviled as a wife-beater, he remarried and remained close to his children and grandchildren.

The outcome was very different for Dorothy Joudrie. She had bought into the prevailing corporate male model — as most North American women did back then — on a subservient, unequal footing, willingly suppressing her own career ambitions for marriage and motherhood. Her husband made the money and she reared the children, and she derived her social status from his position as a rising gas and oil executive. She believed that whatever happened behind closed doors should stay there, and she was determined to keep up the pretence that she and her husband were still a couple, even while living separate lives — he in Toronto with his new partner, the daughter of his wife's cousin, and she in a luxurious Calgary condominium. What she couldn't tolerate was the prospect of being officially supplanted by another Mrs. Earl Joudrie.

DOROTHY DAY JONASON was born in Camrose, Alberta, on March 16, 1935, and grew up in Edmonton. Her father, Joe Jonason, was a Second World War vet who earned a PhD in philosophy at the University of Oregon and taught at the University of Alberta. Dorothy was a lively, high-spirited young woman with an impish smile. She met Earl Joudrie at Westglen High School when she was fifteen and he was sixteen. The elder son in a tough working-class family, he'd left home at sixteen to escape his brutal, authoritarian father and moved in with friends while finishing his secondary education.

Jonason and Joudrie became engaged on Christmas Eve — she was nineteen and he was twenty — and married in August 1957, two months after they had both earned undergraduate degrees from the University of Alberta in Edmonton. As a young married couple, the Joudries lived in Edmonton but were frequently apart because he had a job with Pacific Petroleum in Fort St. John, negotiating drilling rights with farmers.

After they moved to Calgary in 1960, she continued her teaching career at Viscount Bennett High School. Outwardly they seemed a happy couple who went to church together, sang in the choir, played cards with friends, and were active in the community. Nevertheless, they were distraught at their seeming inability to have children, and their frequent fights sometimes turned physical.

After adopting a baby boy they named Neale in 1961, she gave up teaching and focused her energy on her children — daughter Carolyn was born in 1963, followed by two sons, Colin (1968) and Guy (1970) — and her husband's escalating career. By the late 1960s he was president and chief executive officer of Ashland Oil Canada, a subsidiary of a Kentucky-based oil giant, and was making enough money to build a house in an exclusive Calgary suburb. The downside was that he was often away because of business commitments and she was stuck at home rearing four children and managing a large house.

The stress magnified in 1971 when Earl Joudrie was diagnosed with Hodgkin's disease, a cancer of the lymph nodes, and given six months to live. Probably to protect his career prospects, he insisted on keeping his illness a secret, even from her parents, while he underwent aggressive experimental treatment at Stanford University Medical Centre in California. She lived in a nearby motel with four children under ten, returning to Calgary when the school year began. The odds were bad — the other two patients in the treatment program died — but Joudrie survived and continued to sprint up the Ashland Oil executive ladder.

By 1976 he was senior vice-president, group operating officer, and chair of Ashland Oil at its headquarters in Kentucky, and travelling extensively. Far away from family and friends, she was finding solace in copious amounts of Seagram's rye whisky. A double VO on the rocks was her drink of choice; apparently she could tell with one sip if a bartender had tried to slip her Canadian Club instead.

Privately the Joudries were mired in guerrilla warfare. His homecomings were punctuated by vicious late-night arguments and shoving and pushing matches, and on several occasions — as he admitted at his wife's 1996 trial — the fights ended with him hitting her, evidence that was corroborated on the stand by a former nanny. Two of the Joudrie children, Carolyn and Guy, testified about their mother's drinking and their parents' frequent arguments, but they did not corroborate her allegations that their father beat her so badly in the first two decades of their marriage that she suffered a broken nose, bruised ribs, and blackened eyes.

After a particularly stormy Christmas, he decided to quit Ashland, move everybody back to Calgary to work in the corporate towers that controlled the oil patch, and spend more time at home, skiing with his children at Banff and holidaying at a condo in Scottsdale, Arizona. While he was turning around companies and sitting on corporate boards, including Canadian Tire, Algoma Steel, and Gulf Canada Resources, she was making her own career as a fundraiser, working as a volunteer with Easter Seals and the Children's Hospital Aid Society and sitting on the boards of cultural and artistic organizations and the organizing committee for the Calgary Olympics.

Outwardly she was a wealthy socialite who entertained lavishly and travelled to lush vacation spots with her husband and family. Behind the doors of the couple's seven-thousand-square-foot home in the Bearspaw area of northwest Calgary, they were both miserable, although she continued to believe that her life revolved around the marital vows she had made as a bride in the mid-1950s.

By October of 1989, with their four children grown, he had moved out. Publicly they pretended the marriage was intact. In the early 1990s he began a relationship with Lynn Manning, an executive with Kelly Services and the daughter of his wife's cousin. They had become friendly after he appointed her to the board of the Public Policy Forum, an entity that he chaired.

After Joudrie and Manning began living together in Toronto in 1993, he initiated proceedings to divorce his wife. She was aghast and in denial that her troubled marriage was on the shoals. Earl Joudrie travelled to Calgary on January 20, 1995, and met with her the next morning at her condo to give her copies of the divorce papers. As he turned to leave, she redirected him to the garage, pulled out the Beretta she had hidden under the driver's seat of her Jaguar, and shot him until the magazine was empty. While he lay on the cement floor pumping blood, she sipped her drink and mused aloud about how much she would inherit and where she would dump his body.

After the trial he completed the divorce negotiations. She got $1.9 million plus $2,000 monthly support payments for two years. When she emerged from her enforced stay in the Alberta Hospital in Edmonton, she returned to Calgary and tried to pick up the shards of her former life. She opened an Icelandic wool shop and publicly excoriated the province's mental-health-care system, claiming she had endured mental, emotional, and physical abuse and had seen other patients being "demoralized, degraded and dehumanized on a daily basis" while in the hospital.

As her health declined — she was diagnosed with breast cancer and a thyroid condition — her drinking continued apace. Despite sojourns at the Betty Ford Clinic and other rehab institutions, she never conquered her alcoholism. Nevertheless, she finally reconciled with her four children, all of whom were at her bedside at Foothills Hospital in Calgary when she died, at sixty-six, of liver and kidney failure, on February 14, 2002. She was still wearing her wedding ring, but there was no happy ending to her fairy tale.

PETER JENNINGS

Foreign Correspondent and News Anchor

JULY 29, 1938 – AUGUST 7, 2005

B EFORE 9/11 2001 in New York, there was 5/11 1972 in Munich, and both times, Peter Jennings was there. Those two terrorist attacks, twenty-nine years apart, bracket the stellar career of the Canadian-born ABC foreign correspondent and news anchor.

On September 5, 1972, Jennings was ABC's Middle East correspondent and covering the non-sports events at the 1972 Summer Olympics. Security was deliberately lax at the "friendly games," the first Olympics the Germans had hosted since the infamous 1936 Nazi-dominated competition in Berlin.

Before dawn on that day, eight Palestinian terrorists, dressed in tracksuits and carrying assault rifles and grenades in their duffel bags, climbed over a two-metre chain-link fence surrounding the perimeter of the Olympic Village and stealthily entered two apartments housing members of the Israeli team. The terrorists, who belonged to Black September, shot and killed coach Moshe Weinberg and weightlifter Yossef Romano. They took nine other Israelis hostage and demanded the release of more than two hundred Palestinians held in Israeli jails, as well as the founders of the Baader-Meinhof gang, who were imprisoned in Germany.

Jennings and his camera crew hunkered down close to the compound and reported live throughout the ordeal to anchor Jim McKay. The correspondent drew upon his knowledge and expertise in Middle Eastern politics to explain the *realpolitik* while the camera crew provided footage of the armed guerrillas, including a chilling image of a terrorist, his face obscured by a balaclava, leaning over the balcony of an Israeli apartment. The rescue attempt was bungled and in the end eleven Israelis were murdered, but as Barbara Matusow wrote in her 1983 book, *The Evening Stars: The Making of the Network News Anchor*, ABC's coverage of the Palestinian hostage-taking at the Munich Olympics "was among the most gripping episodes ever shown on live television."

By September 11, 2001, Jennings had been the network's defining face and voice on the evening news for nearly twenty years. At the peak of his popularity, in 1992–93, Jennings, a man of exceptional physical grace and charm, drew an audience of close to fourteen million viewers to ABC's *World News Tonight*. In the days after the terrorist attacks on the World Trade Centre, he anchored ABC's coverage for more than sixty hours, sitting in the anchor chair that first day for seventeen hours as viewers watched his chin grow stubbled and his face paler as the fatigue and strain took their toll. *TV Guide* called him "the center of gravity," while the *Washington Post* said: "Jennings, in his shirt sleeves, did a Herculean job of coverage." ABC News later won both Peabody and duPont Awards for its continuous broadcasting.

Covering the two towers wasn't the first time Jennings had relied upon his legendary stamina to go the distance for the network. Counting down to the turn of the millennium in December 1999, he was on the air for twenty-five hours, winning a Peabody Award for ABC and an audience of 175 million for the biggest live television event ever.

Among his many other resumé-enhancing assignments, he was the first Canadian journalist to arrive in Dallas after the assassination of John F. Kennedy in 1963, and he was in Berlin in the 1960s when the wall went up and there again in the 1990s when it came tumbling down. The same was true of Poland. He reported from Gdansk at the *naissance* of Solidarity in 1980 and at the death of the country's communist government in 1989, and he led the network's extensive coverage of ethnic cleansing and military conflicts in the former Yugoslavia in the mid-1990s.

A high school dropout who loved to learn on the ground by following his nose, he was as restless romantically as he was intellectually. He said "I do" four times: to childhood sweetheart Valerie Godsoe; to Lebanese photographer Anouchka "Annie" Malouf ; to writer Kati Marton, the mother of his children, Elizabeth and Christopher; and finally to former ABC producer Kayce Freed.

He loved the camera as much as it favoured him. In the early part of his career, his crisp good looks and forthright demeanour damaged his credibility as an anchor. Later, after time and wrinkles had weathered his beauty, critics quipped: "He's now as good as he used to think he was." Another said: "He's 10 times better than people have a right to expect because he's so good looking."

Being a Canadian had always set Jennings apart. He had an innate leeriness about the American confidence and enthusiasm for everything American, which made some people think he was standoffish and superior. Back in the mid-1960s, in his early days at ABC, his accent — the way he said "leftenant" instead of "lootenant" and "aboot" instead of "abowt" — irked some viewers. When he mispronounced Appomattox, an iconic Civil War battle, and misidentified "The Marines' Hymn" as "Anchors Away" at Lyndon Johnson's presidential inauguration, critics sniffed blood.

But being a Canadian often helped him understand outsider stories and get access to situations in a way that eluded his American colleagues. For example, he flashed his Canadian passport to enter Cuba and send inside reports at a time when American journalists were barred. And because of his influence, ABC extensively covered the 1995 Quebec referendum; Jennings was the only U.S. anchor to broadcast from Canada on the eve of the cliffhanger vote. The events of 9/11 affected Jennings so profoundly that he finally applied for dual citizenship, having lived in the United States for four decades.

PETER CHARLES JENNINGS was born in Toronto on July 29, 1938, the elder child and only son of homemaker Elizabeth Osborne and Charles Jennings, chief announcer for CBC Radio and later vice-president for regional programming.

Describing his father as one of the pioneers of radio news, Jennings compared him with the legendary Edward R. Murrow. He remembered his father challenging him as a young boy to "describe the sky," and after he complied, telling him to "go out and slice it into pieces and describe each piece as different from the next." He also credited his father and the CBC for teaching him to respect the audience and the ethic that "everybody in the country has a right to hear themselves represented somehow on the national broadcasting system." Living up to (and surpassing) his father's broadcasting credentials laregely accounts for Jenning's extraordinary drive.

Jennings made his own debut behind the microphone at the age of nine, when he began hosting *Peter's People* in 1947, a weekly half-hour CBC Radio show of music and news for children. His father, who had been in the Middle East on CBC business when the program first aired, was outraged to learn that his son was broadcasting for his own employer, because he "couldn't stand nepotism," according to an interview Jennings gave the U.S. edition of *Reader's Digest* in 2002.

At eleven he began boarding at Trinity College School in Port Hope, Ontario, where he excelled at cricket, hockey, and football. Six years later he shifted to Lisgar Collegiate in Ottawa (his father had been transferred to CBC headquarters in the early 1950s). School couldn't compete with sports and the real world, and he dropped out before graduation, much to his parents' chagrin.

Despite his fantasies of being a broadcaster, he ended up in the archetypical Canadian job — bank teller — at the Royal Bank of Canada. He hoped the bank would transfer him to its branch in Havana. Instead he was sent to Prescott, a small town on the St. Lawrence, and then to nearby Brockville, where he was hired by radio station CFJR for his first real job in radio.

He soon gravitated to the CBC, where he hosted *Let's Face It*, a public affairs show, and *Time Out*, an afternoon talk show. In 1962 he moved back to Ottawa for a job with CJOH-TV, where he appeared as a special events commentator and host of *Vue*, a daily late-night interview program that he also co-produced.

CTV lured him away to anchor the first national news broadcast out of Ottawa on the private network in 1962. Two years later he was reporting on the Democratic national convention in Atlantic City for CTV when Elmer W. Lower, then president of ABC News, offered him a job as a correspondent for the network. Jennings had cold feet and declined, thinking he wasn't "ready to leave Canada," as he told *TV Guide* in 1965. About three months later he "woke up in a cold sweat," wondering if he had torpedoed his television career.

Fortunately ABC was still interested. At twenty-six he left his higher-paying anchor job at CTV and moved to New York to go back to reporting. "I decided, ironically enough, that I was tired of being an anchorperson," he told Jeffrey Simpson for his book *Star-Spangled Canadians*. "I was too young and too ill-equipped, and America I perceived as this great new canvas on which to paint, to use the cliché. I was also aware that neither CTV or CBC could afford to send me anywhere."

He'd been on the job for only a few months when ABC executives plunked him behind a desk and made him anchor of the network's fifteen-minute nightly newscast. They were hoping he might entice younger viewers away from CBS's Walter Cronkite and the NBC duo of Chet Huntley and David Brinkley. Jennings took the anchorman reins from Ron Cochran — by coincidence, also a Canadian — on February 1, 1965. Critics were scathing, calling him a "glamorcaster" and complaining that he was too young and inexperienced. He once jokingly asked the ABC makeup artist to draw bags under his eyes so he would look his age.

He lasted three years in the anchor seat before being sent back to the field as a roving correspondent — a decision he never regretted, for it was the making of him as a news broadcaster. Beginning in January 1968, he spent most of the next ten years abroad, working first in the Middle East, where he became an expert on the ongoing Arab-Israeli conflict. His program *Palestine: New State of Mind*, for the ABC News half-hour documentary series *Now*, was considered by many observers to be the most thoughtful analysis of the confused political situation in that area.

As head of the newly established ABC News Middle East bureau in Beirut in the early 1970s, he conducted the first U.S. televised interview with Palestine Liberation Organization leader Yasser Arafat. Two years later he won a George Foster Peabody Award for his dual roles as chief correspondent and co-producer of *Sadat: Action Biography*, a candid profile of Egyptian president Anwar Sadat that aired on December 19, 1974. Among his other scoops was his behind-the-lines coverage of the civil war in Bangladesh in 1971, for which he received a National Headliner Award.

By 1978, Jennings, who was based in London, was chief correspondent and anchor of the foreign news segment of *World News Tonight*. Because he was stationed overseas, he often arrived at events, such as the assassination of Anwar Sadat in 1981, long before his America-based counterparts, and his local knowledge gave depth to his reports. He was one of the few reporters to detect in the usually demonstrative Egyptians' subdued reaction to Sadat's death a sign of the former president's estrangement from his countrymen.

His long-standing interest in Middle Eastern affairs prompted him to interview Ayatollah Ruhollah Khomeini — then a relatively obscure Iranian cleric living in exile in France — several months before he returned to his homeland in triumph after the overthrow of the shah of Iran. He reported on those world-shaking events from the scene early in 1979 and returned to

Tehran the following November, when militant supporters of the ayatollah seized control of the U.S. embassy there, taking some sixty hostages.

He was also on hand for the hostages' release in Frankfurt, West Germany, on January 20, 1981, filing eleven special reports in addition to performing his usual anchor chores. During his tenure as the foreign-desk anchorman for *World News Tonight*, Jennings also personally covered the Falkland Islands war between Britain and Argentina and the Israeli invasion of Lebanon in 1982, as well as Pope John Paul II's historic visit to Poland in June 1983. His penchant for reporting the most important international stories himself annoyed some ABC field correspondents, who resented the repeated invasions of their turf by what they called "Jennings's Flying Circus."

In September 1983 Jennings succeeded Frank Reynolds, who had died of cancer, as anchor of a revamped nightly newscast and also became senior editor for the program. He was now competing head-on with CBS's Dan Rather and NBC's Tom Brokaw. Jennings, who reportedly earned an estimated $10 million annually, outlasted his rivals: Brokaw retired in December 2004 and Rather stepped down in March 2005.

He also wrote two books with Todd Brewster. *The Century*, a bestseller that provided a breezily informative if egocentrically American perspective on key events, was accompanied by a multi-part documentary series hosted by Jennings. The duo also produced a much more personal book, about values, called *In Search of America*, which became the basis of a television series.

Like many veteran journalists, Jennings was a reformed smoker. He had started sneaking puffs at eleven and it soon became compulsive. He consumed three packs a day until he quit in 1980, after his first child was born. He relapsed for a few months after the terrorist attacks in 2001, but conquered his addiction for a second time. In the spring of 2005 he appeared frail and was said to be suffering from a cold and then an upper respiratory ailment when he didn't travel to Rome to anchor ABC's coverage of the death of Pope John Paul II early in April. Then, looking weak and speaking in a raspy voice, Jennings appeared at the end of the newscast on April 5 to tell viewers he was undergoing treatment for lung cancer. He died at home in his New York apartment, surrounded by his family, four months later, on August 7. He was sixty-seven.

Eight days before his death, Jennings was informed that he had been inducted into the Order of Canada; his daughter, Elizabeth, represented him at the posthumous ceremony in October 2005. After cremation, Jennings's ashes were divided, with half resting at his home on Long Island and the rest at his summer home in the Gatineau Hills outside Ottawa. It was a more than symbolic commemoration of his dual citizenship.

SERVICE

REAL VERSUS PSEUDO EVENTS

U NAWARE THAT HE had been declared dead in the national media,
Gordon Lightfoot emerged from his dentist's office on a Thursday afternoon in February 2010, climbed into his car, and turned on the radio. That's
when he heard he had departed this mortal coil, possibly as long ago as the
previous night — an ingenious way to avoid the dentist's drill.

"I was quite surprised to hear it myself," the singer-songwriter of such
iconic tunes as "Canadian Railroad Trilogy" and "If You Could Read My
Mind" joked in calls to media outlets. "I'm fine. I'm in great health. I've been
doing just fine. The whole thing's a hoax," he said, noting with pleasure that
"all of a sudden, my music is in heavy rotation."

The hoax began with a prank call to musician Ronnie Hawkins's management from a person claiming to be Lightfoot's grandson. The caller solicited
some tributes and then broadcast them on Twitter. Other outlets re-tweeted
the news, adding fillips and details, spurring on the hoax until it went viral
and was reported on several national news sites. Few, with the notable exception of the *Globe and Mail*, bothered to ask the fundamental questions: Is this
true? What is the source?

The spiral from "Lightfoot is dead" to "Lightfoot is alive" took about an
hour. The aftermath was huge as analysts questioned how the hoax could have
been perpetrated and the gulled fell all over themselves in the blogosphere,
trying to justify how and why they had been pranked.

David Akin, then a national affairs correspondent for the CanWest News Service, explained at length in a blog that he had merely tweeted an alert that had caught his eye: "Ontario-born singer-songwriter Gordon Lightfoot has died, according to sources close to the singer." Akin argued that because he hadn't included a link to another source or an attribution, people wrongly assumed that he was the source of the bulletin, when in fact he hadn't done any reporting. He had merely passed on something he had seen in the blogosphere. That used to be called gossip.

Lightfoot is not the first nor will he be the last person to be killed off prematurely. Former Quebec premier Lucien Bouchard was reported dead in September 2005, when he was in hospital suffering from flesh-eating disease. Former Toronto Maple Leafs hockey coach Pat Burns was declared dead in several media outlets before he phoned the *Toronto Star*, one of the culprits, and said in a frail voice, "I'm alive and kicking. I'm hanging in." Comedian Bob Hope was twice reported dead and his advance obituary was posted on the Internet, while Pope John Paul II's death was pronounced three times in the media — a record — before his actual demise on April 1, 2005. Mark Twain, who was twice declared dead, is famous for his quip "reports of my demise are greatly exaggerated."

The frequency of these false reports will probably increase in the age of 24/7 news and the cut-throat competition for viewer hits by reporters who bypass traditional editorial safeguards to claim bragging rights for breaking news on Twitter feeds and websites. It is all part of media outlets' attempts to prove to advertisers and subscribers that news "happens" first on their websites.

I'm not the the only one to bemoan the hair-trigger journalism of unsourced hits and manufactured events. Daniel J. Boorstin, the American historian, librarian of Congress, and author of *The Creators* and *The Discoverers*, wrote a book fifty years ago called *The Image, or What Happened to the American Dream*. It was published later as *The Image: A Guide to Pseudo-Events in America*. The book is about the melding of perception and reality in American culture. On one level it's a history of public relations in the nineteenth and twentieth centuries; on another level it's a prediction of a future in which invented, packaged, and massaged news takes precedence over the real thing, so that "newsworthy" events gradually become products that are manufactured like soap. If the trend continues, Boorstin points out, there will come a time when journalism and entertainment will merge, where the goal is no longer to tell the truth but to get and maintain the attention of an audience. Boorstin first made that argument in 1962, after watching television coverage of the presidential debates between John F. Kennedy and Richard Nixon.

One of the concepts Boorstin talks about in *The Image* is the pseudo event: the hyped press conference or anniversary story that really isn't news at all but is staged to look like it is by flashy massaging and catchy headlines. You have no idea how many end-of-year and end-of-decade retrospective pieces I have written over the years. The purpose is to have stuff in the bank over Christmas so that journalists can have time off and publishers don't have to pay double overtime on statutory holidays. Of course, every so often real news does happen and throws the system into spasm — the tsunami on Boxing Day 2004; the death of Oscar Peterson on December 23, 2007; the assassination of Benazir Bhutto four days later, on December 27, 2007.

The fact that the news spiral about Gordon Lightfoot's supposed death collapsed within an hour shows that pseudo events have no staying power — "no legs," as we used to say about a puff piece. The very same day that a prankster invented the death of this cultural icon, another newsworthy Canadian really did die: John Babcock, the last surviving veteran of the First World War.

There had been a huge push, led by the Dominion Institute, to recognize the passing of an era — the death of the last Canadian veteran of the First World War — by giving him a state funeral. There were three contenders: Lloyd Clemett, Dwight Percy Wilson, and John Babcock, all of them old men who had lied about their ages to go overseas to fight for king and country. The problem was that none of them made it to the front lines before the fighting stopped and none of them wanted to win the tontine of a state funeral.

As early as 2006, the Dominion Institute, an organization dedicated to arousing interest in and knowledge of our collective past, launched a petition (eventually signed by ninety thousand Canadians) lobbying the government to "honour" the last veteran with a state funeral. Parliament was easily persuaded. Not so the veterans and their families. They all valued Canada and its valorous military tradition, but they didn't want to call attention to themselves as heroes based merely on longevity. They had too much respect for the concept of the Unknown Soldier, in which an unidentified body symbolizes all those who fought, with none claiming precedence or glory over the others.

The pressure mounted on John Babcock and his family after Lloyd Clemett died in February 2007 and Dwight Percy Wilson a few months later in May 2007. "I just happened to be at a certain place at a certain time," Babcock said at the time, brushing off the clamour to turn him into a symbol. There was another complication. Babcock had relinquished his Canadian citizenship many decades earlier, when he moved to the United States looking for work, and had actually volunteered for the American armed forces in the Second World War. No problem. In a special ceremony, his Canadian citizenship was reinstated. Still he and his family balked at becoming the focus of a pseudo event, showing the quiet dignity and unassuming integrity that we like to boast is the backbone of our national character.

Foiled, the Dominion Institute, which morphed into the Historica-Dominion Institute as the years passed, retreated from insisting on a state funeral to urging that one be "offered" to Babcock and his family. Again they said no, politely but firmly. How about a day of commemoration? How about giving the next gold medal won by a Canadian athlete to Babcock's family? The suggestions escalated like something out of a *Mad Men* advertising campaign, while Babcock quietly lived out his days in Spokane, Washington, finally dying, ironically, on the very day that the media had whipped itself into a frenzy about the non-death of cultural icon Gordon Lightfoot.

There are many ways of serving your country. Lyle Creelman, a nurse who cared for the survivors of Nazi concentration camps; Kay Gimpel, who monitored the safety of Allied agents behind enemy lines during the Second World War; and Smoky Smith, the last surviving Canadian winner of the Victoria Cross, fit the traditional narrative of volunteering in times of war. But not all forms of service occur on battlefields. The ten lives I have written about in this chapter include Helen Allen, a journalist who helped children find adoptive families, and Anna Maria de Souza, who raised millions of dollars for medical research through her annual Brazilian Ball. Some, like Donald Marshall, Lucien Saumur, Israel Halperin, and Rudolf Vrba, were victims themselves — of a racist justice system, of religious persecution, of Cold War paranoia, and of the German genocide of European Jews — but they surmounted their own suffering to help others. Finally, John Weir, like Babcock, was a kid seeking adventure and glory. Unlike Babcock, though, he endured more than he could possibly have imagined, as a fighter pilot and a prisoner of war.

The lesson of these lives is that life is what you make of it: each of them refused to succumb to tragedy, happenstance, or fate. And in doing so, they made society a bit more tolerant, a bit more caring, and a lot better for the rest of us.

HELEN ALLEN

Journalist and Children's Advocate

AUGUST 16, 1907 – NOVEMBER 9, 2006

F OR THREE DECADES Helen Allen was a news-hen for the *Telegram*, a Toronto newspaper. She was stuck in the women's pages until a chance assignment turned into a life-changing vocation: finding parents for needy children. Her newspaper column, "Today's Child," featured pictures of orphaned children and heartrending tales of their deprivation, culminating in a naked appeal for people to come forward to adopt them.

We are used to seeing that kind of thing on late-night cable television — for dogs and cats and children from famine-ridden and war-torn corners of the Third World — but Allen made her adoption pitches for children right here in Canada. Bizarre as these public appeals may sound today, in an era when protecting personal privacy is a primary concern of child welfare authorities, her column was an innovative force in improving the lives of thousands of emotionally needy and often physically damaged children.

In the early 1960s, having a child "out of wedlock" was socially and morally unacceptable. So, at a time when reliable contraception and legal abortions were virtually unprocurable, many young women with unplanned pregnancies left town to "visit an aunt" when their baby bumps began to show. After giving birth, the young women, willingly or not, typically gave up their babies for adoption and returned home to resume their lives as though nothing had happened. We now know how traumatic that socially acceptable practice was for mothers, children, siblings, and grandparents.

The ranks of healthy infants available for adoption were swelled by older children, who had been abandoned by parents unable or unwilling to raise their own offspring, or who had been apprehended by child welfare authorities because they were living in unhealthy or even dangerous situations. Many of these "hard-to-place" children had been trundled from one foster home to another or had marked birthday after birthday in orphanages and other residential institutions.

Helen Allen believed that all children deserved parents and a home to call their own. For nearly twenty years she devoted her energies to the task through her column and the long-running television program *Family Finder*. Although nobody knows for certain how many of those adoptions were successful, there is enough anecdotal evidence to suggest that many, many children were happier and healthier because of her actions.

The late media mogul John Bassett, who was the last publisher of the *Telegram*, considered Allen's long-running adoption column "her real life's work." She "has helped this country enormously by giving new hope and new opportunities to the nation's richest resource, our children," he wrote in a tribute to her in 1982, and "nothing has given me greater pride than being associated with her in this task."

HELEN KATHLEEN ALLEN was born on August 16, 1907, near Saskatoon, the only child of a Presbyterian minister and a schoolteacher. Her father moved from one congregation to another, until the family eventually settled in Aurora, north of Toronto. He died of meningitis when Helen was five, and her mother worked as a supply teacher to support them both.

Allen thought her childhood was happy, although she did regret that her single mother never had enough money to buy her the bicycle she craved. Later, looking back as an adult, she realized that it had been tough to grow up without siblings or a father, but she never exploited her own situation as a motivating force in her crusade to find adoptive parents for needy children.

After high school she did a four-year degree in modern languages (French and German) at University College at the University of Toronto, financed with $2,000 from her mother's savings. Allen joined the German Club, which turned out to be a lively collection of people, including Professors Geoffrey Holt and Barker Fairley, who got together on a weekly basis to sing German songs.

An older cousin who worked on the student newspaper, the *Varsity*, introduced her to its editor, a young man named Charles Stacey. A year older, he was destined for a stellar career as a military historian and biographer of Mackenzie King. His revealing study *A Very Double Life*, based on the stuffy and politically astute former prime minister's diaries, showed the lifelong bachelor to be a mama's boy who walked the nighttime streets of Ottawa imploring prostitutes to abandon their trade, and a spiritualist who communed beyond the grave with Leonardo da Vinci, Sir Wilfrid Laurier, and Franklin D. Roosevelt, among other historical giants.

Stacey and Allen dated but went their separate ways after graduation — he to Oxford and Princeton, she to a reporter's job at the *Telegram* after earning her BA in 1929. For the next three decades she did general assignment reporting, reviewed movies, edited the women's pages, and covered select political events, criminal trials, and the 1939 royal tour of King George VI and Queen Elizabeth.

What made her name, however, was the adoption column, an assignment she had taken on reluctantly. The idea came about in a confluence of incidents, experience, and inspiration dating back to a front-page story in the early 1960s, about a young boy being publicly beaten by his father on a downtown street corner. *Telegram* publisher John Bassett assigned reporter Andrew MacFarlane to investigate and write an article on child abuse — a foreign concept in an era when many parents, especially fathers, thought beating their offspring was a routine part of child rearing.

MacFarlane contacted the office of James Band, the deputy minister of welfare in Ontario. Band supplied huge amounts of information on child protection services and took MacFarlane to visit an orphanage that housed dozens of children three years of age and under. The journalist quickly realized that many of those children had short attention spans, played aggressively, and, despite being "cuddled" by volunteers, appeared to lack warmth and curiosity. Both the reporter and the civil servant believed the children needed families and permanent homes if they were to have any chance of growing up emotionally healthy.

A few years later, in 1964, Band sought out MacFarlane, who by then was the *Telegram*'s managing editor, and suggested he run an "advertising" feature to make the public aware of the plight of those forgotten children. Both MacFarlane and Bassett took up the idea enthusiastically and assigned the column to Allen, telling her to contact the more than fifty regional Children's

Aid Societies that operated in Ontario under the Child Welfare Act, find some children who were waiting for families, and run their pictures and write about them in the paper. The plan was to run "Today's Child" for a few weeks and check the response.

Children's Aid Societies, which are protective by definition, were largely horrified at the idea of parading children along with their physical and emotional problems in a public newspaper. To them the column reeked of "freak shows" at carnivals. Only three were willing to participate: Hamilton, Kenora, and Toronto. Although disappointing, the response was sufficient to give Allen enough children to produce a daily column for three weeks.

The first child was a fifteen-month-old girl of mixed race named Hope, a difficult placement in those homogeneous days before immigration rules were relaxed and Canada had an official multiculturalism policy. Nevertheless, forty prospective adoptive parents wrote in response to Hope's story. Their letters were passed along to the Children's Aid Society for screening, assessing, and processing. "I wrote about twenty-three children in those first Today's Child columns that summer," Allen recalled years later, "and when the results were finally assessed, eighteen of those youngsters found homes."

After three years of daily columns, "Today's Child" expanded to other daily and weekly papers throughout Ontario. The following year, Allen proposed doing a television version of the column based on a California program that delivered commercials for a variety of products, reserving one day a week for children wanting to be adopted. Armed with a tape of the American show, Allen and social worker Victoria Leach, then Ontario's adoption co-ordinator, approached CFTO, the Toronto television station that was partly owned by Bassett. "It took them all of fifteen minutes to make up their minds," Allen reported later. *Family Finder*, which ran commercial-free, debuted in the fall of 1968 and became the longest-running program on the channel.

When the *Telegram* folded in 1971, the Ontario government hired Allen as an information officer in the Ministry of Community and Social Services. She continued to write the column three times a week — it was syndicated by the government to more than twenty daily newspapers, including the *Toronto Star* — appear on the television program, and speak about adoption to community and service groups.

In the early 1970s, television and newspaper reporters publicized the plight of the many children who had become victims of the ongoing conflict in Vietnam. The orphanages in Saigon were overflowing with abandoned or parentless children. Social changes, including the widely available contraceptive pill and the zero-population-growth political movement, had decimated the baby surplus of a decade before in the West. That fact, plus the human desire to help needy children, had lots of North Americans flying to Vietnam and trying to pick up babies in exchange for cash or services.

The local adoption agencies were floundering, so the Ontario Ministry of Social and Community Services sent Leach and Allen to Saigon to work with the Vietnamese. As the north Vietnam army advanced and the Americans were pulling out, the two women rescued close to sixty children, brought them to Canada, and found homes for them.

Allen received many honours, including being named to the Order of Canada (OC), an honorary doctorate from York University, and the Award of Merit from the City of Toronto. In the late 1970s she was at an OC reception when she encountered Charles Stacey, a fellow laureate and her beau from back in the 1920s.

Allen, who had never married, and Stacey, by then a widower, renewed their affection for each other and were quietly married on October 3, 1980. The bride was seventy-three and the groom seventy-four. A little more than a year later, she officially retired from "Today's Child" and *Family Finder*, although she continued to spend two days a week answering mail and writing adoption bulletins.

The Staceys were a very companionable couple. They loved to entertain at small dinner parties, read Jane Austen novels aloud to each other, and travel. After he died suddenly of a heart attack in November 1989, she continued to live in their Rosedale apartment until late in 2002, when she moved into a retirement residence. That's where she died of congestive heart failure on November 9, 2006, at the age of ninety-nine.

LYLE CREELMAN

Public Health Nurse

AUGUST 14, 1908 – FEBRUARY 27, 2007

H ER NAME IS barely known, but Lyle Creelman set the standard for public health nursing both here and abroad. She led the first nurses into Bergen-Belsen after British and Canadian troops liberated the diabolical Nazi concentration camp in April 1945. They found thousands of unburied corpses and more than fifty thousand prisoners, many of whom were dying of starvation and typhus.

After the war, Creelman co-wrote a hugely important report on public health nursing in this country that established teaching criteria for two decades, and in 1954 she became the first Canadian to serve as chief nursing officer of the World Health Organization. When she retired from WHO at age sixty, the journal of its International Council wrote in an editorial: "In these fourteen years, she has probably achieved more for nursing throughout the world than any other nurse of her time."

Over her long career, Creelman developed and broadcast a vision of health care based on a philosophy of offering medical knowledge to health practitioners in developing countries, rather than imposing her views on their cultural practices. An intuitive and quietly ambitious woman with great intellectual and diplomatic skills, Creelman thrived in situations that combined travel, exchanging ideas, and deploying her medical training and expertise in new and innovative grassroots organizations.

LYLE MORRISON CREELMAN, who was born on August 14, 1908, was known in her family as the "youngest of the youngest" because she had eleven older half-siblings, the children of her father, Samuel Prescott Creelman, and his first wife, Marianna (née McDonald). The Creelmans lived in Upper Stewiacke, a farming community near Truro, Nova Scotia, where her father was a well-driller. After he was widowed he married a distant cousin, Laura Creelman, with whom he had Lyle, his twelfth and final child. Her father, who was in his late fifties when she was born, moved his reconstituted family to Steveston, British Columbia, a fishing community located at the mouth of the Fraser River, probably during the First World War.

After graduating from high school in Richmond, B.C., she trained as a teacher, receiving her first-class certificate in 1931. Four years later she realized that her ambition demanded larger scope than teaching successive generations how to read, write, and do sums.

Her father had left her $200 in his will when he died in 1926. That money, plus her savings from teaching, enabled her to enter the nursing program at Vancouver General Hospital and the University of British Columbia, from which she graduated with a bachelor of applied science in nursing in 1936.

Older than the other students, she had a commanding, determined presence and, unlike many of them, she was independent-minded and keener on a career than marriage and children. In those days teaching and nursing were the preferred — and often the only respectable — options for intelligent young women. Combining them with marriage and motherhood was not only discouraged, it was usually forbidden by employers. It wasn't until after the Second World War that married nurses were allowed to practise in hospitals.

She worked as a public health nurse in Revelstoke for a year and then moved to Richmond as one of two public health nurses at the newly established Metropolitan Health Committee (later the Vancouver Health Department). In 1938 she won a Rockefeller Scholarship to study for a master's degree in nursing at Columbia University in New York City.

Equipped with all of the available academic and professional tools, she returned to Vancouver in 1939 just as war was declared. She was eager to serve overseas, but public health nurses and nursing instructors were designated "official home front personnel," both to train nurses for the front and to care for Canadians in case the country became an active war zone.

By 1944, when an Allied victory seemed certain and Canada was clearly in no danger of an enemy invasion, she joined the United Nations Relief and

Rehabilitation Administration, which had been formed the year before at a forty-four nation conference at the White House in Washington, D.C. Charged with providing economic and repatriation assistance to refugees in the aftermath of the presumed defeat of the Axis powers, UNRRA (which became the International Refugee Organization in 1948) reported to Supreme Headquarters Allied Expeditionary Forces (SHAEF) and was largely funded by the United States.

Creelman was sent first to England and a year later to Germany as chief nurse of the British Occupied Zone, which included the Bergen-Belsen concentration camp. This was not a part of her life that Creelman liked to talk about, arguing that it was only one of many aspects of a long nursing career, but it must have been a devastating experience to be among the first medical personnel to see, smell, and care for the thousands of dying and dead victims of the Holocaust.

The Nazis created Bergen-Belsen in April 1943 as a sorting and transfer centre for labour and death camps. By 1945 it had become a concentration camp, incarcerating thousands of prisoners who were too weak for forced labour. Many prisoners, including the young Dutch diarist Anne Frank, who had been transferred there from Auschwitz, died from starvation and typhoid before the Allied troops arrived in April 1945.

Creelman's job, as director of the neophyte International Nursing Brigade, was to care for the physical, social, and mental health of her horribly damaged patients. Their deprivations were so overwhelming that her instinct was to do the hands-on nursing herself, but she quickly realized that the real job was to train everybody else. The nurses reporting to her came from more than twenty countries and didn't share a common language, training, or tradition, while the INB itself was too new to have a developed organizational infrastructure. So, after training her INB colleagues, she combined forces with them to offer ad hoc nursing courses to young women in the displaced-persons camps so that they could provide medical care and also, perhaps, find a way to rehabilitate their own war-ravaged personalities and learn new skills.

All of her listening and diplomatic expertise was called upon in devising ways to care for her traumatized patients. Many kept "escaping" from hospital because they couldn't bear to be confined any longer; others who had been severely malnourished hid portions of their meals, convinced that each serving would be the last; and some, especially dissident Russian Jews, were unco-operative and disruptive because they were afraid of pogroms if they were sent home.

After two intense years, Creelman returned to Vancouver. She was almost immediately granted leave from her nursing job to serve as field director of an extensive study of public health services in Canada that was being conducted by the Canadian Public Health Association. She was co-author, with J. H. Baillie, of a highly acclaimed report that served as a guide to a more open and flexible direction for public health nursing in Canada. It was used for many years as a reference work for public health professionals.

Her final career, with the newly formed World Health Organization, came through a Canadian connection. Brock Chisholm, a Canadian doctor who was a highly decorated veteran of both world wars, inaugural deputy minister of health in Mackenzie King's government, and the first executive secretary of WHO, knew Creelman and her work both at home and abroad. A psychiatrist and a strong advocate of religious tolerance and holistic medicine, Chisholm had been one of sixteen international experts involved in drafting the World Health Organization's constitution in 1948. He invited Creelman to work with him the following year as a nursing consultant in maternal and child health.

Five years later, Creelman became WHO's chief nursing officer, replacing her British colleague Olive Baggallay. She held the position for the next fourteen years, spending nine months of the year in Geneva developing nursing standards, planning missions to developing countries, and preparing responses to outbreaks of cholera, malaria, and other epidemics. The other three months, she put theory into practice in developing countries. Even after she retired in 1968 she wasn't ready to quit; she accepted a WHO appointment to study maternal and child health services in Southeast Asia.

Afterwards she settled on Bowen Island, near Vancouver, where her apartment became a place of respite for friends, colleagues, family, and nurses she had mentored from across the country and around the world. In the late 1980s she moved into Hollyburn House, a seniors' residence in West Vancouver. Despite two strokes that impaired her ability to walk and speak, she maintained an elegant appearance and a lively social life until she died of pneumonia on February 27, 2007, at age ninety-eight.

Israel Halperin

Mathematician and Human Rights Activist

January 5, 1911 – March 8, 2007

M OST MATHEMATICIANS FIND their calling early, when their minds are uncluttered, their vision sharp, and their energy boundless. So it was with Israel Halperin, the son of Russian immigrants, who studied under the legendary Johann von Neumann at Princeton in the 1930s.

Halperin was being quietly celebrated among scholars for his work on operator algebras when treachery intervened during the Cold War and yanked him out of the ivory tower and into the mire of *realpolitik*. Unjustly accused as a spy by Canadian authorities, Halperin was suspended from his academic job and brought to trial.

Albert Einstein, his former professor at Princeton, was one of the scholars who came to his defence. Instead of making him bitter, the ordeal confirmed Halperin as a human rights activist. Until the end of his life he campaigned relentlessly for others, especially wrongly incarcerated Jewish dissidents, such as Anatoly Sharansky, in the former Soviet Union.

ISRAEL HALPERIN WAS born in Montreal on January 5, 1911, but grew up in Scarborough, an eastern outlier of Toronto. After Malvern Collegiate, Halperin entered Victoria College at the University of Toronto, graduating with a bachelor's degree in 1932, having won a mantelful of awards that included top marks in mathematics and physics. Two years later he had earned his master's degree and was at Princeton University, registered for his PhD.

Princeton was an academic mecca for refugees fleeing from Europe, especially mathematicians, who were drawn to the university's Institute of Advanced Study. Among them were physicist Albert Einstein and mathematician Johann (John) von Neumann, the father of computer science and inventor of robotics and game theory. Naively but boldly, Halperin asked Neumann if he would direct his doctoral thesis, not realizing that the man had such an exalted research position that he was not required to supervise graduate students. Nevertheless, Neumann, who was doing work on operator theories and continuous geometries, took him on, giving Halperin the distinction of being the great Neumann's only PhD student. After completing his doctorate, Halperin worked at Yale as a research fellow in 1936–37 and spent the next two years as the Benjamin Pierce Instructor at Harvard University.

He wanted to come back to Canada, so he accepted a position in the fall of 1939 as an assistant professor of mathematics at Queen's University in Kingston. He was twenty-eight and had already published several mathematical papers on operator algebras (a combination of algebra, geometry, and quantum mechanics), a field that he established here and kept alive for the next thirty years. It became a hot topic internationally in the 1960s in noncommutative geometry, mathematical physics, and numerical analysis.

Shortly after embarking on his research and teaching career at Queen's, he married Mary Esther Sawdey, the sister-in-law of a Harvard colleague, physicist Wendell Furry. The Halperins eventually had four children, Stephen (1941), Constance (1944), William (1945), and Mary Elizabeth (1948).

Along with his academic work, Halperin was active politically in those twitchy times. In the United States he and Furry were both actively involved with the American Association of Scientific Workers, a liberal and progressive organization founded during the Depression with the aim of involving scientists directly in debate about social and political issues. (Later Furry ran afoul of U.S. Senator Joseph McCarthy's anticommunist witch hunts of the 1950s and was indicted for contempt of Congress for refusing to name names before the House Un-American Activities Committee.) At Queen's, Halperin was developing a reputation as an agitator. He wrote eloquently, publicly, and futilely in defence of geophysicist Samuel Levine, a classmate from his undergraduate days at the University of Toronto. Under the far-reaching powers of the War Measures Act, Levine had been arrested, jailed for six months for possessing subversive literature, and dismissed, in 1941, from his teaching job at U of T.

In 1942 Halperin took military leave from Queen's to enlist in the Royal Canadian Artillery and was commissioned as a second lieutenant. Mostly he worked at the Canadian Army Research and Development Establishment in Ottawa on artillery problems, explosives, and secret intelligence research into rockets and other issues. He attained the rank of major before being discharged at the end of the war and resuming his teaching career at Queen's, moving his family back to Kingston and building a house in the west end of the city.

That's when his life went haywire. Igor Gouzenko, a cipher clerk at the Soviet embassy in Ottawa, defected in September 1945, bringing with him a list of names of alleged spies and fellow-travellers. One of them, a left-leaning British immigrant and advertising copywriter named Gordon Lunan (about whom I wrote in Rogues, Rascals, and Romantics), fingered Halperin as a Soviet spy.

The two men had met in Ottawa late in the war. Lunan, a sympathizer of anti-fascist causes, a friend of union organizer and communist MP Fred Rose, and a lieutenant in the army, worked on *Canadian Affairs*, a newsletter that provided a summary of news and editorials for troops stationed here and abroad.

The Communist Party had been banned at the outbreak of the war but had re-formed as the Labour Progressive Party. Rose had run under its banner, won a by-election in 1943, and retained his seat in the working-class riding of Cartier in Montreal in the 1945 election. Through Rose's connections to Colonel Nikolai Zabotin, head of military intelligence at the Soviet embassy in Ottawa, Lunan was recruited as a low-level spy. He covertly supplied his handler, Colonel Vasili Rogov, with information gleaned from casual encounters with scientists and mathematicians.

One of Lunan's sources was Halperin, whose Soviet code name was "Bacon." Lunan mentioned him in four reports to his Soviet spymaster, although never as a source of any secret information. On the contrary, Lunan wrote in frustration to his handler in July 1945: "this fellow is a mathematician, and not a chemist or physicist, which may account for his remoteness from the details of explosive research."

Halperin was probably known to the RCMP because of his previous political activity and his work with organic chemist Raymond Boyer, president of the Canadian Association of Scientific Workers, an offshoot of the American organization. They swooped down on Halperin on February 15, 1946, raided his office, and whisked him away in a shocking abuse of civil liberties, especially as it was peacetime. The War Measures Act had expired at the end of the Second World War, but the Mackenzie King government had secretly extended one of its provisions — giving the prime minister and the justice minister the power to arrest and detain people suspected of passing secrets to the enemy — in a special order-in-council, PC 6444, in October 1945, a month after Gouzenko's defection.

At the time, Canadian, British, and American military officials were worried that key scientific discoveries were being shipped to the Soviets. Their main quarry was the British physicist Alan Nunn May, a genuine Soviet spy — like the notorious Kim Philby, he had been recruited at Cambridge — who was working at the Anglo-Canadian Laboratory in Montreal and at the atomic research plant in Chalk River, Ontario. Instead of apprehending May and turning him over to the British, the RCMP went after Canadians, most of them guilty of nothing more than sharing already published scientific information and harbouring sympathy for our former ally against the Nazis.

Halperin, like the other accused, was held incommunicado, without access to legal counsel or his family, by the RCMP at its Rockliffe Barracks in spartan accommodation — even the windows were nailed shut — pending an appearance before the Kellock-Taschereau Royal Commission. The commission, headed by two Supreme Court judges, Roy Kellock and Robert Taschereau, had been struck on February 5, 1946 (ten days before Halperin's detention), to investigate Gouzenko's allegations that a spy ring of Canadian communists was handing over state secrets to the Soviets.

Halperin's situation only became known to the public after he covertly sent a letter to John Bracken, the Progressive Conservative Party leader, which was read in the House of Commons on March 21, 1946. "For the past five weeks I have been held in solitary imprisonment, denied access to legal counsel and newspapers; in short, cut off from the outside world," Halperin wrote. "I charge the minister of justice with using his authority in a way which sets a dangerous precedent, one which should alarm every Canadian citizen." He then described himself as coming from a family "whose concern for our country was sufficient to put two sons in uniform. One of them is writing this letter; the other is at the bottom of the ocean."

When Halperin was summoned to appear before the royal commission, he refused to make any statement without legal representation. His hearing was adjourned until March 27, 1946. Meanwhile, Halperin's wife, Mary, and his sister, lawyer Clara Halperin (later Muskat), presented a habeas corpus petition to Mr. Justice Walter Schroeder in his chambers at Osgoode Hall in Toronto, arguing that Halperin's detention was "irregular, illegal, defective, insufficient."

On March 26, 1946, the judge granted the writ and Halperin was released, but he was required to appear in Ottawa Weekly Court four days later, where he was represented by A. H. Lieff, a Jewish lawyer who later became a renowned family court judge. When Halperin's hearing before the commission was reopened, he refused to answer what he described as a "cross examination." A month later he was charged with conspiracy and violating the Official Secrets Act and was committed for trial in December 1946.

Halperin's trial came to a halt when the Crown called Lunan as a witness and he refused to testify, pending the outcome of his appeal against his own conviction on spy charges. When the court reconvened in March 1947, the charges were dismissed for lack of evidence when Lunan again refused to testify.

After thirteen harrowing months, Halperin was legally a free man, but he was still under suspicion in the groves of academe, where several of his colleagues wanted him fired. The person who came to Halperin's defence was Robert Wallace, principal of Queen's, who quickly moved to reinstate his salary, academic status (coincidentally, Halperin had been on unpaid research leave since October 1946), and sabbatical privileges. When a member of the university's board of trustees wrote to the principal declaring that "some Alumni" felt that "a Communist fellow-traveller" was not the "the type of individual who should be teaching in a Canadian university," Wallace replied that "until a man is proved guilty, he has to be deemed as innocent."

Nevertheless, Halperin's continued employment at Queen's was only happily resolved after a heated debate of the board of trustees in May 1948. Among the testimonials sent on Halperin's behalf was a letter from the Institute of Advanced Study at Princeton, signed by Albert Einstein and eleven others, describing him "not only as a mathematician of high standing but also as a man of greatest integrity" and finding it "impossible to believe" that he could be guilty "of any real breach of trust or honour."

For the rest of his life Halperin refused to discuss his ordeal with family, colleagues, or historians working on academic freedom. He concentrated on his academic work and on helping others whose rights had been trampled by overweening authority. He was elected a fellow of the Royal Society of Canada in 1953 and given its Henry Marshall Tory Medal in 1967. He continued to teach at Queen's until 1966, when he was hired away by the University of Toronto. At least one of his Queen's students — George Elliott, now a distinguished mathematician — followed him down the road to Toronto.

During Halperin's long career — which extended far past mandatory retirement at sixty-five — he published more than a hundred papers and influenced waves of younger mathematicians, including Peter Rosenthal, who was attracted to the University of Toronto largely because of Halperin's work on Hilbert space (a kind of infinite dimensional space). Halperin also completed two substantial manuscripts that his mentor Neumann had left in an inchoate state when he died in 1957: *Continuous Geometry* (1960, 1980) and *Continuous Geometries with a Transition Probability* (1981).

In the late 1960s, Halperin founded an international newsletter to broadcast and monitor developments in operator algebras and established the first Canadian Annual Symposium on Operator Algebras and Their Applications in 1972. Many of the participants who gathered for these informal discussions were former students. Eight years later, those same mathematicians set up the Israel Halperin Prize in honour of his seventieth birthday; it is given every five years to a younger mathematician who has done significant research in the area of operator theory or algebras.

Halperin, who had always been a vocal defender of academic friends whose human and civil rights were being trampled, became a committed campaigner on behalf of a much wider community of scholars who were being repressed by their own governments. He was really a committee of one, acting on one case at a time and conducting his campaigns in a very dignified letter-writing mode. Typically he would write to Nobel laureates asking them to add their names to his campaign literature.

With French mathematician Henri Cartan, he formed a committee of scientists and scholars at the International Congress of Mathematicians in Vancouver in 1974 to lobby for the release of Leonid Plyushch, a Russian mathematician who had been incarcerated in a psychiatric hospital and subjected to insulin therapy. Plyushch was released in 1976, at least partly because of the ten-thousand-name petition that Halperin helped to accumulate.

He became secretary of the Canadian Committee of Scientists and Scholars and campaigned successfully for the release of José Luis Massera from prison and torture in Uruguay in 1984, and for Anatoly Sharansky's discharge from a Soviet labour camp in 1986 and permission to immigrate to Israel. The New York Academy of Sciences gave Halperin the Heinz R. Pagels Award in 1999 in recognition of his work in advancing the human rights of scientists around the world.

Halperin continued as an active scholar well into his eighties and was having "serious mathematical thoughts" until the last year of his life, when he decided to stop doing mathematics and gave away many of his papers. Complications from a genetic heart condition caused severe circulatory problems, forcing him to enter hospital, where he died of organ failure on March 8, 2007. He was ninety-six.

ERNEST ALVIA ("SMOKY") SMITH

Winner of the Victoria Cross

MAY 3, 1914 – AUGUST 3, 2005

A ROWDY, SPUNKY fellow who liked drinking, smoking, and roistering, Smoky Smith wasn't the romantic Victorian ideal of a dashing hero on a white charger. A private in the Canadian Army, he was promoted to corporal nine times and demoted back to private just as often, until he showed his mettle at the River Savio in the brutal Italian campaign of the Second World War.

In real life, heroes typically don't come off an assembly line. They are usually ordinary folk like Smith who step into the fire, driven by a mixture of guts, circumstance, and adrenalin. Instead of blustering, they willingly sacrifice their own safety for the benefit of others. That's what Smith did. He single-handedly destroyed a German tank, forced the enemy to retreat, and saved the life of a wounded comrade. That alone should have earned him a medal. But Smith's bravery went further than personal valour: he inspired his fellow soldiers to demonstrate their own heroism.

That's why he deserved the Victoria Cross, the only private of the sixteen Canadians who won the award during the Second World War. The citation read in part: "By the dogged determination, outstanding devotion to duty, and superb gallantry of this private soldier, his comrades were so inspired that the bridgehead was held firm against all enemy attacks, pending the arrival of tanks and anti-tank guns some hours later."

Queen Victoria introduced the VC on January 29, 1856, to honour acts of valour during the Crimean War. Supposedly the medals were struck from metal extracted from Russian cannons captured at the siege of Sebastopol in 1854–55, but recent research has cast doubt on that swelling narrative. Be that as it may, the VC even now is the ultimate award for bravery in the face of the enemy. It was reconstituted in 1993 as the Canadian Victoria Cross, but no Canadian has received it since the end of the Second World War.

Smoky Smith was famous in Canada because he was the last surviving recipient of the VC, but that is not why he was loved. He was loved because he wore his heroism simply and he didn't glorify war. "Even Germans do not like to be shot," he said sixty years after winning the medal. "I don't take prisoners. Period. I'm not prepared to take prisoners. I'm paid to kill them. That's the way it is."

There was no swagger about Smith as he attended Remembrance Day ceremonies and represented his country at poignant anniversaries both here and on the battlefields of Europe. He was the known soldier, to be sure, but he was also a regular guy who could relate to young and old with a quip and a wink and a modesty that did him and us proud. "I am not the hero," he was fond of saying. "The real heroes are the ones left over there buried in the ground."

ERNEST ALVIA SMITH was born in New Westminster, British Columbia, on May 3, 1914, a few months before the outbreak of the "war to end all wars." The elder son of John Alvia and Barmarie Smith's four children, he grew up in a working-class family. His father was a truck driver and his mother a homemaker.

After elementary school he went to T. J. Trap Technical High School. Sitting behind a desk was not nearly as interesting to him as athletics, especially track and soccer. His nickname "Smoky"(which later became "Smokey" in the popular press) may date from those days because of the speed with which he left rivals in his wake, or smoke, as he raced around the track. On the other hand, he was a smoker who only gave up cigarettes in his fifties, although he continued to indulge in a nightly cigar. Smith, who knew the value of a smokescreen, always claimed he didn't know how he acquired the moniker.

Smith entered the workforce just as the Depression had ground the economy into dust. He worked sporadically in a cannery, a cedar shake mill, and an electrical shop and even rode the rails from one community to another looking for work. The Second World War offered him an opportunity to serve his country and earn a steady paycheque. He enlisted in the Seaforth Highlanders in Vancouver on March 5, 1940, at the age of twenty-five. After basic training he was shipped overseas and was stationed in England and Scotland in the early years of the war. His real fighting came with the bloody Italian campaign.

The Seaforths landed in Sicily on July 10, 1943, as part of the First Canadian Infantry Division attached to the Eighth Army. They spent the next eighteen months pushing German forces back up the boot of Italy. Smith suffered a shrapnel wound in the chest in the fighting and spent two months in hospital in North Africa before he was back in the line.

By October 1944 the Seaforths had made their way as far north as the Savio River. That's when Smith entered the history books. The Canadians needed to establish a crossing over the river but the enemy and the weather were against them. Torrential rain had caused the water to rise some six feet in five hours and turned the riverbanks into mush.

To advance, the troops would have to wade or swim through the raging current and rising water levels and then fight the Germans without the protective cover of their tanks. "It had been raining for days and the rain pelted down in sheets," Smith said in a CBC interview in 1956, one of the few times he talked publicly about his wartime experiences. "The ground was one big bog."

That was the situation on the eastern bank of the Savio late in the afternoon of October 20, when the first troops were sent into the river. A shower of gunfire and grenades came from the opposite bank, pinning down the troops until they were able to retreat under cover of darkness. The next morning the enemy began pounding the Canadians on the eastern approaches to the river. That night another group of soldiers, including Smith, made it across the river and took cover.

That's when Smith learned that the forward company was under attack from three German Mark V Panther tanks supported by two self-propelled guns and some thirty infantry. With cunning ingenuity, he led his PIAT (a British-designed anti-tank weapon that had been introduced only the year before in the Sicilian campaign) team of two men across an open field, positioning the weapon in a ditch alongside the road so it could be trained on the enemy. Leaving one man there, Smith crossed the road with his comrade Jimmy Tennant and obtained another PIAT. At that moment a German tank came clanking down the road, firing its machine guns into the ditches and wounding Tennant.

Showing defiance and a complete disregard for his own safety, Smith started firing his PIAT, scoring a direct hit and putting the tank out of commission. Ten German infantrymen jumped off the back of the tank and charged him with Schmeisser submachine guns and grenades. Undaunted, Smith moved out onto the road and started mowing them down with his Tommy gun. He killed four Germans and drove the rest back. Another tank rumbled into view and opened fire, and more infantry were closing in on Smith. When he ran out of ammunition, he ran back to the ditch and grabbed some of Tennant's and held the enemy at bay while protecting his comrade.

In the melee, Smith had destroyed one tank and two self-propelled guns. Yet another tank appeared in the distance, sweeping the area with a longer-range gun. Still under fire, Smith helped his wounded comrade to cover behind a nearby building and obtained medical aid for him before returning to his position beside the road to combat further enemy action. None materialized, so the battalion was able to consolidate its bridgehead and await the arrival of its own tanks and anti-tank guns. This led to the capture of San Giorgio di Cesena and the advance further north to the Ronco River. Later Smith was hailed as a "one-man army" for the way he had single-handedly fought off the German tanks.

King George VI bestowed Smith's VC medal at a ceremony in Buckingham Palace in December 1944. Smith's superior officers were so concerned that he would appear dishevelled, or worse, at the ceremony that they locked him up in a jail cell in Italy the night before he was supposed to board the plane taking him to London for the investiture. That's another story, like the tale about his nickname, that Smith refused to confirm or deny, although he did allow in one interview that he was kept in custody in London before meeting the King. "There's a town full of women out there and here I am in jail," he said with mock chagrin. "It's only because I was good-looking."

After receiving his VC, Smith retreated from the front lines and spent what remained of the war drumming up support for the Canadian War Bonds drive. He was demobilized in April 1945 and returned to Vancouver. Two years later he married photographer Esther Weston. Together they operated a photography studio in New Westminster and raised two children, David and Norma-Jean.

Smith re-enlisted in the Armed Forces in 1950 to serve in the Korean War. He was promoted to the rank of sergeant but was not sent into combat because of his legendary status. Instead he served as a recruiting agent in Vancouver until he retired once again in 1964, at age fifty. He was given the Canadian Forces Decoration for his dozen years of service.

The Smiths opened a travel agency called Smith Travel in 1969, which they operated for more than twenty years, with Smith often taking clients on tours to sites connected with the Second World War. They couple retired in 1992, the year he turned seventy-eight. His wife died four years later, in 1996.

As other veterans died, Smith became iconic as the last surviving recipient of the VC. He was appointed a member of the Order of Canada in 1995 and a member of the Order of British Columbia in 2002. He also made many appearances at veterans' events, Remembrance Day ceremonies, and significant military milestones, including the fiftieth anniversary of the Battle of Vimy Ridge in 1967, the fiftieth anniversary of the Normandy invasion in 1995, and the consecration ceremony of the Tomb of the Unknown Soldier in Ottawa in May 2000.

Smith died at his home in Vancouver on August 3, 2005, at ninety-one, his body was flown to Ottawa to lie in state in the foyer of the House of Commons on August 9. The government flags were flying at half-mast, an extremely rare honour for a citizen who was neither a former prime minister nor a governor general.

Smith's coffin made the long journey back across the country for a second vigil, at Vancouver's Seaforth Armoury on August 12, before a full military funeral the following day. As per Smith's wishes, his ashes were sprinkled at sea, presumably so that his grave could not become a shrine, although friends suggested a different reason: he didn't want to be put in the ground because he had buried too many of his friends.

As a final act of remembrance, he left instructions in his will that his medals, including the VC, which could have been sold for a huge sum, be donated to the Seaforth Highlanders. The regiment has replicas on display in its museum and exhibits the genuine medals on special occasions only, as a memorial to its most celebrated member.

KAY GIMPEL

Secret Service Agent and Art Dealer

AUGUST 14, 1914 – MARCH 19, 2009

K AY GIMPEL FLED the restrictive imperatives of the Depression on the
Prairies for the cultural capitals of England and France. She was seeking culture, excitement, and a larger, more independent life. What she found
was danger, treachery, and sacrifice, working for the Special Operations
Executive (SOE) — a wartime British sabotage organization set up by Winston
Churchill in July 1940 — as an interpreter and liaison for Allied agents
behind enemy lines.

Life in wartime London was acute and fragile. Social niceties such as
chaperones had been suspended, but death was a concrete, full-frontal reality.
As Gimpel said later, "most of the agents who went overseas never came back,
so you lived for the moment." That toll included her friends Frank Pickersgill
and Ken Macalister, Canadian SOE agents in France who were captured by
the Germans, tortured, and hanged with piano wire from meat hooks at
Buchenwald concentration camp in September 1944. Their bodies were then
incinerated.

Salty of tongue in both French and English, which she tended to speak
interchangeably, Gimpel was short, intense, and very sharp. During the war
she roomed with two friends, Mary Mundle, a Scot, and Alison Grant, a
Canadian and the future mother of public intellectual and former Liberal
leader Michael Ignatieff.

All three young women worked for various branches of the secret service;

their flat, located three floors above a dairy at 54A Walton Avenue in Knightsbridge (just behind Harrod's and very close to the SOE veterans' club), was dubbed the "Canada House Annex." Approved as a "safe house" by SOE, it became a meeting place for many agents looking for conversational ease before going to the Continent, or for friendly solace after returning from a mission.

Gimpel, who became Ignatieff's godmother, was his mother's "best, truest, closest friend." He described the war years the two women shared in London as the "the most important" in either of their lives. "There was a strong sense of being where history was happening, bombs were falling, ultimate things were on the line and they were there working with extremely brave men and they were extremely brave women. It was the making of them both. They never glorified it, they never romanticized it; they didn't even talk about it that much."

Initially, the flawlessly bilingual Gimpel was a junior officer in RF, the section of SOE that worked with the Free French Forces supporting General Charles de Gaulle. Her job was to brief agents about what they could expect to find on the ground in France. "This was mere routine, but from the agents' point of view it was jolly useful," said M. R. D. Foot, the official historian of SOE.

As the war progressed, Gimpel moved on to AL (Air Liaison), eventually heading the section, the only woman to hold such a senior position. "Her job, which was very difficult, was to provide the link point between SOE's demands for air help and what the air forces could supply," according to Foot, the acknowledged expert on the organization. "There were two squadrons of Bomber Command practically entirely devoted to working for SOE and eventually four squadrons of the United States Army Air Force," he said in an email after Gimpel's death in London, England, on March 19, 2009. She had "to tell the air men precisely where to go, and when I say precisely, I mean which field in which to drop their stores. Scores of thousands of Resisters in France and Belgium and Holland owed their weapons and their supplies to arrangements made by Kay."

KATHLEEN (KAY) MOORE was born in Strathcona, Alberta, on August 14, 1914, just as the guns began to blaze in Europe in the First World War. She was the middle child and only daughter of Harold Henry Moore, an Irish-born journalist, and his wife, Katherine Helen Chapman. Her parents, who had met at the *Mail and Empire* newspaper in Toronto — he was a reporter and she a secretary — eventually settled in Winnipeg, where he worked at the *Winnipeg Free Press* as a reporter and then as an editorial writer. When Kay was eight, her younger brother died of diphtheria. Not long afterward, her desolate mother began a slow, painful decline from kidney disease, taking to her bed and sometimes holding Kay in her arms as she fantasized about embracing her dead son. She died in an institution in 1930.

In his own grief, Moore's father, who had served as a major in the Forestry Corps in the First World War, tried to run the household on a military model. He used his teenaged daughter as an unofficial second-in-command, a role that she, a high-spirited and independent girl, found onerous. Porridge was only one of the issues that divided them — he insisted there was no better way to start the day, while she loathed the stuff.

Moore went to the University of Manitoba in the early 1930s, where she studied French language and literature. She graduated with such distinction that in 1936 she went to Paris on a scholarship to the Sorbonne. After completing her studies, she stayed on in Paris, working at the British embassy and living in the Hotel Lenox with her colleague Mary Mundle. After Germany invaded France in May 1940, the embassy was evacuated and Moore and Mundle sailed for England.

Moore joined the First Aid Nursing Yeomanry (FANY), which was really a front for her involvement with SOE. She and Mundle, who also worked for the RF Section of SOE, soon met up with Alison Grant, who had arrived from Toronto in the mid-1930s to study art on a Massey family scholarship. After war broke out, Grant had become attached to Military Intelligence Section 5, known more familiarly as MI5.

During the day, Moore worked in Dorset Square, where, besides briefing her friends Pickersgill and Macalister, she also worked with a young man named Ernest Gimpel, a Jewish resistance fighter for the Free French whose code name was Charles Beauchamp.

Born August 5, 1913, in France, Gimpel was the elder son of René Gimpel — an art collector and dealer and friend of Monet, Proust, and Renoir — and his wife, Florence Duveen, the youngest sister of English art dealer Joseph Duveen. After doing his French military service in North Africa as a trooper in the turbaned Chasseurs d'Afrique, Gimpel lived in London, where he worked for an interior design company. After France and England declared war against Germany in September 1939, he went back to France, enlisted in a French tank regiment that November, and was wounded in the defence of the Maginot Line. After the fall of France in June 1940 he joined the Resistance, but he was soon arrested and horribly beaten by the Germans before he managed to escape his captors, only to begin the brutal cycle over and over again.

Through the Resistance network, Gimpel was brought to England by submarine in September 1942. There he joined the Free French Forces, and was briefed by Kay Moore before he returned to France on November 25, 1943. During that fourteen-month respite in London, the two became friendly and fell in love, according to Chrystel Hug, author of the forthcoming book, *RF Is for Real Friends: Snapshots of* soe, *the Free French, and the Alliance Française in London*. Two months after Gimpel returned home, he was arrested by the Gestapo, tortured, and sent to Germany, where he was sent successively to the Buchenwald, Auschwitz, and Flossenbürg camps. When he was released on April 24, 1945, by the advancing Allied troops, his first words were, "Where is Kay Moore?"

Not too far away, as it turned out. After the liberation of Paris in August 1944, she had gone back to France with a contingent of Allied personnel and begun the task of sifting through the avalanche of materials about Allied prisoners of war.

"My mother's memory is of Kay going to find Charles and he being down to skin and bones, with the number 185663 tattooed on his left arm," said Ignatieff. The tiny Moore and the towering but emaciated Gimpel were married in London on August 29, 1945. As a honeymoon she took him to see cousins in Westmeath, Ireland, where he began to recuperate from his physical and emotional wounds.

In November 1946, Charles Gimpel — he had retained the first part of his code name but reverted to his original surname — and his younger brother Peter opened the Gimpel Fils gallery on Duke Street (later South Molton and now Davis Street) in honour of their father, René, art collector and author of *Diary of an Art Dealer*. The senior Gimpel, who had also joined the Resistance, died in Neuengamme concentration camp in Hamburg in 1944.

Before the war, the brothers had stored some of their father's inventory — he specialized in French eighteenth-century, Impressionist, and non-representational painting — in a locked garage in a London mews. Amazingly, the London garage was neither bombed nor looted during the war, and the canvases had suffered nothing more serious than several years' accumulation of dust and dirt. This artistic stockpile became the basis of the brothers' first show, "Five Centuries of French Painting," and was then used as collateral to acquire new works and artists. Over the years the gallery showcased postwar avant-garde paintings and sculptures by artists such as Henry Moore, Barbara Hepworth, Ben Nicholson, and Alan Davie.

Kay Gimpel "was the mainspring of the Gimpel gallery" in the early days, according to her former SOE colleague M. R. D. Foot, who pointed out that it was she who insisted that all gallery transactions be conducted in Swiss francs. "No other currency was accepted," he said. "In the period of ups and downs with the pound sterling and for the dollar, the Swiss franc remained dead steady and the Gimpel gallery's income also remained dead steady."

Almost certainly she was the one who sparked her husband's interest in the Canadian Arctic. Only four years after the Canadian Handicrafts Guild in Montreal had its sensational first sale of carvings brought from the North by artist and collector James Houston (for more information about Houston, please see Builders), Gimpel Fils celebrated the coronation of Elizabeth II in June 1953 by presenting the first exhibition of Inuit sculpture anywhere in Europe. Along with a hundred pieces lent by the Handicrafts Guild, the show included *Mother and Child*, a carving by Cape Dorset artist Mannumi Shaqu that had been presented to Princess Elizabeth on her tour of Canada in 1951. And that wasn't a one-time commitment: from the late 1950s through the 1990s, the gallery held an annual exhibition of Inuit prints and sculpture. Charles Gimpel himself made six treks to the Canadian Arctic, beginning in the late 1950s — "rambling with my camera," as he described it.

Generally Kay Gimpel left aesthetic and policy decisions about which artists the gallery represented to her husband and latterly her son René, now director of Gimpel Fils, but she was a key player in approaching and courting artists and clients. She had a discerning eye and a retentive memory, traits that she enhanced with a massive and idiosyncratic card index on which she scribbled telling details about the clients, which she could retrieve and decode with panache and dispatch. She "ran the family and she set the rules" at the gallery, according to her son.

Even after her husband died of cancer in 1973, she continued to work at the gallery, retiring only in the late 1990s, when she was in her late eighties. Throughout her career, her personal and domestic support system was an Irishwoman named Bridget (Bridgie) Ferry. She had arrived as a girl in the late 1940s to do housework and child minding and was still there six decades later, the glue between generations of Gimpel children and grandchildren, and Gimpel's companion and most trusted of family retainers. The two women — both in their nineties — continued to play Scrabble, do the *Times* crossword, and entertain all and sundry until Gimpel died of pneumonia, a complication of heart disease, and emphysema, in Chelsea, London, at the age of ninety-five.

John Weir

Flier and Prisoner of War

July 22, 1919 – September 20, 2009

In a sky as azure as a line from "High Flight," a Lancaster bomber, one of its port engines cut and propeller stilled, flew in sunlit silence over the playing fields of Upper Canada College in midtown Toronto on an afternoon in late September 2009. It was chased by a perky canary-yellow de Havilland Chipmunk, a flypast that was an idiosyncratic but moving tribute to John ("Scruffy") Weir, a veteran of the Second World War, a pilot who loved to restore heritage planes, and a man who had thwarted his German captors as a prisoner of war.

Above all, he was a survivor. A Spitfire pilot who crashed and burned in France in 1941, he endured four years as a German POW, underwent horrendous plastic surgeries without anesthesia, helped plan the "Great Escape" from the infamous Stalag Luft III, and withstood a forced march across Germany in the dying days of the war.

Few people knew better than John Weir how to cherish life.

John Gordon Weir was born in Toronto on July 22, 1919, less than a year after Germany signed the armistice ending the First World War, a war that had scarred the life of his father, Colonel James Gordon Weir. The elder Weir, a Presbyterian of Scottish descent, served in the frontline trenches in a machine-gun battalion. By the time the guns were silenced, he had been gassed twice, awarded the Military Cross and the Distinguished Service Order, and risen through the ranks from trooper to colonel. He was a genuine military hero.

After the war, he married a Canadian nursing sister, Mary Frederica (Freda) Taylor, whom he had met in a convalescent hospital. After Weir's discharge, he and his wife settled in Toronto. He resumed his former trade as a bond salesman, eventually helping to found the brokerage firm McLeod Young Weir (now part of Scotiabank).

Everything that Weir had absorbed and accumulated — affluence, the horrors of trench warfare, Germany's festering imperial ambitions — he expended in structuring a training and survival framework for his only son. Young John was sent to Upper Canada College, an elite private school, but the classroom was merely a humdrum part of a much larger education orchestrated by his father: how to survive in the natural and political wilderness. As the 1920s turned into the '30s, Weir was convinced that a second world war against the old foe was inevitable.

He wanted to hone his son's wilderness and strategic skills, so he sent the boy to Algonquin Park in the summers under the tutelage of an Ojibwa fishing guide. He sent him to France during school breaks when he was a teenager to learn the language and customs, and took him along on European business trips in the mid-1930s to observe the rise of Nazism.

On a couple of occasions, Weir had his son carry covert messages to desperate McLeod Young Weir clients who were trying to escape from Germany. In the final stage of this idiosyncratic boot camp, he sent his son to Timmins, in northern Ontario, in July 1938 to work underground in the gold mines. Ostensibly the teenager was earning tuition money for university, but the real goal was to toughen him up with hard physical labour.

On September 4, 1939, the day after Britain declared war on Germany, John Weir, then barely twenty, enlisted in the nascent and ill-equipped Royal Canadian Air Force. He was called up in November, sent to a civilian flying school in Winnipeg, and then shipped back east. He was eventually posted to Trenton, Ontario, to train on fighters. After he appeared on dress parade wearing a uniform stained with the engine coolant glycol, a visiting RAF group captain observed that Weir was "rather a scruffy looking individual" — and "Scruffy" he remained.

About this time he met Fran McCormack on a blind date. They danced together like champions and she brought out the playful side in him —

although it never was far from the surface. On at least two occasions he "bombed" her with notes in handkerchiefs dropped from training planes over her Forest Hill neighbourhood, a courting ritual that today would rouse the institutional ire of aviation authorities.

Weir shipped out in August 1940, arriving on the south coast of England in the middle of the Blitz and at the apogee of German invasion fears. He was posted to 401 Squadron, which had sustained heavy losses in the Battle of Britain, and was then reassigned to Thurso, Scotland, to regroup while protecting the skies over Scapa Flow, the main British naval base.

By October 1941, Squadron 401 had been posted to Lancashire and re-equipped with Spitfires, which were faster than Hurricanes and more agile than Messerschmitts. By then Weir had accumulated a thousand hours of operational flight time, far exceeding the life expectancy for new fighter pilots, which was approximately six combat hours. But his luck was about to expire.

Flying sweeps over Abbeville, one of the main Luftwaffe bases in Picardy, he was shot down by a covey of Messerschmitts. When the Spitfire's cockpit and fuel tank burst into flames, he bailed out at 26,000 feet, a dangerously high altitude without an oxygen mask, and landed — burned, battered, and bootless — about thirty kilometres southwest of Caen.

His eyes were almost fused shut and the skin on his hands, face, and neck was seared. A French farmer led him, nearly blind and in shock, to a tree stump and told him to wait for the Germans. That's how he began his nearly four years as a POW, first in a German hospital and then in Stalag Luft I, on the Baltic. After a couple of short-lived escapes followed by brutal beatings, he, along with three hundred other prisoners, was transported by rail to Stalag Luft III, the allegedly escape-proof camp near Sagan, Poland (about 160 kilometres southeast of Berlin), in mid-April 1942.

He immediately joined the X, or escape, committee. Hatching escape plots was a universal conversational currency for bored and frustrated POWs. Carrying out these brave but often foolhardy schemes — sneaking under the wire, jumping from trains while being transported from one camp to another, or tunnelling under the prison walls — was as commonplace an activity as stamp collecting in peacetime. But Stalag Luft III had been specifically designed to thwart tunnelling. The barracks in the four compounds were raised two feet off the ground so guards could observe covert digging; the sandy subsoil, which was structurally fragile, was bright yellow and easily detected against the grey surface soil; and seismograph microphones had been embedded around the perimeter of the camp to amplify the sounds of digging.

But the Germans hadn't anticipated the determination and organizational skills of RAF squadron leader Roger Bushell, who later became immortalized in print and on screen as the mastermind behind the Great Escape. Since being shot down in May 1940, Bushell had survived at least four POW camps and several escape attempts before arriving at Stalag Luft III in October 1942. He immediately developed an ambitious master plan for three tunnels — Tom, Dick, and Harry — and an escape strategy to spring more than two hundred men, equipped with civilian clothes or tradesmen's uniforms, identity papers, and travel documents.

Weir's pal Wally Floody, whom he knew from Toronto and the mines in Timmins, was also a POW at Stalag Luft III. He became the X committee's master tunneller and quickly recruited Weir as a digger. The summer that Weir spent in the mines of northern Ontario had taught him the significance of shoring up tunnels so they wouldn't collapse and bury the diggers.

Floody's first decision as master tunneller was to use Klim tins (containers of powdered milk sent in by the Red Cross) as scoops to dig straight down for thirty feet (thereby making a smaller sound field for the guards) before levelling out and extending horizontally. The tins were also modified and strung together to form ducts to bring fresh air from the surface into the tunnel. The row of tins provided a directional marker as well, which was a bonus for Weir, who was inclined to veer left and downwards. They helped keep him from digging in a circle.

Despite the ingenuity and perseverance of the POWs, the Great Escape was stalled more often than not. In December 1943, with Tom and Dick abandoned and all the obvious dumping grounds exhausted for the mounds of yellow sand coming out of Harry, the ambitious escape plans were put on hold. That's when Wally Floody persuaded his Ontario pal to consult a visiting Red Cross doctor about his deteriorating eyesight. Because Weir's eyelids were gone, he did everything — including sleeping and digging — with his eyes wide open, leaving them vulnerable to disease, damage, and fatigue. The doctor convinced him that he would eventually go blind if he didn't seek treatment. Consequently, Weir agreed to be transferred to a German hospital for plastic surgery.

He thought he would be away for a couple of weeks. In fact, he was there for several months, serving as a guinea pig under the experimental care of

David Charters. A Scottish ophthalmologist serving with the Royal Army
Medical Corps, Charters had been captured in Greece in 1941. By 1943, having
turned down an opportunity to be repatriated in a prisoner exchange, he was
the chief medical officer of Stalag IXB, at the spa town of Bad Soden, near
Frankfurt. The Germans had so few medical supplies and medical personnel
by then that they used qualified Allied POWs to treat civilians and perform
experimental surgeries on prisoners.

Charters did a series of experimental skin grafts on Weir, slowly rebuilding his upper and lower eyelids — without anaesthetic. Before operating, he
trained Weir in self-hypnosis, as that was the only way the patient could withstand the pain of the scalpel and keep his eyes still enough to avoid being
blinded during the multiple surgeries. It took until late spring 1944 for Weir to
heal enough to be sent back to Stalag Luft III.

Charters saved Weir's sight, and probably also his life, for without the long
hospitalization in Bad Soden, Weir would have been crawling through Harry
on Friday night, March 24, 1944, in the Great Escape. Of the seventy-six men
who slithered through the tunnel before the Germans discovered the escape
attempt, only three made it to safety. Defying the Geneva Convention, fifty
captured prisoners were executed, either singly or in pairs. Weir arrived back
in Stalag Luft III in early June (about the same time as the Allied D-Day landings in Normandy) knowing that many of his fellow prisoners had been
murdered.

By late fall, as the Allies advanced through France, the Germans were
clearly facing defeat. Camp conditions deteriorated, and Red Cross parcels of
food and medicine frequently disappeared into German mouths. Open hos-
tility erupted between the guards and the prisoners. As the Soviets marched
from the east in the bitter January weather, the Germans, fearing retaliation
for earlier atrocities, forced the hungry and ill-clad prisoners to march west-
ward, deeper into war-ravaged Germany.

Weir, his survival instincts in overdrive, decided that making a break for
freedom would greatly increase his chances of staying alive until the end of
the war. He bribed a guard to organize a cart and horse and to pretend he was
escorting four POWs to a prison camp near the coast. In exchange, Weir
invented an amnesty agreement, scribbled it on a piece of paper, had his three
pals sign it, ripped it in half, and gave one portion to the guard.

If they made it to Lübeck, on the Baltic, the POWs would rejoin the pieces
of paper and vouch for the guard. After a horrific march through war-ravaged

and SS-infested Germany, Weir nonchalantly tossed the other part of his fake amnesty to the guard after they linked up safely with the invading Allies.

After the war, Weir, like many veterans, was reluctant to talk about the horrors he had witnessed or what he himself might have done to survive that trek. Considering that he left the POW camp near Sagan weighing 124 pounds and had gained nearly 40 pounds by the time he was liberated by the Allies in Lubeck three weeks later, he had clearly drawn upon his father's enforced training in survival techniques.

Weir returned to Canada, married his sweetheart Fran, cashed in nearly four years of back pay from his truncated flying career, and embarked on a profitable career as a bond salesman for Wood Gundy—his father's strict rules against nepotism meant that the doors of McLeod Young Weir were firmly closed to him.

The Weirs eventually had three children. In an extraordinarily close marriage, they travelled extensively and enjoyed weekends and vacations at a large farm they bought in the mid-1950s, in the Mulmur Hills north of Toronto. By the time Weir finally retired from Wood Gundy, long past the age when most people call it quits, he had helped found the Canadian Warplane Heritage Museum in Hamilton and African Lion Safari, near his father's birthplace in Flamborough, Ontario. He died at home in Toronto on September 20, 2009, at age ninety.

LUCIEN SAUMUR

FEBRUARY 6, 1921 – MARCH 22, 2007

&

GLEN HOW

MARCH 25, 1919 – DECEMBER 30, 2008

Jehovah's Witnesses and Civil Rights Activists

W E LIKE TO think we live in a tolerant society, but many of the rights we take for granted only became enshrined after dogged legal battles against bigoted politicians and censorious bureaucrats. As Jehovah's Witnesses, Lucien Saumur and Glen How may seem unlikely champions, but these two men, in fighting for the right to worship according to the tenets of their faith, helped ensure that religious freedoms were encased in the Bill of Rights and subsequently in the Charter of Rights and Freedoms.

Saumur was arrested more than a hundred times for distributing religious tracts and canvassing door to door for converts in the late 1940s and early 1950s in Quebec. How was a lawyer with only one client, the Jehovah's Witnesses. From the time he was called to the bar in Ontario in 1943 until the day he stopped practising, well into his eighties, he spent his entire professional career protecting, defending, and promoting the interests of the Jehovah's Witnesses, all the way to the Supreme Court. In the 1950s, he acted on behalf of Witnesses, including Saumur, who were routinely arrested, especially in Quebec, for going door to door proselytizing their faith and criticizing the Roman Catholic Church and its priests.

After Canada declared war against Germany in 1939, the War Measures Act was invoked to empower the government to take whatever actions it deemed necessary to confront its enemies abroad and at home. Less than a year later, Prime Minister Mackenzie King's government, terrified by the fall of France in June 1940, fearing the German invasion of England was imminent, suspicious that fifth columnists might be operating in Canada, and wanting to placate generally anti-conscription and Roman Catholic Quebec, passed an order-in-council outlawing a number of organizations in Canada, including the Witnesses. "This ban ranks as the single most serious interference with religious liberties by the state in all of modern Canada's history," argues William Kaplan in *State and Salvation: The Jehovah's Witnesses and Their Fight for Civil Rights*.

At the time, Nazi Germany was the only other country to have issued such an edict against the Witnesses. After the war, Maurice Duplessis — who was both Quebec premier and attorney general — actually declared "a war without mercy against the Witnesses of Jehovah," a faith he saw as a serious threat to the dominance of the Roman Catholic Church.

Duplessis feared the Witnesses for a number of reasons. Many of them spoke French, so they melded into the majority population, unlike Protestants and Jews, who were mainly English-speaking and so easily identified as the "other." Yet the Witnesses were also outsiders in that they studied the Bible rather than the Scriptures and they refused to acknowledge temporal authority. Finally, they were strident in their condemnation of the Roman Catholic Church, its nuns, priests, and Pope, and relentless in their proselytizing on street corners, preaching in people's homes, and assembling in large gatherings.

The Quebec premier waged his campaign against the Witnesses with all the authority in his administrative and legal arsenal. Between 1946 and 1953, Witnesses were involved in more than 1,500 criminal prosecutions, ranging from disturbing the peace to sedition, even though there were fewer than five hundred Witnesses in the province. Three legal cases — one of them Saumur's — involving basic rights to freedom of speech, of religion, and of association made it all the way to the Supreme Court of Canada.

The Witnesses emerged out of the Bible Student movement, led by Charles Taze Russell in the 1870s in Pittsburgh; the religion spread through the evangelistic Watchtower Society, which was formed a decade later. Russell's successor, Joseph Rutherford, expanded the group and its theological basis. He gave the name Jehovah's Witnesses to Bible Students who were faithful members of what later became the Watchtower Bible and Tract Society.

Witnesses believe that two worlds exist simultaneously. There is Satan's old world, to which the vast majority of humanity belongs, and Jehovah's new world, to which the Jehovah's Witnesses, the chosen people of God, belong. Witnesses deny the existence of the Trinity and believe that Jesus established his kingdom in heaven in 1914 and ousted Satan, who came down to earth to live amongst us. They use the Bible to interpret the past and predict the future and believe that the world will be destroyed, as the Bible states, at Armageddon, in a conflagration whose anticipated date has shifted from 1925 to 1975 and then to an indefinite time in the future.

While waiting for God's kingdom, Witnesses recognize that they must live in Satan's world, but they do not consider themselves citizens of any particular country, as their loyalty is to God alone. They pay taxes but choose not to vote, salute a national flag, or serve in the armed forces. Once a year they meet at huge international conventions that form the highlight of their religious year, similar in importance to Yom Kippur and Rosh Hashanah for Jews and Good Friday and Easter for Christians.

LUCIEN SAUMUR WAS born February 6, 1921, in the Gatineau Hills in western Quebec, north of Ottawa, one of fourteen children of an illiterate Roman Catholic farmer and his wife. He grew up attending Mass, taking Communion, and confessing his sins to the parish priest in an era when the Church dominated most aspects of life in the province, including education.

When he was eighteen, he left the farm and moved to Ottawa. That's where he discovered the public library and shelves of books just waiting to be read. He began devouring the works he had been denied, and in the process he learned some of the more unsavoury aspects of the Catholic Church's long history, including the Inquisition. The more he read, the more his suspicion and mistrust grew, especially after a cousin introduced him to the Catholic Action movement, which he described later as a political group with fascist and anti-Semitic leanings.

In 1943, a Montreal friend showed him a newspaper article about a man named Hector Saumur, who had been given a three-month prison sentence in

Timmins, Ontario, for being a Witness and thus a member of a banned organization. Recognizing the convicted man as his own brother — he had left home years before to work in the mines of northern Ontario — Saumur wrote to him and in reply received a Bible and some booklets about the Witnesses.

It was the first Bible that Saumur had ever seen, and he showed it to his parish priest, who promptly confiscated it. Undaunted, and fascinated by what he had been reading in his brother's pamphlets about the life of Jesus and the missionary work of the Apostles, Saumur bought another Bible and read it avidly.

He moved to Timmins to join his brother so that he could learn more about the Witnesses and improve his English. For some time he continued to attend Mass while studying with the Witnesses, but he incurred the wrath of his local parish priest when he began asking leading questions about hell, the Trinity, and the immortality of the soul.

After hearing his priest denounce the Witnesses from the pulpit, he gave up Roman Catholicism and resolved to commit his life to upholding the teachings of the Bible and modelling himself on Christ's early followers. Saumur was baptized as a Witness, probably in a secret ceremony, on July 1, 1944.

A year later he was in Montreal, witnessing from door to door as a missionary for the church, working mostly with Marcel Filteau, a bilingual Witness who had been educated in English Protestant schools after his father rejected Roman Catholicism and became a Witness. The two men were frequently harassed and arrested by the police. One autumn day they climbed the outside spiral staircase on a Montreal triplex and were speaking to the owners of the upper flat when the police showed up. One officer stayed at the bottom and the other climbed the stairs and arrested the two Witnesses.

Filteau descended first, with Saumur following and the policeman in the rear, administering kicks and blows on the way. Two steps from the pavement, Saumur, a husky guy who worked out with barbells, turned, grabbed the officer by the shoulders, lifted him up and put him down on the ground again, and said: "Be thankful that I am one of Jehovah's Witnesses." The policeman, according to Filteau's account, went white as a sheet. That didn't stop the officers from throwing the two Witnesses in jail, however.

One of the mainstays of the Witnesses during this period in Quebec was Frank Roncarelli, an Italian immigrant and affluent Montreal businessman who ran a Crescent Street café called Quaff that his father had opened in 1912. After Roncarelli posted bail for nearly four hundred Witnesses (including

Saumur) who had been arrested for distributing religious pamphlets, the police cracked down and, on the orders of the premier, Maurice Duplessis, revoked his liquor licence in December 1946. Six months later he had to close the restaurant because his business had declined so precipitously. He sued the premier for damages with the assistance of legal heavyweights F. R. Scott and A. L. Stein. The case went to the Supreme Court, which finally ruled in Roncarelli's favour in 1959, some thirteen years later and long after he had gone bankrupt.

Meanwhile, Saumur was sent to Quebec City to minister with John (Joe) How. That brought him in contact with How's elder brother Glen, a lawyer and a prime defender of Witnesses embroiled in the justice system.

GLEN HOW WAS born in Montreal on March 25, 1919, but moved to Toronto with his family when he was about a year old. His father, Frank, was an accountant and personnel manager at paint manufacturer CIL, and his mother, Bessie, was a homemaker. When Glen was five and his younger brother Joe was three, his mother answered the door of their Toronto home, fell into conversation with a Jehovah's Witness, and soon began attending meetings of the Bible Students, as Witnesses were called in those days. By 1929 she was a pioneer — a full-time minister — a calling she followed until she died in 1969. Initially Frank How was opposed to his wife's conversion, but he gradually condoned it, although he never became a Witness himself.

After graduating from Vaughan Road Collegiate in 1936, Glen enrolled at the University of Toronto, graduating with a bachelor's degree in 1940 before proceeding to Osgoode Hall Law School. By his own account, How was "not very interested in spiritual things" as a teenager. His conversion can be traced directly to Mackenzie King's use of the War Measures Act to ban Jehovah's Witnesses.

It was "the turning point in my life," How wrote sixty years later in a biographical article in *Awake!*, a magazine published by the movement. "When the full power of the government targeted this tiny organization of innocent, humble people, it convinced me that Jehovah's Witnesses were Jesus's true followers." He was baptized, also probably in a secret ceremony, on February 10, 1941.

Following his call to the bar in Ontario two years later, he began working as general counsel for the still-illegal Witnesses and subsequently qualified in

Quebec, Alberta, and Saskatchewan. He relentlessly argued that ministers in the Jehovah's Witnesses, many of whom had been interned in labour camps, were, like other clergy, entitled to conscientious-objector status. He also defended the right of children of Jehovah's Witnesses to refuse to sing the national anthem at school ceremonies. Some of those children were expelled from school and put into foster care. Late in 1943, he travelled to New York to seek help with his appeals from the wily and experienced Hayden Covington, the Watchtower Society's legal counsel, who eventually won thirty-six out of the forty-five cases he argued before the U.S. Supreme Court.

The federal government rescinded many of its strictures against the Witnesses after the war ended, but there was one jurisdiction — Quebec — where religious freedom was still not observed. How spent so much time commuting to and from Quebec to act in criminal prosecutions, ranging from disturbing the peace to sedition, that he moved there in the late 1940s to set up a law practice. Every morning, his first job was to find out how many Witnesses had been arrested the day before and then try to arrange bail for them. A frequent client was his brother, Joe, who ministered with Laurier Saumur on the streets of Quebec City.

The provincial capital, which was Duplessis's political stronghold, had enacted a bylaw forbidding the distribution of "any book, pamphlet, booklet, circular, or tract whatever without having previously obtained...the written permission of the chief of police." In response, the Witnesses produced "Quebec's Burning Hate," a four-page tract listing names, dates, and places of violence against Jehovah's Witnesses, and began distributing it across Canada in late 1946.

Within days, Duplessis declared his infamous "war without mercy against the Witnesses of Jehovah" and ordered sedition charges laid against anyone caught distributing the pamphlet. In the first sedition case to go to trial, How, who had still not been called to the bar of Quebec, worked under Jewish lawyer A. L. Stein to defend a Jehovah's Witness named Aimé Boucher. Meanwhile, Saumur, who had been arrested some hundred times for violating the flyer bylaw, filed a civil suit against Quebec City and its bylaw restricting his right to canvass door to door.

The Boucher, Saumur, and Roncarelli cases went to the Supreme Court in the 1950s. The Boucher case, which used truth as a defence, eliminated an archaic Quebec law defining sedition as criticism of the government and led to the dismissal of nearly 125 sedition charges. The Saumur case, which relied on a defence of freedom of expression and religion, established that issuing licences to restrict a person's right to practise his or her faith went beyond municipal or provincial authority, and it led to the dismissal of more than a thousand bylaw charges. And the Roncarelli case established that publicly elected officials cannot arbitrarily invoke the law against individuals, as Duplessis had done in personally revoking the restaurateur's liquor licence.

In the midst of the legal turmoil, Saumur had married Yvette Ouellette, a Witness from Montreal, in 1949. They decided not to have children because their missionary work was more important, especially since they believed the end of the world was imminent. That decision left them free to devote themselves to furthering the work of the Witnesses.

Eventually the couple ministered all over Canada. In one case, after discovering that one of his potential converts was illiterate, Saumur taught her to read and write so that she could study the Bible on her own. After his wife died in 2002, Saumur moved into a Witness retirement home in Grimsby, Ontario. He died there of pneumonia on March 22, 2007, at the age of eighty-six.

Meanwhile, How, a slight, dapper man with a thick shock of hair, kept on promoting the interests of the Jehovah's Witnesses. Looking almost biblical despite his short stature, he thundered about the rights and entitlements of his co-religionists in courtrooms across the country and around the world. "He was a very hard-working and tenacious lawyer, but he was wise enough to know that he couldn't do all the heavy lifting himself, so he would prepare the briefs and the submissions and then enlist others, such as constitutional expert Frank Scott, to help him argue cases before the court," according to lawyer and writer William Kaplan.

How was an anomaly. He practised his faith devoutly while using the country's institutions to win guarantees for Witnesses' rights. He respected the courts and was willing to accept the rewards of Canadian society if they didn't overtly violate the tenets of his faith. For example, in the late 1950s he agreed to accept the honorary designation Queen's Counsel after he received a guarantee that he wouldn't first have to swear an oath recognizing the Queen as head of state.

It was this ability to navigate between the religious and legal worlds that made How such a powerhouse lawyer for the Jehovah's Witnesses. In winning freedoms for them, he helped establish implied rights for everyone. In doing so, he influenced legalists, intellectuals, and civil libertarians, including future politicians such as Pierre Trudeau, whose government enacted the Charter of Rights and Freedoms in 1982.

Not all of the cases How argued were celebrated in the larger world. Some, especially the ones in which he fought for the right to refuse blood transfusions, especially for children, are medically and ethically problematic for many people. Jehovah's Witnesses believe the Bible prohibits the consumption of blood, a stricture that encompasses transfusions and most blood products, even in life-threatening medical emergencies. How was counsel for the Jehovah's Witnesses in controversial and unsuccessful appeals to deny blood transfusions for underage children and in an Ontario Court of Appeal case that confirmed an adult's right to make health-care treatment decisions.

In 1954 he married Margaret Biegel, a British Jehovah's Witness. Like many Jehovah's Witnesses, they had no children, and she worked as his secretary as his law career expanded. She died of cancer in 1987. Two years later, in November 1989, he married Linda Manning, a much younger American lawyer and Jehovah's Witness who had moved north to work in the Canadian organization's legal department. Until well into his eighties he continued to represent the Witnesses' legal interests, appearing as a consultant counsel in Osaka, Japan, in 1993 and in Singapore from 1994 to 1996.

The American College of Trial Lawyers gave him its Award for Courageous Advocacy on September 8, 1997, the first time a Canadian lawyer had received this distinction. He was awarded the medal of the Law Society of Upper Canada in 1998 and a certificate of appreciation and recognition from the Bar of Montreal the following year. In 2000 he was named an officer of the Order of Canada for "consistently and courageously" fighting legal battles to advance civil liberties and helping "pave the way" for the Canadian Bill of Rights and Charter of Rights and Freedoms. Calling him a "man of conscience," the citation lauded him for working at "minimal compensation" to defend clients "in every province of Canada, many American states and several other countries."

He died December 30, 2008, in Georgetown, Ontario, of pneumonia as a result of complications of prostate cancer. He was eighty-nine.

Rudolf Vrba

Auschwitz Survivor and Biochemist

September 11, 1924 – March 27, 2006

Auschwitz was the largest and most notorious of the five Nazi death camps. More than a million people, overwhelmingly Jews, were slaughtered there in gas chambers, on scaffolds, or before firing squads, or were allowed to perish from disease, beatings, and starvation. Walter Rosenberg was an exception. He escaped and survived to raise the alarm about what was really happening to Hungarian Jews behind the barbed wire in the most sophisticated and industrialized extermination facility of Adolf Hitler's nefarious campaign to engineer "the final solution of the Jewish question in Europe."

Rosenberg was only nineteen when he and his older friend Alfred Wetzler eluded the guards and their vicious dogs on April 7, 1944, and escaped from Auschwitz. Three weeks earlier, German forces had invaded Hungary. The infamous Adolf Eichmann had established headquarters in Budapest to oversee the deportation to Auschwitz of the country's Jewish population. Mass transports began on May 15, 1944, at a rate of twelve thousand people a day. The victims were told they were being resettled, but most were sent straight to the gas chambers.

Rosenberg and Wetzler were not the only people to slip out of Auschwitz, but they were the most important escapees from that hellhole of murder and depravity because they brought with them detailed descriptions of the layout and function of the gas chambers and crematoria. They hoped that their copious eyewitness testimony to Jewish authorities about what was really happening behind the iron gates adorned with the slogan ARBEIT MACHT FREI ("Work shall make you free") would make Jewish victims rebel and fight back rather than passively accepting their fates. That didn't happen, but the alarm did eventually reach the Allies, and many lives were saved.

A prickly man who tended to be a moral absolutist, Rosenberg hated being thought of as a victim or a survivor, and with good reason: nobody had rescued him — he had beaten Auschwitz. For the rest of his life, even as an acclaimed biochemist at the University of British Columbia, he lived under the name Rudolf Vrba, the *nom de guerre* that he adopted after Auschwitz, and every year he celebrated his birthday on April 7, the day of his escape.

Instead of rejoicing that the "Auschwitz Protocol," as his detailed report was called, saved an estimated 150,000 Hungarian Jews, he remained angry that more lives hadn't been saved. He believed to the end of his life that Hungarian Jewish leaders had knowingly sacrificed more than 400,000 of their own countrymen in order to negotiate safe passage for themselves and their families.

The past is not a simple place, especially for those who scrape away the myths that spread like moss over horrific events to make moral complexities more palatable for the living. Vrba was a troubling character to many because he threatened the solidarity of the post-Holocaust Jewish community with his accusations of complicity in his memoir *Escape from Auschwitz: I Can't Forgive*. As a result, it was easier for many to ignore Vrba's heroism than to honour it.

Ruth Linn, dean of education at Haifa University and a native-born Israeli, had never heard about anybody escaping from Auschwitz — and neither had her students — until she watched French director Claude Lanzmann's 1985 documentary, *Shoah*. How was it possible, she asked herself, that Vrba's memoirs had never been translated into Hebrew? Why had he never been recognized by Yad Vashem, the Holocaust Martyrs' and Heroes' Remembrance Authority? Linn was a key player in having Vrba's memoir translated, in seeing him awarded an honorary doctorate at Haifa University in 1998, and in rectifying his absence from popular accounts of the Holocaust by detailing those omissions in her 2004 book, *Escaping Auschwitz: A Culture of Forgetting*.

Over the years Vrba had made crucial depositions against Nazis trying to escape retribution, whether it was the members of the "final solution" leadership at the Nuremberg trials, Adolf Eichmann after his capture in Argentina in 1960, or former concentration camp guards living undercover in Germany. He was also a feisty witness in the trial of Holocaust denier Ernst Zundel in Toronto in 1985. When Zundel's lawyer accused Vrba of lying about Auschwitz and demanded to know if he had ever seen anybody gassed, he replied that he had watched people being taken into the buildings and seen SS officers throw in gas canisters after them. "Therefore, I concluded it was not a kitchen or a bakery, but it was a gas chamber. It is possible they are still there or that there is a tunnel and they are now in China. Otherwise, they were gassed."

Holocaust historian Sir Martin Gilbert was so impressed with Vrba's heroism that he supported a campaign to nominate him for the Order of Canada and solicited letters from well-known Canadians, including law professor and former justice minister Irwin Cotler. "I fully concur with you that Vrba is a 'real hero.' Indeed, there are few more deserving of the Order of Canada than Vrba, and few, anywhere, who have exhibited his moral courage," Cotler said in a handwritten letter to Gilbert on February 18, 1992. "Canada will honour itself — and redeem itself somewhat — by awarding him the Order of Canada."

It didn't happen, and now it is too late. Rudolf Vrba died of cancer at the age of eighty-one in Vancouver, on March 27, 2006, a week before the sixty-second anniversary of his escape from Auschwitz.

WALTER ROSENBERG WAS born in Topol'čany, Czechoslovakia, on September 11, 1924, one of five children of Elias Rosenberg, a steam-sawmill owner, and Helena Grunfeldova. He was fifteen when the Germans began their murderous march through Europe.

After he was expelled from high school in Bratislava under the local version of the Nuremberg anti-Jewish laws, Rosenberg studied at home and worked as a labourer. His fervour rising, he fled his homeland, hoping to join the Czechoslovakian forces in exile in Britain. Before he crossed the border into Hungary, he tore the yellow star off his shoulder. Nevertheless, he was arrested in March 1942 and escaped, only to be apprehended again by a policeman who was suspicious of a young man wearing two pairs of socks. Two months later he was deported to Majdanek, a concentration camp on the outskirts of Lublin, Poland, and from there transferred to Auschwitz on June 30.

Largely because he was strong and healthy, Rosenberg survived as prisoner number 44070 for almost two years in a place where the average life

expectancy was a few months. At first he was assigned to dig up dead bodies so they could be incinerated in the ovens at nearby Birkenau. When the guards learned he could speak German, he was forced to become a clerk in the storage facility named "Canada" — so called because the country was considered a land of plenty. It housed the food, medicine, clothing, and other valuables confiscated from prisoners on their arrival at Auschwitz and its sat-
.ellite camps.

Work in "Canada," while soul-destroying, was a privileged position in the camp hierarchy, for the food rations were better and the work was not as physically arduous as hard-labour details. Using his capacious memory and analytical powers, he memorized the architecture of the camp and, especially after he became registrar, computed the numbers of people arriving on the transports and roughly calculated how many were set aside to be used as slave labour or sent to be gassed.

Early in 1944, Rosenberg observed that the camp was ramping up to pre-pare for the arrival of huge deportations of Hungarian Jews. With Alfred Wetzler, an older friend from his hometown, he escaped with the help of the prison underground. Knowing that the prison guards typically abandoned a search after three days, the two men hid for that many days and nights in a space hollowed out of a woodpile just outside the first of two barbed-wire inner perimeters. Other prisoners had sprinkled the woodpile with Russian tobacco dipped in gasoline to camouflage the duo's scent and thwart the sniffer dogs.

Wearing suits, overcoats, and boots they had smuggled out of "Canada," they made their way to Žilina, Slovakia, where on April 24 they told their har-rowing tale to the local Jewish council. Rosenberg and Wetzler were put in separate rooms as they wrote out their reports, which were then compared, checked for accuracy against available records, and compiled. The thirty-two-page report testifying to the atrocities at Auschwitz-Birkenau was sent to the Allies, the Vatican, the International Red Cross, and the Jewish leadership in Hungary — the next victims on Hitler's extermination list.

The Jewish council gave Rosenberg identity papers and he became Rudolf Vrba, a name he later adopted legally. The "Auschwitz Protocol" reached the Hungarian Jewish leadership in early May 1944, but they didn't raise the alarm. Instead they negotiated with Adolf Eichmann in an effort to exchange Jews for trucks and other goods needed by the depleted Nazi war effort on the eastern front against the Soviets.

"Basically, Eichmann deceived them," says Gilbert, by promising the Hungarian Jewish leadership that the trains would take the Jews to holding camps, where they would be transferred to trucks that would convey them to safety in Spain. That's why they kept silent. Between mid-May and early July 1944, nearly 440,000 Hungarian Jews (including future Nobel Peace Prize winner Elie Wiesel) boarded "resettlement trains" in good faith and ended up in Auschwitz, where most were immediately gassed. Vrba always believed that if the Jewish leaders had broadcast the truth about Auschwitz, the deportees would have fought back or tried to flee instead of numbly climbing into the railcars.

By June 1944 the Allies had received the "Auschwitz Protocol" — almost two months after Vrba's first meeting with Jewish authorities, an unconscionable delay in his view. The BBC broadcast details on June 15, and the *New York Times* published the first of three articles about the gas chambers at Birkenau and Auschwitz five days later, on June 20. Coincidentally, there was an American air raid on Budapest on July 2, 1944. Hungarian regent admiral Miklós Horthy believed the attack was the beginning of an Allied retribution in response to the publication of the Auschwitz Protocol. On July 7 he ordered a halt to the deportations; they stopped two days later. According to Gilbert, that alone made Vrba "totally and extraordinarily successful."

Vrba warned his own relatives to flee before they too were taken. After that, he joined the Czechoslovak partisan units in September 1944. He fought with them until the end of the war and was decorated for bravery.

After Czechoslovakia was liberated, he went back to school and did a series of degrees in chemistry, receiving his doctorate in 1951 and a further postgraduate degree from the Academy of Science in 1956. He undertook biochemical research at Charles University in Prague from 1953 to 1958. His choice of academic discipline might seem ironic considering that he had escaped death in a Nazi gas chamber, but he was probably always interested in chemicals — how else would he have discovered the odorous and beneficial side effects of combining Russian tobacco and gasoline?

By then he had married a childhood friend, a medical doctor in Prague named Gerta Verbova. They had two daughters, Helena (now deceased) and Zuza. Vrba and his wife separated in 1958, when she defected to the West and he went to a conference in Israel and simply didn't return home.

He worked as a biochemist in Israel for two years but never felt at ease there because of the tensions between what historian Ruth Linn called "survivor discourse" (actual experience that can be hard to document and is therefore easily questioned) and "expert discourse" (sourced accounts by scholars). Vrba also resented what he felt was pandering to Hungarian Jewish elders, such as Rezsö Kasztner, who had used their wits and their financial resources to escape the Holocaust while others perished.

As a Jewish relief leader in Budapest, Kasztner had successfully negotiated with Eichmann to allow 1,685 Hungarian Jews (including members of Kasztner's family) to travel by train to Switzerland instead of Auschwitz, in exchange for money, gold, and diamonds — what came to be called the "blood for goods" proposal. Kasztner, who settled in Israel after the war, was accused of collaboration with the Nazis and assassinated in 1957.

In 1960, Vrba joined the British Medical Research Council and moved to London. Seven years later he was appointed to the Canadian Medical Research Council, and from there he began teaching in the pharmacology department of the faculty of medicine at UBC. In the mid-1970s he went on sabbatical to Harvard Medical School in Cambridge, Massachusetts, where he met his second wife, Robin. She became a successful real estate dealer in Vancouver.

Vrba lived in Canada for nearly four decades. He forged a successful academic career as a biochemist at the University of British Columbia and was the author of more than fifty scientific papers on the function of proteins in the brain in relation to cancer and diabetes. Before he retired in the early 1990s, he liked to say that he spent ninety-five percent of his time on biochemistry and only five percent on the Holocaust. But it was that five percent that made him so memorable.

Anna Maria de Souza

Fundraiser

1941? – September 18, 2007

T HERE WERE TWO secrets that Anna Maria de Souza, the much-married creator of the fabulously successful Brazilian Carnival Ball, kept closely guarded: her age and the nature of her final and catastrophic illness. Italian and Brazilian in ancestry, she heated up the staid fundraising climate in Toronto with an annual fancy-dress ball that for decades was one of the most significant philanthropic galas on the Canadian social calendar. A warm-blooded, energetic outsider, she had the entrepreneurial zeal, organizing skills, and shrewd ambition of a self-made CEO. Instead of starting a company or a launching a hedge fund, she camouflaged her business skills under the patina of a society hostess. Using old-fashioned influence rather than naked power, she forged alliances with charitable foundations in campaigns that raised their profiles, her status, and close to $45 million for Toronto hospitals, universities, and arts and culture organizations for more than forty years.

For all her flamboyance, de Souza was intensely private. Nobody knew her real age — not even her husband, Ivan, as she loved to boast. "I've known her for thirty-five years and it never occurred to me to wonder. She was one of those people who was ageless," said her friend Catherine Nugent after de Souza's death from an undisclosed form of cancer on September 18, 2007. The best guess is that she was sixty-six.

Along with de Souza's success came complaints about her management style. She was unapologetic in response to criticisms that she was territorial and a micro-manager who autocratically chose the event's annual beneficiary. "This is big business, and the organization requires that we have a good board to sell the ball, a recipient who will pay for our computers, our secretarial staff," she told *Maclean's* magazine in 2006. "This work requires a huge infrastructure."

Even knowing how much work was involved, "there was absolutely no reason to say no," said Paul Alofs, president of the Princess Margaret Hospital Foundation, if de Souza asked if you wanted to be beneficiary of the BCB, "because it is such a massive fundraising and awareness-generating opportunity for a not-for-profit."

Although the ball was her biggest activity, it wasn't her only one. She also volunteered on the Women's Committee of the Canadian Opera Company and was curator of the Henry Birks Collection of antique Canadian silver in the late 1970s. A passionate gardener and a keen tennis player, she loved to entertain and to cook for her guests. "She was the most generous, vivacious person I know," said Nugent. "She loved to introduce people to each other and to grow her circle of friends, but she was also shy."

ANNA MARIA DE Souza, the daughter of Amadeu Guidi and his wife, Honorica (née Marcolini), was born probably in 1941 — or at least in the early 1940s — in São Sebastião do Paraíso, in the mountainous state of Minas Gerais in the interior of Brazil. She grew up in a family of four brothers and one sister. Her grandfather on her mother's side had emigrated from Genoa, Italy, as a teenager and found a job as a construction worker building homes for plantation workers.

When money was scarce, her grandfather was paid in land. Eventually he accumulated enough acreage to start his own plantation and enough wealth to take his family back to Genoa on a trip. There he bought a villa. For the rest of his life he spent half the year in Italy and the other half in Brazil. When his daughter Honorica married, Marcolini handed over control of his Brazilian plantation to her husband, Amadeu Guidi. That's where his granddaughter, Anna Maria, grew up, in what she later compared to paradise. It was a time in which life "was gracious and slow and everything was looked after." She was educated at the Colégio Paula Frassinetti, where she earned a teaching degree, before attending the Escola Técnica de Comércio.

At eighteen she married William John Griffiths, an English mining engineer for Wimpey Construction, a British firm that had a contract to build a dam in Brazil. Anna Maria went into labour with their first child on Good Friday, a holiday in Brazil. Her doctor was away, the birth was arduous, and the baby, a daughter, lived for only twenty-three days. Anna Maria survived but was unable to bear more children. To compound the tragedy, her husband died in a work-related accident ten months later.

Widowed and still in her teens, Anna Maria went to live with her grandmother in Italy, where she attended finishing school. Afterwards, sailing back to Brazil on a cruise ship, she met a Brazilian plantation owner who recognized her marketing skills and urged her to get into the coffee exporting business. As chance would have it, at a party in Rio de Janeiro on New Year's Eve in 1964, Anna Maria met a man named John Marston who said he imported bulk foods into Canada. If she had products to sell, he was interested in seeing them.

With an insouciant entrepreneurship, she gathered some samples from the family coffee plantation and set out for Canada, arriving in gloomiest Toronto in February 1965. She looked up Marston — and married him three months later in a Protestant ceremony, which her mother, a Catholic, boycotted. "I fell in love with Toronto and the only thing I could do to stay was to get married," she once confided. By 1974 the Marstons had divorced, with Anna Maria complaining later that her husband was a workaholic who had little interest in married life.

Anna Maria had long since found ways to make her own life more interesting. The winter after she arrived in Canada, in 1966, homesickness propelled her to "kill the longing" by organizing her first Brazilian Carnival Ball, in a church basement at Dundas and Grace Streets, a largely Portuguese area of Toronto. Tickets cost five dollars, the food for the fifty guests was prepared by Anna Maria and her friends, and the aim was merely to cover costs and bring a little Mardi Gras colour to the dreary Toronto winter. The ball quickly became a tradition.

By the early 1970s the ball, which had quickly moved above ground to the Sutton Place Hotel and then the Sheraton Centre, was making a small profit, with the proceeds going to a Brazilian orphanage. That tradition continued with 5 percent of the annual profits benefiting leper colonies, old-age homes, and other causes in or around her hometown. When Toronto charities began asking if they could reap the ball's annual largesse, Anna Maria astutely decided to bestow the fundraising benefits on a different cause every time, thereby hooking into a fresh network and set of volunteers annually.

Krystyne Griffin attended her first Brazilian Ball in 1977, the year she left Paris, married businessman, Griffin Poetry Prize founder, and benefactor Scott Griffin, and moved to Toronto. "Everybody told me this was the party to go to because it showed that Toronto could be fun." They were correct. "A guy in drag dressed like Queen Alexandra walked up and smacked Scott right on the lips. That was my introduction to Anna Maria's parties," said Griffin. "I liked her without knowing her well."

The ball celebrated its fourteenth anniversary in 1980 at the Four Seasons Hotel on Avenue Road in Toronto and netted $50,000. It stayed in that location until 1988, when it moved to the yawning depths of the Metro Toronto Convention Centre, the only venue that could accommodate crowds upwards of a thousand.

Anna Maria met the late Montegu Black at the BCB in the early 1970s, when she was feeling disaffected with her globe-trotting, work-obsessed second husband, John Marston. Black thought she should meet his younger brother, Conrad, who was then plying his way as an aspiring tycoon and researching his biography of Quebec premier Maurice Duplessis. They dated for about two years after her 1974 divorce. "She was a delightful, refreshing, and enterprising person, and was a very popular and respected person in a community where she started as a stranger and, at first, hardly spoke the language," Black wrote in an email message. "I saw her a lot at the time my parents died, ten days apart, in 1976, and she could not have been more supportive."

Anna Maria's lasting love, however, was businessman Ivan de Souza. Introduced by Marvelle Koffler, wife of Murray Koffler of Shoppers Drug Mart, they had much in common, both being Portuguese-speaking and Catholic. They were married on December 22, 1982, and were devoted to each other.

More than the venue of the ball changed over the years. As it became more lavish and raised more money (much of it matched by government programs, with costs underwritten by corporate sponsors), so too did the entertainment. Instead of handmade decorations on a Carnival theme, de Souza began importing Carnival dancers from Brazil. That meant switching the date from Mardi Gras (the carnival on the eve of Lent, the forty-day period of penance preceding Easter in the Catholic calendar) to April or May, so that the dancers could travel to Toronto in their off-season. At the fortieth anniversary of the ball in 2006, the $2 million in net proceeds went to York University's Accolade Project, and the 1,600 guests were entertained by a thirty-minute samba parade from the Rio Carnival, including fifty dancers in feathered, beaded, and bejewelled costumes processing on foot or on wooden horses to the beat of a *batucada* rhythm supplied by the Cocktail Brazil Band.

That November, de Souza was diagnosed with rampaging cancer and underwent rigorous treatment, which included chemotherapy, at Princess Margaret Hospital in Toronto. She looked frail but valiant at the 2007 ball, which raised $2.6 million (net) for the Arthritis and Autoimmunity Research Centre in Toronto. "She and the ball were a brand, and for a very small organization like us, she had a tremendous impact. She did a great job," said Gerri Grant, executive director of the AARC.

In late summer 2007, de Souza went back into hospital for more treatment, but she was well enough to decide that oncology nursing, through the Princess Margaret Hospital Foundation, should be the focus and the beneficiary of the 2008 Brazilian Ball. Supported by her devoted husband, Ivan de Souza, she died while the ball was still in the planning stages — the first one that occurred without her dominant presence. Five years later the ball itself was gone after a final extravaganza in September 2012.

DONALD MARSHALL

Torchbearer for Native Rights and the Wrongfully Convicted

SEPTEMBER 13, 1953 – AUGUST 6, 2009

L IKE MANY TEENAGERS, Donald Marshall drank, smoked, and hung around the local park with rowdy friends. He might have outgrown these habits and matured into a stalwart citizen, a Native leader, an entrepreneur. We will never know what his potential might have been, because he lost the chance to realize his dreams when he was convicted of murder at seventeen and imprisoned for eleven years for a crime he didn't commit.

By the time he was finally released on parole in 1982, he was forever damaged by the miscarriage of justice and years of detention. Another eight years passed before he was exonerated by a royal commission that had been called in 1982, when Jean Chrétien was justice minister. The royal commission, which handed down its final report in 1990, recommended an overhaul of the entire provincial justice system in Nova Scotia and found that Marshall was a victim of the racism and incompetence of a criminal justice system that had failed him "at virtually every turn from his arrest and wrongful conviction for murder in 1971 up to and even beyond his acquittal by the Court of Appeal in 1983."

And yet, despite the tragedies of his later life — addictions to alcohol and nicotine and a series of troubled romantic relationships — his name is synonymous with the struggle for fairness and equality in this country. A proud Mi'kmaq, Marshall was a leader in two essential legal campaigns: justice for the wrongfully convicted and recognition of the historic treaty rights of First Nations.

Marshall broke the trail for other innocent men, including David Milgaard, Guy Paul Morin, Thomas Sophonow, and William Mullins Johnson — all of whom eventually had their wrongful convictions overturned — but he was also a hero in the battle against racism towards aboriginals in this country. He spent six years challenging the federal government's denial of the treaty rights granted to his people by the British Crown during the Seven Years' War, a case that was argued successfully before the Supreme Court of Canada. "He had a huge potential for leadership, which was never crushed by his imprisonment and which enabled him to contribute to the native community in Canada," said lawyer Clayton Ruby, a member of Marshall's legal team before the royal commission.

"He was a really shy person, but he was brave enough to go through the limelight a couple of times to change both the provincial systems and the federal ones and to make very significant changes," said Terry Paul, chief of the Membertou First Nation, after Marshall's death in 2009. "It is a tragic loss not only for me, being a personal friend, but for the aboriginal people across the country. He did so much and a lot of people benefited from his difficulties."

DONALD MARSHALL JR. was born on September 13, 1953, on the Membertou reserve in Sydney, Nova Scotia, the eldest of thirteen children of Donald Marshall Sr., Grand Chief of the Mi'kmaq Nation, and his wife, Caroline. Called "Junior" by his family and friends, he was in line to inherit his father's honorary title.

A rebellious boy and a wild youth, he was expelled from school at fifteen for striking a teacher and sent to family court. Given the choice of working with his father as an apprentice plasterer or going to the Shelburne School for Boys, an infamous provincial reformatory, he quit school with barely a Grade 6 education. That gave him lots of free time to join the Shipyard Gang, a bunch of Mi'kmaq toughs who generally made nuisances of themselves around Sydney.

Tall for his age and physically more intimidating than some of the other gang members, Junior was the designated panhandler when money was short for rum and cigarettes. Although he shunned violence, Junior was not above petty thievery and was well-known to the law, having spent four months in the county jail when he was barely seventeen for giving liquor to minors.

Those skirmishes were negligible compared to the legal quagmire that was about to engulf him. Sandford (Sandy) Seale, a seventeen-year-old African-Canadian, was on his way home from a dance on May 28, 1971, when by chance he met Marshall in Wentworth Park, in the centre of Sydney. The two teenagers, who knew each other casually, were chatting when Roy Ebsary, fifty-nine, a former ship's cook who had been drinking that night with an unemployed companion, Jimmy MacNeil, age twenty-five, hailed them and asked for a light. Seale and Marshall approached. In the ensuing encounter, Ebsary, who was later described as "drunken and dangerous," with a "fetish" for knives, fatally stabbed Seale in the stomach. The young man died of his wounds the next day.

Five days later Marshall was arrested and charged with murder. He was processed through the justice system with such haste that he was convicted, after a three-day trial, fewer than six months after his arrest. Even when the Nova Scotia Court of Appeal finally acquitted Marshall in 1983, the judgement was miserly, absolving the police of any responsibility and saying that the innocent man had contributed in large measure to his own conviction and that any miscarriage of justice was more apparent than real.

Eventually Ebsary was convicted of manslaughter and sentenced to three years in prison, a sentence that was reduced to one year by the Court of Appeal in 1986. He died two years later, having served less than one-tenth of the time Marshall had spent behind bars for the crime Ebsary had committed.

Marshall had to wait until January 26, 1990, to be completely exonerated. That's when the royal commission released its final report. The inquiry, which had been chaired by Alexander Hickman, then chief justice of the trial division of the Supreme Court of Newfoundland and Labrador, concluded that, far from being a perpetrator, Marshall was the victim of racism and incompetence on the part of the police, judges, lawyers, and bureaucrats. After submitting the final report to the Nova Scotia Cabinet, Justice Hickman said: "I really hope that at long last one Donald Marshall Jr. will stand high in the eyes of Nova Scotians, where he deserves to stand." Later that year the provincial government awarded Marshall, who by then was thirty-six years old, a mere $250,000 in cash and a small annual stipend in compensation for an ordeal that had lasted nearly two decades.

The most significant recommendation produced by the commission called for the establishment of an independent body to review cases of alleged wrongful conviction, something the federal government has never acted on.

Instead, victims of the justice system still have to petition the courts for appeals and new trials, in a laborious and costly process. However, another key finding resulted in important changes in the way evidence is disclosed to the defence. At the time Marshall was prosecuted, in 1971, the Crown had to provide the defence only with evidence that the prosecution considered relevant. Now prosecutors are constitutionally obliged to make full disclosure of all evidence that might be relevant to the guilt or innocence of the accused.

In the mid-1990s Marshall was in trouble with the law once again. He was caught catching and selling eels with illegal nets, out of season and without a licence, in Pomquet Harbour, near Antigonish, Nova Scotia, in August 1996. When officials from the federal Department of Fisheries and Oceans told him and his companion to stop fishing, he didn't comply. Instead, Marshall, who had learned the hard way to be wary of authority, phoned his friend Chief Paul and asked his advice. "I told him to keep fishing," Chief Paul said later. "I felt strongly that he had a right to be there and gain a livelihood."

The real difficulty occurred when Marshall left the shore and sold his catch — 210 kilograms of eels — for $787.10. That exchange of money and goods led to his conviction for fishing out of season, fishing with illegal nets, and selling eels without a licence, but it also initiated a legal battle that lasted six years, involved three courts, and provoked learned discussions in the Supreme Court of Canada about the treaty rights that the Mi'kmaq had been granted in 1760 by the British to help secure their loyalty during the Seven Years' War with France. Eventually, for the second time in his short life, the proud Mi'kmaq with a Grade 6 education won a landmark legal victory.

In a decision that enshrined Native treaty rights, the Supreme Court ruled that the 1760 treaty allowed Native people to take fish and game and trade them for "necessaries" at a local trading post. The court wrote that recognizing those rights was important in order to uphold the honour of the Crown in its dealings with the Mi'kmaq people.

The decision was greeted with jubilation in Native communities. It instantly made Native fishermen big players in the East Coast commercial lobster fishery, which led to angry protests by non-Natives that coalesced around Burnt Church, New Brunswick. The unrest led to a second Marshall case at the Supreme Court in 1999, in which the court clarified that it had not created "open season in the fisheries" and that the Crown retained the right to limit the size of the catch if necessary.

Once again the man at the centre of a broader controversy, Marshall accepted the spotlight reluctantly, saying he hadn't gone to the Supreme Court for himself but "for my people. It was more touching than anything else." After saying that he was too old to go fishing, he admitted that he had thought about giving up the fight, but kept going because "I knew that I had dealt with bigger problems."

His past problems were compounded by serious addictions to drink and cigarettes. In 2003 he had a double lung transplant in an eight-hour operation in a Toronto hospital to try to overcome the ravages of chronic obstructive pulmonary disease, a progressive and ultimately fatal lung condition whose symptoms are chronic bronchitis and emphysema. Marshall later said that the recovery was tougher than two trips to the Supreme Court.

He was feeling well enough in June 2007 to celebrate his marriage to non-Native Colleen D'Orsay, but the honeymoon was short-lived. Less than a year later she complained to the *Cape Breton Post* that her husband had received only $156,000 of the $2 million the thirty-three eastern Canadian chiefs of the Atlantic Policy Congress of First Nations Chiefs Secretariat had pledged to pay him in 2001 in recognition of his long struggle on their behalf to establish their historic fishing and hunting rights. One of the exceptions was Chief Paul, who had given him at least $100,000. "All I can say is that when I make a commitment, I stand by it," he told the *Cape Breton Post*, suggesting that Marshall was facing continuing health problems from his double lung transplant. "We felt it was the honourable thing to do, to be able to assist him."

Then, in October 2008, Marshall appeared in a Sydney court accused of assaulting and threatening his wife and her former husband, lawyer Luke Wintermans. His wife was at Marshall's side when he pleaded not guilty in January 2009. His lawyer argued that there had been an abuse of process when a local Crown attorney telephoned a police sergeant seeking an update after some of the charges were laid.

Before the matter could be resolved, Marshall was admitted to hospital in Sydney, suffering from kidney failure, probably as a consequence of the anti-rejection drugs he had been taking since his lung transplant six years earlier. He died on August 6, 2009, at age fifty-five. His roller-coaster ride through the Canadian criminal justice system was finally over. "We pay the money, we have the public inquiry," his former lawyer Clayton Ruby said at the time, "but we can't make them whole again."

CONCLUSION

Ways of Saying Goodbye

THERE ON THE computer screen was the familiar wide-mouthed grin of one of America's favourite humorists. Instead of a riff on presidential foibles or a chuckle about the absurdities of everyday life, Art Buchwald, the widely syndicated columnist, beamed benignly and delivered his ultimate punchline: "I'm Art Buchwald and I just died."

It was January 17, 2007, and the obituary world had just changed as dramatically as the cinema had back in the 1920s, when filmmakers figured out how to incorporate sound into moving pictures. You've heard about living wills; welcome to living obituaries, in which the deceased speak openly about their lives and their legacies from beyond the grave.

Most major newspapers had websites by the beginning of this century. The Internet had made it possible for people around the world to read and compare obits of celebrities, politicians, and even small-town heroes. It had given locally written obituaries a diverse international audience, which was good for writers, readers, and usually the subjects, even though they weren't around to enjoy or assess the accounts of their lives. The *New York Times*, which had already launched an obituaries site with archival features and slide shows, did something much more revolutionary with the Buchwald video.

At first it seemed like a prank. After all, Buchwald had cheated death for almost a year since refusing dialysis and entering a hospice. Before long he seemed so robust that he was kicked out of palliative care and sent home. He took such delight in writing about *not* dying — in his syndicated newspaper column and a book called *Too Soon to Say Goodbye* — that his celebrity reached new heights.

But the video was not another joke. Buchwald really was announcing his own death, at eighty-one, from kidney disease. Before finally going "upstairs," as he put it, he had recorded an interview for the *New York Times* website — the first in an ongoing but irregular video series called "The Last Word."

As I've said earlier, the goal of a modern obituary writer is to bring the subject alive for readers — warts and all. Journalists use any and all legitimate tools to achieve that end. The video camera is only the latest in a series of visual enhancements that began with newspaper sketches and photographs. But its interactive quality and its ability to create the illusion that the subject is talking directly to a viewer in real time blurs the lines between life and death, reality and fantasy, journalism and narcissism.

Buchwald, the only son and youngest child of Jewish immigrants from the former Austro-Hungarian Empire, was born on October 20, 1925, in New York City. His childhood was traumatic: his mentally ill mother was institutionalized, he was sent to an orphanage after his father's curtain manufacturing business failed during the Depression. Things didn't improve after he was reunited with his father and older sisters. He dropped out of high school and ran away from home when he was seventeen.

Although underage, Buchwald enlisted in the U.S. Marine Corps during the Second World War and served in the Pacific for two years before being demobilized as a sergeant. He went to the University of Southern California on the GI Bill, began working as a writer and editor on the campus newspaper, and in the late 1940s went to Paris, where he was eventually hired by the European edition of the *New York Herald Tribune*. His chatty, irreverent columns about characters and incidents became a big hit on both sides of the Atlantic.

Despite his fame as a humorist, Buchwald, unbeknownst to most of his readers, suffered from depression. To them he was the genial everyman. So when he spoke about his approaching death in matter-of-fact terms, discussing his living will — which stipulated he was not to be resuscitated if he fell into a coma — he was reassuring rather than ghoulish. Buchwald demystified death by defying his medical prognosis until even he seemed a bit impatient to get on with the big goodbye, and then by finally going into the great unknown with a smile on his face.

Watching him cheerfully recording the announcement of his own death before it happened changed the dynamics and the protocols of obituary writing. Instead of journalists assessing and describing the life that had just concluded, here was the subject of the obituary offering his own commentary on his life. Is that bad? Not necessarily. Everything depends on the context. The Buchwald video, which was made by NYT journalists, was posted on its obituary website after the humorist's death, not before, along with an explanation of this new feature and accompanied by the newspaper's print obituary.

Having interviewed people in advance for their obituaries both for print and the Web, I am still troubled by one aspect of the confidentiality clause that is part of the deal. "Talk to me about your life and I promise it won't appear during your lifetime" is the offer I always make. That pact is easy to uphold if the confidence involves admitting to a long-ago affair that many people already suspected. What happens if your subject reveals a state secret or a criminal activity? Are you going to sit on a huge scoop for five or ten years? Will your editors let you? Forget journalism — what about the law? Does a promise to a source override an obligation to bring a felon to justice while there is still time to hold him or her accountable? That's a moral and legal dilemma that will become more and more troubling as we find new ways to help the dead communicate with the living.

Another danger comes from the other side of the ledger: the insatiable demand for video uploads and links to enhance traditional reporting can undermine the objectivity of obituaries. There are already lots of legacy sites offering to produce online obituaries for grieving friends and families with the inconvenient truths obliterated. These are testimonials, and they have their place, but they are not obituaries.

These testimonials dressed up as editorial content have their roots in the local-hero obituaries that have long been a feature of small-town newspapers. American journalist Jim Nicholson gave the form a big-city flavour when he began writing "ordinary Joe" obituaries for the *Philadelphia Daily News*, a large-circulation metropolitan daily, in 1982. The *Globe and Mail* followed suit with the launch of its "Lives Lived" column, as did many other papers on both sides of the Atlantic.

Over time, though, there has been a noticeable shift from staff- or freelance-written material to unpaid submissions from family and friends. Discerning readers can tell the difference between pieces that used to be researched and written by journalists and are now produced by grieving loved ones. Many complain of a gnawing feeling that obituaries were better written, as with everything else, in the good old days. The truth is that you usually get what you pay for — an old adage that explains the diminution of quality and objectivity that comes with running free editorial content, even if you gloss over that reality by saying you are connecting with the community.

Lurking in the shadows, ready to pounce on that endangered species editorial integrity, is the ravenous Internet maw demanding novel and robust revenue streams to boost the precarious finances of media outlets. Already many newspapers have outsourced the classified death notice business to digital companies, such as Legacy.com and Tributes.com, that link funeral parlours and grieving families to produce memorial sites and guest books.

Launched in 1988 with backing from the owners of the *Chicago Tribune*, Legacy.com survived the dot-com collapse and is now the leader in the online memorial and paid death-notice market (they also do pet and wedding announcements, organize flowers, and liaise with funeral parlours and grief counsellors). It has "partnerships" with more than eight hundred newspapers in North America, including the *New York Times*, the *Washington Post*, the *Toronto Star*, and the *National Post*, and is a partner with the *Times* of London, among other international newspapers. According to its website, Legacy.com creates death notices and memorials for more than two-thirds of people who die in the United States.

Legacy.com sponsored a research study undertaken by graduate students at the Medill School of Journalism at Northwestern University. The study, "The State of the American Obituary," recommended that "collaborations" between newspapers and Legacy.com should expand. Otherwise newspapers could find themselves out of the lucrative death-notice market: the classified advertising revenue that adds to newspaper bottom lines and supports editorial obituary pages. How long will it be before Legacy.com and similar sites supply editorial content as well as paid notices? I'm not a Luddite. Partnerships are the way of the future, but we need to be steadfast in preserving editorial objectivity and integrity in editorial content. Otherwise we will jeopardize a long and venerable tradition to maximize page views.

The same year as the Buchwald video, another farewell speech hit the Internet and went viral. This video was a film of Randy Pausch, a charismatic computer scientist at Carnegie Mellon University in Pittsburgh, speaking in a university series called "The Last Lecture." The idea behind the program was to invite distinguished alumni to come back to Carnegie Mellon to enlighten students and faculty with the thoughts and ideas they would like to impart in a final address.

Pausch, however, was not an aged sage. Instead he was a Jim Carrey look-alike with a similar patter and demeanour. He was forty-six and had recently been diagnosed with pancreatic cancer when he stood in front of the lectern on September 18, 2007, to deliver a lecture titled "Really Achieving Your Childhood Dreams." He spoke about his own life, illustrating his talk with slides, jokes, and pathos, and concluded by telling the audience of four hundred friends, students, and colleagues that the lecture wasn't really about childhood dreams but about his own life. Furthermore, he hadn't really prepared the lecture for his students and colleagues but as a keepsake for his own young children.

It was an inspirational talk that was recorded for people who couldn't make the lecture and then uploaded to YouTube. More than eight million people viewed the presentation, which was subsequently adapted into a book, *The Last Lecture*, with co-author Jeff Zaslow, a columnist for the *Wall Street Journal*. The book has sold millions of copies and spent years on best-seller lists.

The impact was an enormous wave of empathy for the dying computer scientist and his family. Pausch, a pioneer in the field of virtual-reality research, went from unknown academic — in the public sense — to a celebrity philosopher. In May 2008, *Time* magazine listed him as one of their 100 Most Influential People in the World. And when Pausch died two months later, on July 25, media outlets responded with huge obituaries, turning his life into a supernova that may well guarantee him immortality.

Would we have done that if he hadn't given an inspirational lecture that was posted, without copyright restrictions, at Pausch's own request, on the World Wide Web? Probably not. Was it a bad thing that Pausch manipulated the media into guaranteeing him a virtual life after death? Not entirely, because besides ensuring his legacy, his talk affected many people in positive ways.

The Buchwald and the Pausch videos represent two obituary streams that are now everywhere on the Internet: the digital enhancement of a journalistic obituary and the self-generated video designed to create a post-mortem digital legacy. But Buchwald and Pausch aren't the first and they won't be the last to reach beyond the grave with a farewell letter.

The impulse to leave a message that expresses your final thoughts and gives comfort to mourners is a very human one. But making those sentiments

public catapults final messages into another dimension. It allows all of us —
admirers, rivals, and foes — to creep closer to the deathbed, share in the grief
of immediate friends and family, and explore the nebulous boundary between
life and death. Some condemn the farewell letter as a narcissistic attempt at
immortality or the final act of a control freak, but it offers benefits to both the
dying and the bereaved. And thanks to the pervasiveness of social media, it
forces the subject of death into the public discourse.

Memories fade or become altered with time, but a letter is a literary document that retains its original text and ensures that your words — rather
than somebody else's interpretation of them — are passed on. As with the
prospect of hanging, as Samuel Johnson famously said, a terminal diagnosis
concentrates the mind. Writing a farewell letter, even in conjunction with
others, forces you to think deeply and hard about the message you want to
send and how you want to express it. For mourners, the letter can become a
talisman. You can carry it in your pocket, consult it when grief wallops you,
and reread it like a gospel to help you make decisions in keeping with the
deceased's wishes

In August 2011, marketing genius Steve Jobs posted a final goodbye, camouflaged as a resignation letter, on the website of Apple, the computer technology company he had co-founded twenty-five years earlier. Deeply eccentric
and secretive about his personal life and his health, Jobs was being as open as
he could be with followers and colleagues when he posted: "I have always said
if there ever came a day when I could no longer meet my duties and expectations as Apple's CEO, I would be the first to let you know. Unfortunately, that
day has come."

He wasn't walking away — he wanted to stay on as chair of the board and
he identified his choice of successor as CEO — but he was acknowledging,
however covertly, what most people already knew: he was dying of pancreatic
cancer. Jobs, known for his arrogance and abrasiveness, ended his brief letter
on a tender note: "I have made some of the best friends of my life at Apple, and
I thank you all for the many years of being able to work alongside you." Fewer
than two months later he was dead, at fifty-six.

His death, even though it was anticipated, dominated the news media for
days and in some cases weeks, with reaction pieces, obituaries, business anal-
yses, and lifestyle commentaries. Some pundits compared him to Thomas
Edison, the inventor of the light bulb, among many others whose discoveries
changed everyday life. Perhaps in some instances the reaction was

overwrought, but my point is that, unlike Pausch's "The Last Lecture," Jobs's farewell letter sparked speculation but didn't unleash public mourning. After his death it was something else. It was almost as though we couldn't allow ourselves to admit that Jobs was dying, and then, when he did die, we reacted with the shock that accompanies an assassination or a sudden heart attack or an accident. Even though most of us had never met Jobs, he had changed our lives in the way we communicate and interact with the world. Because he was such a hugely significant person, we had to figure out how we were going to carry on without him, and that, I think, explained the coverage.

Canadian politician Jack Layton wrote a "Dear Friends" letter that was sent as an email and went viral within hours of his death at age sixty-one, from an undisclosed cancer, on August 22, 2011. Layton achieved his greatest success while fatally ill. After leading the New Democratic Party into the 2004, 2006, and 2008 elections, he really came into his own in the 2011 election, which he had sparked by a no-confidence motion against the minority government of Conservative leader Stephen Harper. Using a cane after surgery for a mysterious hip fracture, Layton campaigned relentlessly. His easy manner and rapport with crowds, combined with his feisty performance in the English- and French-language debates — he spoke French like a Montrealer, which appealed to Quebeckers over Harper's functional but stilted French and Liberal leader Michael Ignatieff's Parisian accent — appealed to younger voters, especially in Quebec. As did the way he waved his cane, like a crusader stamping out corruption and waste. When the ballots were counted on May 2, Harper had his long-sought majority, the Liberals had been trounced, and the NDP had won enough seats — 103 — to form the Official Opposition.

Layton's public persona as "*le bon Jack*," the smiling, cane-waving trooper who connected like sticky tape even with people who would never consider voting NDP, made his impending death all the more shocking. A gaunt and raspy-voiced Layton called a press conference in the middle of the summer to announce that he was taking temporary leave to fight a "new" cancer, unrelated, he said, to his 2010 diagnosis of prostate cancer. The country was still reeling when he died, four weeks later, at his home in Toronto. The response was driven partly by the Shakespearean tragedy of watching the precipitous plunge in his health at the pinnacle of his electoral success, and partly it was the timing and manner of the letter's electronic release, mere hours after the news bulletin announcing his death.

He'd been thinking about the letter for several weeks, and then he called together his wife, politician Olivia Chow, and two of his closest colleagues to "craft the final form" of the letter if "things didn't go well" with his treatment, according to Brian Topp, who later ran for leadership of the party. In some ways Layton was tidying his metaphorical desk, telling the caucus and the party how to go about finding his successor and encouraging other cancer patients not to lose hope because his "journey" hadn't ended the way he had hoped. For many the decision not to reveal details of his "second" cancer and his treatment had seemed discordant, even false, in a man who prided himself on his openness.

Within seconds, chunks of the letter — especially the final paragraph, urging all Canadians to be "loving, hopeful, and optimistic" — were being tweeted, shared via Facebook, and digitally cut and pasted into Internet posters. Suddenly people were using social media for political conversations about Layton, his political party, and his cause. He was controlling the message even after death.

As the population ages, death becomes a growth industry. That's the six-foot-deep secret that even the most insecure of obituary writers holds dear, as a glance at the burgeoning paid death-notices in daily newspapers will confirm. The median age of Canadians went up by approximately two years from the 2001 to the 2006 census, with the number of people fifty-five and older rising by more than one million in the past five years.

Not only are people getting older, they want to read obituaries, according to a readership survey conducted by the Media Management Centre at Northwestern University. It found that "obituaries — along with community announcements and life stories about ordinary people — have the highest potential of all news items to grow readership." Researchers interviewed nearly forty thousand consumers in a hundred newspaper markets in the U.S. and concluded that newspaper obituaries were "important" to forty-five percent of readers, "very important" to twelve percent, and "somewhat important" to thirty-three percent.

It is hard not to conclude that the reason people want to read obituaries has a lot to do with the aging population. People are interested in the lives, mores, and final outcomes of their own cohort, and they want to reminisce about their own times, and perhaps even feel a moment of satisfaction that they are still here to read about the ones who have gone before. What people don't seem so interested in reading about, however, is one of the most pressing issues of our times: how people die. Medical technology has made it possible for us to linger on machines until our organs can be harvested, or our off-spring can be persuaded by busy and cost-conscious medical personnel that it really is time to pull the plug on the life support systems. Faced with those choices, many aging people are seeking to control their deaths as they once tried to manage their lives.

Whether obituary readers want to know about doctor-assisted suicide is moot. Finding a comfortable way out is a preoccupying issue for people who have been given dreadful diagnoses: patients with terminal cancer, degenerative diseases such as ALS, or various forms of dementia, among other illnesses. How an obituary writer deals with these situations is a disturbing ethical issue.

More than a dozen years ago, Oregon became the first jurisdiction in North America to pass a "death with dignity" act. Since then more than 350 terminally ill people have taken advantage of the law to end lives that were physically untenable. (Since then, two other American states have passed similar legislations and the right to die is again before the courts in Canada and in the National Assembly in Quebec.)

Journalists Rob Finch and Don Colburn, from the *Oregonian* in Portland, created "Living to the End," a multimedia presentation in the newspaper and on its website. The subject was Lovelle Svart, a sixty-two-year-old terminally ill woman who worked through her decision to end her life in a series of diary and video interviews in which she talked about her life, her terminal lung cancer, and how she decided to end her own life rather than waiting for cancer to claim her. The hard part was determining the point at which the morphine she needed to control her progressive pain had also destroyed her independence and quality of life. Wait too long and she wouldn't be able to swallow the lethal dose; take it too soon and she would lose some precious living time.

The dying-with-dignity process, which is not called suicide, is complicated. To qualify, you have to be at least eighteen, a resident of Oregon, have less than six months to live according to two doctors, and pass a psychological evaluation testifying that you have no overriding medical issues (aside from coping with your own demise). But that's not all. You must make the request either verbally or in writing, wait fifteen days before filling the prescription for the toxic potion, and be capable of ingesting it without help — injections are not allowed.

All of which gives most people a very small window between the time when they realize they don't want to live anymore and when they are so debilitated they are not capable of swallowing the potion. By those standards Sue Rodriguez, the B.C. woman suffering from Lou Gehrig's disease who unsuccessfully petitioned the Canadian government to end her own life in 1992, might not have been able to lift a beaker to her lips and so would not have qualified to end her life under the Oregon law.

In taking on the assignment, *Oregonian* reporter Don Colburn and a team of editors and photographers were assured by their senior editors that "if we felt weak in the knees, we could drop it without rancour." In other words, no letters in employment files about reporters refusing an assignment. Watching over another human being's demise is a way of ushering a loved one from this mortal coil, but voyeuristically observing a complete stranger breathe her last breath could be like watching a snuff film. The *Oregonian* opted for delicacy and, wisely, I think, froze the video image of Svart sitting up in bed surrounded by her loved ones and let only the audio run as she grew progressively sleepier.

The NYT broke the print mould with Art Buchwald's legacy-making video obituary, but this multimedia presentation about an ordinary woman with an unfamiliar name brought me and thousands of readers and viewers closer to understanding the choice that an increasing number of people will face in our ageing society. There was the intimacy of hearing a dead person speak about her own life, but encased in objective reportage. And yet I empathized when Colburn, the journalist, admitted later that he still occasionally asks himself: "If we weren't there, would she [Svart] still have done it?"

That is the sort of ethical question all journalists must ask themselves as we push the boundaries of what can be asked and shown in reporting on the final frontier of human existence. You might even call it a matter of life and death.

EPILOGUE

The Enduring Power of Obituaries

AFTER AMERICAN ACTOR James Rebhorn died of melanoma in March 2014, his church posted a final message from the character actor on its web site. Rebhorn wrote poignantly about his family in a third-person narrative. "Without them, always at the centre of his being," he said of his wife and children, "his life would have been little more than a vapor." He also entreated his daughters to "grieve his passing only as long as necessary" because they "have much good work to do, and they should get busy doing it."

Only a cold-hearted cynic could be unmoved by Rebhorn's message, which went viral on the Internet, creating an online legacy for the hawk-nosed actor best known for cameo appearances as an assistant district attorney in the final episode of *Seinfeld* and as FBI agent Carrie Mathison's father on *Homeland*, as well as for his supporting roles in the films *The Talented Mr. Ripley*, *Independence Day*, and *Basic Instinct*.

Though touching and eloquent, Rebhorn's message wasn't, as many Internet wits insisted, a "self-penned obituary." Rather, it falls into the tradition of a deathbed letter, a combination of comfort and spiritual guidance for grieving family and friends from beyond the grave. A recent example was politician Jack Layton's final email exhorting Canadians to be "loving, hopeful, and optimistic." These are not obituaries because they are self-written; they tend to ignore career achievements and character flaws, and they assume an emotional rather than a journalistic bond with the reader. That doesn't

deny their power, especially when they are broadcast far beyond the mourn-
er's circle. They are still rare, but I wager they will become far more common
as social media displaces the telephone as a communication tool.

Emotional appeals are persuasive, but obituaries use facts and arguments
to make the case about a dubious or worthy legacy. Here's an example. Alfred
Nobel changed his own behaviour and affected the lives of many other people
because of a powerful obituary. A Swedish chemist and armaments manufacturer, he was the inventor of dynamite. Today, though, he is remembered for
the Nobel Peace and other prestigious prizes, which are awarded annually in
Sweden.

Less well known is why Nobel left his fortune to philanthropy. In 1888, his
older brother Ludwig died, but a French journalist thought it was Alfred who
had expired. That's how Nobel got to read the critical headline, "The Merchant
of Death," over his own obituary: "Dr. Alfred Nobel, who became rich by
finding ways to kill more people faster than ever before, died yesterday."
Nobel was so shocked that he determined to rehabilitate his legacy, while he
could, and rewrote his will to establish the Nobel Prizes, thereby turning the
merchant of death into a philanthropist for peace. That is the enduring power
of obituaries.

THERE WAS A time when news of a death travelled slowly. A family placed a
mourning wreath on the front door or draped the porch in black bunting and
sent a letter to inform relatives who lived in other parts of the country or
overseas. Newspapers, radio, and television speeded up the process, but were
bound by broadcast schedules, time zones, and datelines. All of those warps
have gone the way of the passenger pigeon in today's globally connected universe. That's why everybody seems to learn the news at the same time and the
world seems to stop when an icon dies.

We may be only half listening to the radio or the television or routinely
scrolling a mobile device when the newsflash jolts us into hyper-awareness,
taking precedence over anything else we might be doing. Invariably, thanks
to the pervasiveness of news media and celebrity stalking, we think we know
the person, even though the closest we have come is watching him or her on
television or cheering an achievement from the sidelines. Never mind that we
have never actually met the icon, the death seems a personal loss. Where was
I when I first heard the news, we may think afterwards, as we try to connect

our lives and our grief with the death of somebody who has had a super-charged effect on our times.

Media organizations try to capture that mood and back it up with solid news-gathering and analysis, which is why obituaries make it on to the front page and top the broadcast agenda — no matter what else is happening anywhere else in the world. A well-written and deeply researched obituary will live far beyond the 24/7 news cycle. It sets the framework and stands as the final word until a biography or a scholarly monograph comes along to confirm or reassess an icon's place in history.

In our celebrity-saturated age, icon — which technically refers to a shrine in the form of a religious figure before which devotees worship and pray — has developed a secular definition to denote a political, athletic, artistic, or business figure whose fame has transcended the local and the everyday. In the process, the term has sacrificed its luster. That's the price of ubiquity — until somebody of the stature of Nelson Mandela dies. Then the word icon resumes its mystery and its power, and like Niagara Falls transcends the tawdry human follies in its environs.

I had updated Mandela's obituary a dozen times and assured a slew of editors that, yes, his last official public appearance really was at the end of the FIFA World Cup Football championship in Johannesburg in June 2010. That same stadium in Johannesburg was the venue for his first public address after his release from prison in 1990, an appearance he reprised at the 1995 World Cup the year after he became the first democratically elected president of South Africa. Back then he had impulsively donned a Springbok Jersey, once the exclusive costume of white players, and walked on to the field to present the cup to the winning and integrated South African football team. By 2010, he was old and frail, so instead of bounding onto the field, he smiled beatifically and waved happily to the roaring crowds as he and his wife Graça Machel were wheeled around the stadium in a motorized gold cart. Yes, Mandela had received famous visitors since then, including Hillary Clinton, and yes, he had visited his boyhood home, but those were private not official occasions and there was no need to update the obituary to account for each time his name was mentioned in a news bulletin. Notably the stadium was also the site of the public memorial after Mandela's death in December 2013.

The *Globe* had embarked on its Mandela memorial project in 2008, using as a template the long-standing print tribute to the Queen Mother, who had died in 2002 at 101, having outlived her husband by half a century, her younger daughter by six weeks, and most of her contemporaries by decades. That solid world of banner headlines and swathes of type over several pages was about to disappear. In the five years following the decision to initiate the Mandela supplement, the *Globe* had rotated correspondents in South Africa and appointed a new editor-in-chief. More important, a financial and economic crisis had engulfed the world and an industrial revolution had discombobulated the newspaper industry and made print an endangered commodity. The Mandela memorial was transitioned from an eight-page print supplement to a downloadable e-book.

Not knowing how much to write, when it might be needed, or what form it will take is one of the reasons I write long when I am doing an advance obituary: it is a lot easier to trim than to fill in gaps on the fly. Besides, who can remember all those details as the years stream by? Even so, I barely recognized my own voice on the script that I had written and recorded for the slide show to accompany my 8,000-word web obituary.

We were so prepared for Mandela's death that we had a digital and a print plan. Alas, some genius had decided — pre-Twitter — that we needed a news story to trigger our coverage. Until we had a wire story or a file from our own correspondent, we couldn't post my "related" obituary. Finally a web editor typed, "Nelson Mandela has died. More to come…," posted it to the web, and pressed the button on my primed and waiting obituary. Somebody else forgot to remove the warning in block capitals: "DON'T PUBLISH." I'm all for planning, but sometimes outdated protocols get in the way of delivering the news.

The world had been anticipating Mandela's death and worrying about the political consequences for years. Personally, I thought his long decline was a final gift to his people. It gave them time to get used to the idea of life after Mandela. There was grief and uncertainty, but not shock or rage. Mourners celebrated his extraordinary life with song and flowers, not riots or gunshots. It was a testament to the man and the power of reconciliation, and I for one was very happy to have my obituary sit on a back burner until it was needed.

SINCE MY BOOK was published in hardcover in 2012, we lost political leaders, including Peter Lougheed and Ralph Klein of Alberta, Inuk artist Kenojuak Ashevak — *The Enchanted Owl*, her bold graphic image of a red and black stylized figure on a white background, has the same emblematic power as the maple leaf on the Canadian flag, which it predates by five years — and Mavis Gallant, the literary master of the chilling short story.

The biggest change in that time has been the accelerated ascendency of social media as a breaking news tool. In an earlier chapter I mentioned the death of Hamilton Southam, journalist, diplomat, founder of the National Arts Museum, and a key figure in establishing both the Canadian War Museum and the Valiants Memorial, the fourteen bronzes of Canadian historical heroes that stand in Confederation Square, adjacent to the National War Memorial in Ottawa. Southam died at the grand age of ninety-one, fittingly for such a patriotic man, on Canada Day. Alas, the holiday meant that there were few people on the news desk; consequently, Southam's demise slipped under the radar and, even though I had a long obit waiting in the morgue, we were a day late in reporting his death. Hard to imagine that happening today, given all-encompassing social media; somebody, including the family, would have bypassed the telephone and the newswires to tweet the news to the twitterverse.

Certainly that is what I did when I learned early on February 18, 2014, that Mavis Gallant had died in Paris. First I double-sourced the facts and then I sent the following tweet: "Sad news from Paris that #Mavis Gallant, the superb short story writer has died. Her work lives on." In the old days I would have phoned or emailed the news to the news desk. Now I tweet it and supply a sourced news story to the web, followed by a reaction piece, a revised and updated obituary for the web, and a much shorter print version late in the afternoon for the next day's newspaper readers. The style and the first paragraph change with each iteration. Here's the lede of the first web hit: "Mavis Gallant, one of Canada's most distinguished literary figures, died in Paris early on Tuesday. She was 91.

"The funeral was planned for Saturday in Montparnasse Cemetery in Paris, the city where she had lived for most of her adult life. She had no children, and was unmarried, but had legions of literary fans and a close group of stalwart friends."

The fact of her death takes second place to an interpretive comment in the print obituary because "the web is for news, the paper is for comment" is the rule of the day. By the time the newspaper thuds on your doorstep, the news has long since been delivered. The print obituary opened this way: "Mavis Gallant had a journalist's nose, a cinematographer's eye and a novelist's imagination. Her narratives about outsiders trying to insinuate themselves into alien situations and cultures move in waves of dialogue, observation, and lashing tension. That's why reading her stories gives one a sense of a clock ticking, a door creaking open or of an emotional wound about to be inflicted."

By contrast with Mandela and Gallant, the people who do die unexpectedly are the ones you haven't written about, as I have said before. Taking the time to reread books, watch films, review legislative careers, interview admirers and critics, and immerse yourself in the biographical details of an icon's life are basic but essential tasks before sitting down to craft what you hope will be a definitive obituary. But death can sneak up and knock you sideways, which is what happened with Mordecai Richler on July 3, 2001. It was a Monday and I was returning from vacation in British Columbia to my job as a feature writer in the arts section. I thought I would spend the day adjusting to the time difference, catching up on emails, and researching story pitches.

My home phone rang at 8:00 a.m., wrenching me awake from a West Coast reverie.

"Are you coming in to work today?" an editor asked peremptorily.

"What's up?" I replied sleepily.

"Mordecai Richler has died," was the terse response.

I hadn't yet embarked on my stint as an obituary writer, so I did what most neophytes do: I phoned everybody on all sides of the undefended border collecting memories, anecdotes, and tributes; I persuaded Margaret Atwood to write a short appreciation; and I conducted and typed out a Q and A with a grieving Guy Vanderhaeghe, who was too upset to hit his own keys.

At the end of a very long day I had lots of stuff, much of it interesting, some of it drawn from my own knowledge of Richler from having read his books, interviewed him a few times, and even written a prize-winning profile of him a dozen years earlier. But I hadn't produced what I now know is an obituary, by setting his satire in the context of cultural nationalism in Canada and local rage in Quebec when he had the effrontery to ridicule his native province — in the pages of *The New Yorker* no less. There were biographical details but not a comprehensive portrait. So I was glad to have a second chance to write about Richler in *Great Canadian Lives*.

By then, Richler had been dead for more than a decade. Unlike so many celebrity authors whose fame dies with them, his books were still being read and his work debated. His reputation as a curmudgeon and a satirist was as contentious as ever, especially in Quebec.

Writing about Richler so long after his death gave me a couple of advantages. At least three biographies had appeared, including Charles Foran's exhaustive and prize-winning book, titled simply, *Mordecai*. But I had also learned more about the craft of obituary writing and how the work and the life influence each other. And in Richler's case, there was a lot of both. I was able to add many more details about his journalism and film work and the primary role played by his wife, Florence — his first reader, his muse, his lover, and the primary guardian of his legacy.

Comparing the reaction piece I wrote on the day of Richler's death with the biographical essay I wrote a decade later made me realize how much obituaries reflect the time in which they are written. The facts are the same but the subject is in a less emotional and more contemplative light. Nobody ever argues that obituaries should be revised with the passage of time, but I found this experiment both arduous and rewarding.

AS AN OBITUARY writer in an electronic age, I have been jolted by email messages from readers with new information when it is too late to add a paragraph or revise an opinion. After the fact, I have heard deliciously unvarnished tales from disgruntled stepchildren, long lost friends, former lovers, and even a painter convinced he had been swindled by his celebrated art dealer. Sources that are supposedly dead have on occasion risen Lazarus-like to announce their continued existence and to offer a new slant on the life I have diligently tried to capture in print. All of which has made me dismiss the widely-held assumption that a newspaper obituary is the "final" word. There is always more to discover, more to consider.

Using Twitter, Facebook, and other platforms, I can connect with sources and uncover facts that I couldn't possibly have learned using traditional search engines. And then I can use those same platforms to spread the word about the life I've just commemorated. That's the boon and the folly that social media offer the modern obituary writer.

Technology is a tool, but, for all the advantages of downloads and social networking opportunities, there are also ethical dangers lurking in cyberspace. Even while embracing technological wizardry we must safeguard the journalistic principles that gave authority to print obituaries. Balancing speed versus credibility and objectivity versus melodrama are huge considerations if we are to keep the best of print in new narrative modes geared to a more expansive audience.

Facebook is a case in point. Lots of friends and families bypass paying for death and memorial notices in newspapers these days to post grieving messages on the social networking site. It makes sense. With more than a billion users globally, Facebook is the predominant platform for creating and curating a digital identity and sharing it with "friends." In their article, "Virtual Mourning and Memory Construction on Facebook" in the *Bulletin of Science, Technology & Society*, Toronto academics Rhonda N. McEwen and Kathleen Scheaffer made a study of how people grieve and mourn on Facebook, noting that the social networking site is a "dominant, global site with multi-generational and *increasingly older users*." (My emphasis.) That suggests that Facebook will grow exponentially as a means of communicating the news of somebody's death because older people die far more frequently than younger ones. Posting a notice on Facebook, which is free, is also easier because there are virtually no editing or other filters, including cost, to make posters weigh the wisdom, impulsivity, and the consequences of their messages.

McEwen and Scheaffer argue that "the immediacy of publishing comments, messages, wall posts, and photos provides Facebook mourners with a quick outlet for their emotion and a means of timely group support; however these actions directly affect the online curation of the deceased's self and memory and also creates an environment of competition among mourners." By "the online curation of the deceased's self and memory" they are referring to the phenomenon of survivors taking over the administration of a Facebook page and amending and augmenting it. By "competition among mourners" they are noting the tendency to repackage and reinterpret elements of the deceased's Facebook profile on memorial sites in which contributors vie for supremacy in a self-indulgent display of grief. "Thus, the profile of the deceased reflects no longer the work of the user," write McEwen and Scheaffer, "but rather the remembered life of the user's Facebook friends, and the individual's memory archive becomes a social archive" in which the "online self-curation of the deceased is overridden."

In a way these memorial sites are similar to old-fashioned eulogies in which faults are ignored and achievements are glorified, sometimes to the mystification of survivors. McEwen and Scheaffer conclude by recommending a series of policy changes to Facebook, including offering digital estate options to users and freezing the profile of deceased members so that new content cannot be added (although pre-existing friends can still visit the page). Obituary writers, who already troll Facebook for sources and reaction, should be as wary of these manufactured memories as they are of any other tributes they collect in their pursuit of accuracy and authenticity. As Margaret Sullivan, the public editor of the *New York Times*, wrote in a column about the shifting journalistic landscape: "Integrity. Challenging the powerful. Truth and fairness. No matter what the technological changes, these are never going to go out of style."

The past is a different country, but if we don't know its geography and its values, we can't map our way forward into the unknown. Obituaries are one of our surest guides in navigating what went before and chronicling history's influence in shaping our lives in the future. That's why maintaining high standards in this "lowliest" form of journalism is crucial to a country's on-going sense of itself.

SELECTED BIBLIOGRAPHY
A Note on Sources

T HE LIVES, CAREERS, and deaths of the fifty (and more) individuals discussed in this book are the result of extensive research. Not all the evidence of that research can be found in the body of the work, and I have chosen
purposefully not to incorporate proof of the hundreds of telephone calls and
emails that I made in researching and writing these lives. That would have
made the narrative unwieldy and the book as weighty as a tombstone.

I interviewed many of my subjects during my working life as a journalist,
followed their careers over time, talked with some of them specifically for
their obituaries, and spoke, after their deaths, to a wide variety of family
members and colleagues. In writing this book I have re-researched the obituaries I wrote for the *Globe and Mail*, turning them from reportage into biographical essays; added several people I hadn't written about — including
Pierre Trudeau, "Rocket" Richard, Oscar Peterson, Maureen Forrester, Ted
Rogers, and Smoky Smith — and revised everything to reflect additional
research and thinking about the recent past and the history and future of
obituary writing.

What follows is a select bibliography.

General References

The Canadian Encyclopedia
CBC Archives
Dictionary of Canadian Biography
Encyclopedia of Music in Canada
Encyclopædia Britannica
Factiva
Library and Archives Canada
The Oxford Anthology of Canadian Literature
Who's Who
Who's Who in Canada
Who's Who in America
Wikipedia

Books

Allen, Max, ed. *Ideas That Matter: The Worlds of Jane Jacobs*. Owen Sound, ON: Ginger Press, 1997.

Anderson, Doris. *Rebel Daughter: An Autobiography*. Toronto: Key Porter Books, 1996.

Anderson, Ellen. *Judging Bertha Wilson: Law as Large as Life*. Toronto: University of Toronto Press for the Osgoode Society, 2001.

Andrews, Audrey. *Be Good, Sweet Maid: The Trials of Dorothy Joudrie*. Waterloo, ON: Wilfrid Laurier University Press, 1999.

Ariès, Philippe. *The Hour of Our Death*. London: Oxford University Press, 1991.

Aubrey, John. *Brief Lives: A Selection Based upon Existing Contemporary Portraits*, edited by Richard Barber. London: Folio Society, 1975.

Avery, Donald H. *The Science of War: Canadian Scientists and Allied Military Technology During the Second World War*. Toronto: University of Toronto Press, 1998.

Barris, Alex. *Oscar Peterson: A Musical Biography*. Toronto: HarperCollins, 2002.

Batten, Jack. *Honest Ed's Story: The Crazy Rags to Riches Story of Ed Mirvish*. Toronto: Doubleday, 1972.

Berton, Pierre. *Drifting Home*. Toronto: McClelland & Stewart, 1973.

_____. *My Times: Living with History, 1947–1995*. Toronto: Doubleday, 1995.

_____. *Starting Out, 1920–1947*. Toronto: McClelland & Stewart, 1987.

Bishop-Gwyn, Carol. *The Pursuit of Perfection: A Life of Celia Franca.* Toronto: Cormorant Books, 2011.

Boorstin, Daniel J. *The Image: A Guide to Pseudo-Events in America.* New York: Harper & Row, 1964.

Bowering, George, and Jean Baird, eds. *The Heart Does Break: Canadian Writers on Grief and Mourning.* Toronto: Random House Canada, 2009.

Brodie, Paul. *Ambassador of the Saxophone.* Bala, ON: Paul Brodie, 2000.

Brown, Adele O. *What a Way to Go: Fabulous Funerals of the Famous and Infamous.* San Francisco: Chronicle Books, 2001.

Bruce, Robert V. *Bell: Alexander Graham Bell and the Conquest of Solitude.* London: Victor Gollancz, 1973.

Buchwald, Art. *Too Soon to Say Goodbye.* New York: Random House, 2006.

Callwood, June. *Love, Hate, Fear, Anger, and the Other Lively Emotions.* Toronto: Doubleday, 1964.

_____. *Twelve Weeks in Spring: The Inspiring Story of Margaret and Her Team.* Toronto: Key Porter Books, 2003.

Cambon, Kenneth. *Guest of Hirohito.* Vancouver: PW Press, 1990.

Cameron, Elspeth. *And Beauty Answers: The Life of Frances Loring and Florence Wyle.* Toronto: Cormorant Books, 2007.

_____. *Irving Layton: A Portrait.* Toronto: Stoddart, 1985.

Careless, J. M. S. *Brown of the Globe.* Vol. 1, *The Voice of Upper Canada, 1818–1859.* Toronto: Macmillan of Canada, 1959.

_____. *Brown of the Globe.* Vol. 2, *Statesman of Confederation, 1860–1880.* Toronto: Macmillan of Canada, 1963.

Carrier, Roch. *The Hockey Sweater,* translated by Sheila Fischman. Montreal: Tundra, 1984.

_____. *Our Life with the Rocket: The Maurice Richard Story,* translated by Sheila Fischman. Toronto: Viking, 2001.

Chan, Anthony B. *Gold Mountain: The Chinese in the New World.* Vancouver: New Star Books, 1983.

Clarkson, Stephen, and Christina McCall. *Trudeau and Our Times.* Vol. 1, *The Magnificent Obsession.* Toronto: McClelland & Stewart, 1990.

_____. *Trudeau and Our Times.* Vol. 2, *The Heroic Delusion.* Toronto: McClelland & Stewart, 1994.

Cohen, Andrew, and Jack Granatstein, eds. *Trudeau's Shadow: The Life and Legacy of Pierre Elliott Trudeau.* Toronto: Vintage Canada, 1999.

Cohen, Leonard. *Book of Longing.* Toronto: McClelland & Stewart, 2006.

Colquhoun, Keith, and Ann Wroe, eds. *The Economist Book of Obituaries.* London: Profile Books, 2008.

Cook, Ramsay. *Canada and the French Canadian Question*. Toronto: Macmillan of Canada, 1962

_____.*The Teeth of Time: Remembering Pierre Elliott Trudeau*. Montreal and Kingston, McGill-Queen's University Press, 2006.

Cormier, Michel. *Louis J. Robichaud: A Not So Quiet Revolution*, translated by Jonathan Kaplansky. Moncton, NB: Faye Editions, 2004.

Darnton, Kate, Kayce Freed Jennings, and Lynn Sherr. *Peter Jennings: A Reporter's Life*. New York: Public Affairs, 2007.

Davies, David Twiston, ed. *Canada from Afar: The Daily Telegraph Book of Canadian Obituaries*. Toronto: Dundurn Press, 1996.

Deedes, W. F. *Brief Lives*. London: Macmillan, 2004.

de Pédery-Hunt, Dora. *Medals*. Toronto: Canadian Stage and Art Publications, 1973.

_____. *Sculpture*, translated by Raynald Desmeules. Toronto: Prince Arthur Galleries/Canadian Stage and Arts Publications, 1978.

Drabinsky, Garth, with Marq de Villiers. *Closer to the Sun: An Autobiography*. Toronto: McClelland & Stewart, 1995.

Dublin, Anne. *June Callwood: A Life of Action*. Toronto: Second Story Press, 2006.

English, John. *Citizen of the World: The Life of Pierre Elliott Trudeau, 1919–1968*. Toronto: Alfred A. Knopf Canada, 2006.

_____. *Just Watch Me: The Life of Pierre Elliott Trudeau, 1968–2000*. Toronto: Alfred A. Knopf Canada, 2009.

Erickson, Arthur. *The Architecture of Arthur Erickson*. Vancouver: Douglas & McIntyre, 1988.

Foran, Charles. *Maurice Richard*. Toronto: Penguin, 2011.

_____. *Mordecai: The Life and Times*. Toronto: Vintage Canada, 2011.

Forrester, Maureen, with Marci McDonald. *Out of Character: A Memoir*. Toronto: McClelland & Stewart, 1986.

Frayne, Trent. *The Tales of an Athletic Supporter*. Toronto: McClelland & Stewart, 1990.

Frye, Northrop. *The Bush Garden: Essays on the Canadian Imagination*. Toronto: House of Anansi Press, 1971.

Galbraith, John Kenneth. *The Affluent Society*. Boston: Houghton Mifflin, 1998.

_____. *The Great Crash, 1929*. Boston: Houghton Mifflin, 2009.

_____. *A Life in Our Times: Memoirs*. Boston: Houghton Mifflin, 1981.

_____. *The Scotch*. Toronto: Macmillan, 1964.

Gibson, Douglas. *Stories about Storytellers: Publishing Alice Munro, Robertson Davies, Alistair MacLeod, Pierre Trudeau and Others*. Toronto: ECW Press, 2011.

Gillan, MaryEllen. *Obits: The Way We Say Goodbye*. Burnaby, BC: Serious Publishing, 1995.

Gimpel, René. *Diary of an Art Dealer*, translated by John Rosenberg. London: Hodder & Stoughton, 1966.

Goldenberg, Eddie. *The Way It Works: Inside Ottawa*. Toronto: McClelland & Stewart, 2006.

Gotlieb, Allan. *The Washington Diaries, 1981–1989*. Toronto: McClelland & Stewart, 2006.

Graham, Ron. *The Last Act: Pierre Trudeau, the Gang of Eight and the Fight for Canada*. Toronto: Allen Lane Canada, 2011.

Gray, Charlotte. *Reluctant Genius: The Passionate Life and Inventive Mind of Alexander Graham Bell*. Toronto: HarperCollins, 2006.

Greenspon, Edward, and Anthony Wilson-Smith. *Double Vision: The Inside Story of the Liberals in Power*. Toronto: Doubleday, 1996.

Grosvenor, Edwin S., and Morgan Wesson. *Alexander Graham Bell: The Life and Times of the Man Who Invented the Telephone*. New York: Harry Abrams, 1997.

Gwyn, Richard. *The Northern Magus: Pierre Trudeau and Canadians*. Toronto: McClelland & Stewart, 1980.

Harris, Michael. *Justice Denied: The Law versus Donald Marshall*. Toronto: Macmillan of Canada, 1986.

Harris, Paul. *R.I.P.: A Light-Hearted Look at Life Through Death*. London: Harrap, 1983.

Hershorn, Ted. *Norman Granz: The Man Who Used Jazz for Justice*, foreword by Oscar Peterson. Berkeley: University of California Press, 2011.

Hickman, Tom. *Death: A User's Guide*. New York: Bantam Dell, 2003.

Horn, Michiel. *Academic Freedom in Canada: A History*. Toronto: University of Toronto Press, 1999.

Houston, James. *Confessions of an Igloo Dweller*. Toronto: McClelland & Stewart, 1995.

_____. *Zigzag: A Life on the Move*. Toronto: McClelland & Stewart, 1998.

Hume, Janice. *Obituaries in American Culture*. Jackson: University of Mississippi Press, 2000.

Huth, Angela, ed. *Well-Remembered Friends: Eulogies on Celebrated Lives*. London: John Murray, 2004.

Iglauer, Edith. *Seven Stones: A Portrait of Arthur Erickson, Architect*. Vancouver: Harbour Publishing, 1981.

Jacobs, Jane. *The Death and Life of Great American Cities*. New York: Vintage Books, 1961.

———. *The Question of Separatism: Quebec and the Struggle over Sovereignty.* New York: Random House, 1980.

Jennings, Peter, and Todd Brewster. *The Century.* New York: Doubleday, 1998.

Johnson, Marilyn. *The Dead Beat: Lost Souls, Lucky Stiffs, and the Perverse Pleasures of Obituaries.* New York: Harper Perennial, 2006.

Kaplan, William. *State and Salvation: The Jehovah's Witnesses and Their Fight for Civil Rights.* Toronto: University of Toronto Press, 1989.

Keane, David, and Colin Read. *Old Ontario: Essays in Honour of J. M. S. Careless.* Toronto: Dundurn Press, 1990.

Kent, Tom. *A Public Purpose: An Experience of Liberal Opposition and the Canadian Government.* Montreal and Kingston: McGill-Queen's University Press, 1988.

Knight, Amy. *How the Cold War Began: The Gouzenko Affair and the Hunt for Soviet Spies.* Toronto: McClelland & Stewart, 2005.

Kramer, Reinhold. *Mordecai Richler: Leaving St. Urbain.* Montreal: McGill-Queen's University Press, 2008.

Layton, David. *Motion Sickness: A Memoir.* Toronto: Macfarlane, Walter & Ross, 1999.

Layton, Irving. *The Collected Poems of Irving Layton.* Toronto: McClelland & Stewart, 1971.

———. *A Red Carpet for the Sun.* Toronto: McClelland & Stewart, 1959.

Layton, Irving, with David O'Rourke. *Waiting for the Messiah.* Toronto: McClelland & Stewart, 2006.

Lees, Gene. *Oscar Peterson: The Will to Swing.* Toronto: Lester & Orpen Dennys, 1988.

Linn, Ruth. *Escaping Auschwitz: A Culture of Forgetting.* Ithaca, NY: Cornell University Press, 2004.

Lunan, Gordon. *The Making of a Spy.* Montreal: R. Davies Publishing, 1995.

———. *Redhanded: The Spy Scandal That Shook the World.* Maxville, ON: Optimum Publishing, 2004.

Martin, Patrick, Allan Gregg, and George Perlin. *Contenders: The Tory Quest for Power.* Scarborough, ON: Prentice-Hall, 1983.

Massingberd, Hugh, ed. *The Daily Telegraph Book of Obituaries: A Celebration of Eccentric Lives.* London: Pan Books, 1996.

———. *The Daily Telegraph Second Book of Obituaries: Heroes and Adventurers.* London: Pan Books, 1997.

———. *The Daily Telegraph Third Book of Obituaries: Entertainers.* London: Pan Books, 1998.

———. *The Daily Telegraph Fourth Book of Obituaries: Rogues.* London: Pan Books, 1999.

Matusow, Barbara. *The Evening Stars: The Making of the Network News Anchor.* Boston: Houghton Mifflin Harcourt, 1983.

McCall, Christina. *Grits: An Intimate Portrait of the Liberal Party.* Toronto: Macmillan, 1982.

McKillop, A. B. *Pierre Berton: A Biography.* Toronto: McClelland & Stewart, 2008.

Millar, Nancy. *The Final Word: The Book of Canadian Epitaphs.* Victoria, BC: Brindle & Glass, 2004.

Melançon, Benoît. *The Rocket: A Cultural History of Rocket Richard,* translated by Fred A. Reed. Vancouver: Greystone, 2009.

Mirvish, Ed. *Honest Ed Mirvish: How to Build an Empire on an Orange Crate, or 121 Lessons I Never Learned in School.* Toronto: Key Porter Books, 1993.

_____. *There's No Business Like Show Business, But I Wouldn't Ditch My Day Job.* Toronto: Key Porter Books, 1997.

Mulroney, Brian. *Memoirs: 1939–1993.* Toronto: McClelland & Stewart, 2007.

Neatby, Hilda. *Queen's University.* Vol. 1, *1841–1914: And Not to Yield.* Montreal and Kingston: McGill-Queen's University Press, 1978.

Nemni, Max, and Monique Nemni. *Trudeau Transformed, 1944–1965: The Shaping of a Statesman,* translated by George Tombs. Toronto: McClelland & Stewart, 2011.

_____. *Young Trudeau, 1919–1944: Son of Quebec, Father of Canada,* translated by William Johnson. Toronto: McClelland & Stewart, 2006.

Neufeld, James. *Passion to Dance: The National Ballet of Canada.* Toronto: Dundurn Press, 2011.

Nicholson, G. W. L. *Official History of the Canadian Army in the Second World War.* Vol. 2, *The Canadians in Italy, 1943–1945.* Ottawa: Queen's Printer, 1956.

Outram, Richard. *Selected Poems, 1960–1980.* Toronto: Exile Editions, 1984.

Palmer, Richard, ed., with Oscar Peterson. *A Jazz Odyssey: The Life of Oscar Peterson.* New York: Continuum, 2003.

Parker, Richard. *John Kenneth Galbraith: His Life, His Politics, His Economics.* Toronto: HarperCollins, 2005.

Pausch, Randy, with Jeffrey Zaslow. *The Last Lecture.* New York: Hyperion, 2008.

Phillips, John, with Jim Jerome. *Papa John: An Autobiography, 1935–2001.* Garden City, NJ: Doubleday, 1986.

Phillips, Michelle. *California Dreamin': The True Story of the Mamas and the Papas.* New York: Warner Books, 1986.

Poles, George, and Simon Littlefield. *As a Dodo: The Obituaries You'd Really Like to See.* London: Summersdale, 2007.

Posner, Michael. *The Last Honest Man: Mordecai Richler, An Oral Biography.* Toronto: McClelland & Stewart, 2004.

Powell, Georgia, and Katharine Ramsay. *Chin Up, Girls! A Book of Women's Obituaries from the Daily Telegraph.* London: John Murray, 2005.

Rachman, Tom. *The Imperfectionists: A Novel.* New York: Dial Press, 2010.

Radwanski, George. *Trudeau.* Toronto: Macmillan of Canada, 1978.

Reed, J. D., and Maddy Miller. *Stairway to Heaven: The Final Resting Places of Rock's Legends.* New York: Wenner Books, 2005.

Reid, Stephen. *Jackrabbit Parole.* Toronto: McClelland & Stewart/Bantam, 1986.

Richler, Mordecai. *The Apprenticeship of Duddy Kravitz.* Don Mills, ON: André Deutsch, 1959.

———. *Barney's Version.* Toronto: Alfred A. Knopf Canada, 1997.

———. *Home Sweet Home: My Canadian Album.* Toronto: McClelland & Stewart, 1984.

———. *Hunting Tigers under Glass: Essays and Reports,* Toronto: McClelland & Stewart, 1968.

———. *Joshua Then and Now.* Toronto: McClelland & Stewart, 1980.

———. *Oh Canada! Oh Quebec! Requiem for a Divided Country.* Toronto: Penguin Books, 1992.

———. *St. Urbain's Horseman.* Toronto: McClelland & Stewart, 1971.

———. *Shovelling Trouble.* Toronto: McClelland & Stewart, 1972.

———. *Solomon Gursky Was Here.* Markham, ON: Viking, 1989.

———. *The Street.* Toronto: McClelland & Stewart, 1969

Robinson, Ray. *Famous Last Words.* New York: Workman Publishing, 2003.

Roblin, Duff. *Speaking for Myself and Other Pursuits.* Winnipeg: Great Plains, 1999.

Rogers, Ted, with Robert Brehl. *Relentless: The True Story of the Man Behind Rogers Communications.* Toronto: HarperCollins, 2008.

Ross, Judy Smith. *Good Grief, I Have to Plan a Funeral.* Thornbury, ON: Valley Girls Publishing, 2004.

Rule, Jane. *The Desert of the Heart.* Toronto: Macmillan of Canada, 1964.

———. *Lesbian Images.* Garden City, NJ: Doubleday, 1975.

———. *Loving the Difficult.* Sidney, BC: Hedgerow Press, c. 2008.

———. *Taking My Life.* Vancouver: Talonbooks, 2011.

Scrivener, Leslie. *Terry Fox: His Story.* Toronto: McClelland & Stewart, 2000.

Sheeler, Jim. *Final Salute: A Story of Unfinished Lives.* New York: Penguin Press, 2008.

———. *Obit: Inspiring Stories of Ordinary People Who Led Extraordinary Lives.* Boulder, CO: Pruett Publishing, 2007.

Siegel, Marvin, ed. *The Last Word: The New York Times Book of Obituaries and Farewells.* New York: William Morrow, 1997.

Simpson, Jeffrey. *Star-Spangled Canadians: Canadians Living the American Dream*. Toronto: HarperCollins, 2000.

Smith, Martin, ed. *The Daily Telegraph Book of Sports Obituaries*. London: Pan Books, 2001.

Stanley, Della M. *Louis Robichaud: A Decade of Power*. Halifax: Nimbus, 1984.

Starck, Nigel. *Life after Death: The Art of the Obituary*. Melbourne, Australia: Melbourne University Press, 2006.

Symons, Scott. *Civic Square*. Toronto: McClelland & Stewart, 1969.

———. *Combat Journal for Place d'Armes: A Personal Narrative*. Toronto: McClelland & Stewart, 1971.

———. *Helmet of Flesh*. Toronto: McClelland & Stewart, 1986.

———. *Heritage: A Romantic Look at Early Canadian Furniture*. Toronto: McClelland & Stewart, 1971.

Talese, Gay. *The Gay Talese Reader*. New York: Random House, 2004.

———. *A Writer's Life*. New York: Alfred A. Knopf, 2006.

Taylor, Charles. *Six Journeys: A Canadian Pattern*. Toronto: House of Anansi Press, 1977.

Tippett, Maria, with photographs by Charles Gimpel. *Between Two Cultures: A Photographer among the Inuit*. Toronto: Viking, 1994.

Tracey, Lindalee. *Growing Up Naked: My Years in Bump and Grind*. Vancouver: Douglas & McIntyre, 1997.

———. *On the Edge: A Journey into the Heart of Canada*. Vancouver: Douglas & McIntyre, 1993.

Trudeau, Margaret. *Beyond Reason*. New York: Paddington Press, 1979.

Vance, Jonathan. *Unlikely Soldiers: How Two Canadians Fought the Secret War against Nazi Occupation*. Toronto: HarperCollins, 2008.

Van Hasselt, Caroline. *High Wire Act: Ted Rogers and the Empire That Debt Built*. Mississauga, ON: J. Wiley, 2007.

Vorano, Norman. *Japanese Inspiration: Early Printmaking in the Canadian Arctic*. Gatineau, QC: Canadian Museum of Civilization, 2011.

Vrba, Rudolf, and Alan Bestic. *Escape from Auschwitz: I Cannot Forgive*. London/New York: Grove Press, 1986.

Vulliamy, C. E. *Immortality: Funerary Rites and Customs*. London: Senate, 1999.

Weston, Greg. *The Stopwatch Gang*. Toronto: Macmillan of Canada, 1992.

Whitman, Alden. *The Obituary Book*. New York: Stein & Day, 1971.

Williams, Andrea D., ed. *The Essential Galbraith*. Boston: Houghton Mifflin, 2001.

Williamson, Ronald F., and Michael S. Bisson, eds. *The Archaeology of Bruce Trigger: Theoretical Empiricism*. Montreal: McGill-Queen's University Press, 2006.

NEWSPAPERS

Daily Telegraph (London)
Globe and Mail (Toronto)
Guardian (London)
Independent (London)
Montreal Gazette
National Post (Toronto)
New York Times
Toronto Star
Sunday Times (London)
Times (London)
Vancouver Sun
Washington Post
Winnipeg Free Press

PERIODICALS

Antigonish Review
Books in Canada
Chatelaine
Downbeat
Gentleman's Magazine
Grand Street
International Journal of Cultural Studies
London Library Magazine
Maclean's
Nieman Reports
Opera Canada
The Post-Angel
Quill & Quire
Saturday Night
Toronto Life
Walrus
Vanity Fair

ACKNOWLEDGEMENTS

M Y FIRST THANKS must go to the more than fifty people I have written about in this book. Their lives and their times inspired, fascinated, and even disturbed me at times. In writing about them I learned a great deal about humanity, the past, writing short biographies, and the history of Canada and its place in the larger world. I'm extremely grateful to the hundreds of people who agreed to speak with me in person, by e-mail, and on the telephone during the course of my research both as a journalist at the *Globe* and for this book. And to those who had a fright, thinking they were in my sights when I sent an e-mail, asking, "Can we talk?" I apologize. I quickly learned to add the words "not about you" in the subject line.

I am grateful to the *Globe and Mail* for giving me the opportunity to write obituaries, for supporting me in my writing and reporting, and for listening attentively to my frequent suggestions for improving the way we cover obits. I would particularly like to thank Publisher Phillip Crawley and the editors, both past and current, with whom I have worked on the dead beat, especially John Stackhouse, David Walmsley, Sylvia Stead, Patrick Martin, Colin Mackenzie, Colin Haskin, and Susan Smith. A special thanks to librarians Celia Donnelly, Rick Cash and Stephanie Chambers — an obituary writer's best friends. I have also used the research libraries at the Universities of Toronto, Western Ontario, and Victoria, among other repositories, and have come to treasure their open stacks and generous lending policies.

438 SANDRA MARTIN

The University of Victoria honoured me as the Harvey Stevenson Southam Lecturer in Journalism and Nonfiction in 2010, which gave me the splendid opportunity to spend four months in the Writing Department, teaching a course about obituaries as a biographical form to third- and fourth-year students. I'm sure I learned as much from the students as I taught them, especially when it came to developing multi-media obituary websites. The Ontario Arts Council gave me a Writers' Reserve Grant in 2011, which helped immeasurably in giving me time to work on the book in the early stages.

The House of Anansi Press, with its stellar reputation as a Canadian publisher, was a lucky and a welcome home for this project. I'm particularly grateful to Scott Griffin, a generous and careful reader; Sarah MacLachlan, a nimble and resourceful publisher; and Janie Yoon, an editor who climbs down into the writing trenches without losing sight of the goal and the schedule. My thanks also go to my publicist, Laura Repas; the sales team, Barbara Howson, Emily Mockler, and Eva O'Brien; and the marketing duo, Fred Horler and Trish Osuch. I would also like to thank designers Brian Morgan and Alysia Shewchuk for their beautiful work on this book, as well as copyeditor Gillian Watts and proofreader Peter Norman for their careful reading of the manuscript.

Many people gave me valuable advice and support. They include Mary Janigan and Tom Kierans, Margaret Atwood, Charlotte Gray, Jeanne Cannizzo and David Stafford, Robert Jan van Pelt, Michael Marrus, Marci McDonald, Michael Bliss, Michiel Horn, the walking women and my obituary writing colleagues around the world. Several generous souls read parts of this book and took me seriously when I asked them to pick nits and identify howlers. They include in alphabetical order, Katherine Ashenburg, Don Avery, Geoff Beattie, Carol Bishop-Gwyn, Jack Chambers, Pat Feheley, Ron Graham, Jack Granatstein, Blake Heathcote, Bill Kaplan, Kirk Makin, Joe Martin, Sarah Murdoch, and David Stimpson. My husband, Roger Hall, has been my first and last reader for more years than either of us probably cares to remember, but he remains my best and most faithful sounding board. He and my children, Jeffrey and Louisa, have lived this book with me, and I thank them with love and gratitude.

Finally, thank you to McClelland & Stewart for use of the following excerpts:

AUTHOR PHOTO: NIGEL DICKSON

S ANDRA MARTIN is a features writer, and the former obituary columnist at the *Globe and Mail*. She has won writing prizes from the Society of
Professional Obituary Writers, gold and silver National Magazine Awards,
the Atkinson and William Southam Journalism Fellowships, and the Harvey
Southam Lecturership at the University of Victoria. The co-author of three
books, including *Rupert Brooke in Canada* and *Card Tricks: Bankers, Boomers,
and the Explosion of Plastic Credit*, which was shortlisted for the Canadian
Business Book Award, she is the editor of the bestselling and critically
acclaimed collection *The First Man in My Life: Daughters Write about Their
Fathers*. She lives in Toronto with her husband, historian Roger Hall, and is
the mother of two children.